SAINTS AND SERVANTS IN SOUTHERN MOROCCO

SOCIAL, ECONOMIC AND POLITICAL STUDIES OF THE MIDDLE EAST AND ASIA
(S.E.P.S.M.E.A.)

(Founding editor: C.A.O. van Nieuwenhuijze)

VOLUME 67

SAINTS AND SERVANTS
IN
SOUTHERN MOROCCO

BY

REMCO ENSEL

BRILL
LEIDEN · BOSTON · KÖLN
1999

Publication of this book has been made possible with the financial support of the African Studies Centre, P.O. Box 9555, 2300 RB Leiden, the Netherlands

This book is printed on acid-free paper.

Library of Congress Cataloging-in-Publication Data

Ensel, Remco.
    Saints and servants in southern Morocco / by Remco Ensel.
      p.   cm. — (Social, economic, and political studies of the
    Middle East and Asia, ISSN 1385-3376 ; v. 67)
    Includes bibliographical references (p.   ) and index.
    ISBN 9004114297 (cloth : alk. paper)
    1.Ethnology—Morocco—Ktawa Oasis.   2. Marginality, Social–
    –Morocco—Ktawa Oasis.   3. Ktawa Oasis (Morocco)– Ethnic relations.
    4. Caste—Morocco—Ktawa Oasis.   I. Title.   II. Series.
    GN649.M65E57   1999
    305,8 ' 00964 ' 6—dc21   99-27414
                                                                                    CIP

Die Deutsche Bibliothek - CIP-Einheitsaufnahme

Ensel, Remco:
Saints and servants in Southern Morocco / by Remco Ensel. – Leiden
; Boston ; Köln : Brill, 1999
    (Social, economic, and political studies of the Middle East and Asia ; Vol 67)
    ISBN 90-04-11429-7

                            ISSN   1385-3376
                            ISBN   90 04 11429 7

© Copyright 1999 by Koninklijke Brill NV, Leiden, The Netherlands

PRINTED IN THE NETHERLANDS

CONTENTS

LIST OF FIGURES

LIST OF ILLUSTRATIONS

PREFACE

On the very last morning of my sojourn in the oasis community in the Moroccan Dra River Valley, I saw a picture on the wall of the living room of the house in which I had spent the night. Since the mud-brick walls of the village houses in southern Morocco are rarely decorated by their occupants, I was somewhat surprised to see the picture; moreover, I had never noticed it before. It was an advertisement. I saw two smiling men, one dark-skinned and one light-skinned, holding instruments, a trumpet and a guitar respectively, in their hands. The text below the picture made clear it was an ad about cigarettes: *Fine, le rythme d'aujourd'hui*. The young Abdelhadi Hazzabin had put it on the wall. He told me it was from one of the French magazines I had left two years earlier after the fieldwork period in the village had come to an end. Abdelhadi explained how the picture had struck him immediately as a comment on his own life. He imagined that he was the dark-skinned man, a 'Hartani', playing together with his light-skinned friend, Sharif Mulay Fidadi. He explained that unlike the hierarchical relationship between Haratin, dark-skinned cultivators of humble descent, and Shurfa, descendants of the Prophet, in his natal village, there did not exist any problems between him and his friend; sometimes they indeed were having fun just like the two people in the picture. That was how his life should be, without problems disrupting these short moments of happiness.

Abdelhadi had captured the global meaning of the advertisement without being able to actually read the text. In the region, skin colour played a prominent part in the respective images and self-images of the inhabitants of the oasis communities, but only as an element of a more wide-ranging set of cultural ideals and practices that divided the population into strata such as Haratin, Shurfa (sing. Sharif), *Ahrār* (freemen) and *'Abīd* (descendants of slaves). In Abdelhadi's village, social opposites meet: Both Haratin and Shurfa occupy a special place in the oasis hierarchy as they are considered to be 'not quite like other people'. Disrepute fixes the identity of the Haratin in such a way that they are put below the 'commoners' who live in neighbouring villages; the Shurfa on the other hand are lifted above the 'commoners' because of their stringent compliance to the rules of

civility, as well as their control over the supernatural force called
baraka.

At present, the social hierarchy is no longer as self-evident as it
used to be. In the words of the advertisement, 'today's rhythm' has
brought the hierarchical relationships between the different strata to
the fore as a topic for public discussion and critique. Villagers now
pitch social equality against the 'racism' implied in the oasis hierarchy. 'Modern' ideas or religious fundamentalism are set against the
so-called 'traditional' ritual qualities of the Shurfa. The picture on
the wall and Abdelhadi's comment exemplify these new ways of inter-
preting the village dichotomy of Haratin and Shurfa. In Abdelhadi's
view the village dichotomy has been divested of its sharp edges but
has not disappeared completely. Similarly, for most villagers the
dichotomy continues to be a meaningful element in the ensemble of
cultural ideals that shapes their self-images and outlook on life; it
also provides the models by which they lead their lives. In this respect,
even the division of musical instruments in the ad, the trumpet for
the dark-skinned musician versus the guitar for the light-skinned, corresponds to an enduring local division.

How can we understand the ideology and the social structure in
which hierarchy and friendship coalesce as exemplified in the bond
between Abdelhadi and his Sharifian friend? How is this socio-cultural
complex reproduced, maintaining its force through time? The present
book tries to provide answers to these questions through an analytic
description of the hierarchical, yet interdependent, relations between
Haratin and Shurfa in one oasis community. The ad incident illustrates the ambivalent juxtaposition of Haratin and Shurfa. It is this
double-bind between the social opposites of an oasis hierarchy that
provides the framework for my investigation into the social marginality of Haratin on the northern fringe of the Sahara.

Research

This book is mainly based on conversations, interviews and participant
observations in Abdelhadi's village Aduafil. From June 1993 until
May 1994 I had rented a house in this village in the Ktawa Oasis
in the Dra River Valley. The relatively large oasis of 7797 hectares
and 25,000 inhabitants is situated 400 kilometres south of Marrakesh
and 25 kilometres northwest of the Algerian border (see figure 1).

The village is named after a 16th-century religious teacher and descendant of the Prophet and consists of about 50 Sharifian households and 10 Hartani or, as they are called in public, Drawi households, living concentrated in three quarters encircled by walls or dispersed throughout the palm gardens. The village is characterized by the coexistence of only two social categories, Shurfa and Drawa. In other villages one may find freemen (*Aḥrār*) to be part of the population. This coexistence of the social opposites of the oasis hierarchy provides an apt case to consider the hierarchical ideology in the Moroccan oasis societies and the particular features of marginal groups such as the Haratin.

Morocco is a multilingual country. The village belongs to a group of Arabophone villages in the Ktawa Oasis that is situated in an area where also two Berber languages, Tashelhit and Tamazight, are spoken. Most older people in the village do have some passive knowledge of Berber. We conversed, however, in Moroccan Arabic. With one or two educated younger people conversations were sometimes held in a mixture of French and Arabic and now and then only in French.

I did not use any electric recording devices in the collection of the data presented in this book. For conversations two strategies were followed. When I had more or less formally asked a villager to discuss a certain topic with me, I took notes during the conversation, especially when it was held at my home. Interviews also took place spontaneously outside my home, during a dinner at which I was a guest, while going out for a walk or during the afternoon gatherings on the village square. For these chance sessions notes were made afterwards, yet sometimes in the presence of the interlocutors. These strategies were modified according to the willingness of a person to discuss certain issues with me. Two villagers, belonging to one Drawi family, have acted as research assistants, although they were never appointed as such officially. They helped to gather information on genealogy, the social map of the village, landownership and water rights, and village affairs in general. Other regular informants were members of 15 different village families.

For reasons that will be spelled out in the coming chapters, the inhabitants of the, mainly Sharifian, oasis community were extremely sensitive to outsiders, especially with regard to contact with female Shurfa (called Sharifat). For several weeks I enjoyed the company of my wife who had the opportunity to gather some information on the experiences of the Sharifat. Contact with female Drawa (called Drawiat) was somewhat easier, although also for them it was considered inappropriate to enter into conversations with a male stranger.

Besides the material collected from conversations, impromptu interviews and participation in village life, I have used some fieldwork material collected outside the village community, but still within the same oasis. Earlier research for my M.A. thesis had provided me with good contacts in an adjacent village of Ait 'Atta Berbers and Drawa. During my year in the oasis, I regularly visited friends from this village to ask their opinion on the subject matter of my research. Furthermore, data from this village were used to make comparisons with my data in Aduafil.

With respect to written sources, I have consulted the unpublished manuscript collection of the *Centre des Hautes Études sur L'Afrique et L'Asie Moderne* (CHEAM) in Paris, including the 'customary law documents' pertaining to the Ktawa Oasis that were added, without the Arabic originals, in the CHEAM *mémoire* of captain Niclausse (1954). The customary law documents pertaining to the Tafilalt Oasis between the 17th and 19th centuries, were published and annotated by Mezzine (1987). Lastly, I have consulted reports and maps of the *Office Régional de Mise en Valeur Agricole* (ORMVA; Ministry of Agriculture) in Ouarzazate.

The holdings of several libraries were of central importance to the research. In Morocco, these were in Rabat *La Source* and the *Centre des Études Arabes* of the French Embassy. In Paris, the collections of the *Centre d'Études et de Documentation sur l'Afrique et d'Outre-Mer* (CEDAOM), the *Bibliothèque Nationale* and the *Institut du Monde Arabe* were consulted. In London, a visit to the library of the *School of Oriental and African Studies* (SOAS) yielded interesting references. In the Netherlands, the libraries of the *Instituut voor het Moderne Nabije Oosten* (IMNO; University of Amsterdam) and the *Royal Tropical Institute* in Amsterdam and the *Afrika Studiecentrum* in Leiden proved to be of great help.

Acknowledgments

The research for this book was subsidised by the University of Amsterdam (*The Amsterdam School for Social Science Research*). Two travel grants from *The Netherlands Organization for Scientific Research* (NWO) made further research in Morocco and France possible. I am grateful to these sources for their support.

For obvious reasons, anthropological research in a small community like Aduafil would not be possible without the trust and cooperation of its inhabitants as well as of the authorities involved. I would like to thank the national and local authorities in Morocco for granting me permission to conduct research in the oasis. I am very much grateful to the inhabitants of Aduafil and neighbouring villages, and their family members in Casablanca for their understanding and assistance in every possible way. Special thanks go out to all members of the Hazzabin family, the Yassine family, the Zazuli family, Šafay family, and the Budihar family for their hospitality. I returned home not only with the information they provided but also with memorable experiences that will last a lifetime.

This book is a revised version of a Ph.D. thesis defended at the University of Amsterdam in 1998. I wish to express my deepest gratitude to my supervisors, Anton Blok and Willy Jansen, for their unwearying interest in the project and their constructive comments on all of my written efforts. I thank the staff, secretary and fellow graduate students of *The Amsterdam School for Social Science Research* for the feedback and encouragements in the years I joined their ranks.

In the course of working on this book, several colleagues and friends read sections or provided me with comments and references. I would like to thank in particular Muhammad Aït Hamza and Abdallah Hammoudi for presenting me with useful references on research in Morocco, and Jeremy Boissevain, Léon Buskens and Paolo De Mas for commenting on the very first research proposal. I am grateful to Joop Goudsblom, James Scott and Ineke van Wetering for their careful reading of two papers presented in the school, and to Muhammad Saadouni, Harry Stroomer and Alison Fisher for their linguistic advice. I thank Charles Benjamin (whose field notes I was allowed to consult), Zachary Hinchliffe, Joris Rijbroek and Jaspar Winn for acting as 'sounding boards' while working in Morocco. I am much obliged to Dale Eickelman, David Hart, Ferdinand de Jong and Marja Spierenburg for their valuable comments on the thesis manuscript. Finally, I wish to acknowledge my debts to Dale Eickelman for introducing me to E.J. Brill Publishers.

With all these contributions it remains to be said that for any flaws in this book I alone am responsible.

Transliteration

Words and geographical names that have found their way into the English language are spelled without italics according to *The Concise Oxford Dictionary* (1990 edition; Oxford: Clarendon Press): Couscous, Fatiha, Hadith, hajj (and subsequently hajja) et cetera. Arabic words and sentences are spelled following J.M. Cowan (ed), *The Hans Wehr Dictionary of Modern Written Arabic* (New York: Spoken Languages Services, 1976) and written in italics: *Ajr, kammās*. These Arabic words are included in the glossary. Spelling in quotations remains unchanged. French transcription predominates in older writings on North Africa (with ch for š and ou for u). For the sake of readability all Dutch, French and German quotations have been translated. The original transcription of Arabic words in the translated quotations has been maintained.

In anthropological texts written in English, the complex Arabic plural forms are usually not used. Instead, one writes the singular form plus -s or -at. I follow this usage; thus, *qsar* becomes the plural *qsar-s* instead of *qsur*. Exceptions to this rule are the ethnonyms: *ʿAbd ʿAbīd, Ḥurr Aḥrār*.

Of the ethnonym 'Haratin' various spellings exist. Most common is (1) *Ḥartānī* pl. *Ḥarāṭīn* (for example in *The Encyclopaedia of Islam*), yet one may also find (2) *Ḥartāni* or (3) *Ḥarṭāni*. The spelling is not neutral. The first variant could possibly read as mulatto from the (Mauritanian language) *Ḥassanīyya* root Ḥ-r-ṭ-n. Variant two evokes their dark skin colour (*aḥarḍan* = dark brown in Berber) and variant three suggests Haratin to be either 'freedmen' (*Ḥurr ṭāni*; e.g. a manumitted slave) or agriculturalists (from the verb *ḥaraṭa* = to plow the soil) (cf. Teine-Cheikh 1989: 95; Pandolfo 1997: 325; cf. Leriche 1951; Marçais 1951). Here the ethnonyms Hartani (pl. Haratin), Drawi (pl. Drawa) and Sharif (pl. Shurfa) shall be written in simplified form without italics. This also accounts for personal names.

Following Wehr's dictionary, the Arabic emphatic consonants are written with a subscript dot (ṣ, ḍ, ṭ, ẓ); long vowels are noted by a superscript hyphen (¯). The consonant *ʿayn* is symbolised by a superscript c (ʿ).

The following guidelines may help in the pronunciation of Arabic words.

The ʿayn is a guttural sound, produced by lengthening the glottal stop; this should deliver a somewhat 'sheepish' sound (ʿabd).

The ḏ is pronounced like th in mother (ḏabīḥa).

The g, typical for Moroccan Arabic, is pronounced as the g in goodbye (Gnawa).

The ġ is pronounced as the r in Paris (ġusl).

The ḥ is pronounced with a deep sigh and sounds like a loud whisper (ḥmar).

The j is pronounced as the j in the name Joan (jallāba).

The ḵ is pronounced as ch in Bach (ḵali).

The š is pronounced as sh in shoe (šahāda).

The ṯ is pronounced like th in thing (ṯulṯ).

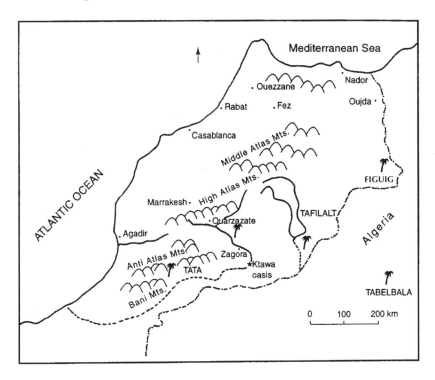

Figure 1: Morocco and the Ktawa Oasis

CHAPTER ONE

INTRODUCTION

> We assume that men are born equal. We must remember that
> this is a judgment and not a fact (Leach 1967: 14).

Ever since anthropology's pristine beginnings, its rather ambitious
enterprise has consisted of the description and understanding of the
practices of people living in other societies to make sense of one's
own or shed light on the *condition humaine* in general. In this endeav-
our, observers are repeatedly being asked to engage with value systems
not their own. This request becomes a demand when it concerns the
theme, social hierarchy, that according to Louis Dumont is 'at the
heart of the "unthought" (*l'impensé*) of modern ideology' (1980: xvi).
We encounter everywhere in this world people who are portrayed and
treated as different from the rest of the population from the time of
their birth; people who are confronted with an ascribed body of
information on their psychic and somatic features and for whom
only circumscribed roles have been reserved in society on the basis
of this fixed identity. It may be that they are avoided as much as
possible or encountered in ritualized ways. Often mentioned examples of such 'special status people' are the Japanese Burakumin and
the Indian Untouchables. The latter most clearly exemplify the task
of the anthropologist to steer between involvement with and detachment from the subjects of his study. In this respect, the ongoing discussion on Dumont's seminal work *Homo Hierarchicus* (1980; cf.
Appadurai 1986, 1988; Dirks 1994; Khare 1984; Parish 1996) is illu-
minating: How to conduct an analysis of the structures of caste society and do justice to the multiplicity of voices, learn about the
viewpoints of the people at the lower end of the hierarchy, to 'unmask',
as it is called, the 'representational inequalities' embedded in ethnographic writings (Webber 1997: 11; cf. Gal 1995; Guha 1982; Ortner
1995; Scott 1990; Wertheim 1964: 23–37)? The present study takes
up this problem by focusing on a category of people that shares
some of the characteristics of the afore mentioned Asian status groups.

From the Atlantic Ocean to the Ahaggar Mountains in Northwest

Africa, the ethnonym 'Haratin' (sing. 'Hartani') designates a specific
category of dark-skinned agriculturalists and occupational specialists
of humble descent (Colin 1971; Mercer 1982; Spencer 1978: 102).
In Moroccan society, the name Haratin connotes an image of disrepute and subordination and is therefore usually replaced by 'Drawi'
(pl. 'Drawa') and other local names. The pejorative connotation of
the name Hartani indicates the enduring disrepute that clings to the
people known as such. Equally striking is their ambivalent status:
The Haratin are indispensable to the functioning of the oasis societies
yet fellow villagers treat them with a mixture of awe and contempt.

   The Haratin are in anthropological literature often defined as descendants of slaves. Since a dark-skinned population lived in southern Morocco before the slave trade from the region south of the
Sahara to Morocco even started (Camps 1970; Bellakhdar et al. 1992:
160) and people clearly differentiate between descendants of slaves
and Haratin they should be distinguished from the former slave population. Thus, Dwyer's interlocutor in his Moroccan Dialogues has this
to say on the Haratin: 'Oh, your pleasure can hardly tolerate them
at all. You don't know their measure: they appear servile, but you
don't know what they are thinking. They are not like that black
mechanic who was working on the well. You remember. He was
black, but not a Haratin' (Dwyer 1982: 116).[1]

   The Haratin live in Mauritania (De Chassey 1977; Marchesin
1992; Mercer 1982; Ruf 1998a, 1998b; Teine-Cheikh 1989) and
Morocco;[2] in Algeria they live in the oases near Morocco (Champault

---

[1] Casajus spoke of the Inadan, occupational specialists living among the Tuareg,
as 'free men of a special category', being 'needed, but also despised' (Casajus 1987:
291, 305). As we will see, this qualification equally applies to the Haratin.

[2] See Camps (1970), Jacques-Meunié (1958), Leriche (1951) and Marçais (1951).
Several unpublished reports of colonial civil servants and military officers make mention of the low reputation and socio-economic status of the Haratin in the Moroccan
oasis societies (Azam 1946, 1947; St Bon 1938a, 1938b; De La Chapelle 1929;
Monteil 1948; Moureau 1955; Niclausse 1955; cf. Spillman 1931, 1936). These
reports provide a great deal of information on the social organization of the oasis
societies, but do not really focus on the place of the Haratin. Probably, the initial
lack of attention from anthropologists is due to their interest in long-standing social
groupings. This at least would explain why the diffuse and only loosely organized
Haratin have been largely ignored, while the descendants of slaves in Moroccan society, organized into religious brotherhoods, are treated in two monographs (Pâques
1991; Welte 1990; cf. Dermenghem 1954: 255–302). A second factor might be the
hegemonic perspective that pervades the literature. With respect to the large-scale
immigration of Haratin from Morocco to the oases of the Algerian Ahaggar Mountains
in the 19th century, Keenan (1977: 144) notes that, '[w]hen we consider the scale

1969) and around the Ahaggar Mountains (Bourgeot 1975; Keenan 1977). The *Šwašīn* in Tunisia, Libya and the eastern Sahara resemble the Haratin. Evans-Pritchard (1949: 42) described them as 'descendants of Arab men and Negresses', in between Arabs, Turks and 'full-blooded Negroes'. Bédoucha (1984: 83) pointed out how just like the Haratin, the *Šwašīn* do not form one or several well-organized social groupings but constitute small pockets of endogamous population groups, even isolated families or individuals, 'a huddle of small groups without mutual affinities'. Out of necessity they live as dependants in the proximity of other population groups.

In the oasis societies along the northern fringe of the Sahara, the low status and disrepute of people known as Haratin and *Šwašīn* has been interwoven in an elaborate social hierarchy which may include traditional literati and religious specialists, nomadic and transhumant population groups, freemen and slaves. Although the oasis societies 'cannot truly be said to be mere copies of each other' (Hart 1984: 123), striking family resemblances can be observed. The social and cultural unity of the region, reflected and most impressively demonstrated in Pâques' *L'arbre cosmique* (1964), can also be seen from the status of Haratin and the persistence of unequal social categorization. Haratin and *Šwašīn* alike are located between the self-proclaimed freemen (*Aḥrār*) and descendants of slaves (*'Abīd*). In this respect, the social categories have been denoted as 'castes' (Jacques-Meunié 1958), 'quasicastes' (Pascon 1979: 111), 'classes' (Pascon and Ennaji 1986), 'estates' (Maher 1974: 13, 24–39) and 'ethnic groups' (Hart 1984: 124). From notes in the literature it seems that Haratin are not only held in low esteem but may face what has been called *eine klare und kaum überwindliche soziale und menschliche Barriere* (Hergemöller 1990: 14, 25). In this study the question shall be asked whether or not Haratin, as social marginals[3] face such a 'self-evident, scarcely surmountable, social and cultural barrier'.

---

of this immigration it is surprising that the history of the Harratin settlement received virtually no documentary attention during the French period'. Instead, the host of publications deals with the politically dominant nomadic population. In a number of recent studies the status of Haratin in the Moroccan oasis communities is discussed (Bellakhdar *et al.* 1992; Dunn 1977; Hammoudi 1993; Hart 1984; Herzenni 1990; Maher 1974; Mezzine 1987; Ouhajou 1986; Pandolfo 1989, 1997).

[3] Social marginals are people who are bereft of specific rights or honour and given a 'special taxonomic status' in society, hence the name 'special status people' that was introduced by Tax-Freeman (Ohnuki-Tierney 1990: 105; cf. Tax-Freeman 1979 and Berland 1982). 'Marginal' is here a variant of anomaly in a classificatory

Following the supposition that disrepute and esteem are interdependent (Dumont 1980: 54),[4] the reputation of the Haratin is here considered in connection with that of their social opposites, the Shurfa, descendants of the Prophet. In southern Morocco, Haratin and Shurfa constitute, respectively, the base and the apex of the social hierarchy. Shurfa are highly respected for their piety and affiliation with the House of the Prophet. People attribute to them a sacred quality, called *baraka*, which they can transfer to other people. Haratin are like Shurfa considered to be 'not quite like other people',[5] but they are so in an inauspicious way: Non-Hartani inhabitants of the oasis communities refuse to marry Haratin and prefer to live separately from them. An 'aura of taboo' (Carnegie 1996: 473) surrounds members of both categories. Through an exploration of the, sometimes divergent, interpretations of the cultural ideals that circumscribe the encounters of Shurfa and Haratin in their daily life, this study aims to unravel the close interdependence between the taboo-loaded reputations of the high-status Shurfa and the low-status Haratin. Central focus shall lie on the ways in which this and other interconnected structural dichotomies are evoked, reinterpreted and contested (cf. Mitchell 1990), attesting to the inherent ambivalence embedded in a hierarchical relationship and offering opportunities to both parties to assert themselves (Van der Veen 1971: 310).

The field of opinion

In 1955 the French colonial military officer Moureau provided his superiors with an inside view of recent events in the Moroccan Protectorate. In particular, Moureau expressed his opinion on the recent

---

system (Ohnuki-Tierney 1981: 121–124). For examples of French *marginaux* see Vincent (1979) and for German *Randgruppen* see Hergemöller (1990).

[4] 'It is clear that the impurity of the Untouchable is conceptually inseparable from the purity of the Brahman. They must have been established together, or in any case have mutually reinforced each other, and we must get used to thinking of them together' (Dumont 1980: 54). More general, Dumont defines hierarchy as the 'encompassing of the contrary'. Since what 'encompasses is more important than that which is encompassed', whatever happens at the extremes of a hierarchy is essential for its understanding (idem, 76).

[5] The phrase is from Briggs (1960: 87) and denotes the 'red ones' (*Hamria*), people of mixed descent and low esteem in the Algerian Mzab. Note that this colour qualification for Haratin is widespread (Keenan 1977: 100).

période troublée, during which urban-based extremist parties had organized violent manifestations against the French colonial government. He wrote that '[i]n the first row of these manifestations, one has noticed a significant proportion of the coloured population, people who in the oases constitute the social class of "Harratins"'. These Haratin, dark-skinned agriculturalists of the southern oases, went to work in Casablanca, sending part of their salary to family members left behind in the southern oases to finance the construction of a house or the purchase of land. The 'subversive ideas' that migrated Haratin had come in contact with in the streets of Casablanca were brought back to the oases: 'Youngsters on leave return home and develop in their village the themes that [extremist parties] taught them. They scandalize the elders who have maintained their servile mentality and who refuse to follow them on their revolutionary path'. Even so, Moureau pointed out how down south some Haratin had started refusing to carry out the collective agricultural services, which according to customary law were the sole task of Haratin: 'This has never been seen before (. . .). This emancipation has produced a genuine revolution, peaceful as it may be, in the oases. *Little by little the established social order is being turned upside down* (1955: 1, 10; italics added). Moureau's objective was to present some background information on the Hartani population for the French administration, since thus far all the attention from researchers and civil servants had been directed to the Berber tribes in the pacified and oppositional areas of the country. As a result, not much was known about the Haratin who were participating in the riots in Casablanca. Reading Moureau's report one still feels his excitement at being a witness of the revolutionary changes in urban and rural Morocco, changes he compared with the revolt of African-Americans in the USA. It was the conviction of French officers such as Moureau and St Bon (1938b: 15) that the revolutionary spirit of equality among the Haratin was stimulated as an unintended consequence of the benevolent French presence in the country; in the course of the present book it will, however, be argued that the persistence of hierarchical notions, albeit in altered forms, in the oasis societies should not be overlooked.

Since independence, achieved only a year after 'the troubles' described by Moureau, the transformation of the oasis societies has continued at an even more rapid pace. Article five of the first Moroccan constitution in 1962 mentions the juridical equality of all citizens before the law: *Tous les Marocains sont égaux devant la loi* including the

Haratin living in the oases. Equally important was the growing availability of paid labour, mainly outside of the oasis. Sharecropping
Haratin were offered a chance to escape the long-term labour contracts with landowning families; Hartani day labourers could find
permanent jobs in boomtown Casablanca. Hart, the ethnographer
of the once powerful Ait 'Atta pastoralists, suggested some Haratin
had become 'fairly prosperous' after independence in 1956 (1984:
149). Given the fact that racism was 'a basic sociopolitical fact' in
southern Morocco, Hart predicted that the changing economic status of Haratin would constitute a source of conflict in the future of
the southern regions of the country (Hart 1972: 55). These impres-
sions were affirmed through in-depth socio-economic research in one
oasis. Herzenni observed that notwithstanding radical socio-economic
changes, 'the kernel of the social relations' between Haratin and
their fellow villagers persisted. This researcher was confronted with
the paradoxical simultaneous existence of 'veritable changes of the
social structure and (. . .) the continuous application of the referen-
tial framework from the past' (Herzenni 1990: 14, 20–21).

The enduring disrepute of the Haratin resembles that of marginalized population groups elsewhere in the world. It has been observed
that post-independence processes of state formation have not always
altered local social hierarchies (Migdal 1988: 36), in particular, they
have not led to the actual emancipation of groups whose collective
identity hinges on a ritual impure condition. Parish (1996: 27) notes
with respect to the low status of the Newars of Nepal that '[a]lthough
legal and political constraints have eroded, the social and cultural
constraints of caste life continue to have power, to be central to people's lives'. Similar situations exist for Untouchables in the Indian
'caste system' and the status of the Burakumin in Japan (cf. Donoghue
1957; DeVos and Suárez-Orozco 1990: 174). In the Middle East,
the persistence of hierarchical structures in Yemen is a case in point.
With descent and occupation as main criteria, a Sharifian élite and
a broad category of agriculturalists and occupational specialists of
humble descent constitute here respectively the apex and base of the
social hierarchy (Bujra 1971: 13–53; Dostal 1985: 185–195; cf.
Gerholm 1977). Recent research established that '[i]n spite of the
introduction of the term "citizen" for all Yemenis by the Government,
and the occasional lip-service being paid by the "citizens" to the
abandonment of social distinctions based on descent, to an extent
the old categories have continued to persist' (Vom Bruck 1996: 148).

Nevertheless, in agreement with findings on the theme of caste in Indian society, the observations of Hart and Herzenni do indicate that the identity of Haratin in Morocco has departed, in Bourdieu's words, 'the universe of the unsaid'—where the prevalent social relations were never mentioned, let alone discussed. Instead, in the emerging 'field of opinion', a public sphere of face-to-face and long-distance exchange of ideas (Taylor 1997: 217–220, 259), people can name the unspeakable and come up with alternative views (Bourdieu 1977: 168–171). To register this discursive field, one needs a perspective that respects complex social realities without reducing it to a uniform structure and that prefers polyphony over monotony, devoting attention to divergent interpretations and 'the everyday drama by which cultural ideologies [pertaining to hierarchy] are constructed and debated' (Appadurai 1986: 750). Jokes (Douglas 1975), riddles (Hamnett 1967), nicknames (Blok and Buckser 1996) and rituals of reversal (Babcock 1978) are the typical cultural forms in which an alternative social order can be imagined and expressed. In this sense these forms may be seen as ultimately ambiguous, that is, as points of transition 'between two or more frames of reference' (Hamnett 1967: 381), leaving room for more than one interpretation.

Comparable attention, however, should be devoted to that which has remained in the universe of the unsaid: The commonsense notions that continue to construct the 'master-categories' of 'the Hartani' and 'the Sharif', determining the lives of a large group of oasis inhabitants and overriding other categories linked to age, gender or personal qualities (cf. Hughes in Becker 1973: 32–33). These master-categories are made to look natural and permanent in daily encounters and conversations, in the division of labour and Islamic calendrical rituals. It is exactly this intertwinement with a variety of more or less systematized domains of the social order from which the prevailing social classifications derive their taken-for-granted character (Bourdieu 1977: 164; Eickelman 1981: 86; cf. Carnegie 1996; Gilroy 1997; Howe 1991).

Bourdieu argues in *An Outline of a Theory of Practice* (1977) that human beings are endowed with a repertoire of mental dispositions, schemes of perception and thought to communicate with other human beings. These dispositions which inform and guide people in their daily life are historically formed and culture-specific. To a certain extent, the basic assumptions underlying these structures of dispositions are held implicitly and as such instilled in daily life (idem, 72).

However, in the field of opinion that accompanies the development
of mass-education and the spread of various media in the modern
nation-state, practical ideologies can be made explicit and become
the subject of intense debate. Eickelman, who coined Bourdieu's
approach 'a political economy of cultural meanings' (1979: 386) has
noted 'practice theory' could correct American interpretive anthropology
as it has been used to gain insight in Moroccan society by Geertz
and associates (Geertz, Geertz and Rosen 1979; but see Free 1996).
Instead of focusing on collective representations and cultural systems,
a political economy of meaning would devote attention to production
and reproduction of patterns of meaning, to the social location of actors,
and to the introduction of innovative ideas, given that meanings not
only are shared but can also be denied and altered (Eickelman 1985a:
136; Hayeur 1991; Marcus 1983; Roff 1987; cf. Gilsenan 1982).[6]

Bourdieu's 'conceptual schemes immanent in practice' (1977: 96–
158) hark back to a long-standing theoretical tradition in symbolic
classifications. Similarly, concerning the juxtaposition of social opposites in an oasis society, the seminal work of Durkheim and Mauss
(1963), Van Gennep (1960) and Lévi-Strauss (1962) into culture-
specific systems of symbolic classification as well as the work of
Douglas (1966, 1975), Leach (1964, 1978), Turner (1974) and Ohnuki-
Tierney (1981, 1984, 1990) are of particular relevance. In these
studies, it is assumed that the meaning of cultural elements can only
be understood by analyzing them as parts in a structured whole. Whenever humans tend to think in clear-cut categories, usually in clusters
of contrastive pairs, the constructed, though objectified, boundaries
receive special attention. They become the focus of a 'taboo'—defined as a rule of conduct, supernaturally sanctioned, that prescribes
avoidance or prohibition—or are attributed with a sacred status and
numinous power (cf. Leach 1978; Ohnuki-Tierney 1981: 119–129).
This also accounts for those cultural elements that are difficult to classify—because they fall in between two classes or share character-
istics of two classes simultaneously (cf. Douglas 1966, 1975; Leach
1964). In particular, studies in which these insights have been applied

---

[6] There is a parallel discussion with respect to South Asian caste systems (Robb
1995: 47). In a review of Daniel's study *Fluid Signs* (1984), Appadurai (1986: 757)
notes the pastoral quality of the study and suggests this kind of interpretive ethnography needs elaboration in the direction of 'a political economy of semiotics'.

to the occupational activities of social marginals or 'special status people' to show how they act as mediators or 'brokers' between social and cultural categories have greatly influenced the original plan of the research project as well as the outline of the present book. I have coined the schemes of classification and patterns of meaning in which the categories of 'Hartani' and 'Sharif' are embedded, 'cultural ideals'. Cultural ideals summarize man's relationship with and control over the natural world, his fellow humans, and his bodily functions and feelings. It shall be argued that it is their mediatory position in this 'triad of basic human controls' (Elias 1971: 176; cf. Goudsblom 1987), which determines the reputation of Haratin but also enables them to obtain *power chances* vis-à-vis their fellow inhabitants in the oasis society (Blok 1981, 1989, 1996; Jansen 1987; Ohnuki-Tierney 1984; cf. Geertz 1960; Wolf 1956). The social and cultural power of Haratin as brokers defies the conceptualization of them as dependants only and supports Leach's argument that it is exactly 'taboed ambiguity' that can become powerful.

Double-bind

Social distance has often been brought forward as an aspect or cause of stigmatization and discrimination (cf. Allport 1958). Social distance can be expressed in explicit or implicit rules of segregation. Dollard observed how after the abolishment of slavery, 'Southerntown' in the American Deep South became 'bisected by a railroad, and its tracks divide people according to color, the whites living on one side and the Negroes on the other' (1949: 2). Closer to the locus of the present study, captain Moureau observed in 1955 how the houses of the Haratin were grouped inside the walled village in a quarter sharply separated from the remaining habitation: '[T]hey live on their own, marry among themselves and celebrate their own feasts. In short, they form a distinct community from which the clear-skinned community keeps aloof' (Moureau 1955: 6). However, when concentrating on spatial segregation, we should not overlook the interaction and often close interdependence between members of distinctive social categories. It has been observed that '[s]trictly speaking, there is no segregation of *haratn* from other social groups; they are often close friends and confidants of Berbers and Arabs. But especially in rural communities, there is an elaborate protocol which defines them as political inferiors' (Maher 1974: 25). The quotation does not point to social distance but, in the words of Genovese (1972: 5), to the existence of 'a fragile bridge across the intolerable contradictions' of social bondage; a complex interdependent relationship between social marginals and others. As already noted, in the social hierarchy Shurfa and Haratin represent opposite poles; yet in the community that is central in this book, they coexist and maintain close relations. Awareness of the interdependent relationship paves the way to an exploration of the power chances Haratin are able to gain as a consequence of their marginal position in the village.

A concept that highlights the mutual interdependence between established inhabitants and social marginals is that of a 'double-bind'. This concept originates in psychology and denotes the simultaneous reception of multiple contradictory messages from one or more persons with whom a person stands in a close relationship. The common case is a family in which a child receives contradictory messages, or orders, from both parents. It is hypothesized that in extreme situations the child might develop a schizophrenic attitude (Jackson 1968). Research into double-bind relations has been conducted by Gregory Bateson (cf. Bateson and Bateson 1987). Since then the concept has been used to pinpoint various paradoxes inherent in human communication.[7] As a sociological concept, double-bind refers to an intense interdependent relationship between two or more persons that cannot be interpreted unequivocally. The concept has been elucidated in a theoretical essay by Norbert Elias that introduces the sociological case study *The Established and the Outsiders* of which Elias was co-author:

> [T]he socio-dynamics of the relationship of groups bonded to each other as established and outsiders are determined by the manner of their bonding, not by any of the characteristics possessed by the groups concerned independently of it (. . .). [O]ne cannot grasp *the compelling force of this kind of bonding*, and the peculiar helplessness of groups of

---

[7] The concept has been used in feminist literature and family studies. The novel *De vriendschap* (Friendship) of the Dutch novelist Connie Palmen evolves around the double-bind relationship between two girlfriends who cannot live with or without one another. Another interesting literary application can be found in the plays of the Swedish playwright Lars Norèn in which family relations are analyzed in painful detail as double-bind relations (Florin in Norèn 1985).

people bound to each other in this manner, unless one sees clearly
that they are trapped in a double-bind (Elias 1994: xxx–xxxi; italics
added).

Elias notes here that the power of the double-bind fluctuates. This
means that in relations where an outsider group fulfils a function
for the established, the 'double-bind starts working more overtly...'
(ibidem). Here the term will be used to express the inherent dialogical dimension of identity formation as well as the coincidence of
practices aimed at the exclusion of Haratin with their sociological
and psychological indispensability. The concept thus pinpoints the
ambivalence that is implicit in the hierarchical configuration of Shurfa
and Haratin. In previous research in a nearby village of Ait 'Atta
Berbers and Haratin I had come across the intimate relations and
regular, ritualized, exchanges between families of both population
groups. Here, I have tried to give this exchange relationship its
proper place. The conceptualization of hierarchical interdependence
as an exchange relationship is furthermore in agreement with recent
criticism on Dumont's thesis on the centrality of the purity-impurity
dichotomy in inter-caste relationships. According to Raheja, Dumont's
emphasis on this 'single overarching principle' obscures the importance of 'prestations' and exchanges in constituting relations between
castes (Raheja 1989; cf. Parish 1996: 88–93). This book tries to make
clear how the existence of dyadic, asymmetrical relations between
Shurfa and Haratin, including fictive kinship bonds, create lasting,
trustworthy relations between the two parties.

Leitmotif in this study is the construction and contestation of the
double-bind relationship between Shurfa and Haratin. Thus, throughout the book we will encounter ideas and practices in which rapprochement and dissociation, inclusion and exclusion, compete for
ascendancy. The recognition of both similarity and difference is the
fundamental feature of every human relationship. As such, the present study presents this ambivalence in an accentuated manner, a
blow-up as it were, by way of an exploration of the hierarchical interdependence between Shurfa and Haratin in the social and ideological fields of the oasis society. The identity of the Haratin has become
the subject of critical examination by villagers. People dispute the
hierarchical social order and the ideological principles on which it
is based. We will see in the discussion of the cultural ideals, relating to rules of etiquette (*adab*) and views on purity and pollution, a
repetitive practical realization and reproduction of established social

and cultural categories vis-à-vis the presentation of alternative interpretations. A second motif in this book is the occupational specialism of Haratin. As pointed out in several chapters, an examination
of the special features and quasi-monopolization of certain tasks by
Haratin in the oasis, illuminates the deepseated conceptions and categories of thought that I denote as the prevalent cultural ideals of
an oasis society in southern Morocco.

CHAPTER TWO

LATENT DESTINY
IMAGERIES OF HARTANI AND SHARIF

If the difference were only a word, what an awful form it would take. If it be only an illusion, what significance and conjuring power it would have! (Memmi 1962: 79)

This chapter introduces the symbolic forms that establish and reproduce the personae of 'Sharif' and 'Hartani'. Central aim is to examine the affinities between ancient hierarchical categorization and the emergence of new forms to impress and contest social inequality in the modern nation-state. Referring to Migdal (1988: 36), one may speak of a 'hard-nosed persistence' of hierarchical structures notwithstanding egalitarian policies of modern nation-states. Yet, to what extent does nationalist ideology indeed represent all of its citizens in equal terms? It will be shown here how the creation of cultural difference within the localized arena of the southern oasis society is tied up with the construction of the imagined community of Moroccan society as a whole. Nationalist ideology contains a deep-rooted conception of identity as a fixed, 'latent destiny' inscribed on the body (Gilroy 1997: 308) and set within the nation (cf. Carnegie 1996). Haratin and Shurfa hold opposite positions regarding this, to some extent, implicit discourse on people, places and cultural ideals. A second theme of this chapter is the analogy and possibly explicit connection between contemporary conceptions of ethnic identities and those contained in anthropological texts, indicating that 'the manifestations of ethnicity we study today contain within them the ghosts of previous academic formulations' (Banks 1996: 189).

Language games

Oh, son of another man from the Dra (Moroccan curse; Westermarck 1926 i: 483).

At least since the second part of the 18th century, numerous European travel writers and *philosophes*, ethnologists and fieldworkers, diplomats and colonial civil servants have mapped, classified and evaluated the confusing, though appealing, world on the southern shores of the Mediterranean (Burke III 1972; Lorcin 1995; Pouillon 1993; Thomson 1987). A recurrent problem in their activities concerned the extent to which prevalent ethnonyms coincided with the actual population groups in the Maghreb. Did names such as Moor, Arab, Berber and Hartani refer to separate races, corporate or ethnic groups? Or should the names be conceived as linguistic devices with a merely contextual meaning? Could they even be pure inventions of European writers without any local connotation whatsoever? In the beginning of this century, the first generation of ethnologists and historians working in Morocco approached the social categories which the terms were supposed to denote as objective entities. In this sense, ethnic or tribal identity—being a Hartani, 'Attawi or Sharif—is a permanent and essential condition that carries with it certain circumscribed character-istics which are incarnated in the ethnonyms. A similar assumption of ideal categories as the central focus of study underlay mainstream anthropological structural functionalism. In the Maghreb the preoccu-pation with the unchanging 'mosaic' of population groups lasted until the late 1960s.[1]

The distinctive features of social groupings that were observed by anthropologists were not always neutral. Possibly influenced by political interests, research questions aimed at the classification and objectification of fluid local structures. Individuals were taken as 'rep-resentatives of certain distinct categories of persons, specific sorts of individuals' (Geertz 1973: 5, 363), even illustrative of certain grand historical developments. The division of the population in Arabs and Berbers (Gellner and Micaud 1972), or the timeless subdivision of the Berber-speaking population in three ethnic groups,—northern Sanhaja, eastern Zenata and southern Masmuda (cf. for a critique Hart 1982)—are two cases in point. A next generation of anthro-pologists objected against a prima facie reduction of individual iden-tity to one of the current ethnic denominators. They argued that the existence or relevance of tribe, race and ethnic group should not be taken as *assumption* but as the *problem* of anthropological research. The focus thus shifted to the *formation* of social identities. This was

---

[1] In the work of Evans-Pritchard (1949) and Emrys Peters (1990a, 1990b) on the Bedouin of Lybia, an early revisonist stance toward the structuralist-functionalist paradigm can be found (Eickelman 1981: 48–62).

in accordance with a more general paradigm shift in the 1960s: From durable social groups toward short-term coalitions, factions and cliques; from the dominant influence of values and norms toward individual choice; from static social structures to social processes. Barth in his seminal essay on ethnic boundaries (1969: 10–11) argued against the view of ethnic groups as 'biological self-perpetuating, bounded' groups in favour of an approach that considers the various contexts in which ethnic identity is expressed.   *context of ethnic expression*

In Moroccan anthropology, Clifford and Hildred Geertz and Rosen (1979) theorized on the basis of their collective research project in and around the town of Sefrou that names, be they first names, honorifics or ethnic denominations, constitute the cultural vocabulary in which the fluidity of the process of identity formation in Moroccan society can be expressed (H. Geertz 1979: 339–340; Rosen 1979: 101–106). Instead of taking tribal and ethnic denominations as determinants of social identities, the separate systems of name giving only constitute the raw material for the language games between persons actively involved in the process of identity formation. Labelling individuals with any of the available terms indicates but does not determine their identity. The evocative metaphor used by Geertz is that of a bazaar, where individuals meet each other and exchange information necessary for the creation of a meaningful context from where their social relationship can be developed. In this way an extremely contextual social identity is created, that is, one dependent on the *Geertz* place, time and persons involved:

> Ascriptive distinctions—generated out of language, religion, residence, race, kinship, birthplace, ancestry—run through the whole of the bazaar, partitioning the Muslim community into literally dozens of categories. (. . .) The mosaic quality of Moroccan society, and beyond it Middle Eastern civilization, not only penetrates the bazaar but finds there perhaps its most articulate and powerful expression, its paradigmatic form (C. Geertz 1979: 141, 143).

The interest in social construction and individual choice (or agency, as we now would say), returns in the work of Rosen. In an early article it is argued that '[t]he constant focus in Moroccan society is not, therefore, on corporate groups but on individuals; not on sanctions through which behavior can be channelled and limited but on arranging associations wherever they appear most advantageous' (Rosen 1972: 158; cf. 1984: 165). The quotation implies recognition of the changing relevance of Hartani and Sharifian descent in determining social relations or identities. The label of Hartani, just like Sharif, Arab, Berber or a tribal name, may be used in certain circumscribed contexts, while in others kinship, profession or gender gains prominence.

The interpretive studies on Moroccan society have led us to consider how subjects are created in a specific social and cultural context, how indeed 'reality' itself is situationally constructed and subjected to negotiations (Rosen 1984: 180). Ethnic names cannot be taken at face value but have to be analyzed regarding their inclusion into historically transmitted patterns of meanings that are expressed in everyday practices. This chapter, as the ones following, pursues a similar approach in the exploration of current symbolic practices that shape the 'culturally familiar figures' of Sharif and Hartani, saint and servant (cf. Carnegie 1996: 471). Yet, the caveat to take into account here is the distributive, possibly unequal character of cultural interpretation. People might thus be caught 'in webs of significance', to use a well-known rephrasing of Geertz's felicitous metaphor for the articulation of culture, instead of spinning their own (Geertz 1973: 5). This caveat is in agreement with Asad's early pointed criticism concerning the ingrained 'a priori totality of meanings' in Geertz's interpretive studies which excludes 'the possibility of conflicting conceptions and discourses' (Asad 1983: 251). These critical remarks have been developed in a number of ethnographic studies that appeared after the Sefrou research. The studies of Hayeur (1991) on the urban élite of Rabat and that of Marcus (1983) on rural-urban relations in and around the northern town Taza, show the necessity of taking into account the specific social configurations, developed through time, within which markers of social identity get their meaning. These case studies have led to a more general critique on the notion of fluid social relations. Eickelman (1984: 216; cf. 1985a) stated that in the work of Geertz, Geertz and Rosen (1979) 'Moroccan social identity is represented as more plastic than it actually is'. Bourqia (1991b: 161) concluded that on 'the bazaar of identities' not everyone may be able to use his descent as currency: 'Some choose not to use this currency and even may exert themselves to conceal it from public because their origins are not honourable'. Turning now to the oasis societies in southern Morocco, an examination of the naming patterns bears out the truth of this last observation.

In the southern oases, 'Hartani' and 'Sharif' are part of an elaborate repertoire of social denominations to place individuals in crude categories of class, tribal affiliation, and kin group. The terms point to social status, deny a person certain qualities while suggesting others, and for this reason might be downright offensive. Name-giving is a meaningful act which sometimes coincides with its offensive mirror-image, name-calling. Social denominations are then used against individuals, reinforcing a degrading collective identity with the denial of individual autonomy and social change. Where in the anthropological literature the name Haratin is mentioned without reservations, people in southern Morocco usually avoid using the term. They do employ alternative terms that refer to birthplace or, possibly imagined, origin. This discrepancy between texts and local practices directs attention to the sensibility involved with the usage of names, be they first names, honorifics, or ethnonyms, and their importance in current processes of identification and identity formation (cf. Charsley 1996).

Identity formation works by creating clear-cut differences, in particular through valued binary oppositions. The name Haratin thus acquires meaning in a 'relationship of resemblance' to names like Drawa, *Qablī* and *Assūqī*, and in an 'oppositional relationship' to the repertoire of names to classify a non-Hartani. In the most complete list of ethnonyms in southern Morocco, compiled in the 1940s and published in 1958, it is said that '[s]ome words might be impressed with a certain contempt, others on the contrary with prestige' (Jacques-Meunié 1958: 243). Sharif is an example of the latter category. The name is the title for the descendants of Prophet Muhammad and has the connotation of 'distinguished', 'eminent' and 'high-bred'. The name is a cognate of the noun *šaraf*, 'honour', and the verb *šarufa*, 'to be highborn' (Wehr 1976: 466–467). The name 'Sharif' implies a specific relationship to the prevalent cultural ideals. The noble descent of Shurfa (pl. of Sharif) holds the promise of a superior status in society and a respectful approach by 'commoners'. People like to make clear to others they are Shurfa and wish to be treated accordingly. 'Hartani' evokes an opposite attitude toward hegemonic cultural ideals. The name conveys contempt and circumscribes the relationship between the people named as such to their fellow humans, as well as their appearance and inner self. People prefer not to be addressed with the ethnonym Hartani or with one of the various equivalents that have a similar negative connotation. One might even speak of a verbal taboo with respect to the name Hartani. Among

Berber-speaking Ait 'Atta 'it is very bad to see a Hartani or even pronounce the word before breakfast' (Hart 1984: 110–111). Elsewhere a similar practical taboo on the word exists.

In the southern Dra Valley, 'Drawi' is the most common synonym and euphemism for 'Hartani'. It is not entirely cleared from all offensive associations either and its meaning is therefore contested. The name Drawi is a linguistic form called *nisba*. Geertz (1983: 65–68) and Rosen (1984: 19–30) have singled out this linguistic form as an important device to classify human beings in Moroccan society. In Arabic, the root word *nasaba* evokes a range of words which have to do with linkage and relation. In the specific form with which I am concerned here, it ascribes a particular attachment or quality to a person (Rosen 1984: 19). By placing the suffix -i on to a characteristic, a *nisba* describes and denominates a person: 'Thus one may speak of an individual who comes from Sefrou as a *Sefrawi*, a Beni Mtir tribesman as a *Mtiri*, a bowlegged man as *qawasi*, or derive from the word *yahûd* (the Jews as a people) the *nisba* for a single Jew, *yahûdi* (ibidem). Similarly, a person whose origins lay in the Dra Valley may be known as a Drawi. In the work of Geertz and Rosen, the situational meaning of the *nisba* functioned as an important link in their general argument concerning the construction of social identities in Moroccan society. In '"From the Native's Point of View": On the Nature of Anthropological Understanding' (1983: 55–70), Geertz notes that a *nisba* makes of a Moroccan a contextualized person: '[B]ut as contexts themselves are relative, so too are nisbas, and the whole thing rises, so to speak, to the second power: relativism squared' (Geertz 1983: 65–66).

In the Dra Valley, the *nisba* Drawi is only used as a substitute for those people otherwise known as Haratin and not for non-Haratin. Since this last term is considered to be more offensive, using 'Drawi' has the effect of euphemizing the identity of the individuals involved. A local schoolteacher in the oasis noted that when he would denominate a person as a Hartani or *Qablī* ('southerner'), it is as if he would deny him true origins. Drawi instead suggests some sort of a fixed origin. His opinion is illustrated by another common synonym for Haratin. *Assūqī* is a *nisba* based on the word for market (*sūq*). The origins of an *Assūqī* thus lie at the market instead of in a tribe, village or town. As Kapchan (1996: 36) notes, in Morocco the market is 'the most prominent social metaphor for a site that embodies dirt, confusion, and shameful enactments'. Haratin when called *Assūqī* are

Hartani No origin, clear descent
Assuqi origin in the market — disorder, dirt

thus associated with the Moroccan symbol of disorder *par excellence*. In a more general sense, then, *Assūqī* pinpoints a person without clear origins, a mongrel (*wuld al-ḥarām*). A *nisba* like Drawi refers to a person's birthplace, tribal origin, or social milieu. It suggests that although a person may be a stranger in a certain setting—and, as we will see below, the name Hartani indeed conveys this meaning—the *nisba* Drawi gives him his essential identifiable background. Because it provides a context to ascertain a person's identity, assigning a *nisba* is the first step in getting to know someone. Yet, Drawi is a euphemism for Hartani and in many cases stands for a dark-skinned person. The negative connotation of 'Drawi', although less than 'Hartani', is illustrated by the curse (*Á bin drawi al-akur*, 'son of another man from the Dra') cited at the beginning of this section. Westermarck (1926 i: 483) significantly brackets the curse together with 'son of another Hartani', 'son of a foundling on the streets', et cetera. Similarly, in Casablanca Drawi is a pejorative name for someone from the southern oases. Thus, while there is indeed space for negotiation or manoeuvring regarding meaning and application of names, this takes place in an arena, or market if you like, where not all of the actors involved are able to negotiate on an equal footing. They may be called Drawa but are still treated as Haratin (that is, a dark-skinned person without clear descent), while negotiation that removes the Hartani stigma altogether seems even more difficult to accomplish. The constructivist line of approach on Moroccan society as presented in the work of Rosen and Geertz does not leave room for the existence of a 'masterstatus', defined as that aspect of a person's identity that overrides other, more subordinate aspects (like gender, residence and language), determining his or her identity in different social contexts (cf. Hughes in Becker 1973: 32–33). Here this masterstatus is the attributed membership in the category of Haratin. Thus, the schoolteacher's explanation illustrated that some Drawa have disputed the meaning of Drawi as a dark-skinned person (i.e., as a Hartani), arguing instead that the name suggests they are the original inhabitants of the valley (cf. Ennaji 1994: 105). Since, as we will see below, knowledge of your origins is a valuable cultural asset, this would give the denomination a more honourable ring. In subsequent chapters we shall also come across people who negate the ethnic names altogether. This is however less common. The reason for this lies in the subscription of most Drawa to the prevalent set of cultural ideals, especially with regard to the importance of descent in the

Drawi is a euphemism

not everyone negotiates on equal footing

Knowledge of origin is valuable

assessment of status differences. This brings me to the contemporary
field of opinion in the oasis society. In the next two sections the
historically transmitted patterns of meanings that form the context
in which the ethnonyms of Sharif and Hartani/Drawi get their meaning, are considered.

Roots in the nation

'Remco, you know he is not a Moroccan, he is a donkey'
(comment by a Sharif on the presence of a Drawi).

The formation of identities in southern Morocco works through symbolic forms that derive their meaning beyond the geographical boundaries of the oases. The first identity marker to be discussed, origin,
is linked to the discursive connection between identity and place,
as most strongly formulated in nationalist ideologies. At stake here
is a belief in the naturalizing and essentializing convergence between
place, culture and people (Gupta and Ferguson 1992). How does this
seemingly indissoluble triad, to which I shall add 'race' in the following section, informs the representation of 'Sharif' and 'Hartani'
as culturally familiar figures?

   The discussion of the *nisba* Drawi made it clear that naming is
related to one's origins, a crucial asset in Moroccan culture. *Aṣl* is
the Arabic term used here. In conversation, the term might be
brought up as an explanation of someone's behaviour, for example
when a person remarks that one should live in accord with one's
origin (cf. Rosen 1984: 23–30). Because origin binds man in time
and space, it is one of the distinguishing assets that sets him apart
from nature. Thus, when I was questioned one day about my origins and answered that I was Dutch, the questioner returned the
answer by saying that 'a cow might be Dutch, but I suppose you
are not a cow'. From the man's answer we should not infer that
nationality comes second or even is contrary to origin, a persistent
survival of pre-independence tribal times. It is rather the case that
nationality is expressed or heightened through one's origins. Thus,
once in discussing the marriage of a Drawi with a woman of a higher
status, one man jokingly remarked how this Drawi had swapped
nationalities (*jinsīyat*).

   In the *guide des communes*, a guide and list of state officials published

by the government, the population of the commune of Tagounite
in the Dra Valley, where fieldwork took place, has been described
as follows:

> The Drawa, originally from the Sudan, Arabs, ʿAlawī Shurfa coming
> from the Tafilalt Oasis, Idrissī Shurfa coming from Marrakesh, Zerhoun,
> Figuig and Tlemcen, and Berbers in particular belonging to the Aït
> ʿAtta.

In the text, the origins of the different population groups determine
their identity, whereby remarkably enough the Drawa, 'people of the
Dra', are said to be the only people originating outside Morocco—
namely in bilād as-sūdān, that is, the regions south of the Sahara.
The short text of the guide induces to go deeper into the connection between roots and nation in Morocco. I shall go into the suc-
ceeding social categories in review whereby the text fragment acts
as the lead for an examination of the relationship between local
viewpoints and ethnological topoi.

In the text, the Shurfa are said to come mainly from Moroccan
oases and not from abroad. In the oasis, the Shurfa from the village
of Aduafil gain their elevated status primarily from their common
ancestor, a religious teacher whose tomb lies at the centre of the
village, and from there down to the genealogy of Prophet Muhammad.
The claims of local Shurfa are strenghtened by the dominant, yet
contested, political ideology that puts prophetic descent at the centre of the origin myth of the Moroccan nation: In the 8th century,
Sharif Idriss bin Abdallah, direct ancestor of the Shurfa of the village, migrated from the Arabian peninsula to Morocco and founded
the first national dynasty. Since the 16th century, Sharifian dynas-
ties have ruled Morocco as 'Sharifian Sultanate'. The present-day
royal house is of Sharifian descent, albeit from a different genealogical branch (i.e., ʿAlawī) than Idriss. The nationalist ideology is founded
on the Sharifian origins of the country, which according to Combs-
Schilling (1989: 291–309) is instilled in everyday life at all important
Islamic rituals. King Hassan II is 'Prince of the Faithful, the center
of Moroccan political identity for over a millennium, the definer of
the nation, the definer of man . . .' (idem, 309). Munson raised serious
doubts about the ritual centrality of the king as political leader (caliph):
'[O]ne should not confuse the religious significance attributed to the
king by Morocco's government-controlled media with the religious
significance attributed to him by ordinary Moroccans' (Munson 1993:

124). Moreover, '[t]he king's status as sharif, carries far more weight
in the popular imagination than does his status as caliph' (idem,
128). Shurfa in the oasis do point out their close relationship with
their 'nephew' King Hassan II.

Other oasis inhabitants emphasize in a similar way as the Shurfa
do, the close connection between their origins and the Moroccan
nation. In the text, the Berbers are characterized by a tribal affiliation, not by a geographically specified origin. This at least suggest
the Berbers are indigenous to the region. Members of the Berber-
speaking Ait 'Atta Confederacy claim descent from their ancestor
Dadda 'Atta (whose tomb lies only a few kilometers from the oasis)
or, more commonly, from a renowned ancestor of one of the segments of the confederacy. At school, young 'Attawi children are
taught that the Berber population is the original population of
Morocco. Here, again, descent and nationality reflect on one another,
although this is again not uncontested. The origins of Shurfa and
'Attawis bring them 'close' to the Moroccan nation in a temporal,
social and geographical sense, in the same manner as the humble
or unknown origin of the Drawa is related to geographical distance.
Thus, although the name Drawi suggests an origin in the valley, it
is nevertheless said that the origins of Drawa are uncertain, unclear
or located outside of Morocco. Drawa are mocked for not being real
Moroccans, but Africans instead (referring to the sub-Saharan region).
Since descent links an inhabitant of the oasis to the national state,
lacking knowledge of it denies a person a national identity and even
questions his humanity (hence the abusive 'donkey nationality' of
Drawa and my 'cow nationality').

In the text, the 'Arabs' constitute a problematic category as well.
The guide is silent on their tribal or geographical origins. Are we
supposed to conclude from the singular 'Arabs', that the Arabic-
speaking population is, similar to the Berbers, indigenous to the
region and close to the Moroccan nation? Taken the connection
between origin and closeness to the nation, the author could very
well have been afraid that in referring to foreign origins of the Arabs
or Arabic-speaking population groups, he unwillingly revived the
much-disputed division of the Moroccan population into Arabs and
Berbers. In order to understand the contentious national identity of
Shurfa and Haratin it is necessary to go somewhat deeper into this
Arab-Berber divide.

Arabs and Berbers revisited?

The people who were living in the Maghreb before the immigration of Arabic-speaking groups in the 7th century are usually called Berbers in European languages; they are also known under the Berbername 'Imazighen'. Their distinct, yet related, languages are grouped under the same name (Berber or Tamazight). In Morocco, the three major areas where Berber is spoken are the Rif, the Middle Atlas and the Sous regions. In Algeria the major areas are the Mzab, Kabylia, Aurès and the Ahaggar region in the south where the Tuareg live. In the early ethnological literature of the Maghreb recognition of the social and cultural differences between the Arabic- and Berber-speaking populations was the starting-point for research. In Algeria, where the protracted paradigm of the Arab-Berber divide came into being in the 19th century, Berbers were supposed to constitute isolated communities, living more or less apart from the urban Arabs on the coast or the nomadic Arab population down south. They were only superficially touched by Islam and had retained their ancient beliefs and practices (Lorcin 1995: 159–160). When brought to the Moroccan context, the Arab-Berber divide was further developed and interwoven with a dichotomous model of state formation, dividing the country into the pacified western plains and the uncontrolled mountain areas. From 1920 on, it came to be the dominant model for ethnographic research and policy making in Morocco (cf. Burke III 1972).

The paradigm of the Arab-Berber divide was underpinned by a physical anthropological discourse that distinguished Arabs and Berbers as separate races. For example, 'the classic work on Moroccan history' (idem, 177), Henri Terrasse's *Histoire du Maroc* (1950), which summarizes decades of historical and anthropological research in colonial Morocco, assumed the purity of the three Berber races and their culture before the defilement via intercultural contact with the Arab population. Using a physical anthropological vocabulary (e.g., 'perfect', 'homogeneous', 'contaminated'), Terrasse considered the Arab-Islamic invasion as the major turning-point in Moroccan history. Before that time, the Moroccan population was 'united and almost perfect' (1950: 20).

The fate of the Arab-Berber divide has been documented quite well. The scientific discourse gained the status of official colonial policy after the First World War, culminating in the promulgation of

Berber
dahir

the 'Berber Dahir' in 1930 (following a decree in 1914). With this decree the French administration tried to institutionalize the alleged distinction between Arabs and Berbers in a separate schooling and juridical system. This led to nationwide resistance against the colonial divide-and-rule policy that denied the unity and equality of the population as Muslims and Moroccans. After independence nationalist ideology propagated the Arab and religious (Sharifian) foundations of the country.

The author of the *guide des communes* may have felt haunted by the ghosts of colonial academic formulations of ethnic identity (Banks 1996: 189), in particular because in post-colonial Morocco the place of Arabs and Berbers in the nation-state continued to be a delicate issue. Distinctions between Arabs and Berbers on the basis of religion and race have been largely discarded as unfounded. Instead, Berber *idéologues.* are concerned with having national authorities acknowledge that the language and culture of the Berber-speaking populations are integral components of the nation's patrimony. Since the 1980s, the ideology of 'Berberism' has rapidly spread, partly under influence of activists in neighbouring Algeria (Chaker 1987) and Europe. The activist struggle increasingly put the official Arab-Islamic identity of Morocco under pressure. Since the mid-1980s the national authorities have established closer relations with Berberists, in particular via 'cultural associations' which focus on cultural forms of expression and are thus less threatening to the state than political movements. The formulation of a national charter on Berber language and culture and the distribution of magazines and cassettes has nevertheless helped to disseminate the notion that 'Berber culture' is at least one cornerstone of the Moroccan nation.

The Berber question remains a sensitive issue in Morocco because it is directly linked to the nation's identity and the triad of place, people and culture. I give two brief examples. In a TV documentary of 1994 (Ouali and Derami 1994), Ouzzin Aherdane of the Berber party *Mouvement Populaire* claims to have laid hands on documents that question the Sharifian foundations of the nation. His adversary in the programme, Mohamed Deraoui of Meknes University, points out that all scholars agree on the fact that the Berbers were not indigenous to the country (as 'they came from Yemen') nor its first inhabitants (as 'the Goths preceded them'). Moreover, 'Moroccan *civilization* (*ḥaḍāra*) only truly began with the arrival of Sharif Idriss bin Abdallah'.

An article on the special Berber page of the national newspaper

Al-Bayane (Darif 1993) deals with the accusation that the Berberists try to revive the Berber Dahir (whereas in the 1930s the Berbers were among the first to oppose the colonial policy). Is it possible to eliminate 'colonial culture' (i.e., the Arab-Berber divide) and favour Berberism simultaneously? The solution of the author is to endorse the 'authenticity' of and 'attachment' to the national patrimony while stressing the various contributions of population groups within the territory of the Moroccan nation. The 'national Moroccan Arab culture' is the product of the interaction of different civilizations (Roman, Carthaginian, Vandalic, Byzantine, Andalusian, Jewish, Turkish and French). Berber culture is able to flourish *within* the outcome of this mixture, that is, Moroccan Arab culture, or so the article says.[2] These various statements from different media illustrate the depth, range and sensitivity of questions concerning the linkage between nation and various ethnic categories in the country. Returning to the text fragment in the *guide des communes*, I believe the author indeed wants the reader to conclude that the 'Arabs', as mentioned in the guide, are an original part of the Moroccan population, securing in this way the Sharifian foundations of the nation as well.

In addition to religion and culture, language is a contested marker of identity. If speaking Berber indicates an indigenous origin, then the Arab and Sharifian population would have to be classified as 'foreigners', at least in the southern regions. The Arab identity of the nation is, however, strenghtened by the interconnection between the Arabic language—the language in which the Holy Book was sent down—and Islam, and embodied by Sharif Idriss. Haratin or Drawa are often Berber-speaking in the south. Why then are they not presented as an indigenous population group?

African descent

The explanation for the separate status of Drawa in the text of the guide lies in the association of Drawa with the slaves who have been brought to Morocco over the centuries. The writer of the guide may have had his information from one of the several ethnologists who have argued for a common social origin of Haratin and *'Abīd* (sing. *'Abd*). The word *'Abd* means slave or servant—every Muslim is an

---

[2] Typically, as we will see, a reference to 'African civilization' as an ingredient of Moroccan culture, is missing.

'abd of God—but may also get the general meaning of 'black man'. According to Laoust, the Haratin originated in the Sudan where they were 'once sold as slaves'. 'At present [they] have established themselves in districts where they live in most cases attached to a family in the function of servant or slave' (1934: 156; cf. Maher 1974: 15). The assumed connection between slaves and Haratin returns in a number of etymological interpretations of the ethnonym Hartani. Nicolas (1977) postulated that the people who were sold at the slave market Kaharta in West Africa came to be named Hartani. A second ancient etymological interpretation (Leriche 1951) that can still be heard in the south argues that 'Hartani' should be read as *Ḥarr-ṭānī*, that is, as a contraction of *Ḥurr* (free) and *ṭānī* (second). Just like the Roman *libertus* never lost his manumitted condition, the ethnonym Hartani reminds people named as such of their past as slave (cf. Testart 1998). The etymological interpretation is incorrect (Colin 1971; Marçais 1951; Teine-Cheikh 1989: 95); it does, however, direct attention to the contrast between *Aḥrār* (freemen) and Haratin, with the status of the latter being defined as 'unfree' and 'foreign' because of their lack of connection with landownership and long-standing social networks based on descent, kin and affines.

For people in the oases the relationship between the identities of slaves and Haratin seems more complex than is allowed by the statement that 'Haratin once were slaves'. It is well known, generally recognized and part of the self-image of the *ʿAbīd* in Moroccan society that they descended from Sidi Bilal, a close friend and servant of the Prophet and the first muezzin in Islam. This origin story incorporates the descendants of slaves in the Arab-Islamic history which explains why one Sharif stated bluntly that while slaves 'are just like us', Drawa 'are nothing'. Recognition of the noble descent of *ʿAbīd* is also the reason why a second Sharif, when asked about the difference between Drawa and slaves, answered that 'slaves are better than Drawa . . . [Why?] It's just like that'.

Knowledge of one's descent distinguishes *ʿAbīd* from Haratin. The distinction should, however, not be pushed too far. Given the dark skin colour and alleged geographical origin, both *ʿAbīd* and Drawa are placed by significant others in one subordinate category. Thus, some villagers argued that both Drawa and slaves are 'the children of Sidi Bilal'.[3]

---

[3] The complexity of the distinction between Haratin and *ʿAbīd* also appears from

Displacement

Based on the essentializing convergence between place and people, significant and powerful others displace the Drawi/Hartani population, locating their origins outside of the Moroccan imagined community (cf. Anderson 1993). A discussion between me and two villagers illustrates the displacement of Drawa in relation to the Shurfa. One Sharif named Mulay Mustafa related how in the 1930s a delegation of Shurfa from the village had visited the Moroccan sultan. He suggested a Drawi named Baqerum had accompanied them. The Drawi was one of the villagers who had offered a piece of cloth to the Sultan. For this reason, the Drawi even came to be called 'sultan' after his return. Mustafa remarked that although the nickname was a joke, he indeed had been on an equal footing with the Shurfa throughout his visit. I believe that by way of the nickname the Sharifian villagers tried to neutralize the unusual equality of the Drawi with the Shurfa. Yet, the nickname contained an insurgent connotation as well. It was thus offensive in more than one way: Blok and Buckser pointed out for nicknames in general how they may 'offend people as well as the categories they seek to uphold. Pointing to social distinctions and cultural definitions, nicknames expose them—through the genre of the comic—as essentially arbitrary if not artificial' (1996: 88). This potentially subversive attribute

---

a closer look at the popular religious brotherhoods such as the *Ḥamadša* (Crapanzano 1973) and the *'Aissawa*; Brunel 1926: 67). Both are known for their public dramatic performances involving music, dance, and self-mutilation. The participation of Haratin is explicitly mentioned by authors or can be inferred from the context. Lecoeur (cited in Crapanzano 1973: 85 note 4) notes that the affiliants of the *Ḥamadša* are predominantly blacksmiths, drivers and potters. Crapanzano, researching the brotherhood in the northern town Meknes, did not find evidence to support Lecoeur's statement on the interconnection between occupation and brotherhood membership. Nevertheless, in Meknes the *Ḥamadša* adepts are dark-skinned but 'differentiated from the members of the so-called black confraternity, the Gnawa' (i.e., the brotherhood of descendants of slaves) and to a large extent natives of the southern oases, including those in the Dra Valley (idem, 86). The combination of profession, origin and non-*Gnawa* status makes it likely that these people are indeed considered to be Haratin. Furthermore, even within the *Gnawa* religious brotherhood, Haratin are involved. In Marrakech, the brotherhood can be split up into two sections. The first consists of slaves of *Lalla Krima* or *Lalla Mimuna*, a sect of 'metis Berbers (*zénètes métissés*) of the oases (*harratin*)' (Jemma 1971: 94). The second branch belongs to the sect of *Sidi Bilal*. Members of the first mainly speak Berber, possibly attesting to a rural origin, while members belonging to the second speak Arabic. According to Pâques both sects are distinct but complementary: 'Bilal and Mimuna constitute thus one being; metaphorically speaking, Mimuna is the sex of Bilal' (1991: 64).

of nicknames explains the heated reaction of my Sharifian neighbour Mulay Omar. He said that Mustafa's story certainly was false. A Drawi would never accompany the Shurfa to the sultan. The suggestion that maybe Baqerum went with the Shurfa to serve them was also disregarded by Mulay Omar: 'That is nonsense. Does the sultan not have his own servants?' Then he bent toward me: 'When you would visit the king, you would not let yourself be accompanied by an Englishman or German, would you?' I responded that this is not a correct comparison because both Drawa and Shurfa are Moroccans. Mulay Omar was not convinced: 'There are Drawa and there are Shurfa and the two don't mix! Your story is a lie'.

Whereas the Shurfa epitomize the Moroccan nation, the Haratin are placed outside of the national imagined community. In the process of identification, an imaginary Africa figures here as the original home of the 'others': The one-dimensional individual Hartani appears as the counter-image of an imaginary male, rooted in Moroccan terrritory. An often-quoted dictum, ascribed to King Hassan II, compares Morocco to a palm tree with its roots in African soil, yet receiving rain from Europe. The metaphor reflects the opinion of Sharifian villagers on the ambiguous status of the Haratin but deviates from the Sharifian villagers' self-image: They consider Moroccans first and foremost as Arabs, Berbers or Europeans, contrasting themselves to the 'African' Haratin. References to the Sudan and Somalia (where at the time of this fieldwork the United Nations were active, which was shown on television) testify to a protracted interconnection between the region and subordination.

To some extent both Shurfa and Drawa may be represented as outsiders who elude the clear-cut geographical circumscription of the nation. Both social categories then are positioned at the nation's—temporal, geographical and cultural—boundaries. For Shurfa their ambiguous state has been transformed into sacredness. They brought Arabic and Islamic civilization to the country and came to embody the nation. For Drawa, their ambigous state is seen as endangering the unity and purity of the nation. Following Douglas (1975: 281), the idea here is that seen from 'a continuum of social systems', at one end, outsiders might be excluded completely and irrevocably, and at the other extreme outsiders might be admitted to full membership of the community. Shurfa and Drawa are located at the poles of this continuum.

How do Drawa perceive the attribute of strange descent? Those

[handwritten margin note: Akkawis do not claim ignorance of descent]

[handwritten margin note: Drawi stress independence different from slaves]

living in the village either acknowledge ignorance of their descent or explain how they had migrated from another oasis. Others stressed their origin and regional *cum* national identity as conveyed in the *nisba* Drawi or as printed on their national ID. Drawa mostly objected against an identification with slaves, arguing they have come to the oasis of their free will. In this way they emphasize the cultural ideal of independence instead that of descent. Another strategy was to downplay the worthy origin of ʿAbīd. One man explained that the main difference between ʿAbīd and Drawa was that the first had been sold 'as sheep'; a second agreed that ʿAbīd were sold as livestock and furthermore defined ʿAbīd as 'those people who make music'. He referred to a practice at harvest time when groups of ʿAbīd go along the houses making music and asking for alms. ʿAbīd are here portrayed as dependent people of dishonourable birth. These remarks, however, match the self-image of the descendants of slaves summarized in the statement that 'a man is a slave when he has been bought' (Pâques 1991: 33).

Although Shurfa and others favour ʿAbīd over Haratin, Drawa try to distance themselves from any association with a possible enslaved past. One Drawi did however tell me, when asked about his opinion on the present socio-economic condition of Drawa, that compared with the time when they walked in chains, things definitely had improved: 'They would throw a coin in the fire and then push it onto your arm'. He added that his ancestors were castrated when working inside the patron's house where women were living. Although the castration of slaves seems to have been pursued by some slave-owners in the 19th century (Hunwick 1992: 22), the view of this Drawi on slavery was probably coloured by watching *Roots*, the TV serial on American slavery. Several times I heard villagers make fun of dark-skinned men by calling them after the main character of the serial, *Kunta Kinte*. Thus, curiously enough, *Roots* provided this Drawi with the picture of his own *aṣl* (i.e., roots).

Embodiment

[handwritten note: dislike of hybridity]

A key subtext of the discourse on roots and the nation is the purity of both descent and nation, and the dislike of hybridity. Unlike the descent of Shurfa and ʿAbīd, the descent of Drawa is put forward as anomalous, that is, falling outside of the preferable order (Douglas

[handwritten: Douglas]

1975: 285). This section examines the role of the body and bodily
practices in this imagery. It will be shown how external and internal bodily features are inscribed with meaning, neglecting similarities and fabricating or exaggerating differences. The body can also
actively be worked upon to produce difference (Shilling 1997: 84 *et
passim*). Recall how in the previous section, one Drawi put castrat-
ing and branding forward as common practices to fix the identity
of his ancestors; here less terrifying examples shall be presented.
Central aim is to show the subtle interplay between the symbolic
domains of descent and physical features in the construction of the
personae of Drawa and Shurfa.

The external body

> 'Say Remco, who is the negro (*aswad*) here?'
> RE: 'I don't know'.
> (Speaker points to the only Drawi present) 'He is the negro . . .'
> (I do not laugh).
> 'He doesn't mind being called this way. If we want to make a joke,
> we say negro to them'.
> RE: 'And how do they call the Shurfa?'
> 'They don't call them anything'.
> (conversation with a Sharif on the village square)

The Drawa may be perceived by some as strangers of African descent,
but they have lived in the southern oasis communities for centuries.
I noticed how a regular way to mark out the alleged anomalous presence of a Drawi was by pointing to a passer-by and saying: 'Look
a black man (woman)' as if by naming the anomaly it would mys-
teriously disappear. Also in private, Sharifian villagers sometimes
name the Drawa blacks (sing. *kaḥil* or *aswad*). In the Berber-speaking
villages surrounding the village, similar names in Berber are known.
Calling someone *Kunta Kinte* of course also applies to his colour of
skin. These examples show how naming acts as a discursive device
to come to terms with the alleged anomalous appearance of individuals.
Moreover, as indicated by the piece of conversation, naming silences
the marginal subject who is 'forced into submission even as the power
of the word is imposed on her or him by others' (Carnegie 1996: 483).

Skin colour is regularly mentioned as an attribute to distinguish
Shurfa from Drawa. The imagined community predominantly consists of light-skinned people; the 'one-dimensional individual Hartani'

down south is dark-skinned.[4] Skin colour is also a common differentiating marker of identity between Haratin and *'Abīd*: 'Slaves' are said to have a much darker skin. In individual cases pointed out to me, this seemed to be correct. Haratin are perceived as dark-skinned yet more in between light- and dark-skinned. Mixture of skin colour is of particular concern to inhabitants in the valley. People expressed their concern about my friendship with a Drawi by making jokes about the 'coffee-with-milk colour' a possible marriage with his sister could bring about. In the oasis community, Shurfa objected against the mixing of blacks and whites and expressed their fear of the possibility of a marriage with a light-skinned woman who later turns out to bear dark-skinned children. Whiteness of skin is generally valued by Drawa and Shurfa alike. Male Drawa prefer to marry a light-skinned Drawia. Colour consciousness or prejudice is thus a substantial factor in the fixation of the 'imagined essence' of Drawa and Shurfa, in particular because of its visibility (Goffman 1963). A dark-skinned person may evade questions or lie about his origin or occupation but his skin colour remains clearly visible, possibly betraying his social identity. In case of doubt or possible confusion, e.g., a light-skinned Drawi or dark-skinned Sharif, people joke or express their concern with what they consider to be an exceptional ambivalence.

Descent and skin colour are linked. Dunn observed for the nearby Tafilalt Oasis that basically patrilineal descent, and thus family name, determines the attribution of skin colour (Dunn 1977: 44): A person is 'white by definition' (Domínguez 1986). Spillman (1931: 96) pointed at the impossibility of distinguishing a *Ḥurr* ('freeman') from a Hartani by skin colour. Since dark-skinned individuals can be found in every category, even that of Shurfa, it is possible for a stranger to claim descent from a locally renowned religious teacher (marabout) without the possibility of verification. Similarly, a light-skinned person may 'hide internally' a Drawi identity, something only to be discovered

---

[4] Political criticism, in particular concerning the head of state, can then be voiced in a racist idiom. Munson (1993: 130) relates how an old woman 'who was born in a mountain village, often referred to [King] Hassan II as the *'azzi* (Negro or nigger), a conventional comical insult in Moroccan popular culture' and here meant to express her opinion on the political climate of the country. This form of royal insult goes a long way back. Mulay Ismaïl, the 17th century ancestor of the present king, was like King Hassan II privately called 'son of a slave'.

after a darker-skinned child has been born. Thus it is considered
important to be informed about the origins of the person you marry.

Skin colour as a marker of identity is merged with other bodily
features. One day I visited a village with an 'Attawi when he pointed
to some children, saying you could see by the colour of their skin
they were Haratin. I objected to this as I happened to know non-
Haratin with a darker colour of skin. My companion was not convinced: 'Look at their curly hair, which is unlike our straight hair'.
To explain the difference between Shurfa and Drawa, a Sharif told
me about a member of his family who once made a trip to Morocco's
capital Rabat to visit his uncle. He only knew the name of the quarter where his uncle lived, so he just walked around in it. After a
while he saw some children playing in the street. He guessed they
could be his uncle's children as they had a Sharifian look on their
face. He turned out to be right. The following conversation with a
Sharif on the village square, shows how a somatic feature that is not
innate but acquired through strenuous labour can function as an
identity marker.

> 'You know this man is a real peasant (fellah), he cannot read nor
> write. You will see him digging a canal when the water comes. And
> when you die, he will dig your grave!'
> RE: 'You are a peasant as well'.
> 'No, I am not (the man says indignantly), I am into trade. Only when
> there is water, I irrigate my own fields. (He points to the Drawi) His
> [callous] hands and feet are those of a peasant'.

It appears that emphasizing somatic features is one way to objectify
the identity of Drawa. Moreover, in the example the opposition
between mind and body, which is one between Sharif and Drawi,
is related to the division of labour, with Drawa fulfilling less respected
work. This related strategy reduces the collective identity of Drawa
to their physicality, contrasting it to mental or more general cultural
qualities, in the example the ability to read and write.

Appearance, origin and division of labour are combined in the
story of Ham that an educated non-Drawi once told me to account
for the socio-economic condition of Drawa. Ham's sons were cursed
by Noah (Nūh) and forced to work eternally as servants. The classification of mankind according to the descendants of the three sons
of Noah (Shem, Ham, Japhet) originates in the Bible (Genesis 9:
18). Though the story of Noah is mentioned in the Koran, his son
Ham does not figure in it. However, Ham's curse can be found in

Arabic literature 'in a variety of forms, often with considerable differences' (Lewis 1990: 44, 123–125). In one such a story, 'the descendants of Ham are condemned to be slaves and menials. Some also assign specific roles to the descendants of Shem and of Japhet, the former to be prophets and nobles (*sharīf*) the latter to be kings and tyrants' (idem, 45). The attribution of Haratin to the children of Ham corresponds to a European pre-modern ethnological discourse on mankind and the sons of Noah that tended to attribute to each of the different classes of mankind its own characteristics (Sanders 1969). In the 19th century, this Biblical discourse was transformed into a linguistic and racialist theory about the peopling of the world. The race category of Hamites was invented to account for the civilizations on the African continent that had developed without European assistance. The Hamites were supposed to be of European stock. They lived in northern and eastern Africa and included such population groups as the Berbers, Tibu, eastern African cattle-herding tribes (Nilotic peoples), and Ethiopian and Somalian peoples. According to the best-known advocate of the Hamitic thesis, the British ethnologist Seligman, the Hamites were the 'great civilizing force of Africa' (Seligman 1930: 19). They belonged to a non-African race, yet were not natives of the continent. The Haratin were included in the Hamitic family as a sub-group called Kushites (or *Kouchites*, after Kush, son of Ham and grandson of Noah).[5]

In the Islamic versions of the curse of Noah, skin colour and servitude coalesce. Thus, in a number of early modern texts Ham was originally light-skinned. The dark skin colour of Ham's descendants was God's punishment, complementary to Noah's curse of eternal servitude (Vajda 1971: 104). The morality of a dark skin also returns in the following story on Ham and Haratin:

---

[5] The alleged racial purity of the Haratin as well as their European origin as Hamites, explain why Henri Terrasse's *Histoire du Maroc* (1950) provides us with an ultimately positive image of a category of people whom local inhabitants depict in a rather negative way: 'The elegance of their corporal lines, their pace, the bronzlike green and brightness of their skin, certain asian traits in their face—curved eyebrows, occasionally slit-eyedness and protruding jaws—all distinguishes them from the negroes and the mestizos [*métis nègres*] (. . .). Not to mention their elegant intelligence and flexible adaptability' (Terrasse 1950: 20). See on Hamites and Haratin the work of Brémond (1950), Coon (1951: 34); Julien (1956: 49–52); Murdock (1959: 9, 112, 113) and Camps (1970).

> The Harratin relate that they are the descendants of Noah's second
> son Ham, and that once upon a time they used to be white. One day,
> however, Ham protected his head during a heavy rainstorm by car-
> rying the Koran on top of it. The rain was so heavy that it washed
> all the characters of the holy book on to Ham's skin; these characters
> being sacred, were indelible, and so they turned Ham and his offspring
> black for ever!' (Epton 1958: 161; cf. Leriche 1951).

Ham, of course, misuses the Koran, and is therefore punished. However, the dark skin does have a holy origin, the ink of the Koran (cf.
for Tuareg and Noah's tale, Claudot-Hawad 1990: 17).

  The concern with skin colour, combined with origins, can be witnessed outside of southern Morocco. In ethnographic publications
many condescending remarks on dark-skinned people or Haratin
in particular can be found, indicating that colour prejudice does
exist in Moroccan society at large. See, for example, the comment
of an inhabitant of Rabat, quoted from a study on the 'Rbatis', a
group of families that consider themselves the original inhabitants of
Morocco's capital:

considered themselves Chleuh

> Moroccan society is divided along racist lines: Northern Berbers, Chleuh
> Berbers, Arabs, Blacks or Haratin. The people are very much aware
> of the colour of their skin and guard it very closely (. . .). Thus, the
> Rbatis have a white skin colour, it is a mark of recognition and never
> would a Rbati accept a black man in his family' (Hayeur 1991: 130).

This quotation needs to be nuanced. Skin colour is certainly of concern to some Moroccans and numerous references to colour prejudice can be found in popular culture; yet, observers disagree as to
how much importance should be given to these references. Faath,
in a study on human rights, observes that notwithstanding the absence
of legal inequality, dark-skinned Moroccans are faced with social discrimination in daily life (1992: 384–385). Munson notes, however,
that most 'educated Moroccans' ridicule racist thinking 'and often
stress that Islam does not tolerate any form of racism'. Moreover
'Morocco is by no means rigidly stratified along racial lines' (Munson
1993: 131). I agree with this last observation, yet the combination
of descent and skin colour does produce a significant marker of identity that cannot easily be discarded.

  The quotation on the Rbatis shows awareness of a concept like
'mixed marriage' from which we can infer a preoccupation with the
purity of family and ancestry. In the oasis I observed a similar anxiety about so-called mixed marriages. I give two examples. People

gossiped about the friendship of a female 'Attawi, daughter of a village head, with a Drawi from another oasis. The two youngsters had met during their studies in the provincial capital. One villager pitied the father for his bad luck and scorned the girl for flirting with a Drawi and for leaving 'a good-looking young man from her own family without a wife': 'That's a shame. She should respect the collective consciousness (al-waʿy al-jamāʿī) of the people here'. The second example deals with mixed marriages in general.

> Sitting in front of the village gate, a Sharif who lives most of the year outside of the village read aloud a tragic newspaper article about the war in Yugoslavia. A Serbian man and an Islamic woman wanted to flee the country because as a 'mixed couple' they were threatened by both sides. They were, however, killed by border police. The man who told me this story commented that apparently the same kind of problems seemed to exist elsewhere. I asked him for an explanation. He whispered (while pointing to a Drawi): 'You know, he is black and I am white, there is a difference between us, their wives have the freedom to go out into the fields, while our women have to stay at home'. I asked why they cannot leave their house: 'That's something from the past. You see, we also do not marry each other. When such a marriage however does take place, people talk among each other, saying it is not good and should not be allowed'.

It appears that the possibility of 'mixed marriages' is the litmus test of social change, just like it was for the French capitain Moureau when he considered the conclusion of mixed marriages in Casablanca a demonstration of the Haratin's emancipation (1955: 8; cf. Hammoudi 1997: 106). Whereas in the oasis Shurfa speak of the threat of mixed marriages to indicate the distinctiveness of Shurfa vis-à-vis Drawa and other social categories, Drawa come up with examples of intermarriages between Drawa and higher status groups in neighbouring villages or in Casablanca to signal the wind of change that is blowing in the nation. These Drawa speak out what to Shurfa should remain unthinkable.

Colour consciousness is also translated in public objections against possible discriminatory acts. Racism is seen as foreign to Islam and to Morocco, yet typical of Europe: The treatment of North African migrants in Europe is called racist and also tourists are sometimes branded as racists. Racism is said to hinder the development of a national identity. The Rbati élite is thus accused that in their sectarian behaviour they go as far as preferring foreigners to Moroccans as marriage partners. Moreover, these same people collaborated with

the French authorities in colonial times (Hayeur 1991: 128). Usage
of the French *racisme*—*maiz al-ʿunṣurīya* in Arabic—is widespread
in Morocco. The term is easily-used, also for Moroccans. One of
Hayeur's informants complained about how true Rbatis take him
for a country dweller (*ʿarūbī*) even though he had lived in Rabat all
his life: 'That's racism', and, as he added, Islam forbids any racist
act (Hayeur 1991: 129). In my own research, I also observed how
people sometimes use the term to condemn any attempt in making
unjustified distinctions between humans, as for example between rural
and urban people or even between those invited for dinner and those
not. The concept of racism is part of a global moral discourse of
condemnation. Its use by informants demonstrates the societal changes
in the oasis communities. People discuss and dispute the current
social relations, and some object to or reinterpret the social hierarchy that has been handed down to them by using the powerful concept of racism.

The internal body: Emotions

Implicated in the reduction of Drawa to their physicality, contrasting it to mental or more general cultural abilities of Shurfa, is the
notion that Drawa are less civilized than their fellow villagers. They
have less self-control and are closer to nature. Non-Drawa represent
them as strong, energetic persons, more capable of doing hard labour and more resistant against sickness or other evil. When a scorpion entered my house and I asked for help, a Sharif yelled at me
[the Drawi] 'Hammed will take care of the scorpion. They don't
harm him, you know, he eats them'. With respect to sickness, the
following was reported by two Dutch researchers in their fieldwork
report in the 1950s.

> A somewhat educated Moroccan had told us about the existence of a
> typical dissimilarity between the ancient oasis population and the Ber-
> ber population that had come to settle in the oases only recently. The
> Drawa were supposed to be immune against malaria, while the Berbers
> suffered a lot from this disease. When we made an inquiry after this
> fact with the French doctor, he showed himself indignant: 'Nothing of
> the sort, the very idea!' (Jager Gerlings and Jongmans n.d.: 113).

The doctor considered it a ridiculous idea but 'the educated Moroccan' could well have read in an ethnographic compilation appear-
ing around the time of the Dutch expedition about the different blood

type of Haratin (Briggs 1960: 67), a feature which has led one physical anthropologist to argue that the blood type of the builders of
the pyramids matches that of present-day Haratin in the Dra Valley.[6]

Drawa are attributed not only with physical strength but also with
sexual energy. Male Shurfa mentioned this attribute with respect to
male and female Drawa. The Moroccan folktale 'the Pilgrim's wife
and the Hartani', recorded in the Sous, offers a nice illustration of
this point (Dwyer 1978: 118–119). In the tale, a married woman
begins a sexual relationship with a Hartani after her husband has
left on a pilgrimage to Mecca. When he returns and cannot find
her in the house, the man believes her to be dead. During the night
a saint arrives at his house to tell him his wife has moved into the
house of the Hartani. At first, the man cannot believe the saint's
words but at last he does: He finds them and takes revenge by killing
his wife and taking the Hartani to prison. Dwyer (1978: 118) comments that 'the wife of a *hajj* succumbs to the advances of a *hartani*,
a brown man of servile status. The *hartani* lacks whiteness, the essential mark of beauty'. Yet, 'the wife of the well-to-do pilgrim (. . .)
matches the *hartani*, whose essence is believed to be animalistic: her
blood, like his, proves to be "hot"'.

The following riddle, put to me by a Drawi, captures this dimension of the 'imagined essence' of Drawa as well.

> An *'Abd* and an *'Abda* [i.e., a black man and woman, RE] are inter-
> connected through a cord. They only start to work when it gets dark,
> but then they continue all evening. What is this?

At the explicit level the riddle refers to the cooking of the regular
dinner in the village. The answer is then a couscous pan. Such a
pan consists of two parts. In the lower half one puts water and vegetables and in the upper part, the couscous. The steam of the vegetables rises and enters the upper half through holes in the bottom
of the pan. In this way the couscous in the upper half is steamed.
To avoid the loss of heat, a cord closes off the space between the
two halves. Because villagers use unglazed clay pans and open fire

---

[6] Information on contemporary physical anthropology reached me through inter-
net discussions on 'Afrocentrism', a multidisciplinary paradigm that considers the
central role of African cultures in the development of human civilization. Some
Afrocentrists react against Hamitic ideas that deny true (dark-skinned) Africans a
place in history. Yet, it uses these same Hamitic data to trace the spread of civilization from North Africa to the south of Africa (Roth 1995).

fed by palm leaves (instead of metal pans and gaz), daily use makes
the pan turn black. As with every clever riddle, it tempts to a second interpretation, here one in which humans with a black skin are
portrayed as sexually overactive persons. The metaphor of the couscous pan is well chosen: The two halves represent the two sexes,
with the lower part being the male and the upper part being the
female part. The upper half is penetrated by the steam (*nafs*) of the
'male half' until the couscous is done.[7] In the riddle, sexual drives
and blackness are symbolically linked—not unlike the Saharan proverb
that 'in the night all men are black' (Bourgeot 1975: 84). The linkage
returns in the practice of putting one half of a couscous pan in a field
to stimulate the cultivation. Sometimes the burned and blackened
heart of a palm tree is used. Just like the couscous pan, it is said of
Drawa that they are as black as the ashes of a fire whereas other
non-Drawi blacks are said to be black because of the sun. The linkage of food preparation with sexuality (and fertility) might explain
why in one Moroccan tribe a black earthenware pan should be called
'the white one' in the presence of a Sharif (Westermarck 1926: 37).
This circumlocution reflects the verbal taboo of dark-skinned Haratin
generally known as Drawa.

The internal body: Rationality

The expression of the imageries of Shurfa and Haratin in a cultural
idiom extends to their respective intellectual capabilities. Drawa are
said to be less knowledgeable of differences between the human and
non-human world or to act according this knowledge. The following
four jokes (*nukat*) illustrate this dimension.

> a) A man pays a visit to a Drawi. He parks his car in front of
> the house and goes inside. While the guest enjoys dinner with the
> Drawi host, the Drawi children take care of his 'transporter'. That
> is to say, they go outside and feed the car with wheat.

---

[7] The cord stands for the women's belt that closes the body and holds the energy
(*rūḥ*) together (Pandolfo 1989: 14). In other words, the belt holds the two black
halves together to create more energy. See furthermore Pâques (1991: 150): 'This
identification between man, the universe and barley, permits them to develop a
complete symbolism of food. The couscous pan on the fire becomes a microcosm
with below the firewood (. . .) and on top of that the plate full with beef (the earth)
from which vapour rises that ascends like the mist (. . .) and cooks the grain descended
from the sky, full with *nafs*'.

b) While promenading in front of the *qsar*, a Drawi comes across a hedgehog. He immediately runs back to the village to tell about this discovery. The whole village turns out to take a look at 'the thing'. But what is it? Nobody knows. Suddenly, one Drawi cries out he has the answer: 'It's a needle factory'.

c) The moon disappears when the sun rises. However, one day the moon does not seem very willing to leave the stage for the rising sun. It is then that Drawa start throwing stones at the moon to make him go away.

d) A group of Drawa is busy at the well. Suddenly the bucket with which they bring the water up falls back into the well. One Drawi knows how to get the bucket back. He leaves the scene and returns with a billy-goat. He grabs the animal by the hind legs and lifts it upside down into the well, using the horn as a hook to catch the bucket.

Most striking in these four jokes is the mingling of humans, animals and lifeless objects: A car is thought to be a donkey, a hedgehog is supposed to be a machine, a moon becomes an animal which can be chased away, and finally, a billy-goat is used as a lifeless object. Besides the message that Drawa are 'proverbially stupid', as was pointed out in a 19th-century travel report (Shabeeny 1967: 3), the jokes suggest they do not know proper human classification, while the manner in which they transform nature into culture is ridiculed.[8]

The Drawa appear as an ambivalent category of people, with out-siderhood, appearance and mental capabilities being interconnected. Shurfa are rational and controlled, that is, the opposite of Drawa. Having established the central role of the Shurfa in the alleged Arab

---

[8] Compare the following 'world-upside-down' story: St Bon writes in his *mémoire* on a cluster of oases east of the Dra (1938a: 44) how the Ait 'Atta came to name a group of Haratin as *Baba Aghioul*, 'he who carries a donkey on his shoulders', because when once these Haratin wanted to cross a river, one of them took the young donkey they had with them on his shoulders to save it from drowning, or so the 'Attawis say. Ennaji (1994: 104) presents a joke that contains a similar message by focusing on the anomaly of an educated Hartani. The joke is on the appointment of a teacher at a Koran school. When the only candidate appears to be a Hartani, one of the members of the committee suddenly comes up with a second eligible candidate. And as it would only be fair to give him an equal chance to apply for the job, the Hartani has to wait until the committee has seen this second candidate: So, they let in a black donkey with a turban on his head. The Hartani understands the message and immediately leaves the stage and town.

and Berber origins of the nation, it is not surprising that whereas
the Shurfa are said to speak 'turbo Arabic', it is said Drawa are not
able to speak proper Arabic nor Berber. Or, they are only able to
speak Moroccan Arabic, and not to read and write Standard Arabic.
Non-Drawa make fun of Drawa and imitate their gestures, body
movements and gibberish talk. I wish to conclude this section, however, with a case of public strife in which the mimicry came from
the Drawa: I was driving in a *grand taxi* heading down the oasis road
with two other passengers. The taxi stopped to let an old Sharif step
in. He was dressed in white, rumpled clothes with a white turban
on his head. Once inside, one of the two young passengers asked
for the newspaper that the Sharif had held under his arm. The old
man was not very willing to give the paper and asked them whether
they were able to read it: 'Are you able to read, do you know
Arabic?', he asked. 'Of course', one of the men answered. So they
got the paper from the Sharif. It only took a couple of minutes
before the old man asked the men to return it again. He had seen
they were not reading at all. He was right they could not read, and
as he shouted, this was typical of Drawa: They don't know anything,
not even how to speak and read Arabic. Even so, the young men
had made fun of the man, asking for the paper jeeringly mimicing
the Sharif by seemingly reading it. They continued to make fun of
the Sharif after he got out of the car.

Conclusions

Texts and local practices alike generate a distinct and durable body
of knowledge and evaluations which portrays the people named as
Haratin or Drawa as anomalous, sharing traits of different social categories (cf. Douglas 1975: 282). They are without clear descent, in
between the light-skinned and dark-skinned people. They are said
to come from elsewhere, yet living amidst fellow villagers. Caught
in the web of prevalent cultural ideals, Drawa in particular are identified as marginal people, marked off from the 'normal population'
and attributed with special physical, intellectual and emotional qualities. Likewise, in some anthropological texts, they ultimately are classified in between the European and African populations as Hamites.
    The dispersed remarks and observations relating to ethnicity and
colour prejudice dealt with in this chapter are embedded in a larger

temporal and geographical framework, beyond national boundaries
(cf. Lewis 1990). A number of studies dealing with other areas indicate a close connection between contemporary conceptions of race
and ethnicity and colonial historiography in particular (Carnegie
1996; Robb 1995). For Morocco, Hammoudi has signalled the 'con-
nections between things and words' that colonial ethnoscience invented:
Words, ethnonyms came to embody people with specific features:
'Dichotomous categories produced Morocco anew' (Hammoudi 1997:
107–109, 125). Ancient fluid categories and metaphors were objectified
in nationalist discourses, proving their tenacity after independence.

In my survey of the identities of Drawa and Shurfa I profited
from existing anthropological literature. Since the ethnic names are
used to create meaningful differences, I have tried neither to essen-
tialize nor to deny their forcefulness in defining social identities.
Subsequent chapters shall remain primarily with one oasis community to consider how the ideas pertaining to Drawa and Shurfa as
presented in this chapter are cultural interpretations of a specific
social bonding.

essentialism

* Hammoudi :

CHAPTER THREE

OASIS BOUND
STRANGERS IN A PACIFIED ENCLAVE

> For, to be a stranger is naturally a very positive relation; it is
> a specific form of interaction (Simmel 1950: 402).

After having considered the schemes of perception that shape the
personae of 'Sharif' and 'Hartani/Drawi' in the Moroccan nation-
state in the previous chapter, the present chapter examines how these
dispositions inform and structure the distinctive configuration of saints
of servants in one locality. Central aim is to show the construction
of this locality as a culturally distinctive *place* and from this the *displacement* of one part of its population. Before independence in 1956,
the overall majority of the sedentary population in the oasis societies lived in extremely dense, walled settlements, called *qsar*-s. The
qsar is rigorously enclosed, maintaining the dwellings within four
walls. Inside, one notices a strict spatial division, with Drawa living
at a marginal location. Social groups in the oases live separately
from one another; when forced to live together, like Shurfa with
Drawa, they do so in separate quarters.[1] The peculiarities of the
coexistence within the oasis villages will be pointed out in a historical sketch of the community and local sanctuary of the village of
Aduafil. The village was founded in the 16th century by the religious teacher Mulay Adafal and further developed by his descendants. The shrine of the founder is the pivot around which the
quarters of the present-day village have been built. After the early
years the descendants of the founder extended the meaning and functions of their ancestor's shrine and developed it into a refuge and
market centre. The description of the increase in function and range
of the sanctuary in this chapter centres on the conceptualization of
the settlement as 'a pacified, civilizational, enclave' and the Drawa
as long-term 'strangers', that is, as people without vested rights in
the oasis community.[2]

---

[1] Paraphrase of Jacques-Meunié (1958: 241).
[2] See for the concept of 'pacified enclave', Blok (1981: 117, 123).

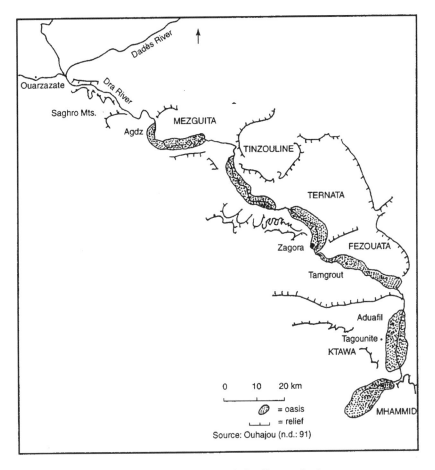

Figure 2: Dra Valley and the Ktawa Oasis

An oasis sanctuary in the making

Along the Dra River is collected the largest cluster of oases in the region south of the Moroccan High Atlas Mountains. The river originates out of a joining of two other rivers, the Ouarzazate and the Dadès, at the southern foot of the High Atlas, and runs 200 km southward along a mountain range to end in the desert near the last oasis of the valley (see figure 2). The empty bed continues westward to the Atlantic Ocean. The river water reaches at best the last oasis Mhammid, after which it evaporates in the desert. Wells supplement the irregular stream of surface water and make human

sedentary life in the oases possible. For a visitor coming from the
north, the southern Bani Mountains constitute the decor that frames
the green stretch of palm trees in the oases—a fifth of all the date
palms in Morocco is located in the Dra Valley. The Ktawa Oasis
is the largest in the valley, with an irrigated surface of 7797 hectares,
a length of 37 km, and about 25,000 inhabitants (census 1982), living in 60 villages. The village of Aduafil is one of the smaller villages on the west bank of the Dra River in the northern part of
Ktawa.

The natural boundaries that circumscribe the valley have maintained the relative isolation of the oasis from surrounding human
habitation. To the east and west the Ktawa Oasis is closed off by
the Bani Mountains, leaving only relatively narrow passes for the
river and the only asphalt road to run through. Twenty kilometres
south of Ktawa lies the small oasis Mhammid, the last one in the
valley. South of Mhammid the Sahara begins. In the north of the
valley, one has to cross the Saghro Mountains and the High Atlas
Mountains with summits above 4000 m to reach Marrakesh, 'capital of the south'. The only pass at an altitude of 2300 m is often
closed in winter because of heavy snowfall. At the other side, in earlier days the difficult barrier of the Sahara was only crossed in winter. In the valley, the Ktawa Oasis can only be reached from the
north by way of a small corridor, the Foum Takkat.

Throughout history the geographic isolation of the oasis has played
a significant role in the upkeep of its relative independence from the
other oases in the valley and from the Moroccan state. This independence has, however, not prevented its inhabitants from keeping
contacts with the outside world, nor has it prevented others from
moving in. Instead, Ktawa profited from its geographic location to
function as a threshold between northern Morocco and sub-Saharan
Africa. The oasis has fulfilled an important role in the caravan trade
between Morocco and the regions south of the Sahara.[3] In the 16th
century, when the village of Aduafil was established, the Ktawa Oasis
had taken over from Sijilmasa (in the Tafilalt Oasis) the position as
the most important stopoff in the Saharan caravan trade to Tagheza
and Timbuctoo (Bovill 1978: 238) and was going through its finest

---

[3] Compare the following note by Jacques-Meunié (1982: 368): 'Beside its fertile
soils, the Dra is situated exceptionally well at the entrance of Morocco, along the
route from Timbuctoo to Marrakesh . . .'

hour. An intricate trade network interwove the interests of the north and south of the country. Ktawa was the regional centre of a trade network that outgrew the oasis. From the south came gold, salt—often used as currency, ambergris, gum, hides, luxury goods (ivory, animals) and slaves. Europe tried to sell cloth, firearms and ironwork. The input of northern Moroccan towns consisted of food and luxury handicrafts for the Arab colonies in the south and the Sudan. In the middle were located the southern oases with dates, figs, sugar (from the Sous), cotton (Tafilalt Oasis), indigo (the Dra), and alum.

In the Ktawa Oasis, Drawa worked as agriculturalists and artisans, Jews fulfilled artisanal work and controlled part of the trade, and nomads traded their pastoral products at specific periods of the year for cereals and dates. Regionally, sedentary agriculturalists and transhumant or nomadic herdsmen were economically interdependent and met at the local markets. Furthermore, the constant immigration of different population groups—Jews from the Middle East and Spain, Berber- and Arab-speaking herdsmen, religious functionaries claiming saintly descent, and slaves (by way of a forced voyage)—led to a multi-ethnic composition of village life in the oases. It was only when the caravan trade stopped being significant and actual national borders were drawn that the northern fringe of the Sahara, including Ktawa, was cut off from the southern regions. The Dra Valley came then to be situated at the margin of the Kingdom of Morocco, its rural economy totally dependent on and directed toward the northwest of the country.[4]

When the village was founded, the oasis had a very mixed population. There were the Drawa and quite a number of Jews who lived in two large qsar-s where they worked as jewellers, leather workers and traders. There were the landowning Aḥrār: From the 7th century on, several groups penetrated the valley, partly under the banner of Islam. They subjected the local population and called themselves 'the free-born' (Aḥrār), making the Haratin their tenants and labourers. It may also be that they who worked as tenants and labourers came to be named Haratin. Mezzine (1987: 194) writes on the early process of subjugation of the 'Haratin' that 'it probably were [Berber tribes] who finished off the subjugation of the black population signalled in the oasis at the eve of the Arab conquest', yet

* Berber tribes subjugated prior to Arab conquest

[4] See for neighbouring oases Tafilalt and Figuig, Dunn's *Resistance in the Desert* (1977: 137–272).

it remains uncertain whether we should transpose the present-day distinction of Haratin and *Aḥrār* to a strict ethnic division in the past.

Slaves form another category of people in the oasis. The trans-Saharan slave trade was operative on a regular basis from the 8th century until the beginning of this century (Swanson 1978). The peak of the trade was from the 17th to the end of the 19th century. It is not known whether slaves constituted a substantial part of the oasis population at the time the village was founded. Leo Africanus, who visited the valley in the beginning of the 16th century, wrote in his report published in 1550 that the inhabitants of Ktawa owned numerous male and female slaves, working as servants in the houses of the élite. The historian Jacques-Meunié (1982: 412) argued that Leo Africanus may have confused slaves with the autochthonous dark-skinned Haratin who were legally free. This conclusion was based on the non-existence of any proof of a significant slave trade between Morocco and sub-Saharan Africa in this period (1982: 224; cf. Hammoudi 1985: 31). Thus, for example already four centuries earlier, the soldiers for the slave army of the Almohad dynasty were recruited from among the Haratin in the Dra Valley instead of among people at the southern fringe of the Sahara (idem, 411–412). In all likelihood, the annual trans-Saharan caravans were bringing a number of slaves to the northern oasis markets at the time the village was founded and some of them probably stayed in southern Morocco. They were involved in agricultural production, working side by side with Haratin. Many of these slaves, however, might in fact have been free-born or manumitted Haratin. Evidence for this conclusion is offered by the confusion that went along with the recruitment of slaves for the slave army of Sultan Mulay Ismaïl in the 17th century (Meyers 1974: 84–115). Recruits were rounded up in the southern oases instead of in regions further south. To justify conscription, the Moroccan state reduced slaves and Haratin to the same denominator: 'Many of the supposed *ʿabīd* [that were rounded up to serve in the slave army, RE] lived as free Muslims, (. . .) either because they had never been slaves, such as the *ḥarāṭīn*, or because their ancestors had been manumitted, or because these or they themselves had been separated from their masters in periods of instability' (De Bakker 1991: 78). Notwithstanding protests, attempts to conscript Haratin into the sultan's slave army continued into the 19th century.[5]

---

[5] In 1697 'all blacks and *ḥarāṭīn* from the Ksar al-Kabir region were impressed

Aduafil did fulfil a considerable role in the 19th century slave trade because of the change of the trade route from Algeria (via Figuig) to Morocco (via Ktawa) in this period. Reason for the change of direction was the French invasion in Algeria (1830), the abolishment of slavery in Algeria by the French government and attempts to stop the slave trade (Dunn 1977: 107–109). The German traveller Gerhard Rohlfs stayed in Aduafil for two weeks mid-19th century, and gathered some information of the caravan trade with Timbuctoo:

> Before I proceeded further on my journey I went to Ktaoua to get some information about the trade with the Sudan. (. . .) I first went to Aduafil, an important place, which has the chief trade with the Sudan; gold (in small quantities), ivory, leather, and slaves, are its chief imports, in exchange for which the drawi [here referring to all the inhabitants of the valley, RE] can provide the blacks with European products only, for the copper which is supplied to the Sudan from Tarudant goes principally through Tenna and Nun. The slaves are purchased in the Sudan at the cheap prices from two to three pounds; though young, pretty and fair-complexed girls are more expensive. They are then resold in Fez and Morocco [Marrakesh, RE] at a considerable profit, fetching from fifteen to twenty-five pounds each. The caravan journey from Aduafil to Timbuctoo takes about eight weeks, and the largest stretch of desert without water (according to the natives, though I think it is an exaggeration) takes ten days in crossing (Rohlfs 1874: 353–354).

Rohlfs' description suggests that the slave trade was an important segment of the oasis economy in the 19th century. Rohlfs' report confirms a second report indicating that the caravan trade in the valley was in the hands of the Shurfa (Shabeeny 1967: 7). This is in agreement with the slave trading activities of the major religious lodge of Tazerwalt in the Sous (Schroeter 1992) and of the *zāwiya-s* south of the Sahara (Klein 1992). The slaves were gathered in the village

Schroeter

---

into the army' and in 1698 the sultan 'ordered the impressment of the *harāṭīn* in Fas al-Bali (. . .), justified by referring to the needs of jihad'. In 1708 a third attempt was made in Fez (De Bakker 1992: 146–152, 178). Slave armies were a common phenomenon in North Africa (cf. Hunwick 1992: 17–20) but the conscription of free Muslims like the Haratin was without any obvious legal justification. Thus, when in the early 19th century, the Moroccan sultan tried to revive the institution of the slave army with the decision to conscript the southern Haratin, he met such fierce resistance that his decision was never put into practice. Without cooperation, it proved impossible by outward appearance alone to obtain a conclusive agreement as to who in fact could be considered a Hartani (El Mansour 1990: 25; cf. Ennaji 1994: 24). See for the trans-Saharan slave trade and the diaspora of black Africans in the Mediterranean, Savage (1992).

of Aduafil, probably on the annual saint's day (*mausim*), and sold and
resold on markets in northern Morocco. In the southern oases, wealthy
families owned some slaves of their own, as is still remembered in
the present-day village. In this century, the slave trade continued at
least until the 1930s (Ennaji 1994: 171–198).

The arrival of the saints

Returning to the time the village was founded, it appears that southern Morocco was divided into separate territories, sometimes without a clear-cut authority, and subsequently faced with a differentiated
use of violence.[6] The sedentary oasis population was not able to
organize an adequate defence without external help. Herdsmen constituted their military force, but also posed the greatest danger. In
addition, there were constant struggles between coalitions within the
settlements in the oasis, as mentioned by Leo Africanus in the description of his sojourn in Ktawa. In this period economic prosperity and
uncertain political circumstances coincided. The establishment of the
Saadian dynasty guaranteed a certain stability in the region. The
powerbase of the Saadians was first restricted to the northern part
of the Dra Valley, but gradually they expanded to the whole of
Morocco (Dahiru 1981: 1–17). The success of the Saadians was based
on a combination of control over the caravan trade and uncertain
political circumstances. Their success was furthermore part of a nationwide political struggle in which prophetic descent and sainthood became critical power sources (Eickelman 1976: 22–29). Until
the beginning of the 16th century, there were few saints in southern
Morocco, but from that moment onwards, numerous religious lodges
were founded in the rural south, some by religious leaders who claimed
prophetic descent through Idriss, the 7th-century religious leader and
founder of the first Arab dynasty in Moroccan society. The family
that came to be known as the Saadian dynasty called itself the
Sharifian dynasty to contest the legitimacy of the reigning dynasty

---

[6] See the following description by Jacques-Meunié: 'In the beginning of the 16th
century the whole of Saharan Morocco is outside the control of the dynasty that
rules north of the Atlas and has Fez as its capital. The major provinces in the
South (. . .) are disintegrated into numerous independent districts of which some
have only a village as capital (. . .) The temporal power is thus broken up into multiple authorities which are—being independent or enemies of one another—factors
of insecurity and anarchy' (1982: 424–425).

(which did not act against the external threat of a Portuguese military force from the Atlantic coast) and gained a nationwide legitimacy.[7] In the oasis, the foundation of Aduafil was linked to these turn of events. The new village developed into a sanctuary, enclave and refuge with its inhabitants becoming scribes and arbitrators.

Like the Saadians, Mulay Adafal, the saint after whom Aduafil has been named, claimed to be of Sharifian (*Idrissī*) descent, while as an arbiter he may have played a role in inter- and intra-village conflicts, a position that according to local tradition his forefathers had already played in Tunisia. The arrival of Adafal in the Ktawa Oasis may also have satisfied the need for scribes because although all inhabitants were Muslim—except for the small group of Jews—the majority still spoke Berber and was not able to read or write Arabic. A scribe was needed to write down the customary law documents that ruled internal *qsar* life (cf. Mezzine 1987) and agreements that had to do with trade, property and inheritance.

From the short family history of the saintly founder of the village, it becomes clear that in the 16th and 17th centuries the village was part of an elaborate network of religious lodges, a network that coincided with that of major trade routes. Remarkable in the family history of Ahmad Adafal is the western migration pattern. Grandfather Ahmad bin Abu Bakr migrated from 'Susana' in Tunisia to the oasis Figuig, now situated on Morocco's border with Algeria. Figuig used to be an intellectual and religious centre in the south that attracted young scholars, from whence they dispersed over rural Morocco.[8] After their few years of education some of these teachers or reciters of the Koran tried to find a permanent position as village imam. Others clung to their travelling life. Father Muhammad bin Ahmad continued in a westerly direction and settled in Ktawa. Here his three sons grew up, although they made several trips across Morocco and throughout the rest of the Islamic world. This was consistent with the commonality of religious scholars leading a peripatetic life

---

[7] The actual leaders, however, mocked the prophetic descent of their so-called Sharifian enemies by calling them the Saadian dynasty, referring to the tribe of the foster-mother of the Prophet (the Beni Saad) (Dahiru 1981: 3–7).

[8] Leo Africanus visited Figuig and wrote the following on its inhabitants: 'The people are very intelligent. Some of them are occupied with trade in the land of the blacks, others proceed to Fez to study letters. When one of them has received the honours of the doctorate, he returns to Nubia to become a priest or preacher' (1981: 435).

in pre-colonial Morocco (Eickelman 1985b: 66). Others settled in a rural community to set up a lodge: 'These rural lodges performed a variety of socially-oriented functions. Some of them (...) helped to disseminate Muslim beliefs and ritual practices among large sectors of the rural population'. Others 'ran Qur'ānic schools or acted as local mosques and were thus instrumental in reducing illiteracy among the predominantly Berber-speaking populations of the countryside' (Rodriguez-Manas 1996: 456). Once settled, these religious leaders were able to initiate collective agricultural works, such as the construction of irrigation channels and the cultivation of wastelands. They organized relief schemes in times of crisis, providing a temporary shelter and regular food to the poor. Sharif Mulay Adafal probably developed similar activities for cultivation of the land and mind of the local population. He became a teacher and legal advisor for the population (Hajji 1977: 609).

In Ktawa the three sons followed the intellectual life of their father and grandfather. At a young age, Ahmad Adafal (d. 1614) was first instructed by local teachers, then went to study in the Naciri lodge of Tamgrout in the Dra Valley and in Fez (Hajji 1977: 609). Later, he left for the *zāwiya* of Tazerwalt in the Sous to be initiated into the religious 'tradition' (*ṭarīqa*) of the most famous religious scholar of southern Morocco, Ahmad bin Musa as-Samlali (ibidem). Eventually, Adafal would write a biography of Sidi Musa (Pascon 1984: 158). After a long journey to the Middle East, Ahmad Adafal settled permanently in Aduafil. Mulay Adafal owned an elaborate library, the surviving portion of which is kept in the lodge in Tamgrout and the national library in Rabat.[9] His two brothers, Abdallah and Muhammad, showed less interest in travel and limited their trips to Tamgrout and Fez. Muhammad (d. after 1556) maintained correspondence on theological issues with imams elsewhere in the country.

The settlement history of the village shows how an exchange relationship developed between the Shurfa and the autochthonous population of the oasis, consisting of material aid for scriptural assistance, legal advice and supernatural mediation. Thus, it is said that when Adafal settled in the oasis, he did not own any parcel of land; present-

---

[9] 'Aḥmad Adfāl left a library filled with precious works he had collected on his long tours across the Maghreb and the East. On his deathbed, he recommended his sons to take responsibility of it and sell none of the copies; at present, however, almost nothing has been left' (Hajji 1977: 610).

day villagers claim that only after his death did his sons start to collect land and palm trees. Adafal himself lived off the gifts of local
inhabitants. This conforms to the kind of life one would aspect of
a Moroccan saint. His position in the oasis was founded on his literacy, piety, impartiality and healing practices, away from the material aspects of life, accumulating only prestige (Pascon 1984: 44).
After his death people started to present plots of land and palms as
donations to the Shurfa. Because the sons did not enjoy the same
symbolic capital as their father, they were forced to use other strategies to consolidate the sacred nature of their authority. In the climate
of numerous claims of Sharifian descent, Ahmad Adafal's son had a
genealogy drawn up to ascertain their claims as *Idrissī* Shurfa descended
from the House of the Prophet (1565). A second document, a *dahir*
dated April 1566 and signed by the Saadian Sultan Abdallah al-Galib
as-Saadi, proved the authenticity of the first document and the loyal
relationship with the Saadian dynasty.[10] The exchange of land and
material gifts for supernatural grace determined the relationship between the Shurfa of the village and lay inhabitants of the oasis.

Mulay Adafal arrived in the oasis as a stranger in the sense that
he introduced qualities and an identity as Sharif that were new to
the inhabitants. The site at which he decided to educate the people
was already occupied by an existing village. In the surrounding
villages, as well, autochthonous Drawa could be found. As with all
strangers in the oasis, Mulay Adafal must have had to ask permission of the owners of the specific irrigation sector in the oasis on
which he planned to settle. This was mostly done by way of an
offering on the threshold of the *qsar*. Religious figures and clerks
were considered strangers, but nevertheless welcomed in their scriptural and ritual capacities (Azam 1946: 24; Monteil 1948: 4). After
the death of Mulay Adafal, a shrine was built on the site, and a
village arose around this shrine. In the end, the new and former village were physically integrated, though nominally and officially they
remained separate. Adafal's children became ritual specialists and

---

[10] These documents seem to disprove the general applicability of the following
statement concerning the religious families in the oasis (Jacques-Meunié 1947: 410;
italics added): 'Some of these families claim to be descending from Mulay Idriss,
others claim to be directly related to Ali. These families derive their pride and prestige from their alleged Idrissid or Alid descent; *in reality, however, they seem for the most
part of uncertain origin coming, as they do, from local marabouts. Here, as elsewhere (. . .), it
seems likely that the Shurfa have been introduced by the Ait Átta at a recent date*'.

scribes of the oasis population. Income was furthermore generated through their control over the surrounding land. Respect from nearby villagers for the Shurfa was based on their symbolic capital consisting of their relationship with a hegemonic cultural (linguistic and urban), religious and political régime outside the oasis, yet beyond the foundation myth, the importance of this relationship remains somewhat unclear. In the oasis the sanctuary constituted a pacified enclave with its inhabitants as trustworthy arbitrators.[11]

The Drawa

Where did the Drawa in the village come from? It is said by the inhabitants of the village they originated in the present-day Algerian oasis Tabelbala. This oasis was a stopoff on one of the trade routes from the Dra Valley and Figuig to the south. The reasons for the migration of the Drawa are not clear. It is certain that the inhabitants of Tabelbala had to deal with an extremely difficult natural habitation. When in the decades before foundation of the village Leo Africanus visited the Tabelbala Oasis on his way to the Sudan he was touched by the poor living conditions:

> There are three highly populated castles around which the arable grounds are cultivated and palm trees stand. Water is extremely scarce and so is meat. They eat the ostriche and its eggs which they hunt. Even though they carry on business with the land of the blacks, the people are poor because they are vasals of the Arabs (Leo Africanus 1981: 432).[12]

The inhabitants of the Tabelbala Oasis and Ktawa kept close contacts as can be seen from the several migratory movements between the two oases. The ancestors of the Drawa who at present live in Aduafil may have migrated to the Ktawa Oasis between the 16th to the 19th century. Similarly, there seems to be no reason to discard the local version in which they arrived with Mulay Adafal in the 16th century. It is known that after Leo Africanus had passed the oasis, in the course of the 16th century, the Saadian army passed Tabelbala

---

[11] Besides acting as pacified enclave, the religious lodge could also function as the pivot of religious struggle (jihad) (cf. El Mansour 1991: 70).

[12] In a travel report from 1447, more or less the same is said: 'After Sidjilmassa we encountered ksours named *Tabelbert*, inhabited by very needy people who had as their only food water and the products of a poor soil' (Antoine Malfaut cited in Champault 1969: 24–25).

on its way to the south. Because of the military incursions, many Tabelballis migrated to the north (Champault 1969: 31). Furthermore, being located on an important trade route, it is conceivable Mulay Adafal visited the Tabelbala Oasis during his travels from Figuig to the valley. In Tabelbala he found or even sought for Haratin to accompany him to Ktawa. At present the name of the quarter and the surname (Belballi) of one extended Drawi family in the village recall their origin. Other Drawi families settled in the village more recently. One of these families figures prominently in the last section of this chapter. Coming from another oasis, people often explicitly or implicitly hint at the difference between them and those Drawa who came from Tabelbala.[13]

Consolidation of the sanctuary

The consolidation of the lodge and the social order in the oasis was determined by two major developments in the 17th century. First, new Sharifian families settled in the oasis. Their arrival was related to the growing importance of a new Sharifian dynasty that ruled Morocco from the mid-17th century onwards and still does today. These *'Alawī* Shurfa originated in the Tafilalt Oasis and belonged to a different genealogical branch than the *Idrissī* Shurfa from Aduafil. Some of the *'Alawī* Shurfa came to live very near Aduafil (in the villages of Knasda, Mansouria, Qsabt Mulay Fdil; see figure 3). They may have taken over some of the already mentioned ritual tasks of the Aduafil Shurfa in the oasis. The lineages of prophetic origin in the separate villages became competitors but also associates with respect to their Sharifian stature and control over supernatural grace that prompted them to live in agreement with the cultural standards required of those belonging to 'the House of the Prophet'.

The second development was the prominent role of a confederacy of pastoralist Berber tribes known as Ait 'Atta from the 17th century onwards.[14] Their arrival changed the power balance again

---

[13] See on the relations between Ktawa and Tabelbala, Hart (1984: 29): '[T]he Ait Isful of Tagunit (. . .) transhume (. . .) as far as Tabalbala in Algeria, 300 km away. . . .' Until recently a signpost in Tagounite gave notice of the direction to Tabelbala.

[14] It would perhaps be more precise to name the Ait 'Atta a 'supertribe' because the individual sections recognized agnatic descent from a common ancestor. It also knew certain institutional arrangements similar to those of smaller units (Hart 1981:

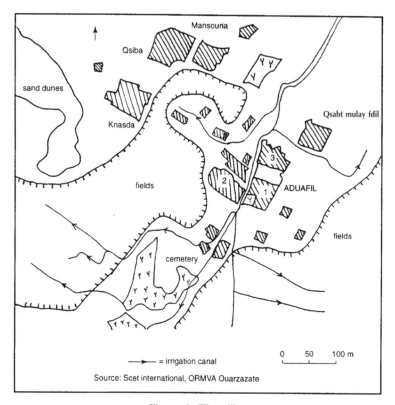

Figure 3: The village

in favour of the *Idrissī* Shurfa, including the descendants of Adafal. In this way, the villagers of Aduafil continued to profit from their Sharifian status and the presence of a sanctuary. The Ktawa Oasis came largely in the hands of the Ait Isful Tribe which was part of the larger confederacy of the Ait 'Atta. With the local population they agreed upon the adoption of protection pacts that regulated the flow of agricultural products toward the herdsmen in exchange for protection against other predators, like, for example, other sections of the same confederacy.[15] About 1900, all the *qsar-s* were divided

71–75; personal communication 1998). This denomination would, however, over-state the structural quality of what was to a large extent a powerful 'folk theory' (Hart 1994: 230).

[15] Compare the following note by Hart (1984: 57): 'The whole history of the region is one of the ousting of the former, largely Arab, protectors by the Ait 'Atta

among several 'Attawi tribes.[16] The Ait 'Atta Confederacy built several protection *qsar-s* next to the ancient villages of Drawa and *Ahrār*. At the end of the 19th century, the Ait Isful Tribe built a *qsar* next to Aduafil, from which they controlled the northern part of the oasis. The division of labour in this *qsar* followed oasis practice. Thus, as in Aduafil, Drawa from nearby oases came to live with the Ait Isful to cultivate their lands.

The Aduafilis and the Ait Isful agreed upon a protection pact (1926; cf. Niclausse 1954) in which the Ait Isful received an annual part of the harvest. With every harvest, the Isfulis were entitled to 1/20 of dates, 1/31 of cereals, 1/20 of vegetables, 1/31 of maïs and broad beans. The additional articles in the agreement between the village and the herdsmen indicate that the relationships between the Isfulis and Shurfa were not as hostile as one would expect.[17] The agreement expressed respect for the Shurfa, which can be explained by the fact that the 'Attawis tended to favour the *Idrissī* Shurfa over the *'Alawī* Shurfa. Since the 17th century, state power was in *'Alawī* hands and throughout the 18th and 19th centuries, the Moroccan state fought battles against 'Attawi domination in the oases, without much success (Hart 1984: 58–61). Most annoying to the *'Alawī* state was that the Ait 'Atta controlled the home oasis of the *'Alawī* Shurfa. Another reason why Aduafilis were treated sympathetically by the Ait 'Atta was that the patron saint of the confederacy was an *Idrissī* Sharif. The Ait Isful expressed their respect through visits and offerings at the sanctuary. The Shurfa were asked to act as scribes and arbitrators in inter-tribal disputes.[18]

Haut: Dadda Atta

and then of a power struggle between the various 'Atta clans now resident in the area to maintain a precarious equilibrium'. For example, the Ait Isful and Ait Kherdi contested each other's right to act as protector of Aduafil. From the early 1920s onwards, the Ait Isful functioned as sole protector (Niclausse 1954: annexe 32).

[16] Mobility, cohesion, the possession of firearms, and a militaristic ethos probably have all contributed to the success of this process of 'the "overcasting" of agrarian society by an upper layer of warriors' (cf. Goudsblom 1989: 88).

[17] One article obliged the Isfuli guard to protect the Shurfa at every spot, a second article prohibited guards camp on village territory, and a third article gave the villagers the right to refuse certain guards (Niclausse 1954: annexe 23).

[18] The antagonism between 'Attawis and *'Alawī* Shurfa can still be observed in the oasis. Jacques-Meunié emphasizes the importance of another sanctuary in the oasis, that of Sidi Salah in the southern most tip of the oasis: 'The descendants of Sidi Salah are consulted in case of disputes between tribes, and their opinion is respected (1951: 410). Compare Gellner's *Saints of the Atlas* (1969).

Other functions of the village as religious lodge strengthened the religious and scriptural specialism of the Shurfa. The village was a juridical enclave where excluded persons or hunted individuals could find refuge. Until recently, the village housed a small school attached to the mosque. Here, children from surrounding villages congregated to learn to read and write and memorize the Koran. Finally, for years the village has organized an annual saint's day in the surroundings of the shrine. This was another occasion to put the village and its inhabitants in the centre of attention.

Lodges such as that of Aduafil were in command of a workforce to take care of actual agricultural services. In the oasis, the Drawa from Tabelbala were going to cultivate the lands obtained, freeing the Shurfa from the material aspects of life, that is, agricultural labour and a number of other tasks. In this way, they ensured that the Shurfa did not have to deal with people from other villagers on an equal footing (for example in collective agricultural labour). The Shurfa offered the Drawa security, protection and prestige linked to their proximity to the sanctuary of a Sharifian saint. As I proceed, the typical features of the status of the Drawa in the village become clear.

Coexistence within four walls

The population of an oasis like Ktawa lives in a precarious state of coexistence. First, alluvial agriculture necessitates a fixed residence and close cooperation between villagers. In an oasis, the rainfall is insufficient and cultivation is dependent on the combination of fertile land and the provision of river water and subterranean sources. Alluvial agriculture and date palm cultivation require the building and constant maintenance of irrigation canals, as well as a strict cooperation between the inhabitants of an irrigation territory. Furthermore, cultivation of the date palm demands patience and is an investment in the future. People cultivate their plots while living closely together on the infertile sand grounds. Water and land are scarce resources and privately owned by descent groups whose boundaries are mostly restricted to only one village. The strategic location of the oasis may offer landholders an opportunity to gain an additional income through trade, in which case landless individuals, possibly from peripheral areas, are appointed to cultivate the lands.

Pointing out some of these ecological *cum* sociological features of oasis societies, Dunn (1977: 87–88) argued that the pre-colonial social organization in the oases was centered around the *qsar* settlements: 'Beyond its high, thick walls political life took on the cast of international relations' while intra-*qsar* politics was comparable to the classic segmentary tribalism of pastoralist groups, in particular with respect to the emphasis on acephalousness and the rotation of political functions. This latter view seems to devaluate the hierarchical notions that permeate social relations in the oasis communities. One is familiar, Pascon notes in an article on social stratification (and against segmentarism) in the villages of rural Morocco, with 'the coexistence of *mrabtins, chorfa, haratin,* and *ahrar*' creating hierarchically placed groups, with the *quasi-castes* in the Dra Valley, and with the distinction between the *éminents* and the *gens du commun* in written sources (Pascon 1979: 111, 113). Likewise, Gellner, known of course as the advocate of the principle of segmentarism applied to nomadic tribal groups, raised serious doubts about Dunn's model concerning the social organization of sedentary agricultural communities:

> By contrast [to mobile pastoralists, RE] oasis-dwellers are more vulnerable—their palm trees cannot move, and they can be cut down; they have to cooperate about water; are not mobile and are compelled to remain in close proximity to each other; by all accounts they are rather more severely stratified, with a stratum of oppressed sharecroppers, identifiable by colour... (Gellner 1981: 229–230).[19]

According to Gellner, social hierarchy, the necessity to cooperate and the vulnerability of crops and settlement determine the precariousness of oasis life.[20] As already suggested in the quotation, these features

---

[19] Also with respect to the nomadic and transhumant tribal groups, the value of segmentary analysis has long been under fire (cf. Hammoudi 1977; Pascon 1979; Hart 1996 and references cited there). Pascon pointed out that seen from close by 'nothing is less egalitarian than a tribe' (1979: 111). From a different perspective, Hart, ethnographer of the Ait 'Atta, recently stated that '[a]s it stands, and contrary to the position I once took, segmentary lineage theory now seems to me to be far too rigid and too exclusive to take proper account of the essential flexibility of many North African and Middle Eastern social structures which may appear at first sight to be "segmentary" in certain contexts' (Hart 1996: 722).

[20] 'Social caging' is the metaphorical term that has been introduced to denote such a process of growing mutual interdependence between people because of certain constraining factors of an ecological and social nature (Mann 1986; Maryanski and Turner 1992). The oasis as a social cage exists there where people simultaneously become dependent on the restricted geographic location of the oasis and on one another. In light of the constant threat of pastoralists, one might conclude that the oasis dwellers were truly caged within their settlements.

of oasis life return in an amplified way in the subject of this chapter, the status of the Drawa in the oasis settlements.

The vulnerability of the sedentary inhabitants appears from their confrontations with nomadic and transhumant herding population groups. Arab camel-herding nomads entered Morocco from the 13th century onwards. In the south they attacked villagers and threatened travellers and traders. Herdsmen belonging to the Ait 'Atta Confederacy constitute a second population group with whom the sedentary population had to find a modus vivendi. The Ktawa Oasis was largely in the hands of the Ait Isful and Ait Wahlim tribes (who were part of the larger confederacy of the Ait 'Atta). It was only in the 1930s that the French army led by captain Spillman finally broke down the defence of the Ait 'Atta Confederacy in the Dra Valley (cf. Spillman 1936). In this way the French army subjugated and pacified one of the last independent strongholds in the country; yet, the protection pacts remained operative until 1956.

Over the years, the camel herdsmen and mainly sheep-herding transhumant Ait 'Atta were integrated into the economic and political structures of the oasis society, and interwoven in the system of social hierarchy. Some became through the acquisition of land part of the landowning class who hired tenants to cultivate the fields and take care of date palms. The Ait 'Atta lived on the territory of the villages they protected and sometimes had their own settlement built. Rarely did they inhabit the already existing villages. This procedure gave rise to the characteristic settlement pattern of 'dispersed concentration' in the Ktawa Oasis with landowning descent groups occupying one walled village. Thus, although the village walls were inadequate for the defence of inhabitants against newcomers like the herdsmen of the Ait 'Atta, they were effective in keeping strangers at a spatial distance. The constant pressure of the herdsmen as well as the persistence of what Dunn (1977: 88) called 'tense and guarded' relations between qsar-s made that the walled qsar constituted in the pre-colonial oasis society 'a pacified enclave' and the nucleus of the social network of oasis inhabitants. In addition, the linkage of qsar territory with family, kin and property constituted the domains around which the complex of prevalent cultural ideals of the oasis society converged. The civil rights of the sedentary population were based on ownership of land and water rights, rooted in common descent, and usually limited to village boundaries. Inhabitants without these rights were economically and socially excluded. Outsiders could be incorporated by way of concluding an agreement with settled families.

The mostly quadrangular-shaped *qsar* is either built of unbaked loam dried in a wooden form or constructed of hand-made adobe bricks. In a typical *qsar* one gate allows entrance to the streets, the homes and the storehouses. The lay-out follows a geometric pattern. Along the inner side of the walls run the main streets. From them side-streets, often blind alleys, lead to the front doors of the *qsar* dwellings. The communal square, mosque and well are positioned near the gate. The *qsar* radiates an urban quality in a rural land-scape. It has been argued that the villages were derived from a fusion of the local loam architecture with the urban architecture and the military castle-like monasteries (*ribāṭ-s*) of the Arab Muslim conquerors (Nijst *et al.* 1973: 132–137). Its skyline has been compared to a mod-ern metropolis, while the geometric pattern of the streets contrasts with the proverbial labyrinths of ancient Arab urban centres.

The population size of *qsar-s* rarely exceeds 1000 inhabitants: 'When more people have to be housed in an oasis, the result is not one larger ksar, but an archipelago of smaller ksour' (idem, 119). As already noted, newcomers are either given permission to build a sec-ond *qsar* or made to live outside the walls in tents or palmleaf huts. Captain Azam (1947: 17) wrote on the habitation of newcomers in the 1940s that '[l]ittle by little their residence becomes permanent. They live in palmleaf huts, because the rule never to build in loam outside of the qsar is imperative'. This observation was confirmed by contemporary villagers in the nearby settlement of Drawa and Ait Isfulis and the settlement of Arabic-speaking Beni Mhammad (cf. De la Chapelle 1929). In the Ktawa Oasis, it was only when the French army arrived in the oasis in the 1930s that the sedentary population started to make small extra entrances in the walls of the *qsar*. After independence in 1956, people could even imagine leav-ing the *qsar* altogether. The process of the *éclatement des ksour*, as it is called in French literature, that is, the departure from the *qsar* and the disintegration of *qsar* life, had begun. This development from *qsar* to village is reflected in the history of Aduafil.

The village was founded by Mulay Adafal, and enlarged by his three sons (see figure 3). They settled themselves near an already existing village that at present is incorporated into Aduafil. The sons of Adafal came to live in the three quarters that constitute the old village. The size and the lay-out of the present village are in many

respects representative of the villages in the Dra Valley and southern Morocco in general. It consists of three ancient mud-brick quarters (*qṣar-s*), a village shrine, Friday mosque, second mosque, cemetery
and a number of dwellings dispersed throughout the palm gardens.

The first quarter is named the Saint's Quarter (1). It is the oldest
and the one that includes the sanctuary of the founder of the village. Opposite it is the Outside Quarter (2). In this quarter one street
is reserved for the Drawa, more or less officially named the quarter of the Tabelbala Oasis (*Zāwiya Tabelbala*), but Shurfa call it Drawi
Street (*Darb Drawi*). The last quarter with a small mosque of its own
is situated further up north, which explains its name, the Upper
Quarter (3). Here, three Drawi families have their home. Some families have built new homes opposite or attached to the *intra muros*
quarter, others built a house further away from the village centre.
During my fieldwork about fifty Sharifian households and ten Drawi
households lived in the village, making up for a population of about
500 inhabitants. In the village we find two social categories within
the walls of one *qṣar*. The simple fact that the names of the quarters reflect the division of the community into two social poles, Shurfa
and Drawa, gives us a clue to the close relationship between the
spatial and social order in the oasis settlement (see figure 4).

A second clue is the internal distribution of Shurfa over the three
quarters. The Saint's Quarter houses the families who are descended
from two sons of Mulay Adafal (lineages 1 and 2); the two other
quarters are inhabited by one other lineage each. This division of
the Sharifian families into four lineages spread over three quarters
is reflected in the distribution of water rights and land between Shurfa
and contact with the Drawa.

In Aduafil the disintegration process of *qṣar* life really began to
have an effect at the end of the 1970s. Since then, a rapidly increasing number of villagers has begun to build a new one-storey home
just outside the three *qṣar-s* or further away in the fields. Because of
this development, the *qṣar-s* have become singular elements of a real
village with houses, barns and a primary school along the streets
outside the *qṣar-s*.

Here, I wish to concentrate for a moment on the period before
the exodus from the *qṣar* to tell a local riddle that evokes the pre-
independence period and makes a commentary on my interpretation of the coexistence of Shurfa and Drawa in one *qṣar*. The riddle
was put to me by Abdelhadi Hazzabin, the young Drawi who became

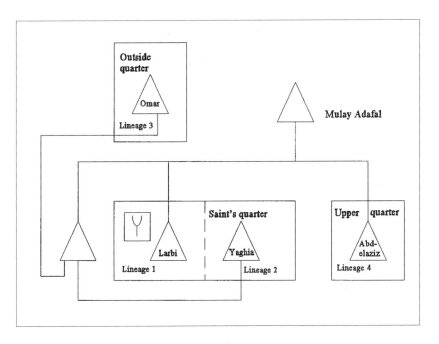

Figure 4: Four lineages in three quarters

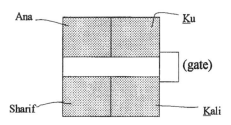

Figure 5: A riddle

an important informant in an early phase of the research. He was
a member of the family who was assigned to look after me during
my stay in the village. On one occasion Abdelhadi asked for a piece
of paper and drew figure 5 (a riddle).

Abdelhadi's drawing refers to the pre-independence period when
all inhabitants were living within the walls of the *qsar*. In the one-
street *qsar* of the drawing, one Sharifian family lives with several
Drawi families. The Sharif wants to leave his house and head for
the gate but unfortunately the Drawa are waiting for him on the
threshold of their home to stab him with a knife the moment he
passes by. The Drawa are related to each other. 'This is my house',
says Abdelhadi pointing to the house opposite the Sharif's. 'The second one is my brother's house (*ku-ya*) and the one next to the Sharif
is my uncle's (*kali*). The question you have to answer is, how can
the Sharif reach the gate without being stabbed to death by the
Drawa'. I did not know the answer. The riddle is a play on words
that hinges on the double meaning of *kali*. In the meaning of 'my
maternal uncle', *kali* corresponds to the other relatives, but in this
particular case it also means 'empty' or 'in ruins'. Thus, to reach
the village gate, the Sharif can cross the uninhabited house next to
his own. The riddle is somewhat simple, and probably the double
meaning of *kali* is used in other jokes. In this case it was cut to size
to fit the local scenery of the Dra Valley. Nevertheless, the riddle is
significant because of its grim portrayal of the relations between
Shurfa and Drawa. It alludes to the cultural theme of the precarious existence in an oasis village, that is, the ambivalent closeness
within village walls vis-à-vis the threat of the natural world outside
the walls. Let us first consider the opposition between *qsar* and outside world.

As already pointed out, the function of the *qsar* during the *ancien
régime* was to protect its inhabitants against the violent attacks of the
pastoral Ait 'Atta, while the covered streets protected the inhabitants
against the burning sun and sand storms (Noin 1965: 102–103). However, I also consider the walls to be 'walls of civilization', meant to
separate its inhabitants from the wilderness and from strangers and
'wild creatures' (Pandolfo 1989: 9; cf. Blok 1981: 117–118; Ohnuki-
Tierney 1984: 295). As far as the last category is concerned, they
are one of the reasons why especially little children are afraid to
leave the *qsar* in the dark. Once Salem, one of the younger brothers
of Abdelhadi, was given an order to invite me for breakfast the fol-

lowing morning. As he was afraid to leave the *qsar* in the evening (to go to the other quarter where my house stood), he walked to the gate, waited there for several minutes and returned home, saying to his parents that he had fulfilled his task. In reality, it was only the next morning, when it was light, that he informed me. Abdelhadi understood the fear of his younger brother. Once when he was young, he had to go to the toilet and went outside the *qsar*, but afterwards could not find the village gate. He was afraid of the dark space and did not dare to walk around. He waited therefore the rest of the night until it became light, only to discover that he was sitting beside the main gate of the *qsar*. The fear of young children but also of adults is primarily directed to a specific wild man, called 'ghoul'. A ghoul is a being similar to man, but slightly different. He is black, covered with hair and dressed in rags. He roams around outside the *qsar* at night, always on the watch for people leaving the *qsar*, whom he likes to eat (cf. Westermarck 1926 ii: 398–400; Chebel 1993: 241). The ghoul represents the danger of the outside world, the space outside of the *qsar* during the night.

During the day, villagers have to deal with human outsiders. Strangers, individuals with whom inhabitants do not develop face-to-face contact on a regular basis, are a common phenomenon in the oases. They might not have a fixed residence because of their itinerant occupation. The religious lodge is visited regularly by strangers, wanderers from outside the oasis who stay for a night or two. People never let them in their home, but they do give them food which is eaten outside of the *qsar*. In winter they are allowed to sleep in the intermediate zone between the gate and the street. This is also the place where itinerant vendors can display their merchandise. In the past several itinerant occupational specialists such as blacksmiths and jewellers served the sedentary population in this region. Day labourers, musicians, craftsmen, tradesmen and ambulant literates roamed the countryside. At present, now and then leather-workers come to the village to buy up the villagers' dried sheep skins. Strangers like these are treated with kindness and given food, but kept at a distance. An indication of the durability of these attitudes is that the customary law of a nearby village in 1910 even fined the person who refused to give mendicants alms when asked for. A second article stated that the mendicant receives a recompense when assisting in the harvest without being asked to do so (Niclausse 1954: annexe 8). In a second, more ancient, customary law of a village in the Tafilalt Oasis, it was explicitly forbidden for a butcher or baker to practise in the *qsar* (Mezzine 1987: 238).

Strangers can be dangerous yet attributed with extraordinary qualities. Therefore they should be approached with kindness. Doutté observed that in Morocco 'generally speaking, the stranger is a sorcerer' (1908: 49). In the oasis village, the itinerant musicians who visit the village during harvest time and, unlike itinerant vendors, do enter the *qsar* streets, are indeed known for their capacity to heal by touch. In this belief, the displacement of these itinerant musicians, moving between the walled village and the outside world, is transposed to a capacity to mediate between humans and the supernatural world.

While *qsar* inhabitants tend to keep outsiders at a distance, the same practice seems to apply when different social groups live out of necessity inside one *qsar*. There one may find a more hidden frontier between social categories, each one in their own quarter and, as Pandolfo notes on life in a village further up north in the Dra Valley, members should not intermingle unnecessarily (1989: 14).[21] Especially Drawa should not walk around without any specific purpose in the quarters of the light-skinned population, while in the previously mentioned pre-independence customary law, inhabitants were fined severely when they sold a house to a Hartani (Mezzine 1987: 193). Thus, even when the outsider comes inside and closer, one has to take care to keep distance.[22]

Spatial marginality characterizes the coexistence of Drawa with other population groups in southern Morocco. The real village of Aduafil, as opposed to the imaginary one in the riddle, presents an example of this general pattern. It consists of three quarters. In the Outside Quarter one street is reserved for the Drawa. Actually, at present one Sharifian family lives in the dead-end street of the Drawa, just like in the riddle. To avoid walking through the street to arrive

---

[21] The concept 'hidden frontier' is taken from Cole and Wolf (1974).

[22] In comparison, in the Egyptian Siwa Oasis a specific category of landless bachelors called *zaggālah*, also known as *kadīm* (servants-workers), acted as labourers and field-guards. Some of them were 'entrusted with the punishment of any person who transgressed against the law': 'When the Siwans were still living inside their walled town, none of these bachelors was allowed to spend the night in the town but had to sleep outside the gates, in caves cut in the rock or in the gardens'. During the day, these same men could enter the houses and private female spaces of their landowners without any problem (Fakhry 1982: 40–41, 44).

at the gate, the Sharifian family made a door in the outer wall which is closed at night. In the Upper Quarter three Drawi families live. Again one finds them near the entrance of the *qsar*. The spatial marginality of Drawa, often not allowed to live within the walls, is a common pattern of southern *qsar* life (cf. for west of the Dra valley, Montagne 1930, and east, Dunn 1977) and a reflection of the marginal status of Drawa in general. In contrast, Shurfa were often invited to live within the walls of a *qsar* because they were said to bring luck and grace (*baraka*) upon its inhabitants. For other *qsar-s* in the south it has been observed that the spatial segregation of Drawa and other social marginals continued even after the population moved out of the *qsar* after independence, in which case families of different social categories came to live apart from one another in *extra muros* quarters (cf. Bisson and Jarir 1988). This enduring pattern of spatial segregation was indeed observed for the neighbouring village consisting of Drawa and Ait Isful Berbers.[23]

By recognizing that everywhere in the pre-Saharan zone Drawa lived in a separate quarter or *qsar*, one can now better understand the topsy-turvy world of Abelhadi's riddle. In particular, its subordinate message is revealed. The riddle is a counterpoint[24] in the village where the word of the Sharif is still the one heard most forcefully in public, and where it is said everybody lives peacefully with one another, Shurfa are honoured and Drawa act as their servants. At the risk of overinterpreting the riddle, one might say it represents the ideal village turned upside-down. In the riddle, the Sharifian family lives out of place, its members, being from another set and surrounded by a majority of Drawa, having to fear for their life because of their proximity to Drawa. As such, the riddle represents a mock-attack on the real world of Shurfa; a world in which they are the majority in the village with a well-knit web of kin and affines. Moreover, the Shurfa might be calling each other *ḵali*, i.e., mother's

---

[23] The Jewish population, living in the oasis until the 1950s, was considered even more outcast. A Jew 'risked his life if he dared to enter a ksar where a *cherif* lived: the Jew was regarded as "unclean"' (Nijst *et al.* 1973: 127). In Aduafil, Jews were only allowed to enter the village ground if they took their foot-gear off. It was only after the Second World War that most Jews left for Europe, America and Israel. The classic work on the southern Moroccan Jewish communities is Flamand (1959; on the oasis communities: 39–63). See for more recent work Goldberg (1984) and Abitbol (1992).

[24] See for the concept of counterpoint Wertheim (1964: 23–37).

brother, because of their common descent from Fatima, the daughter of the Prophet. The riddle is a mock-attack since it is only a joke, 'a play upon form'—a reversal of a main cultural theme in society (Douglas 1975: 94–96; cf. Hamnett 1967)—using and reproducing an alternative discursive space to comment upon the village figuration.[25]

Abdelhadi Hazzabin recognized the social commentary of his riddle. He gave an unsolicited clarification by comparing the attitude of the Drawa in the riddle with the struggle for freedom by blacks in South Africa: 'Do you know Sol Nadela? In his country the Shurfa wanted to colonize the Drawa, but he said no to this. "We want freedom". That is why they put him in prison for 24 years'. Newspapers are not often seen in the village, and even if they were, Abdelhadi would not read them, as he is only able to read and write very elementary sentences. Before I met him, he also had never left the oasis except for two short visits to Zagora, the capital of the district. Radio and television provide him with facts on the outside world, albeit in a slightly modified form. Nelson Mandela's fight against the whites of South Africa and being prisoned for decades exemplified for him the struggle of the Drawa in the walled settlements in the valley.

The imaginative village of the riddle recalls another evocative image, namely Van Gennep's analogy of a society that is similar to a house, mentioned in *The Rites of Passage* (1960). A house consists of different rooms, each belonging to an isolated individual or social group. To go from one room to the other, one must cross the corridor and remain temporarily in a liminal state before entering the next room. However, as Van Gennep remarks: 'An individual or group that does not have an immediate right, by birth or through specially acquired attributes, to enter a particular house and to become established in one of its sections is in a state of isolation' (1960: 26). The analogy aptly describes the relationship between Shurfa and Drawa in the village. The Moroccan rectangular *qsar* resembles the society at large in its separation of social strata—with Drawa placed in the 'corridors' of the *qsar*—and seclusion of individual households. The

---

[25] Westermarck reproduces the following striking saying (1930: 74): When a light-skinned woman marries a dark-skinned man she says that 'for lack of a relative I call a negro my mother's brother' (*ḵali*), i.e., a preferable marriage partner.

village configuration or even the oasis as a whole resembles inner *qsar* life in the incorporation of strangers with whom the residents have to interact and with Drawa living displaced.

Van Gennep's 'isolated individual' can be called a stranger, as defined by Simmel (1950: 402–408), that is, the *'potential* wanderer (. . .) fixed within a particular spatial group, or within a group whose boundaries are similar to spatial boundaries'. Yet, as Simmel remarks, the position of the stranger in the group 'is determined, essentially, by the fact that (. . .) he imports qualities into it, which do not and cannot stem from the group itself' (idem, 402). In particular, when the social group into which the stranger is trying to enter keeps its ranks closed, he remains in a permanent intermediary state and gains the status of a long-term stranger. They—as we are dealing in this book with a plurality of strangers—stay because both the established population and the 'strangers' need one another for certain circumscribed tasks. The strangers (Drawa) are in an anomalous state, assigned to tasks that even reinforce their anomaly, becoming indispensable for the social and cultural reproduction of the social group of the established (Shurfa).

Simmel's definition of a stranger is unlike popular usage, in which the term is mainly used to refer to a person one does not know or is not familiar with and whom one may see once and then never again. Instead, Simmel defines a stranger to be a person who 'comes today and stays tomorrow', i.e., someone with whom we may have contact on a daily basis. It is this 'specific form of interaction' between a group of people and those treated as 'strangers' which is meant here.

Van Gennep's analogy, the riddle and Simmel's definition of the stranger, direct our attention to an important aspect of the 'Hartani-Drawi' identity in the oasis community. The Drawa are attributed with the trait of 'being different' and 'coming from somewhere else', yet live within village boundaries. As we will see, because they are lacking in landed property, water rights, and a clear descent, they are deprived of a birthright to be a full member of the village community. In the village of Aduafil, their right to live in the village was based on the 'qualities' they imported, derived from the tasks they fulfilled in the service of the Shurfa. However, the fulfillment of these tasks, continuing to this day, reinforces their strangeness. The cultural definition of Drawa as long-term strangers is an extreme result of this double-bind and the more general anxiety toward the maintenance of the social and cultural boundaries of the *qsar*.

Occupational specialists

Drawa have lived in the Moroccan oasis communities for centuries as agriculturalists and date palm cultivators, yet from the previous section it appears that they are seen as 'potential wanderers' and strangers, people who lack property and durable bonds in the community, and are not considered to be full-fledged members of sedentary communities. To find a line between these opposed qualifications, I will examine here if the alleged marginal status of Drawa in the oasis communities can be connected to their fulfillment of a so-called 'peripatetic niche', a number of odd and despised, yet sometimes highly profitable jobs shunned by members of the dominant categories (Bollig 1987: 209).

From a volume on 'peripatetics' by Rao (1987b), it becomes clear that North Africa is something of a *terra incognita* with respect to knowledge of itinerant population groups. Bollig mentions an early note by Van Gennep on a group of 'people of dark complexion who travel all northern Africa, including Morocco, from the one end to the other. The men are little seen, but the women wander through the villages, settlements and towns, telling fortunes by means of sugar in the hand' (cited in Bollig 1987: 183). Doutté (1908: 43) furthermore mentions 'Algerian Gypsies', travelling circumcisers and fortunetellers. Bollig (1987: 209) distinguishes five spheres of activity that are typically occupied by itinerant population groups in general: Handicrafts, entertainment, ritual services (circumcising, gravedigging, healing), mediation, begging. Can these peripatetic people, providing services for sedentary communities, be associated with people known as Drawa or Haratin?

First of all, Drawa were, and still are, to a large extent landless and marginal peasants. This implies that in the case of a calamity, they would be the first to be forced to move. Droughts and famines were commonplace phenomena in southern Morocco. Inhabitants had had to deal with droughts in 1903 and 1905, and famines in 1910, 1913, 1922, 1931 and 1937. Pests infested the southern countryside in 1912 and 1915, Spanish flu struck in 1918 (Filali 1984: 98bis). These calamities not only caused many deaths, but induced numerous others to move on in the search for food and shelter. From the villagers' point of view, regional migrants are included in the category of wanderers. Interregional migration in Morocco follows fixed patterns, as testified by the following statement of an inhabitant of the Sous region: 'There have been people coming up here from the oases—from the Bani—as long as anyone can remember. They come during hard times in large numbers, but there has always been a trickle. We use them to build houses and to work our fields' (Waterbury 1972: 29). Some of these migrants decide to stay. As far as the Haratin are concerned, migration indeed seems to be a general pattern. Jacques-Meunié (1958: 259) concludes they are 'often strangers on the territory, coming from other oases where they were unable to find employment'.[26] At the time of harvest, women, sometimes accompanied by children, still wander around looking for left-over dates and asking for alms.

Most Drawa now lead a sedentary life, but it is not unlikely that individuals or groups, albeit under different denominations, at one time or another led a peripatetic life. The Drawa of the neighbouring Ait 'Atta village are an interesting example. The 'Attawis of the village name them *Imalwan*. Originally, this is the name given to a tribe or segment of a tribe in the High Atlas. Laoust qualified the *Imalwan* as pedlars (*colporteurs*), first denoting a group of tribes living in the High Atlas and the southeastern oases, but now dispersed all over the southern countryside (1934: 155; cf. Jacques-Meunié 1958: 245; Mezzine 1987: 27). Hart (1984: 127) called the *Imalwan* 'a curious, darkskinned, relict people (. . .) who, as neutrals and itinerant vendors also came to act as keepers of [the] Customary Law' of the Ait Hadiddu. More recently, Kraus (1991: 9–10; italics added) restated the findings on the *Imalwan*: 'The Imluwan are completely fragmented. The dispersed fragments have joined other tribes (. . .), *where one is fully aware of their foreign origin*'. Some of the *Imalwan* from the nearby village in the Ktawa Oasis have worked as itinerant healers, blacksmiths or vendors and continue to do so for neighbouring communities like Aduafil.

Secondly, Drawa fulfil a number of occupations for which an itinerant way of life was necessary or preferable. They work as welldiggers, guards, musicians, cobblers, barbers, midwives, blacksmiths,

---

[26] See for Algeria Keenan (1977: 100–101; cf. 143–148): '[T]he dark-skinned Harratin cultivators (. . .) came into Ahaggar from the oases of Touat and Tidikelt in increasing numbers after the mid-nineteenth century (. . .). There was no inter-marriage between Kel Ahaggar and Harratin, and contact between them was limited almost exclusively to the economic sphere. They comprised a separate community of dependent clientele . . .'

traditional healers and herbalists.[27] Of some of the occupations performed by Drawa the itinerant or outsider status that comes with
it is well-known. This accounts for ambulant herbalists (Bellakhdar
et al. 1992: 209), blacksmiths who attend the weekly markets in the
region (cf. Doutté 1908: 43), and travelling well-diggers and builders
of subterranean irrigation canals. Furthermore, Haratin fulfil a crucial role as flute-players and buffoons in the itinerant groups of poet-
musicians of the High Atlas called *Imdyazen* (Roux 1928: 232).

For some of these occupations one does not need to live an itinerant existence, yet they are included here because they are performed by migrant Drawa. The first one is that of potter. On Ait
'Atta territory, '[they] are generally held to be southern blacks unable
to find employment at home' (Hart 1984: 127). The profession is
often passed down the generations, and contemporary potters from
different villages claim to form one family. The same hereditary pattern has been observed by Joly (1906) and Herber (1922) in the
north of the country. Herber discovered that the Meknassi potters
originally descended from 'the Sahara', belonging to the same ethnic category as the cobblers and the blacksmiths, i.e., the Drawa.
He added that forging and cobbling were held in disrepute and
quoted Laoust on the reputation of potters: 'The potter . . . is known
as a wretched human being condemned by fate . . . He lives an un-
fortunate, secluded and dispicable life . . .'. In the Ktawa Oasis,
potters are indeed Drawa. Tanning is a predominantly urban occupation. In the oasis, the tannery in the large and most 'urban' *qsar*
of Beni Sbih used to be in the hands of the Jewish population. At
present, a Drawi family has taken over on a small scale. Large tan-
neries exist in towns like Marrakesh and Fez. In the former town it
is also said that originally all its tanners were Jewish, yet most contemporary tanners are dark-skinned people from the south (Jemma
1971: 14, 25). Other occupations often practised by Drawa when
living in the oasis communities fall under Bollig's category of ritual
services and social mediation: Water-rights controllers, water-carriers,
criers, messengers, porters, marriage brokers, gravediggers, circumcisers et cetera.

From my sedentary fieldwork location in the oasis, it became clear

---

[27] Mezzine (1987: 344) concludes in his historical study of one oasis community
that artisanal tasks in service of the agricultural communities were always fulfilled
by Haratin.

that Drawa fulfil numerous occupations. Most have lived in the oasis communities 'from time immemorial' but it was not unusual for them to be starting anew in an oasis other than the one where they were born. As landless and marginal peasants they lack a stable village basis; as occupational specialists they sometimes serve more than one village or even oasis.

Drawa share some traits that have been mentioned as typical of peripatetics. Rao observed that itinerant occupational specialists are predominantly endogamous and often face restrictions on prolonged physical proximity to sedentary communities. They are forbidden to carry weapons and are known for their neutrality in their dealings with customers. They are furthermore sometimes attributed with a certain measure of power in the sphere of rituals and the supernatural: 'Peripatetics are thus despised, yet feared' (Rao 1987a: 4, 9). Drawa are largely endogamous. In the past they were forbidden to carry weapons with the Ait 'Atta Berbers taking them for people 'who do not fight or make war' (Hart 1984: 147–148) and up to this day they are ridiculed for this inability. Furthermore, their marginal state and involvement with transitional processes make them predisposed to fulfil important roles in rites of passage and calendrical rituals. Last, as we will see further on, Drawa are attributed with supernatural powers. The features singled out by Rao as characteristic of peripatetics seem to me to be common to occupants of *disreputable* tasks in general. Likewise, the possible itinerant past is only one dimension of Drawa fulfilling professions that are shunned by others. Thus, the occupations mentioned so far have remained to a large extent or exclusively monopolized by Drawa while, for example, agricultural work has to some extent become a normal occupation for members of the other social strata.

While in early modern Europe the disrepute or *infamy* of occupational specialists could be set out in legal terms (cf. Blok 1981; Hergemöller 1990), this seems not to be true in the pre-modern *Islamic* world. As far as I know, egalitarianism, the basis of the Islamic creed, has never in Morocco been overruled by special legal rules for people of disreputable occupations.[28] Nevertheless, in southern

---

[28] From material presented by Marlow, 'produced in many different regions of the medieval Islamic world' and covering 'a relatively long period of time' (1997: 172), it appears that manual occupations as well as ones involving contact with refuse and organic substances were frequently despised. Some jurists proposed a specific legal status for those fullling the occupations (163, 167). Also, from Brunschvig's

Morocco, the restricted rights of Drawa as a social category were part of the customary law documents that ruled oasis life until the mid-20th century. Until 1962, when the first constitution of the independent Moroccan Kingdom took effect, Drawa in general did not have the same civil rights as members of the other population groups. They were discriminated against in legal and political terms, because true membership of a village community (*qabīla*) was based on the principle of common descent and ownership of land. Customary law, a mixture of Islamic law and common law, ruled *qsar* life in the south (Mezzine 1987). In one such published customary law document concerning life in the neighbouring Tafilalt Oasis, several articles on strangers applied to the status of Drawa who lived with other social groups in one *qsar*. Sometimes Drawa were mentioned specifically. One article stated plainly that the testimony of a Hartani was not valuable in the *qsar*. The blood price for killing a Drawi might be set at half that of another man and equal to that of a woman.[29] Furthermore, the legal system of the distribution of irrigation water in the Dra Valley corresponded with the Drawa's reduced civil rights. From research undertaken by Ouhajou (cf. Hammoudi 1985: 47–51), it becomes clear that a close correspondence existed between the system of social hierarchy and the unequal allocation of water to irrigate the land. Thus, descendants of local saints and Shurfa amassed the largest share of water rights and Drawa, the smallest share.

Besides the special legal treatment, striking family resemblances exist between the core activities of Drawa. In this respect, Pascon already spoke of the 'quasi-impurity' of working with iron, fire and pottery in Moroccan society (1979: 113). The professions involve contact with organic substances and are aimed at the purification of people and places. It will be shown how in this respect Drawa encroach on the rules of civilized conduct in the oasis communities. Moreover, the solitary occupational specialists that go from one village to another are living outside a village and consequently move outside of the civilized village community (cf. Blok 1996: 89). The village tasks of Drawa such as date-palm guard, porter of the *qsar*, messenger, village crier, marriage broker, and porter at communal

---

well-known article on disreputable occupations in the Islamic world (1962) it appears that the activities of the blood-letter, tanner and bath attendant were esteemed poorly by jurists (1962: 47–50).

[29] Charles Benjamin, personal communication.

dinners bring them outside or to the boundaries of village territory, possibly at night, and into contact with outsiders. In chapters six and seven, the consequences of the fulfillment of their tasks for the esteem of the Drawa will be examined more closely.[30]

In the two villages with which I am familiar, some Drawi families are known to have a recent migratory family history. They came to live in the villages dominated by, respectively, transhumant Berbers and Shurfa, and in each of these villages their condition as 'strangers' continues. In the following section one of these families will be introduced.

Social marginality; a family history

Hammed Hazzabin, father of the narrator of the riddle, was quite surprised when I asked him to answer a couple of questions on the history of his family. He replied that unlike the Shurfa of the village, his family did not have any history (tarik). Then, when I explained to him that, although not written down, he must know something on the history of his father and grandfather, he told me to go to his former Sharifian patron. He surely would know these kind of facts. His hesitation, or rather refusal, partly has to do with a definitional deficit: Tarik deals with the story of 'prophets, saints, sages, poets and vanished princes'. And there is a reason, Lévi-Provençal commented with regard to this quotation (1922: 32), why secular history comes last; history, above all, deals with ancestral and spiritual power. Hammed's hesitation corresponded with the hegemonic view in the oasis that because Drawa do not have a clear sense of their own origins, their opinion on the past, even when it is their personal history, cannot be of any value.

In a particular way this notion has been reinforced by Hammed's family name. It was only in the early 1950s that the French bureaucracy introduced a system of fixed surnames for everyone to register and control the Moroccan population. Before that, surnames were confined to an intellectual and religious élite, functioning to fix the family history in time and to testify of one's honourable origins (Chafi

---

[30] For the family resemblances of 'infamous occupations', see Blok (1981, 1989; 1996). For literature on despised occupational specialists, see Casajus (1987); Jansen (1987); Le Goff (1977); Mc. Naughton (1988); Van Nieuwkerk (1991); Ohnuki-Tierney (1984) and Tax-Freeman (1979).

1989: 8) and supernatural powers. Thus, when the Sharifian Aduafilis signed up for their surname, almost all of them chose to formalize their bond with ancestor Mulay Adafal. As this defeated the purpose of assigning surnames, they were asked by the civil servants to name the family after a parcel of land that was most dear to them. In this way the bond with the surrounding land (*blad*) and the family origins would be guaranteed as well. And so, with one exception named after another well-known marabout, all Sharifian surnames point either to the 16th-century saint or to a field or group of fields they own. During my stay this led to amusing misunderstandings on my part when people spoke of going to *Buqiwar* or irrigating *Swasi*, thereby referring to an actual field and not to a family of the same name.

Family names are thus linked to control over the means of production (cf. Wolf 1966a: 9). Of the three large Drawi families, one is named after a plot of land that they own themselves, as was proudly pointed out by the head of the family standing on his field at harvest time. Another family is named after the oasis of origin (the Tabelbala Oasis), while the third is named after their patron's land. Ali, the oldest of the four brothers related to me that the name was chosen by him at the time he needed an official ID to be permitted to travel to Casablanca. As the family did not own any land, he came up with a parcel owned by the family's patron. This nevertheless binds them in an unusual way to the oasis community.

The remarkable characteristic of the surname Hazzabin alludes to their marginal status in the village community. I did not ask Hammed whether he would agree with this qualification but I am sure he would not. He would argue that the members of his family are normal villagers participating in contemporary village life and not treated differently from members of Sharifian families. They are indeed considered to be members of the *blad*, the land and community (*qabīla*) of the Aduafilis. They are part of the distribution and exchange networks in the village. This means they share in rights such as the acquisition of the bi-annual quota of subsidized flour, or when hired for a specific job, they have the right to receive, a well-prepared meal in addition to the agreed sum. In contrast, the privilege of dining together is not granted to workers from outside the village; they are the real outsiders. Likewise, the Hazzabins and the other Drawa share in most collective obligations, such as paying a fixed sum for the renewal of the local mosque or serving in the upkeep of the irrigation ditches. Hammed is not an outsider, nor can he be called a wanderer, as Simmel's definition of the stranger implies. Hammed is very much attached to the village where he was born, and the surrounding land. Only twice has he visited his brother, sister and their son in Casablanca. Both visits did not last longer than two days, which was long enough to acquire a mysterious illness that disappeared immediately after his return to the oasis. He declared to his family he would never return to *Casa* or any other town. Hammed is at his best when he takes a walk across the fields surrounding the village, checking the palm trees and palmleaf fences, built to keep the sheep and goats of the village herd away from the legumes. Hammed's attitude is quite unlike that of two of his brothers, both of whom have sold their small share of the inheritance and left the village for Casablanca and Fez. Just like their great-grandfather, they lacked any permanent economic bond with their region of birth. Throughout the years their ties with the village have weakened further. Most of their children have grown up in urban conditions and probably will never visit the oasis community. Nevertheless, Hammed and his family is considered to be more a 'stranger' in the village than any other Drawi family, as they settled there only four generations ago.[31]

Ali Hazzabin, as I will call him retrospectively, arrived in the village of Aduafil in the second quarter of the 20th century. According to present-day villagers he came from an oasis village about 100 kilometres north from the Ktawa Oasis. Ali's grandson and namesake was quite irritated when I asked him about the exact reasons for his great-grandfather's migration. He found it quite normal that people move to another place when they are unable to sustain themselves in their home village: 'I migrated to Casablanca, you came to Morocco, and our grandfather settled in Aduafil'. Notwithstanding the fact that the mobility of an oasis population is indeed nothing special, it still seems to be primarily, though not exclusively, Drawa who belong to this category of 'potential wanderers' in the southern oasis communities.

Ali came to the village in a period when the oasis was in the hands of a French military government. Between the second half of the 19th century and the 1930s, the Moroccan Sultanate was gradually

---

[31] The stigma of an alleged recent residence is not restricted to this oasis society (cf. Elias and Scotson 1994: 12). For North Africa a striking example is presented in Abu Zahra's study on the Tunisian village Sidi Ameur. In this village, '[l]ater arrivals to a community, who consequently are not descendants of its founder, are not considered as being equal to his descendants'. A local saying points out that 'there is no outsider except the devil' (Abu Zahra 1982: ix, 48).

divested of its autonomous status. In 1912 the colonization was officially instigated through a division of the country into a Spanish and
a French part. In the south sovereignty was relinquished to a French
military government, though indigenous resistance continued there at
least until the 1930s. In 1933, the French founded a new administrative and commercial centre (Tagounite) in the Ktawa Oasis that
deprived the *qsar-s* of Beni Sbih and Nesrat of their market held
there every Sunday and Thursday since the 16th century. The French
built the new village just outside the oasis and equipped it with
the coercive means to end the continuous violent conflicts in the
oasis. Even now Aduafilis still call the village 'the fort' instead of
Tagounite. The oasis was formed into one commune (*caïdat*). The
caïd, appointed by the Ministry of Interior, resides in Tagounite. At
present, the *caïdat* is part of the district (*cercle*) Zagora and the province
of Ouarzazate. The military government gave local powerholders an
official function in the new administrative system, thus perpetuating
the political dominance of the transhumant Ait 'Atta in the oasis.
Yet the French sovereignty, installed after fierce struggles and the
bombardment of one *qsar*, assured peace and was an important step
toward integration of the oasis into the Moroccan state. It opened
the possibility for labour migration to the north. Thus, in the present
century, ever since the French subdued and colonized the country
and especially since the great drought of 1945–1946, people from the
Dra Valley have been migrating to Marrakesh, Casablanca and, from
the second part of the 1960s, to Europe. Older men in the village
have worked in several northern towns, including Casablanca and
Khouribga (in the phosphate industry). Another group of people found
work in other Arab countries, particularly those where oil was found.

    After Ali Hazzabin, came his son Abdallah and daughter, who are
still remembered by the older people in the village. Then came his
grandchild Salem, the father of the present-day Hazzabin brothers.
Unlike the Shurfa and some of the Drawa, the Hazzabins for a long
time constituted a single family without any marital ties. Only the
fourth generation, that is the present one, became related to another
Drawi family through marriage. In this way they also gained control over some parcels of land and the right to use water to irrigate
the land for a few minutes. Still, the lack of father's brothers or similar bonds with fellow villagers reveals the shallowness of their family ties, at least when compared with the intricate family networks
of Shurfa in the village.

At present, the family consists of five households: The four brothers Hammed, Ali (named after his grandfather), Najem and Barka, and Mina. The following short description introduces the family and illustrates the different strategies followed by Drawa to deal with the socio-economic changes after independence.

The oldest brother, Ali, took part in what was the first wave of urban migration. In 1942 he left the village to go to Casablanca for the first time. At the time this was a real adventure, travelling from the oasis to Zagora where one needed to obtain a permit to continue to the north, crossing the Atlas Mountains in a primitive doubledecker ('it had to be pushed when going up the mountains'), to arrive in Casablanca and be held in quarantine for several days. As did so many rural migrants, Ali found a job in road construction. After several years, when he had saved enough money, he bought a three-room apartment in a newly built quarter at the edge of town. He has sons with children of their own and a daughter. His sons have all left town to live in the north of the country. Ali almost never returns to the village.

Ali's migration is typical for the trend in the Dra Valley, stimulated by the opportunity of a better life in Casablanca. Improved health services in the oasis, introduced by the French presence, led to a rapid growth of the population; a growth, which had to be balanced by migration. The first French statistics from 1933 count 47,000 inhabitants in the valley. In 1971 the figure had risen to 111,000, and in the 1982 census the inhabitants numbered 170,069. The Ktawa Oasis had 24,780 inhabitants in the 1982 census. Compared with 1971 this meant an increase in the population of 2.2%. The migration trend that started before independence accelerated in the 1960s. Of all the migrants in the valley, between 15% and 20% left permanently (cf. Pletsch 1971). At present, every family in the village has relatives in Casablanca, some never return to their natal village, others commute between their home in *Casa* and the village, where their family survives because of their migration salary.

As a result of overpopulation in the southern oases, migration became a necessary phenomenon. It had some typical features. In the Dra Valley it was the landless and marginal peasants who migrated, among them many Drawa. The overriding majority of them moved to the western and northern towns. Much less than in other regions, migrants from the Dra Valley went abroad to Europe. A third complementary feature of the migratory process in the valley is the limited attachment to the region of birth. Once their economic circumstances improved, migrants brought their family members over to start a new life. For the Drawa migration became the most important way to escape the labour contracts with landowners. In particular to youngsters the choice between working in the fields as labourer for large landholders or working in road construction in the northern towns for their own benefit was easily made (Moureau 1955: 8).

Labour migration changed the tenacious occupational specialism only to some extent. In agreement with their marginal status in the oasis villages, many found work in a category already occupied by freed slaves on the streets of the northern towns: Milk- and water-carriers, street vendors, and coachmen. Already in the 19th century, liberated slaves and dark-skinned people in general only survived by finding work in the city streets as ambulant musicians and engaging in other disreputable activities such as water-carrying, cobbling, porting, prostitution, and serving in coffee-houses (Ennaji 1994: 98–99). In Marrakesh the corporation of the water-carriers came to be controlled by Drawa of one village in the oasis Taghbalt. As they recruited only among themselves, the monopolization of this trade was complete. At the Paris World Exposition in 1937, the Moroccan pavilion housed a Drawi water-carrier from this village in Taghbalt (St Bon 1938a: 79). Additionally, they found work as domestic servants, weavers (Maher 1974), leather-workers (Jemma 1971), cultivators, well-diggers, tanners, butchers (Noin 1970: 187) and construction workers. They also traded in medicinal plants, henna, peas and broad beans in the streets of the northern towns (Bellakhdar *et al.* 1992: 168).

The head of the second household, the youngest brother Najem, belongs to the second wave of migration, starting in the late 1960s. In the early 1970s, when he was still in his twenties, he left the village to look for a job in the north of the country. His change of regional orientation can be attributed to the massive foreign migration of Moroccans from the Rif and their subsequent investments in their home region.[32] Through irregular construction work in the Rif

---

[32] See McMurray's account of Haddou, a Moroccan migrant worker from the northern town Nador. With money earned in France, Haddou planned to build a dream house: 'He then hired a construction foreman to round up a crew and get started. They came from the region of Ouarzazate in southern Morocco, just like most of the other construction workers in Nador. Haddou liked them because they worked hard for little money and without complaint. They had migrated in search for work just like himself' (1993: 381).

(Nador and Ketama), Najem got to know the patron of a building company in Fez, who could provide him with a steadier job. That was when he decided to migrate permanently to the north and live among the *Fassis*. Thus, when his father Salem died, he sold most of his share of the inheritance to his relatives and started to build his own home in the outskirts of Fez. He returns home once a year to earn some additional money picking dates. He then lives in a small room in a dilapidated quarter of the *qsar*, where his first wife and one of their daughters still live.

Hammed is the head of the third household. His central role in the village shows him to be a truthful descendant of his father Salem. Together with his sons he still cultivates his own few fields and share-crops the palm trees of several owners in and outside of the village. The sharecropping tasks as well as several other functions in the village were inherited from his father Salem. His oldest son Fatih went to Casablanca at an early age to live in the household of Ali, and is now married there.

The fourth household is Mbark's. Mbark, better known as *Barka*, also lives in the village, but in a different quarter. Just like his older brother, he chose to earn a living within the village instead of in one of the northern towns. Mbark and his sons cultivate their own fields and that of one major absentee landholder in the village. A complementary source of income constitutes the sale of vegetables and transport activities at the bi-weekly oasis market. In the village he recently opened a small shop with gas tanks, batteries, matches, sugar, et cetera.

The head of the fifth household is Mina, Najem's first wife, but also the sister of the wives of Ali and Hammed. She and her two daughters try to run their own household by way of a number of odd jobs, of which midwife is one. Her youngest daughter is married to Abdelmzid, son of Hammed and her sister Aisha. Figure 6 presents the kinship relations of Hazzabin family as the family reappears in the chapters to come.[33]

The socio-economic status of the people known as Haratin differs substantially from one oasis to the other. Likewise, the effects of migration for socio-economic change in the oases were not the same

---

[33] One brother, Abderahmane, has lost almost all contact with the family. I do not possess any information about him or his household. He is included in the figure because of his fictive (milk) kinship bond with one Sharif (see chapter four).

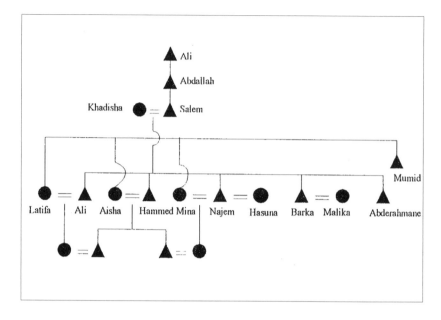

Figure 6: The Hazzabin family

for every Drawi family. Whether migration indeed acted as a 'lever'
to force emancipation in the southern oases (De Haas 1995: 54)
remains unclear from the restricted viewpoint of one oasis community. In the village of Aduafil, Drawa face difficulties investing their
money in landed property as to develop into independent landholders
in their region of birth (see chapter four).

The Hazzabin family's history of residence in the village reflects
the social changes that Drawa as a social category have gone through.
When they first arrived in the village, the family lived in their patron's
stable a few square metres in size. Until this day, they maintain close
relationships with this Sharifian family. Next, they were able to buy
a proper *qsar* dwelling, consisting of three levels and a quadrangular
open space from top to bottom in the Outside Quarter. This dwelling,
in which the family has lived for decennia, is still the only common
property that may be divided among the brothers. In the 1970s,
many Shurfa left the *qsar* to live in *extra muros* houses opposite the
ancient *qsar*. They were able to do so with the help of migration
money. Most succesful example is the first and still largest concrete
house outside of the walled village built by a migrant worker from
France. The departure from the *qsar* gave one of the brothers, Ham-

med, the opportunity to buy more space in the *qsar*. Since at present the ancient Outside Quarter for the most part is a ruin—and in this respect the riddle in the beginning of this chapter refers to an actual situation—Hammed and his family are the only residents. Their dwelling traverses the quarter in such a way that it is possible to enter it from different *qsar* streets. One could say that with the help of migration money and the disintegration of *qsar* life, the Hazzabins have moved from the margin to the core of the *qsar*. Yet, since the Shurfa of the Outside Quarter have at the same time largely moved out into more spacious *extra muros* dwellings, the spatial and social segregation of the two social categories maintains its force to this day.

Conclusions

In the relatively isolated Ktawa Oasis, with a characteristic pattern of very dense settlements that lie dispersed throughout the oasis, different categories of inhabitants came to coexist within the walls of the *qsar-s*. In the pre-independence period, the walls of the *qsar* protected oasis inhabitants against the harsh natural environment and unwanted contacts with outsiders. This type of settlement acted as base of one or two descent groups who owned land and water rights in the direct surroundings. Newcomers to the village who came to live with the established population were usually treated with kindness but kept at a spatial and social distance: Particularly, Drawa who came from other oases were often not able to buy land or gain rights to the use of irrigation water.

Intellectual and religious specialist functions, initially backed by the state, were the major sources of power on the basis of which the Shurfa of Aduafil gained a foothold in the oasis. From there, the acquisition of land secured their position. Drawa in general constituted the reservoir of marginal peasants and ambulant occupational specialists, forced to migrate seasonally or permanently to neighbouring regions. They often lived separately from the rest of the population and were to a large extent forced to remain endogamous. Drawa have been defined here as 'strangers' in the communities where they live. In the oasis, both membership of the village community and dominant cultural ideals have been determined by long-standing relations between families with property rights in the location of birth.

Drawa came to live in the oasis village as tenants, thereby gaining security and stability as well as enjoying a privileged closeness to the saintly Shurfa. From the perspective of the Shurfa, the Drawa kept their marginal status, living inside the village but not belonging to the descent group of the founder of the village. The enduring, although not complete, exclusion from land and water rights is of crucial importance for their marginal status. In the village Drawa furthermore mediated between the walled village and the outside natural world. An identical interdependent relationship developed between Ait ʿAtta Berbers and Drawa in a nearby village and else-where in the oasis.

In this chapter the nature of the long-standing social exclusion of Drawa in the oasis has been pointed out. The following two chap-ters show how Shurfa and Drawa nevertheless maintain close inter-dependent relationships. In chapters six and seven, this will lead to a consideration of Drawa as social and cultural brokers for the Sharifian population.

CHAPTER FOUR

CLOSE ENCOUNTERS
PATRONAGE IN THE VILLAGE

> Relationships between the aḥrār [*nobles*] and the šwāšīn, tenants
> or domestic servants, were built on tenderness and sincere mutual
> affection (Bédoucha 1987: 258).

Notwithstanding the large gap in prestige, families of the two social
categories that in the oasis hierarchy are taken for social opposites,
Shurfa and Drawa, live together and maintain close relations. Eickelman
(1976: 120) has pointed out that 'Moroccans do not conceive of the
social order as consisting of groups in structured relationships'. Instead,
'[e]mphasis is placed on managing personal networks of dyadic relationships'. Central aim of this chapter is to examine how these dyadic
relationships, concurring with enduring patterns of socio-economic
inequality, shape the configuration of saints and servants. The argument evolves around the mutual interdependence, even intimate rapprochement between both parties. The patron-client relations between
Shurfa and Drawa, consisting of asymmetrical arrangements involving loyalty, protection, and reciprocal rights and obligations (cf. Blok
1969: 365), are referred to locally as relationships based on exchange
(*tabādul*). The socio-economic exclusion and consequently dependent
status of Drawa are basic tenets of the relationship; yet the close
encounters between male and female Shurfa and Drawa point to
more complex, inherently ambivalent relationships between families.
The first section considers the alleged agricultural specialism of Drawa
and kind of bonding between landholders and tenants. In the remaining part, I remain with the village to describe how Shurfa and Drawa
maintain close interdependent, and affective bonds.

Agricultural specialists in a sanctuary

Alluvial agriculture and date-palm cultivation are extremely labour
intensive, and in the numerous microcosmic 'hydraulic societies' on
the northern fringe of the Sahara, Haratin constitute the major labour

force. In Morocco they carried out 'most of the menial labor in the oases' (Dunn 1977: 44) and in the oases of the Algerian Ahaggar Mountains, it was thanks to the 'Herculean labours' of Haratin that alluvial agriculture developed among the Tuareg (Keenan 1977: 100). Why are the Drawa in the village likewise so closely connected with agricultural work?

On an afternoon in April, I joined Abdellatif Hazzabin on his assignment to pollinate some date palms. Following the path along the irrigation canal that splits from the main canal, we arrived at the villagers' fields and trees. Next to the canal, just outside the village, Abdellatif approached a tree to pick a few white brushes from it. These brushes are the pollen that have to be put between the orange branches of a female tree so that it will grow dates for harvesting in autumn and winter. Without human intervention, the dates would remain the tiny knobs on a branch that they are in April. But even with human help, villagers consider the chance of producing dates relatively low. According to them, each year only one of every three palms produces mature dates. From among the mass of trees, Abdellatif easily identified those which his father had told him to pollinate. With his plastic slippers as the only protection against the sharp leaves and needles, he climbed the tree, put some of the white pollen between the orange branches and came down again. During the whole process Abdellatif muttered a two-line chant that expresses the wish for the wind to stay away—and not blow away the pollen. In this way we went from one tree to the other. Back in the village, I told my neighbour and former patron of the Hazzabins of my trip with Abdellatif. When I asked after the chant, he sneered at contemporary practices: 'Today they sing without any truthful intention (*nīya*) behind the singing. They mumble one or two lines, say *bismillah*, or don't say anything at all'. Instead, the patron praised Abdellatif's great grandfather Abdallah, whom he remembered as the true 'singing fecundator of date palms'. In those days, the chants were much more elaborate, and because Abdallah had a clear and loud voice, you could hear him singing from a long way away. Then, when you approached him and greeted him or extended wishes for an abundant harvest, he interwove his answer to you in between the lines of the chant, in this way avoiding the interruption of the chant (and thus the pollination).[1]

---

[1] Compare the following note on the Egyptian Siwa Oasis: 'It is a joy to hear

The response of the patron is illustrative of the way some of the villagers I spoke to think and feel about the meaning and importance of present-day agricultural practices and the place of Drawa therein. First, the patron's remarks reflect a nostalgic outlook on the past. It is common belief in the village that in the early days villagers took better care of their fields and young men were physically better equipped, better fed and more willing to carry out hard agricultural labour. It is true that, compared with 'the old days', technological innovation has changed, sometimes improved, and diversified the harvest: In the 1970s, cement inter-village irrigation channels replaced earthen canals, and motor pumps were introduced to bring up the water more easily. Today, tractors plough and level fields more quickly, although less precisely than when done by hoe and hand. On the other hand, the overall importance of agricultural production in the total income of villagers has decreased, and more land lies fallow. The main instigator of this development has been the growth of secondary income sources outside of the village community in combination with the refusal of absentee landowners to participate financially in sharecropping their fields. Furthermore, the droughts of the 1980s once again showed the precariousness of relying on agriculture as the sole source of income.

The patron's response highlights another typical viewpoint in the village, one pertaining to the qualities of Drawa as fecundators and oasis cultivators. Drawa are considered to be pollination specialists and to possess detailed agricultural knowledge. Villagers declare that originally Drawa lived in the village to take care of cultivation in the service of the Shurfa, as was already the task of the first Drawi who accompanied Mulay Adafal in the 16th century.[2] Before the

---

a labourer singing in Siwan as he works on the tree. His melodious tunes are heard from a distance, and the moment he stops another labourer answers him from another garden. For every kind of work there is a special song, and the Siwans can tell right away what the man is doing' (Fakhry 1982: 27).

[2] The patron's story is furthermore reminiscent of the practices of the Hartani adherents of the cult of Sidi Bounou in the Dra Valley. These adherents, the *Wlad Sidi Bounou*, when first observed in the 1920s, were mostly water-carriers, blacksmiths and vegetable sellers; these are the typical occupations of Haratin. This is how Legey (1935: 223; cf. Amard 1997: 51–53; Joly 1905) describes the practices of the members of this brotherhood: 'It suffices to scratch their head or to pretend to scratch one's own head; and they at once throw off all their garments except their drawers, and rush to look for a palm-tree. If they succeed in finding one, they climb to the top, and clinging to the spiky branches begin to weep and to sing'. It is said the *wlad* cannot be hurt by the palm branches. The *Wlad Sidi Bou Nou*

construction of a system of barrages in the Dra River and the introduction of a new irrigation system in the early 1970s, the palm trees
and the fields were irrigated by the river and groundwater, brought
up by mechanical hydraulics and human and animal labour. At the
time, people relied more on wells for the irrigation of their fields
and Drawa were considered to be the outstanding well-diggers, knowing how and especially where to dig a new well. In particular, they
knew how to find fresh water with the aid of a swinging watch or
stick. Small teams of well-diggers, led by one master in the trade
(*mu'allim*), travelled around the oases. They were also much in demand
in the High Atlas Region and even further north.[3] Drawa were furthermore considered to be specialists in the construction of subterranean irrigation canals in northern oases. At present, these well-digging
teams of labourers *cum* patron still exist. Pollination and irrigation
are two typical and long-standing tasks in which Drawa as tenants
of landholding families are involved: One article of the ancient written village law of a nearby oasis stated that the tenant who tries to
leave after the successive pollination of the dates but before the harvest should be prevented from doing so. He will be obliged to irrigate the palms at least once (Mezzine 1987: 241). Because of the
increase in migrant labour and the decreased importance of agriculture, their knowledge of well-digging, pollination and irrigation
practices is not that much used, although still sometimes needed.
Herzenni observed for the neighbouring oasis of Aneghrif that Haratin
'are at present the only ones who master the knowledge on the water
rights of the two sources in Aneghrif as well as the expertise needed
for the pollination of the date palms' (1990: 20).

The agricultural specialization—once perhaps a quasi-monopoly—
of Drawa coincides with the low regard for agricultural labour. For
the Maghrebian oasis societies in general, the geographer Despois
observed in the 1960s that the light-skinned landowners predominantly abstained from agricultural work. They took it as a sign of
moral decline that because of the migration of their labourers they

---

belong to the 'Aissawa religious brotherhood (Brunel 1926: 67) who 'recruit primarily from among the group of harratines' (Bellakhdar *et al.* 1992: 241; cf.
Dermenghem 1954: 293 for a Tunisian Hartani 'society of the shoot of the palm
tree'). See chapter seven for the ritual tasks of Drawa in the cycle of life.
[3] Briggs (1960: 95) mentions the well-diggers of Ouargla in Algeria who 'look
not unlike some of the less negroid Haratin but (. . .) seem to have an even lower
status in spite of their relatively important function'.

were forced to leave their lands fallow (Despois 1961: 582–583). In the early days, as villagers still remember, Shurfa indeed did not engage in fecundation, irrigation, or harvesting dates. Instead, as one Drawi said, '*Drawa šaddū al-akmās*' ('Drawa entered into a tenancy for one-fifth of the harvest'). They also did not fulfil the corvée services (*tiwīza*) that were enforced by the local authorities. The contemporary division of labour in the Ktawa Oasis only partly confirms the opposition between dark-skinned labourers and light-skinned landholders as observed by Despois. Today, almost every village family, Drawi or Sharif, at one time or another has been directly involved in agricultural labour. Drawa, however, are still perceived as the real peasant ('fellah'). Because of their physical strength, it is said that they are more capable of carrying out strenuous irrigation labour. Shurfa consider the presence of Drawa in the village to be directly related to agriculture and date-palm cultivation, but they associate Drawa also in more implicit ways with irrigation work. Thus, one Sharif who generally wore the typical Sharifian white turban changed it for a green one, characteristic for Drawa, when he went to irrigate his fields.

In the Maghreb the low regard for agricultural labour—in itself more of a general characteristic in the Mediterranean zone (cf. Blok and Driessen 1984: 113)—was reinforced by the opposition between a nomadic or transhumant ethos and a sedentary, agricultural ethos. In the Ktawa Oasis, the sedentary population predominantly has contact with a transhumant (instead of nomadic) herding population belonging to the Ait 'Atta. A truthful 'Attawi, captain Spillman observed in the 1930s, abhors agricultural labour: 'Those who cultivate with their hands are scarce. Tenants or harratin fulfil this subordinate occupation' (Spillman 1936: 39). 'Attawis in the oasis now do cultivate the land, but they keep on looking with awe and respect at those 'Attawis, sometimes family members, who still solely or predominantly herd animals.

Although I did not come across an explicit disdain for agricultural activities in the village except for one or two occasions, the majority of heads of larger Sharifian households do avoid agricultural work and leave it to their younger family members. The avoidance is partly connected to a positive attitude toward trade. Almost all of the largest landholding families are also those most involved in trading activities. The number of Shurfa who own a store in the village or commercial centre is remarkable, also in comparison with

neighbouring villages. Others trade dates from the region in Marrakesh, and one even owns a factory there. The trading Shurfa find
in the Prophet their most illustrious example. Numerous Koran verses
and Hadiths[4] encourage trade, provided that it is done without excessive profits or treacherous dealings. In the past, Shurfa of the village and elsewhere in the valley were involved in the caravan trade
from the region south of the Sahara to Marrakesh and Fez.

For the whole of Northwest Africa, ethnologists have reported on
an association of Haratin with agriculture and date-palm cultivation.
What has been said for pre-independence Mauritania, namely that
'agriculture is the task of servile members or tributaries of society . . .'
(De Chassey 1977: 54), also applies to the Tuareg society in pre-
independence Algeria (Keenan 1977: 101–106) and the Moroccan
oasis societies with transhumant Ait 'Atta Berbers and the sedentary
population living side by side (Hart 1984: 123–158). The alleged
agricultural specialism of Haratin has led to an etymological explanation of the term Hartani from the Arab root verb *ḥarrāṯ* meaning
'ploughman' (Nicolas 1977: 101; Maher 1974: 227; but see Teine-
Cheikh 1989). Although the etymology is probably incorrect, I observed in conversations with villagers the synonymous use of the
terms Hartani, Drawi, labourer (*kaddām*) and sharecropper (*kammās*),
suggesting that Haratin predominantly are seen as representing the
much larger category of landless or marginal peasants in the southern countryside who are charged with agricultural labour in the service of landholding families.

The answer to the question of why Haratin are associated with
agricultural work and, although to a lesser extent, Shurfa with trade,
seems to come closer when we include the subordinate, because
dependent, status of most cultivators. In the Maghreb, people who
do agricultural labour on a daily basis usually are not the owners
of the land. Instead, cultivation is organized through a tenancy contract between the worker and the owner. Thus, a vertical bond is
established between the two parties that lasts at least one season
but normally continues for a much longer period. Sharecroppers are
usually landless or marginal peasants as Jamous observes for the
north of the country: 'Those who accept this type of contract are
in general very poor. They either do not possess any land or only

---

[4] A Hadith is an officially authorized tradition relating to the Prophet.

a very small plot and insufficient to live on' (1981:138). This applies equally to the south, with Haratin fulfilling a large proportion of the tenancies.[5]

The low esteem of agricultural labour is to a large extent summarized in the dependency (versus autonomy) of the peasant. In the ancient customary law documents, protection, subordination and servility are interchangeable key terms to denote the status of the Hartani tenant (*ḵammās*). An agricultural labourer or tenant who lacks land and water rights and thus cannot live independently of other families is also lacking the two most important assets of respect and pride. Land and water provide the origins of social bonds between family members and in the past provided the inalienable right to citizenship in the region (*blad*). Land, in short, is a testimony of one's origins. In the customary law documents of the region it was laid down that citizenship could only be gained through the ownership of land. Yet land was seldom sold to outsiders. In one law document of the neighbouring village of Nesrat, for example, 'selling a garden or a field to a stranger is as grave as the killing of a man' (Azam 1946: 63; cf. Niclausse 1954: annexe 2, 15; cf. for the Rif, Jamous 1981: 135). In the law texts, property (*milk*) was synonymously used with origin (*aṣl*) (Filali 1984: 245), which is confirmed in the fact that present-day family names find their origin in plots of land owned by these families.

The lack of autonomy determines the low status of the Drawi tenant. Most Sharifian villagers and some Drawa still agree on the conviction that Shurfa should not work in service of others as this does not fit their status and cultural level (*mustawan*). Working in the field or fulfilling collective services forces a Sharif to mingle with members of other social categories, while it are exactly the social distance and internal social cohesion that constitute the source of power of the Shurfa.

The association of Drawa with agricultural labour must be understood in the context of the disregard for agricultural labour in combination with the entry into a dependent condition as tenant or labourer. It would, however, be wrong to underestimate the mutual

---

[5] Weulersse (1946: 69) spoke of 'the contempt for the sedentary, in particular for the sedentary *par excellence*, the peasant' in the Middle East and noted that 'in the world (. . .) of the oases of western Arabia, to work the soil is by definition and for all time servile labour'.

interdependence of Shurfa and Drawa. It has been pointed out that
in general 'noble men are seen as supposedly non-dependent' and
the 'dependents are ideally seen as "humbly serving only"' (Van der
Veen 1971: 309). As we will see, the concurring processes of inclusion and exclusion, rapprochement and dissociation, that shape the
relationships between Shurfa and Drawa in the village defy such an
'ideologically dichotomous interpretation of the ambivalent reality'
(ibidem).

If the Haratin are associated with sharecropping and agricultural
labour in general, what role was there for other forms of possibly
more bonded labour, in particular slavery? In Morocco the slaves
who were imported until the 1930s did not contribute greatly to the
peasant economy, although in Saharan oases south of the valley they
worked on sugar and salt plantations, and acted as herdsmen and
cultivators for nomads (Hunwick 1992: 20–21). In Morocco, slaves
were owned by a family for whom they worked in and around the
house as marginal members of the household.

The difference between slave and labourer or tenant might not
always have been clearly set. Some authors mention the existence of
a group of servants, sometimes slaves, living close to a few sanctuaries
of national importance. These sanctuaries possessed large tracts of
land, controlled by a restricted number of Sharifian families, living
as squires.[6] Numerous slaves lived near to these sanctuaries. For example, in the north of the country, the sanctuary of Ouezzane possessed 700 slaves (Ennaji 1994: 21). Comparable to the baronial
landlords of Ouezzane were the Shurfa of Tazerwalt. Servants cultivated the land of this most important sanctuary in the southwest
and acted furthermore as concubine, wet-nurse, overseer, and jack-
of-all-trades (idem, 21, 26). The sanctuary of Tamgrout in the Dra
Valley, last in the row of large sanctuaries and the one closest to
the village (at 60 kilometres), also controlled many servants and slaves
(Hammoudi 1980: 626).

It is not clear whether all the cultivators and labourers of the large

---

[6] The *ḥabus* or *waqf* land came under control of the sanctuaries through different
forms of grants, gift-giving and purchase. Some sanctuaries were on good terms
with the Moroccan sultan and were eligible for fiscal concessions and taxing rights
on specific villages and indirect military support. The same concession mechanism
made the institution of private ownership within tribes possible (see for an analysis
of changing landownership structures in Moroccan society from 1500–1900, Joffé
1991).

estates did have the status of slave. In all likelihood, a more extensive repertoire of strategies to bind people to the land existed at the
turn of the century, including the right to demand gifts (*ziyāra*) and
establish irrigation and ploughing services. The historian Ennaji, in
his study of Moroccan slavery, asked the rhetorical question of whether
a sanctuary existed which did not have slaves who were devoted to
it heart and soul but also pointed to a possible confusion of slaves
with freedmen. The innumerable people working in Tazerwalt probably were not slaves but labourers and tenants, certainly since the
end of the 19th century (Ennaji 1994: 27, 51). In Ouezzane, the
same confusion about the exact status of the workers exists. Pâques
(1991: 70–71) mentions the migration of Drawa from the Dra Valley
to the northern town to take care of irrigation, the regular cleansing of the wells, and the upkeep of the canals. In Tamgrout, slaves,
tenants, and temporary labourers who preferred to live in proximity
to the protective surrounding of the sanctuary worked side by side
(Hammoudi 1980: 628). In short, sanctuaries could through fiscal
concessions, rights on gifts and tax-raising and debt relationships,
control the labour of the population of neighbouring villages and
'latifundia' further away.[7]

These three examples of powerful sanctuaries direct our attention
to the kind of relationship that might develop between landholding
descendants of a holy man and marginal peasants in smaller sanctuaries such as that of Aduafil. That relationship, in my view, can
best be denoted as one between patron and client, that is, a reciprocal relationship involving, in the words of Berque (1938: 27), 'material services of the tenant, spiritual services of the Master (*Maître*)'.
This implies that in the case of the Drawa in the sanctuaries, the
agreement may have been set on a voluntary basis. Landless and
marginal peasants, again usually but not solely Drawa, offered their
labour and knowledge in return for a regular and stable access to
agricultural resources, sometimes in combination with protection from
a sanctuary or from a transhumant collectivity. A closer look at the
ideological underpinning of this exchange relationship between saint
and servant will have to wait until the next chapter. First I shall
explore more closely in the remaining sections of this chapter the
social bonding between Sharifian patrons and Drawi clients.

---

[7] See for a comparative overview of various dependency relations between slave
and freeman, Testart 1998.

Drawa were not passers-by but became involved in an intricate exchange of goods and services between members of the village, including the duty to fulfil numerous tasks for the village community or for specific Sharifian families. This brings us to a major difference in the labour relationship of slave and Drawi. In contrast to the slave who mainly worked in the owner's house (and was given a parcel of land in 1956), members of a Drawi family work as tenants or labourers for a cluster of related families, possibly with as its centre one 'big man'. A direct patron-client relationship exists between the family and the 'big Sharifian family'. Additionally, unlike slaves, the Drawa fulfil communal tasks in the village. Below the village of Aduafil will provide us with an example of this pattern.

Of landowners and tenants

Agriculture or date-palm cultivation is no longer the all-distinguishing mark of Drawa. Previously, a veritable adult Sharif would not irrigate his fields by himself, nor carry out other daily agricultural tasks, but leave them to younger family members and Drawi tenants. Nowadays, even the Sharifian imam of the village works in his own fields.[8] One crucial factor in the nevertheless continuing association of Drawa with agriculture has been their dependent socioeconomic status, as seen from the division of land and water rights and the concomitant sharecropping arrangements in the village.

Economic developments

At the time the French Protectorate gained precedence in the oasis in the late 1920s, irrigation agriculture constituted the major source of subsistence for the villagers, if possible in the form of the classic three-layer oasis cultivation of palm trees, fruit trees, cereals and legumes. People grew barley, wheat and several vegetables. Principal constraint on the growth of agricultural production was the incessant lack and irregularity of irrigation water. In the dry periods, people in the southernmost oases Ktawa and Mhammid never knew

---

[8] For women things seem to have remained the same: Drawiat amass dates and cut daily fodder in the fields, married Sharifat remain at home.

whether the water would ever arrive at their fields.[9] I was told that conflicts about the division of irrigation water between villages were abundant. When asked after the major changes in their life with the implementation of French administration, all villagers mentioned first how the French made an end to the inter-village struggles for water by building the present-day partitioning doors in the central canal that runs through the village. It was however only years after independence, in 1970, that a barrage near the provincial capital Ouarzazate was built as part of an ambitious nationwide agricultural programme, that a more continuous flow of water was provided for (*La Charte Agricole*; cf. Ayad and Le Coz n.d.). Currently, concrete channels connect all six oases throughout the Dra Valley into one intricate irrigation system, led by the provincial authorities in Ouarzazate. They decide on the number of days the water will flow from the reservoir into the valley. Unfortunately, even the new irrigation system could not prevent the dry period of the mid-1980s ruining several harvests and thousands of palm trees.

During the colonial period the oasis region was not of great interest for the large-scale agricultural projects set up by the colonial authorities, neither was it attractive to French colonists. After independence this trend continued, reinforcing the already existing regional differences. The south remained one of the poorest regions in the country, yet it acquired the smallest amount of subsidy from the state (De Mas 1978: 287–291). The French geographer Noin summarized the consequences as follows: 'The standard of living [of the Moroccan *qsar* population, RE] remains all in all very low. The majority of the families lives in miserable conditions' (1970: 185). A report on Ktawa from 1981 gives the same picture of poor living conditions when compared with the northwestern part of Morocco (cf. Ministère 1981). Foreign migration has not had the same impact in the Ktawa Oasis as it had in similar marginalized areas like the Rif or the Sous. At the time of my fieldwork (1993–1994), no paved roads led to the villages, which makes normal transport during the rainy season almost impossible, there was electricity for only three

---

[9] Their anxiety was described by Jacques-Meunié when she visited the oasis during the drought of 1946: 'Hanging on the telephone, all await the tidings: Upstream the river starts to fill and to run, but how far shall it get? Shall it reach Zagora? And if so, shall the water be powerful enough to continue to Fezouata and make its way through the beds of the canals which have been choked up by the sand for so long?' (Jacques-Meunié 1973: 178).

hours a day and no running water. Local opinion on the peripheral position of the region and its inhabitants was nicely summarized in the joke that 'Morocco is a fast car and the Dra Valley is
its exhaust-pipe'.

In addition to the inadequate transformations in agricultural production to compensate for the demographic growth between 1933
and 1956, the structures of landownership and water rights remained
largely untouched during the time of French control in the region,
proving their tenacity after independence (Ouhajou 1986: 53, 62; cf.
De Haas 1995: 159). At the time of colonization, Drawa made up
independent households, whose members worked as labourers or tenants on the holdings of landowning families. This trend continued
after independence. Many landless and marginalized peasants, and
among them were many Drawa, left therefore for the northern towns.
Captain Moureau reported in his *fin de stage* study that the landholders in the oases found it increasingly difficult to find Hartani
sharecroppers: 'They consent to many more privileges for the sharecroppers than the customary laws prescribe and they even close their
eyes for the theft of water and dates' (Moureau 1955: 10).[10] In 1971
a ministerial study reported that more than a fifth of the Drawa was
landless and forced to work as tenants or day labourers (Toutain
1971). One way to skirt the refusal of proprietors to sell their land
was to buy the right to cultivate it.

The general pattern in the Dra Valley is the continuance of an
unequal division of water rights between villages to the disadvantage
of Drawi villages and individual Drawa and a comparable unequal
division of land, with 'microfundia' (less than one hectare) as the
rule. For Aduafil, these developments imply that the pattern of ownership of land and water rights that once pushed Drawa into sharecropping contracts with Shurfa continues to influence relations between
Shurfa and those Drawa who stayed behind in the village and did
not migrate to the northern cities.

The land in the village can be divided into three categories:
(1) Close to the village quarters; (2) outside the village territory and
(3) remainder within the village boundaries. The first category con-

---

[10] A similar development has been observed in the Algerian oases where many
Haratin took on salaried jobs in the newly-developed industries set up from the
1950s onwards, leaving the Tuareg patrons with their fields uncultivated (Vallet
1990: 78).

sists of relatively small, walled parcels of land near the village centre on which vegetables are grown or a stable or new *extra muros*
house is built. Almost every household owns such a small, precious
piece of land. The second category consists of inherited land outside the immediate village environment and recently acquired land.
The latter includes in particular land in the surroundings of the
administrative centre, four kilometres from the village. The purchased
land is brought under cultivation with water-pumps. This subcate-
gory is only attractive for those who can afford to make a large
investment in land and pumps. Two Sharifian households own large
tracts of land outside the village; one man has even moved to live
on his land. One of the two men worked in Europe for many years
and invested his money in this kind of new land. The third category of land consists of parcels that are used for the cultivation of
cereals and are irrigated via the smaller village canals which start
from the large channel that interconnects the oasis villages.

I undertook a small survey (300 plots) concerning the ownership
of land falling under the first and third categories (i.e., land for which
irrigation is organized through the village water rights).[11] From this
survey, observations and discussions with villagers, it became clear
that the spatial division of land close to the village largely follows
lineage lines, with the land of the Drawa located in between. Lineage 3
of the Outside Quarter owns land west of the village, Lineage 1 of
the Saint's Quarter owns land east of the village. The two other
lineages own land in both directions, although predominantly east.
The division of land returns in the surnames of the families of the
respective lineages. These names refer to a parcel of land or a remarkable sign in the landscape (open spot, sand dune) on either side of
the village.

Another observation is the large gap in ownership of land between
Shurfa and Drawa. The parcels of land owned by Drawa could be
counted on the fingers of one hand. A cautious estimation of land
division singles out five Sharifian extended families as major landowners, possessing a great stretch of land near the village as well as

---

[11] A registry of landed property does not exist. Data were collected with the use
of the maps that have been drawn in the service of the construction of irrigation
canals in the late 1970s (Scet International-ORMVA, Ouarzazate). I noted for every
parcel of land the owner, sharecropper and usage. Numbered family name lists
which correspond to the numbered parcels of land on the maps seem to exist for
other oases, but not for Ktawa. At least, I was not able to obtain them.

generous parcels outside it. Next comes a large category of Shurfa in possession of land in lots of up to five hectares. The Drawa are the smallest landowners or are landless. The Hazzabin family, for example, only recently acquired land. Neither Abdallah nor Salem Hazzabin owned any land in the village. Once I was walking with a Sharif outside the village, when he stopped and pointed at a piece of land: 'When you put the land of all the Drawa together, it would not even be as large as this field [that was his, RE]'. When I asked about the possibility for Drawa to buy land in the village, the same Sharif stated that 'at present, people don't sell them their parcels'. Besides, referring to one Drawi in particular, 'all he does is sit on the village square, instead of going to Casa to earn money to buy land [outside the village, RE]'. As a general conclusion it can be said that the division of land follows family and lineage lines, which means that large parts on either side of the canal are owned by one Sharifian family or lineage. Land is privately owned and sold separately from the right to use water.[12] Drawa own a few parcels of land but not enough to live from independently.

Since the ownership of a date palm is not necessarily implied by the ownership of the land on which it grows, the ownership of date palms cannot be inferred from the landownership. Moreover, only a few types grow saleable dates, the rest serves for private consumption and fodder. From talks with villagers, the following estimation was made. The average number of palm trees is 50 per household, with again at least five households owning more than 200. The Drawa own per family 10 or less.[13] The number of livestock (sheep, goats) is evenly divided among families. Cows are an exception. At least seven Sharifian families own one or more cows that provide them with sour milk and butter; no Drawi family owns a cow. Without sufficient land, they would not have been able to provide it with daily fodder.

---

[12] That is to say: *Milk* (private ownership) land is the largest category. Other prevalent types of ownership are *ḥabus* (land owned by the *zāwiya*; for example, land that was once given by someone from a neighbouring village and that at present can be sharecropped by every Aduafili), *ḥabas* (privately owned land with a specified condition attached to it; for example, land for which a family has to present annually a collective dinner on the Prophet's birthday), collective land (in ownership of the *qabīla*, i.e. the village community; for example, the field on which the collective outdoor prayers take place).

[13] In the Tata Oasis, west of the Dra Valley, Haratin bought palms from impoverished nomads: Their ownership of palms rose from 12.2% in 1935, 25% in 1945, to 28.4% in 1954 (Moureau 1955: figure 2).

Just as important as landownership is the division of water rights. Surface water is the scarcest resource in the oasis, a fact that is expressed in a strict division of water rights *between* villages as well as a strict regulation of the use of water *within* villages. What has been said for landownership also accounts for the division of water rights: The concentration of rights in the hands of a minority is coupled with the 'pulverization' of rights in the hands of the large majority.[14] In the village, the system of water rights controls the use of the surface water which flows through the main irrigation canal on the days that are assigned to Aduafil (Thursday during daytime and Saturday during the night).[15] Regulations are especially necessary in times of shortage. The only violent quarrels between villagers that took place during my stay in the village concerned the use of irrigation water. Water rights are owned by families and divided as part of the inheritance. In the village, the importance of water can be seen from the detachment of the right to use water from landownership. It is possible to buy land from members of the village, but unlike elsewhere in the valley the use of water is the inalienable right of members of the village community and not for sale. This implies that when a person buys a piece of land or palm tree he may not be able to irrigate his land for lack of water. He may either request the use of someone else's water, or dig a well. However, without a motor pump, irrigation is time-consuming and not without risk. One Drawi who dug a well during my fieldwork hit salinated water and gave up.

The Sharifian families control a larger share of the communal water rights than Drawi families. When we compare the water rights for the two categories, we see that an average Drawi family has control over 4 minutes, while families of the four Sharifian lineages control respectively 8, 17, 23 and 27 minutes.[16] Many Sharifian households have control over at least 20 minutes each; all the Drawi

---

[14] Paraphrase of Ouhajou (1986: 94). From his research in another oasis in the Dra Valley, it becomes clear that 2.5% of all families owns 40% of the water rights (idem, 94). Thirty-seven Drawi families (total: 258) are closed off from any right to use water (see for water rights in the Dra Valley, Hammoudi 1985).

[15] On those two days, the available time between sunrise and sunset is divided into units of two hours, somewhat confusingly named after the days of the week. Thus, after 14 hours, the cycle starts again. The 'week-cycle' starts where one ended at the last irrigation session.

[16] Without correction for the number of families per lineage, the division is as follows: Drawa: 6% of water rights; lineage 4 (Upper Quarter): 8%; lineage 1 (Saint's Quarter): 24%; lineage 2 (Saint's Quarter): 26%; lineage 3 (Outside Quarter): 36%.

families together control a little over 30 minutes, split up into numerous units of less than 5 minutes. The amount of water rights of single Drawi families is not enough to irrigate a field, as it already
takes more time than is available to let the water flow to a field.
Even when Drawa work together 30 minutes is not much. Their
fields are widely spread over the village grounds, and it would be
too time-consuming to reach them all in one round.

The unequal access to the use of water is interwoven with a difference in social cohesion between Shurfa and Drawa. Water rights remain
in one family but are subdivided as part of the inheritance. For
example, one family once owned 30 minutes. When the family split
up, the water rights were divided among the rightful shareholders—
in the case of three brothers, into 10 minutes each. Yet, during irrigation these three brothers continue to work as associates (šarīk-s).
They do so because their rights to use water are sequential (three
times 10 minutes of what once was one 30-minute part), but also
because their lands are close together. They can irrigate their land
much more effectively together than when on their own. Furthermore,
Shurfa have the possibility to gain control over more water rights
via strategic marriages, in which case an associative relationship
between the two families who become related by marriage may
develop.

Drawa have to look for ways to find similar irrigation associates.
One strategy is to ask the owner of a nearby field or a befriended
Sharif if one may use his water. Another is to use the water which
they dispose of as tenants of Sharifian families. For example, Hammed
Hazzabin cultivates as a tenant the date palms of an absentee Sharifian
landowner with 30 minutes of water rights. As the landowner's fields
are not cultivated, Hammed can use a large part of the water to
irrigate his own fields and those of other families. His brother Barka
is less lucky as he shares a tenancy with another Drawi, which tenancy includes the use of the water rights of the landholder. Barka
is now forced to look for other means to use irrigation water. Barka's
problem is more deeply interwoven with the system of water rights.
More than any other brother of the Hazzabin Family he has tried
to improve his economic position in the village through the acquisition of land. Because of the lack of water, he has been forced to
buy parcels of land in a nearby village, where land and water were
both for sale. He has also brought new land into cultivation at the

edge of the oasis with the use of a well. In combination with a motor pump this can be an effective solution to the problem of a lack of surface water. Previously two Sharifian villagers did so already successfully. However, similar to the attempt of the already mentioned Drawi, his well turned out to be too labour-intensive and without a pump unfit to solve the problem of salinated ground water.[17]

Shurfa largely downplay economic differences between villagers by comparing themselves with urban Moroccans or Europeans, arguing that any difference between the rich and poor in the village pales before European richness (e.g., that of the anthropologist). Furthermore, the decision of whether someone is poor and in need of aid does not depend on plain material circumstances alone. Villagers assess whether a person or a family is economically dependent on the support of his fellow villagers on the basis of a combination of considerations. One Sharif is poor and eligible for alms because he is blind and needs external help for all agricultural activities; a second receives alms because he has only daughters and no sons, which means he has to hire men to irrigate his fields; a third poor villager is an unmarried adult man who is considered to be mentally retarded (as seems to be the general opinion on adult unmarried men). Likewise, Hammed receives the alms that are prescribed in Islamic law because one of his adult sons is handicapped. From the explanations of Shurfa, it seems that fate can bestow the burden of economic hardship on every family, regardless of descent. Nevertheless, from my observations concerning the division of land and water rights, it appears that a less incidental inequality draws a clear line between Shurfa and Drawa.

Sharecropping

The socio-economic strategies (marriage and cooperation with irrigation) of Shurfa are directed toward the reinforcement of their mutual bonds to the detriment of the Drawa in the village. To uphold the status of the strong Sharifian families (or 'big men'; see below) and

---

[17] A well with a motor pump is an effective remedy against the salinated ground water as the salination is less harmful when in a short time enough water rinses the soil. One needs a motor pump to achieve this.

maintain social cohesion, the Shurfa, until recently, appointed Drawa to take care of agricultural labour. The strategies of Drawa were even more intensely aimed at entering into an enduring economic relationship with people from outside the family. It was from this partial common interest that the sharecropping system evolved.

The sharecropping arrangement in the strict sense is based on a limited transaction: Money or a part of the harvest in return for the input of the sharecropper's labour, knowledge and experience, and that of his family. Next, the arrangement between landowner and tenant could be extended and diversified to reinforce the mutual interdependence. In the latter instance, the sharecropping arrangement between tenant and owner is encapsulated in more wideranging patterns of reciprocal rights and obligations (cf. Wolf 1966b: 86–87). The direction and value of the exchanges—the rights and duties of both parties—are not specified and written down, which means they are often the subject of negotiations between patron and client.

With dates being the only serious cash crop in the oasis, the palm tree was and still is king in the Dra Valley. Dates are sharecropped according to the well-known _kammās_ system. As the name suggests (_kammās_ means one-fifther) the share of the tenant consists of one-fifth of the harvest. The other four-fifths go to the provider of land, seed, equipment and water. One may opt for a differentiation between saleable varieties and non-saleable ones. The tenancy of the non-saleable dates consists of one-third of the share (_tulṭ_). The picker of dates, normally belonging to the sharecropper's family, receives another ʿabra a day,[18] and the one who climbs the trees and cuts the dates one and a half ʿabra or even two. According to villagers, since the 1970s the sharecropping tariff for cereals (wheat and barley) has been raised from a quarter to one-third of the harvest. In case of a fifty-fifty division, the tenant and owner of the land split the costs. In the past, one day harvesting grain was salaried with one large bundle (_huzma_), but a payment in cash now predominates (35 dirhams a day).

The share for cutting-and-picking is called the _tamašgala_ (from _šagala_, 'to work'). In addition, the workers have the right to a meal provided by the owner in the field. Today, sometimes the _tamašgala_ is paid in cash instead of in kind. This is, however, less favoured by

---

[18] An ʿabra is a measure of capacity (two decalitres) but equals about 16 kilos of dates.

labourers, as they know dates will earn them more than the agreed upon 35 or 40 dirhams a day. In any case the *tamasğala* can be a matter of dispute between tenant and date-palm owner. The owner may argue that only the pick of saleable dates goes with a *tamasğala* share. Once when harvesting a date variety that is only used for private consumption and fodder, the owner argued that Hammed's household should be satisfied with their one-fifth share. When the Hazzabins were confronted with this, they agreed. At dinner, however, they told me they would return and get their share in secret.

The same kind of dispute concerning the *tamasğala* evolved between Barka Hazzabin and his absentee landlord. He considered the possibility to pick dates his right as sharecropper, but the landowner did not. The absentee landlord, living in Casablanca, only came to the village to collect the money for the dates. Thus, he did not want to wait for the dates to be picked and only then look for a buyer. Instead, he preferred to sell the dates while they were still on the trees, in this way hoping for a quick deal. The trader certainly would not hire Barka, who would thus lose a substantial part of his expected salary for picking dates. Barka did not agree with the landowner's proposition, but the second tenant of the owner had already agreed. In the end, they settled upon a compensation in money for the lack of dates. This example shows how tenants might interpret sharecropping as a long-term relationship with multiple functions, while some (absentee) landlords prefer to interpret it as a short-term working relationship, that can be expressed in the exchange of money instead of kind. On the other hand, the landowners who do live in the village stress the durability of the bond with their sharecropper, in particular when they expect the tenant to serve in the house.

Since the late 1970s, the sharecropping system has changed and eroded. The cultivation is increasingly done by the owners themselves, while agriculture as part of the total income of villagers has decreased. The changing interpretation of labour relations and the structural changes since the 1970s can be illustrated by the case of the Hazzabin family. When Ali Hazzabin came to live in the village, he occupied a small room in the Drawi Quarter that was owned by a Sharifian household for whom he started to work. Abdallah and Salem continued the tenancy and joined it with some other tenancies. The Hazzabin brothers still remember how until a few years before Salem's death they went from field to field preparing the ground for cultivation (without tractor), sowing it and harvesting the

crops. The same applied to date palm cultivation. The tenancy of
the land of the very first patron endured three generations. Hammed
still sharecrops a number of the patron's trees and maintains a close
bond with the family to this day. A couple of years ago, Hammed
tried to revive the tenancy relationship with them. One of the sons,
now an old man, was not capable of cultivating his land himself and
asked Hammed to enter into the same relationship as his father
Salem. Both parties could not agree at first on the terms of the contract: The patron was not very willing to hand over money to buy
seed and demanded a financial contribution for the use of a tractor, while Hammed is supposed to have asked a larger share than
the one he was entitled to in the past. In the end they came to an
agreement but after two years the tenancy broke off.

The other tenancies of the Hazzabin family have also been annulled.
Najem went to look for work in the north of the country, while
Barka went to Casablanca and later on started to sharecrop on his
own. The sons did not agree with the way their father dealt with
the patron's infringements of the sharecropping arrangement. According to them, he should have opposed the fact that he never got the
true one-fifth share but was sent home with only half of it. This cut
shows how a patron might consider the part of the sharecropper to
be connected to other services in and around his house. The regular 'gifts' from the patron for these services are then subtracted from
his rightful share as tenant.[19] Najem and Barka quarrelled regularly
with the patron's sons who, as they say now, made undeniably clear
to them, that they were *their* sharecroppers. The brothers preferred
to leave the village, but their father refused permission because, as
one of his sons now states, he attached too much importance to an
intimate bond with the patron's family. After the death of the head
of the Sharifian patron family, he even made himself for its representative, assisting with the division of the inheritance and feeling
responsible for the future of the children (as, later on, his son Hammed
did when another member of the same family died). Hammed inherited his father's tenancies; only one continues up to this day. Hammed

---

[19] See Jamous (1981: 138): 'Not infrequently the owner considers these gifts [to
recompense for the services fulfilled in his house, RE] as a loan, substracting it thus
from the annual part of the harvest that is due to the *akhemmas*. Taken his socio-
economic condition, the latter can hardly protest'.

is still the tenant of a Sharifian family living in Paris, represented by a widow, called 'the hajja',[20] who lives alternately in Casablanca, Paris and the village.

The tasks of the sharecropper extend beyond the irrigation and cultivation of the crops. Whenever there is work to be done on the irrigation channels outside the village, Hammed is asked by the local irrigation controller to send a specified number of men from the village. In the village, men are chosen according to the quantity of water rights they possess. Since Shurfa have the largest share, obviously they form the overall majority. However, they prefer not to work outside their own village, and pay Drawi men to work for them. Since Drawa as tenants already take on a large share of collective labour on the irrigation ditches, normally a third or more of the men called upon are Drawa, representing their own water rights and that of a number of Shurfa.

Landowners and tenants often help each other with odd agricultural and domestic jobs. Not infrequently, Drawa draw the short end of the stick, doing labour-intensive work in return for a light job or the lending of equipment. When construction work is being done, Drawa always perform the most strenuous part, shovelling and hoisting the loam. Male and female Drawa cook and serve in the Sharifian household at communal dinners or small parties. Both run messages for their patrons (cf. for Tunisia, Bédoucha 1984: 95; 1987: 254).[21] Shurfa provide Drawa with fresh water. Since Drawa living in the village do not own a second house in the commercial centre, they would be without access to the much desired fresh water of the commercial centre; they are, however, free to gather water in the homes of their patrons. These are some illustrations of the extended relationship that has been built around the sharecropping contract. In the next section this relationship will be examined more closely.

---

[20] A honorific used for a woman who has fulfilled the pilgrimage to Mecca.

[21] Maher (1974: 49–52) mentions with respect to the women of the *qsar-s*, that 'peripheral members' of households, that is, 'those who have no property or kinship rights in the household', often help with odd jobs. These female helpers and clients are in particular 'widows and *hartaniyin*' (see for the marginal status of widows in the Maghreb, Jansen 1987).

Exchanges

As we saw in the discusson of sharecropping arrangements, the nature of the relationship between Sharif and Drawi can be interpreted in different ways by both parties. General agreement, however, does exist on the *credo* of the exchange relationship, that is, a hierarchical interdependence with the input of bodily labour by Drawa.

In the village, Drawi households maintain special relations with only one or two Sharifian households. In this respect, it is said that a relationship of *tabādul* (exchange) between the two families exists.[22] The *tabādul* relationship not only consists of the exchange of gifts but includes every interchange of services and material goods between patron and client. *Tabādul* expresses, together with trust (*tiqa*), the *emic* view of the patron-client relationship. According to Drawa, trust between Sharif and Drawi implies a friendly and confidential relationship in which secret information is not revealed and, as Drawa often pointed out to me, an acceptance on the side of the Shurfa to let male Drawa into their homes and eventually into contact with Sharifat. According to them, trust between the two parties is a necessary precondition for the development of workable relations and the exchange of information between patron and client. The emphasis on the element of secrecy on the side of Drawa establishes and strengthens the relationship between patron and client. Trust, however, can be interpreted in different ways. It testifies to the confidential bond between the two parties, but the interpretation of the confidentiality possibly differs. Thus, the Drawi may in fact act as a 'mediator' between two families with whom he maintains confidential relations and to whom he is 'loyal' as well. On the side of the Sharifian patron and his family, trust may exemplify the status of the Drawi as a serving 'non-person', who is allowed to enter 'the forbidden domains' of house and household but whose transgressions of these social boundaries are taken lightly because of his subordinate status and, when it concerns men, even unmanliness (cf. Goffman 1959: 149–53; see chapter six). This feature accounts for the present-day patron-client relationship in the village in general: It

---

[22] In his discussion of debt relationships, Peters (1990b) speaks of *tabdil* (exchange) in contrast to *dain* (debt) relationships. It is the latter variant that creates familiarity and long-term bonds.

hinges on the hierarchical social order, yet involves close encounters between the participants.

The multi-strandedness of patron-client bonds

Hammed is involved in a long-standing conflict between two Shurfa whose date palms he sharecrops. One party is 'the hajja', while the other is a man from Marrakesh. The Marrakshi claims that the date-palms of the hajja are his. So far, he has not been able to back his claim with the presentation of property papers, and having grown-up outside the oasis, he cannot point out which trees in particular are his. Nevertheless, at every harvest the problem arises anew. In the year of my stay in the village (1993–1994), the Marrakshi arrived at the village to have his dates cut and sold immediately. Hammed, however, preferred to wait until the hajja was present as well. Hammed argued that otherwise he could be accused of stealing the dates. The Marrakshi then asked him to cut only the dates of his trees. Hammed explained this would be impossible as he did not know which tree belonged to whom. At the end of their discussion, which turned into a noisy public quarrel, the Marrakshi decided to cut all the trees with the help of Hammed's former patron, who acted as interme- diary, but who would also be the first candidate to buy the Marrakshi's trees once the problem had been solved. Hammed had to give in, otherwise he would lose his cut-and-pick share, but the problem remains unsolved up to this day.

In the quarrel, Hammed stood up for one of the date-palm owners. He knew the history of each tree in detail and had lied, his sons confessed, of his ignorance about the ownership of the trees. Hammed's loyalty to the hajja in the date-palm conflict can be understood in terms of the vertical dyadic relationship between the Hazzabin fam- ily and her. This means that the bond between them goes further than just the sharecropping arrangement of one of the brothers. It is, so to speak, many-stranded. All households of the family were affected by Hammed's position in the quarrel. The bonds between the two families are long-standing, dating from the time the hus- band of the hajja was still alive. At present, when she visits the vil- lage, the hajja spends most of the daytime in Mina's house and, afraid to sleep alone, also at night. Furthermore, she quite often vis- its Hammed with whom she behaves most amicably. Hammed's son and the daughter of Mina and Najem live together in one of her

houses in the Outside Quarter. Another couple, consisting of a second son of Hammed and a daughter of Ali, rents an apartment of
hers in Casablanca. One of Barka's daughters works as her housemaid (*kaddāma*) in Casablanca. In short, between the two families
exists an extensive and continuous exchange of labour, agricultural
products, financial and moral support. Additionally, time has forged
bonds of affection between the Sharifa and the Hazzabins. The
younger children approach her as a wealthy aunt and grandmother.
The Hazzabin family acts as the hajja's intermediary: In Casa the
young housemaid, Barka's daughter, shops outside for her patron;
in the village Hammed's family members perform this task. The relationship between Hammed and the hajja was made clear to me in
a funny scene in her house: Two traders from a nearby village had
come to discuss the sale of her dates. The middle of the ground
floor was filled with sacks full of dates, with Hammed standing in-
between them, acting as middleman. He talked with the traders, ran
upstairs to the hajja to discuss the offer with her, came down again
to inform the traders of hajja's answer. This act was repeated until
the two parties had agreed on the price. Meanwhile, the hajja, who
lives in Casablanca and Paris, complained to me—I was also allowed
to go upstairs—about how 'tradition' kept her from negotiating with
the traders directly.

Hammed's household maintains close bonds with two other Sharifian families. For both of them, Hammed has been, or still is, their
tenant. For one of them, namely that of the head of the village,
Hammed's father acted as advisor in the division of the inheritance
between the three remaining children when their father died. Likewise,
Hammed fulfilled the same role for the family of one of the children. The families invite each other to all major parties and ritual
occasions. Hammed and his sons serve at their communal dinners,
while the women assist in the kitchen.

Similar multi-purpose relationships, in which the exchange of services, goods, and mutual support are central, exist between other
Sharifian 'big families' and particular Drawi families. Hammed
Hazzabin maintains close bonds with the village head and lineage 3
in the Outside Quarter and to a lesser extent with lineage 1 in the
Saint's Quarter; Barka Hazzabin married into a Drawi family of the
Upper Quarter and is now the most important Drawi family there
with a second Drawi family also providing services. Barka is also
close with a few households from lineage 2. The (Drawi) Belballi

family is closely related to lineage 2 in the Saint's Quarter. The Zdarni family is intimate with the imam and through him with lineage 1 in the Saint's Quarter; The Burari family is close with lineage 3 in the Outside Quarter; Finally, one other Belballi household is close with lineage 1 in particular.

The general picture is that in the village the four lineages that occupy the three quarters are represented by four or five Sharifian 'big families', that own large tracts of land and whose head possibly fulfils honourable tasks (village head, imam, member of the village council). Such a 'big man' has authority, expressing his stature by his control over 'the word', that is, 'the art of public speaking', and lavish expenditure (Jamous 1992: 173). Between the 'big families' and one Drawi family in particular a dyadic bond exists, similar to that of Hammed Hazzabin and his patron family. This means that the relationship is based on a past or still-existing sharecropping arrangement, reinforced through regular gift-giving and the creation of fictive kinship bonds (see below). Drawa and Shurfa remark that a certain Drawi family belongs to a certain Sharifian family or group of families; 'he is theirs', they say, pointing at the head of a certain Drawi family.

Around the 'big families' clusters a numbers of less powerful Sharifian families of the same lineage. In this way, every lineage in the three quarters is served by one Drawi family at least. The less important families of the lineage are also entitled to the services of that Drawi family, although to a lesser extent. For example, having Drawa serve dinner is for them limited to important occasions like marriage parties. The Drawi that is at the centre of this cluster of Sharifian families may then be respectfully addressed as *Baba.* The close relationships between the Sharifian 'big families' and the Drawi family do not exactly copy one another, but recurrent family resemblances in the patterns of gift-giving, serving, and fictive kinship bonding between patron Sharifian and client Drawi families justify them being put on a par. Moreover, when asked, villagers agree on the existence of a particular exchange relationship between the above-mentioned couples of patron and client families.

In the light of wider socio-economic change, the tenancy contracts for the cultivation of land between Shurfa and Drawa have changed considerably. The traditional one-fifth share for the tenant has by some been turned into one-third with an increase in the financial involvement of the owner of the land. Access to land as a source of power for a potential Sharifian patron has diminished. Furthermore, with the availability of motor pumps, people are able to circumvent the traditional division of water rights and bring new land under cultivation. Drawa, however, have to look for outside sources of income to acquire the money needed for such a pump. People who look for jobs in Casablanca and not just access to agricultural goods, have to contact middlemen who know how to find jobs and urban housing. The large Sharifian families in the village are still in a better position than Drawa to provide for these mediating services between village and town (cf. Wolf 1956: 1072). They have usually built one or two houses outside the village (in the administrative oasis centre, Marrakesh or even Casablanca), own a car, and act as traders of local dates. Services provided for by Drawa in the village may thus be compensated by favours in town. The hierarchical interdependence between Drawa as workforce and service personnel and Shurfa as landholders and ritual specialists is based on an actual and still continuing exchange of services and goods.

There does not seem to be a direct linkage between services performed by Drawa for their patron families and a reward in money or kind. The reward is not specified and rarely paid out in money. Instead, at certain ritual occasions in the year patron and client exchange goods for services performed. These 'gifts' are generally presented on top of the already agreed share of the harvest for the sharecropper and his family. The additional gifts perpetuate the bonds between the two households, but for the Drawa they also constitute a substantial contribution to their income.

The first gift takes place at the feast of the ʿīd al-fiṭr; the feast that celebrates the end of the Islamic month of fasting. The fiṭra (that what is given before fṭur, breakfast) is a regular and obligatory gift to the poor, prescribed in Islamic law. In the village, every member of a household should be represented by one fiṭra part. Thus, ideally, a household of ten members should send ten parts to ten different eligible persons. The fiṭra should not be given to those who not deserve or need it; only those persons are eligible who are 'poor'. In the village, the donation of fiṭra is a cascade of gifts: The richer Shurfa give to poorer Shurfa and Drawa; they, in their turn, give to relatives and poorer Drawa. Thus, a 'big man' Sharif might give to Hammed Hazzabin, who, in his turn, gives to the poorest Drawi in the village. The gift consists of dates or grain of at least two and a half kilos (or 12 dirhams). In the village, a wooden box of about

one kilo is used to measure the minimum volume of grain. Its use
by Drawa implies that they receive more than they give away. Usually,
Hammed receives one to one and a half *'abra-s* (max. 16 kilos of
dates, which equals the salary of one to two days) from his patron
family. Even the poorest man in the village sends out *fiṭra* in contrast to two villagers, both Shurfa, who receive alms from villagers
on the village square in the morning of the *'īd al-fiṭr*. The first of
these is an older man who has never been married, does not work,
and is generally considered to be somewhat retarded. Of the second, the muezzin, it is not clear whether he sits on the square
because of his task as muezzin or because of his poverty: The former muezzin did not ask for alms in this manner, and the present
one only does so from the moment he was appointed as muezzin.
The *fiṭra* gift is accompanied by the exchange of small bowls of boiled
food between relatives, friends and neighbours of one quarter. The
reciprocal transfers of food between patron and client also take place
at calendrical rituals and other rites of passage, including marriage
(at which money or a substantial material gift is given).

Another form of alms giving is the *'ušr*. This gift is the obligatory
one-tenth part of property one is supposed to give annually according to Islamic law (although the gift does not nearly attain one-tenth
part of their harvest). In the village the gift (*sadaqa*) is given at harvest time. People from the oasis and neighbouring regions walk
around with sacks to ask for a part of the harvest. Usually they are
handed over as many dates as can be taken out of a basket with
two hands. The *'ušr* is also given to Drawi clients by their Sharifian
patrons.

Myth or exchange?

Various authors have pointed out that 'patronage' as a hegemonic
ideology covers up unequal and possibly exploitative socio-economic
relations. According to Scott (1977), patronage is a legitimizing ideology of the status of the powerholders in society that camouflages
structures of exploitation. Likewise, Gilsenan argued in an article
'against patron-client relations' that the term obstructs a deeper analysis of social structures (1977: 168). Here I have tried to relate the
socio-economic dependence of Drawa to the existence of patron-
client relations between landless and marginal peasants and landowners. It remains difficult to determine the exact nature of the

social relationship that existed between Drawa and landholders in the past. From the perspective of the Drawa, the patron-client relationships were probably born out of their overall lack of landownership or right to use irrigation water. Economic security and possibly physical protection made the tenancy an attractive option for landless and marginal peasants. One should guard against drawing an idyllic picture of mutual aid and teamwork in the village community (cf. Miller 1984: 69–71), sidestepping the unequal exchange patterns within the village; yet, the possibility of a voluntary bonding and mutual agreement between patron and client should not be ruled out.

Today, bonds between patron and client still contain elements of protection and mutual exchanges. Patronage is also to some extent a publicly debated issue among people in the oasis. Some indeed seem to think in terms of exploitation. The different appreciation of Shurfa and Drawa can be seen in the use of a kinship idiom. Both parties refer to the interdependent relationships as one of father and son, but the evaluation differs. Shurfa stress how 'we treated them as our sons' to express their dissatisfaction at the ingratitude of present-day Drawa, who supposedly turn their backs against their ancient patrons. Some Drawa, on the other hand, complain that 'in the past we were treated as the young sons of the family' who could be commanded at will. They point to the hierarchical element in the relationship and the subordinate status of Drawa. These critics were in particular younger Drawa and older people who have left the village and stepped outside of the exchange relationship. Thus, Ali Hazzabin, the older brother who lives in Casablanca, mocked at his own past by saying that 'we were like goats ... yes, we were made of cardboard' to help the Shurfa. He added that 'luckily youngsters of today don't do that any longer'. His young nephew Abdellatif, still living in the village, did not believe his father and laughed when he talked of all the arduous work he had to fulfil for Shurfa and for the corvée services of the local authorities, when a youth. Abdellatif, however, does still serve while his older brother often refuses to do so. Other Drawa accept the relationship but all pointed out that 'in the past' Shurfa were much more generous with their gifts.

The exchanges of material goods and services between Sharifian patrons and Drawi clients are dissimilar, with Drawa basically providing services for goods (cf. Wolf 1966a: 16–17). Furthermore, where access to agricultural goods and rightful shares are presented as ritual gifts prescribed by Islamic belief, Shurfa are put in a morally superior position. With respect to the 'cultural capital' of Shurfa in the exchange relationship, one may paraphrase Mauss that 'in this game of exchanges the property of the Sharif is the Sharif himself'.[23] As we will see in chapter five, living in the proximity of the Shurfa enhances the esteem of the Drawa of the village. The services of clients lend weight to the esteem of the Shurfa, when they abstain from agricultural work and let people serve at collective dinners (see chapter six). Drawa know of course that sometimes they are recruited to lend status to the visit of a guest to a patron, or to give support in the case of small conflicts and political rallies. When one Sharif in the village ran for a political seat, he invited every person who could testify to his loyalty by showing the coloured election card of his opponent. A Drawi told me that he understood the Sharif's intentions but did not want to support him. He attended the free dinner which he did not want to miss, by simply laying hands on two cards: One he threw into the ballot box, the other he showed the 'patron'.

The notion of *tabādul* pinpoints an actual interdependence with the Drawa providing indispensable services for patrons who choose to act as honourable Shurfa. The Drawa constitute the serving personnel and take care of most physical labour. In the neighbouring village of Drawa and Ait 'Atta Berbers, a classic drama occurred that exemplifies the generational conflict in Drawi families when this long-standing relationship between 'body and mind' is turned upside-down. An old Drawi had been a client of one of the most important Ait 'Atta families of the oasis. He was tenant, worked in and around the house of his patron, and fulfilled other odd jobs in the village (crier, gravedigger). One of his sons followed him in his footsteps and is now a tenant of the patron. A second son was sent to school. This son successfully passed primary and secondary school with the patron's aid; he even stayed several years in the patron's house in another oasis in the valley to crown his schooling career with a teaching degree. 'In the house of the patron he was treated as a son of the family', an informant remarked. 'Yet the moment he had found a job,' the same informant stated disapprovingly, 'he turned against the patron's family'. The son, however, argued that he and his father had been kept in their place for years, as servants. He demanded from his father that he turned his back against the

---

[23] 'The property of the Brahmin is the Brahmin himself' (Mauss 1969: 56).

patron. The father refused, and the father and son broke up. The son continued in his struggle and even ran for a political seat against his former patron (but lost).

Thus far, it has been shown how in the village, the enduring division of land and water rights between Sharifian and Drawi families continues the interdependent relationships involving exchange of goods and services between the two parties of unequal status. The construction of these patron-client relations is closely related to the continuance of socio-economic bonds between Sharifian kin and affines. In the following section, the affective dimensions of this interdependent relationship are illustrated by an examination of the practice of colactation and milk kinship.

Fictive kinship

> He who has no milk, has no friends (Moroccan proverb; Westermarck 1930: 102).

A couple of days after the marriage of Latifa, the daughter of my Sharifian neighbour, with her nephew from Casablanca, I took another walk through the palm gardens with the Drawi Abdellatif Hazzabin. His family is very intimate with Latifa's family and since I had noted a greater openness of contacts between men and women in an urban context, I asked whether it would be possible for him to visit Latifa in Casablanca: 'Of course, I can visit her, but I could already speak with her in the village'. Abdellatif explained to me that their families were as one. Latifa was like his sister because once her brother had come into contact with the mother's milk of Abdellatif's grandmother. This had forged a permanent brother-sister bond between them.

In this section I will try to show that the creation of bilateral milk kinship arrangements between Shurfa and Drawa is an important mechanism for the creation of lasting multi-stranded relationships between Sharifian and Drawi families. The milk kinship ties express and reinforce the bonds of trust between families of patrons and clients. In this respect milk kinship is not unlike the institution of god- or co-parenthood (*compadrazgo*) in the Mediterranean (cf. Mintz and Wolf 1967: 185; Pitt-Rivers 1976: 317–334). In both, we deal with a fictitious kinship relationship between people of unequal status that is part of a larger long-term exchange of goods and services. Milk kinship bonds are based on the practice of 'colactation': A person becomes kin when he or she is breast-fed; usually, the mother of one nurses both children. In Arabic one speaks of a nursing bond (*riḍāʿ*) and of milk siblings (*ḵud min ḥlīb*). Naming the institution milk kinship follows the existing literature on this topic (Altorki 1980; Delaney 1991: 157–158; Khatib-Chahidi 1992; Maher 1992; Jansen 1996; Long 1996). Even so, I would argue that colactation *cum* milk kinship provides a confidential, and sometimes amical, bond that does not copy but is alternative to kinship bonds.

At least until the beginning of this century, when slavery was still a common practice among the rural and urban élite, the enslaved wet-nurse (*dada*) was allowed to go behind the family façade and fulfil an intimate role in many a Moroccan household. The unequal status did not obstruct but rather constituted the impetus for the development of lasting, faithful relationships between the wet-nurse and the son or master of the house (Ennaji 1994: 52–53). The traveller James Grey Jackson gives an extensive account of wet-nursing in the beginning of the 19th century:

> When circumstances oblige [women] to take a nurse, she is not treated as a servant, but becomes one of the family, and passes her days among the children she has suckled, by whom she is *ever afterwards* cherished and protected; the children are taught to consider her as their own relation, and she is called (*Emuh d'el Hellib*) the milk mother (Jackson 1968: 156–157).

Unfortunately, apart from a few remarks in the work of Fernea (1975) and Maher (1974; but see Maher 1992), information on the continuance of wet-nursing in present-day Morocco does not exist. My own experiences in the Dra Valley and a monograph on a Tunisian oasis, where the Hartani-like *Šwašīn* acting as wet-nurses are affectionately addressed as 'maman' (*ummī*) and referred to as 'my *dada*', suggested that the practice is far from dead in the Maghreb (Bédoucha 1987: 244; cf. 1984: 99).[24]

---

[24] An interesting comparison can be made with the prevalence of parallel cousin marriages in the Arab world. This practice seems to have been overemphasized in the literature, in comparison to actual prevalence. Milk kinship is largely overlooked, but seems an important way of constructing life-long bonds (cf. Heine 1990: 259).

Collective milk bonds

Moroccan ethnographic studies deal with colactation arrangements exclusively as part of collective tribal peace agreements. In pre-independence Morocco, these agreements either served to settle (a temporary) peace between tribes or to incorporate individual outsiders into a tribal faction or village community. According to Lesne (1966: 144), in these agreements colactation functioned as one powerful way to create durable 'artificial ethnic bonds' between potential enemies. Tribes in the Central Atlas knew two forms of alliances in particular, the *amur* and the *taḍa*. The *amur* was a pact of protection 'drawn up between two individuals, one of whom was usually a stranger to the tribe' (Vinogradov 1974: 72). The temporary pact granted the opportunity to travel freely in a certain area without having to fear assault. Another form of *amur* 'was always contracted between two individuals of unequal status, and was in the nature of a patron-client relationship. This *amur* was also known (. . .) by the Arabic term, *khuwa*, meaning brotherhood' (1974: 73).[25] The second form of alliance, *taḍa*, was a collective alliance involving rival clans or tribes. Through a ritual in which the slippers of the men of both parties were mixed, a lifelong peaceful bond between the rival groups was created. The word taḍ means 'to nurse' in Berber and 'at one time in their past, certain taḍas involved ceremonies of colactation' (idem, 74). The slipper ritual was of the same kind as the more ancient colactation ritual: It forged and sanctioned an enduring bond between two social groups through a taboo on intermarriage and established close friendship and intimacy between the participants.

Throughout pre-independence Morocco we find the same repertoire of symbolic practices to bring individuals and collectivities together in peace agreements but the same terms did not always cover the exact order of practices. For example the tribal confederacy of the Ait 'Atta in the south practised the bilateral *amur* or *ḵuwa* (Niclausse 1954: annexe 17), between people of unequal status, which consisted of the sacrifice of a sheep in front of the house of the

---

[25] 'A stranger [who could be a member of the tribe] desiring to reside for a time in a particular douar, would inquire about a strong and respected *akhatar* [elder] of the community. He would then take a sheep and sacrifice it in front of the akhatar's tent declaring loudly, "I wish to become your amur" and the akhatar would say, "*mrhbannek*" [I welcome you]' (Vinogradov 1974: 73). See for a discussion of protection pacts in relation to the complex of honour and shame, Brown (1982).

chosen protector. The *taḍa*, however, did not have the ritual closing ceremony or lasting quality as in the Central Atlas. This was reserved for the *tafargant*, which resembled the northern *taḍa* in its collective character and use of colactation.[26] Likewise, the *tafargant* served to transform hostile tribes or clans into allies. For example, in the 1930s, two tribes belonging to the confederacy agreed on such a peace agreement. The responsible men of the Ait Isful and the Ait Unir decided to collect the milk of 20 women from each side. At the ceremony, first the peace agreement was written down by a scribe. Next, the document was suddenly whisked into the air without there being any wind, thereby assuring those present of the divine consent to their agreement. The milk was subsequently mixed into a large bowl of couscous. By eating a bit of the meal, all male participants became each other's milkbrothers. From that day on, they would respect one another and their women. This agreement came down to a taboo on intermarriage.The account of the peace agreement was related to me in the neighbouring village of Ait ʿAtta Berbers where since this last ceremony had taken place only bilateral colactation bonds had been arranged.[27]

In the collective peace agreements the same motifs prevail as in the milk kinship arrangements between specific families within the village: (1) The creation of a bond which parallels kinship bonds based on blood in the conclusion of a taboo on intermarriage; (2) the incorporation of strangers into a larger social group (a household or family); and (3) the contract-like nature of a reciprocal arrangement involving two parties of unequal status.[28]

Milk bonds between families in a village quarter

In contrast to what has been suggested by the lack of reports on bilateral colactation in Morocco and furthermore explicitly stated in reports from the rest of the Middle East (cf. Altorki 1980: 238;

---

[26] *Tafargant* alliances could also be concluded without the use of mother's milk.

[27] Hart refers to the same *tafargant* in his study on the Ait ʿAtta (1981: 188; personal communication 1998).

[28] More information on peace agreements and forms of multilateral fictive kinship alliances in northern Morocco can be found in Belghazi (1997), Lesne (1966), Marcy (1936; 1949) and Vinogradov (1974: 72–75); for the western plains see Eickelman (1976: 11–18, 163–68, 266); for the Ait ʿAtta in the High Atlas and the Pre-Saharan zone see Hart (1981: 183–210; 1993: 31–34) and Dunn (1977: 75–76).

Khatib-Chahidi 1992), bilateral colactation is still practised in the Dra Valley. In the village many milk kinship arrangements exist between members of Sharifian families and between Shurfa and Drawa.

Given the inequality in status between Drawa and Shurfa, the topic of this study, the question is why this kind of colactation arrangements and subsequent milk kinship bonds between Shurfa and Drawi women exist. A complicating factor here is that nursing, colactation and milk kinship arrangements were not regular conversation topics for me and my male informants. Some men considered it inappropriate to talk about something which so clearly belongs to the domain of women.[29] Others denied the existence of milk kinship bonds in the village, while a third category condemned the practice as old-fashioned, impure (*harām*) and thus non-Islamic. This last qualification must be disregarded as unfounded. In Moroccan family law, based on Malikite Islamic law, no disapproval of the practice can be found. Moreover, the Prophet Muhammad himself was as an orphan nursed by a wet-nurse and rules concerning milk kinship are explictly mentioned in the family law of many Islamic countries, including Morocco (Jansen 1996: 62).

In all cases of a colactation bond between a Sharif and a Drawi, Shurfa were nursed by Drawa. That is, the mother's milk flows only in one direction. The same pattern was found in the neighbouring village of 'Attawis and Drawa and in isolated cases presented to me elsewhere in the Dra Valley. Additionally, milk kinship arrangements between the same Sharifian and Drawi families might be concluded in subsequent generations. These general patterns are illustrated by the milk kinship network of one Drawi family. Figure 7 presents seven milk kinship bonds with the (Hammed) Hazzabin family at the centre as donor of milk.

The Sharif of the first household (1) was nursed by Hammed's aunt Khadisha who acted as nursemaid. She took care of the little Sharif during the day and had even given him a typical Drawi name (*Najem*) temporarily. The milk bond between this Sharifian family and the Hazzabins was renewed through the Sharif's son (2). At

---

[29] The following note by Creyghton (1992: 44) shows that female anthropologists may encounter a similar wall of silence when they raise the topic of milk kinship: 'Ideas and other mental constructs concerning breast feeding are hardly ever directly expressed by the Khmir [in Tunisia, RE]. They hide them behind dark hints, evocative stories, behind ritual and symbolic behaviour'.

present, the relationship between the two families is confidential and intimate. The same accounts for the relationship between the Hazzabins and the second Sharifian household (3). Here as well the milk kinship bond is repeated in the next generation (4). In the same manner as between the Hazzabin family and the two Sharifian families, colactation bonds exist between several major Sharifian and Drawi families in the village. Also in the nearby village of Ait 'Atta and Drawa I found this pattern of more than one milk kinship bond between two neighbouring families of unequal status combined with great intimacy between male and female members of the two families (figure 8).

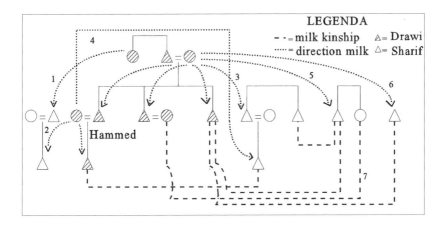

Figure 7: Milk kinship A

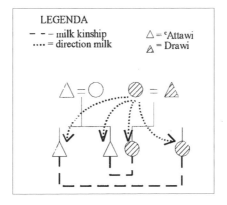

Figure 8: Milk kinship B

Formal and folk models of meaning and consequences of colactation
and milk kinship bonds do not always match. The legal rules as to
who exactly becomes a forbidden marriage partner after the act of
colactation has taken place are extremely complicated and vary from
one school of Islamic jurisprudence to the other. Furthermore, as so
often is the case, on the ground the rules are not applied by everyone to the same degree. Thus Altorki (1980: 238) observed discrep-
ancies in the interpretation of legal aspects of milk kinship between
two provinces in Saudi Arabia. Also in the oasis, and even within
the village, people did not agree on crucial aspects of colactation
and milk kinship.

To learn something about the rules for nursing and the assertion
of kinship in the village, I visited the imam of the second mosque.
I asked him if he knew something about the topic of milk brothers:

> Answer: 'Yes, it is written of in Sura *Nisā'* of the Koran'. (He quotes
> the verse).[30]
> q: 'Who will become kin?'
> a: 'Only those who have nursed at the same time will become kin'.
> q: 'So that means that unlike the actual milk siblings, their brothers
> and sisters can marry each other?'
> a: 'Yes (he frowns) . . . but it is not good. It is allowed in the Koran,
> but they have always moved in and out of one another's houses, and
> thus basically have grown up like kin'.
> q: 'Will the mothers become like milk sisters?'
> a: (He laughs) 'No'.[31]

The imam belongs to those who disapprove of nursing someone else's
child. He argues that with so many cross-cutting milk ties, kinship
bonds might become too complicated to unravel. For example the
above-mentioned milk kinship arrangements regarding the Hazzabins
are not the only four in which they are involved. Moreover, none
of these milk bonds has been registered. Especially under the present conditions of migrating young couples with parents staying
behind, the danger of being unaware of existing milk bonds between
potential marriage partners looms large. The imam told me of a

---

[30] Sura *Nisā'* (4, 23): '*Ye are forbidden to marry your mothers, and your daughters, and
your sisters (. . .) and your mothers who have given you suck, and your foster-sisters, and your
wives' mothers . . .*'

[31] This question was inspired by a passage in Fernea's *A Street in Marrakech* (1975)
wherein she explains the special relationship between two women by mentioning
the fact that the child of the first woman had been nursed by the second.

couple in Tangier who had only recently become aware they had lived in an incestuous relationship for years. Authentic or not, the story certainly serves as a deterrent for contemporary practices of villagers.

When asked about the reason for the milk kinship bonds, other villagers explained how their children were nursed by a woman from another household because the biological mother had insufficient or poor quality milk. Since people lack the financial means to buy fresh or powdered milk, they turn to a female friend with the request to nurse their child. In their stories, colactation is presented as an instrumental act, one that will disappear—and already has, as some incorrectly add—when all villagers are able to feed their children in another, preferred way. Here, the milk kinship bond is taken as an unintended result of the healing power of mother's milk. Some, however, stated that women also exchange milk to create or testify to a lasting friendship.[32] This is in agreement with the observation that girlfriends exchange mother's milk obligating one another to reciprocate (Champault 1969: 279) and thus to ensure a lasting friendship. In the oasis, mother's milk is furthermore used as a medicine, especially for eye diseases. Contrary to what is stated in Islamic law, some people in the oasis take the position that in this way milk bonds are created as well.

Villagers argued that ties based on contact with mother's milk (*riḍāʿ*) are not as powerful as blood ties (*nasab*). In legal terms, a milk bond indeed only restricts one's marriage partners. Milk siblings do not take part in the inheritance, nor is there an obligation to take care of the child. In turn, milk children are not obliged to care for their milk parents (cf. Jansen 1996: 65). Although at this point local practices follow scriptural rules, this is not always the case. In particular, I observed how villagers disagree on how many feedings are needed and for whom exactly the incest taboo has effect. Some declare that only with three to four feedings does a durable milk bond between mother and child develop, while others argue that one drop of milk might be enough. In contrast to the first view, one

---

[32] Pandolfo (1997: 61) cites a woman who speaks of the close relationship between her grandmother and her neighbour in the *qsar*: '"[I]f one had a baby, the other gave her the breast, and vice versa. They shared the roof, that is, they shared the breast". For, "had they not shared the breast, they would have had to build a limiting wall . . ."'.

can bring in that locally it is believed that every contact with mother's milk creates a bond. I already mentioned that mother's milk is considered to be a healing substance, especially with regard to eye diseases. Quite a number of milk kinship bonds started off in this way. Although he hesitated slightly, the imam stated that only those individuals who colactated at the same time become kin. It is indeed true that between these direct milk siblings a special bond develops, strengthened through the exchange of gifts. *Contra* the imam's opinion, others argued that all siblings born after the nursing has taken place also become milk kin.

Men, as some confess, have only a limited control over the alliances that women may create through the exchange of milk. It is therefore logical that my male informants downplay its importance. Compared with a blood tie, a milk bond definitely does not lead to similar social and economic obligations.[33] It is basically a relationship of sentiment and affection that may result in ritual exchanges between milk brothers but should not be reduced to it. Some were appalled by my question of whether the gift of mother's milk was compensated financially. The following anecdote exemplifies this aspect of the mother-child bond. One day, a villager told me about an older, unmarried Drawi man who had worked in France for several years. Though he earned quite a lot of money, the man did not invest it in something substantial, like a new house or durable consumer goods. He returned to his home village as poor as the moment he left it. To illustrate the man's loathsome character, the villager told me about an enduring quarrel this man had with his mother. One day, the man went to his mother to tell her that from that day forward he did not want to have anything to do with her. To seal his decision, he intended to go to the market and buy the same quantity of milk she had given him when he was nursed as a child. In this way, he argued, he would have bought off his obligations towards her. The villager explained to me that, regardless of what this incident suggests, the nursing bond between mother and child never can or should be broken, and trying to do so is extremely shameful. The anecdote suggests that the man not only forgot about his future and that of his children in France but also, and that was even worse, tried to erase his past in the village.

---

[33] Compare note 22 in chapter three on the ridicule of the Sharifian ancestry of the Saadian dynasty.

Whatever the exact rules, villagers agreed that between *all* members of the two families involved, an enduring and intimate bond develops. Where a blood tie may be seen as a formal bond embedded in socio-economic obligations, a milk tie creates an affective bond. In combination with the theme of exchanges, this is the dimension which links the topic of milk kinship to the larger issue of patronage with which this chapter deals. Thus, in the words of Creyghton, '[l]ove is fostered only between siblings who drank from the same breast' and milk kin are supposed to 'comfort you, encourage you [and] be your intermediary' (1981: 4, 68). The implicit notion underlying this opinion is the generally accepted belief in the power of mother's milk to 'bind' people. Basically, this integrative power of mother's milk functions together with the common nursing experience as the cornerstone of the bond between mother and child. In contrast to procreation, generally held to be a predominantly male activity, nursing is considered to be the female way of creating affectionate lifelong ties between children, women and families. For Drawa and Shurfa the exchange of mother's milk can function as an important vehicle for entering into the long-term exchange relationships that I have outlined above.

Colactation brings outsiders into the intimate sphere of one's family. Altorki, in the article that brought the topic of Islamic milk kinship to the attention of an anthropological audience, suggested that in the past social reasons may have been a ground for the establishment of milk kinship bonds, in particular when it concerned an enslaved milk mother. Male servants and female members of the household could more easily interact when the social barrier that forces women to veil before a man other than a kinsman had been removed. The arrangement of milk kinship bonds between people with a marked status difference thus made 'domestic life more convenient' (Altorki 1980: 240; Khatib-Chahidi 1992: 121). Turning from the past of the urban élite in Saudi Arabia to that of Morocco, we find that the wet-nurse 'was so much part of the domestic circle' of élite families that when she was forced 'by disgrace or vicissitude' to leave the family behind, everyone in the family was deeply affected by the separation (Ennaji 1994: 52).

Altorki's argument also explains the existence of milk kinship bonds between Sharifian and Drawi families in the present-day village. Milk bonds are indeed one dimension of the patron-client relationships. Part of the patron-client relationship is the development of amical and fictive kinship bonds that create an atmosphere in which reciprocal aid becomes self-evident instead of imperative.[34] Milk siblings are free to walk in the patron's house and face Sharifat. This gives Drawa as tenants, servants and assistants of bride and groom more leverage. As Sharifat may not be touched by non-kin, even after their death, Drawi milk kin are also in this case qualified to act as gravediggers (a profession usually performed by Drawa).

The example presented in figure 7 indicates that in the village milk kinship bonds have created durable bonds between Drawa and Shurfa within one quarter, suggesting that these are part of a wideranging ensemble of reciprocal rights and obligations between the two parties, one that is referred to as an exchange relationship (tabādul). The example furthermore shows how milk kinship bonds may move beyond a purely dyadic relationship and link many families of one quarter, here the Outside Quarter, belonging to one Sharifian lineage (lineage 3) and one Drawi family. As I observed already, almost every major Sharifian family and Drawi family in the village is connected by way of an actual or past milk kinship bond. Moreover, the annual gifts between patron and client families are influenced by possible milk kinship relations between them. Thus, one Sharif stated that he presented the still living milk brother of his dead father annually with about 30 kilos of dates (two ʿabra-s). The Drawi 'milk uncle' regularly assisted his Sharifian 'milk nephew' at collective dinners.

Similar to the collective milk bonds, colactation involving two families may function as a rite of incorporation, bringing Drawa and Shurfa together. At the same time, colactation imposes an incest taboo which prevents milk siblings and their family members from developing sexual or marital relations. Milk kinship thus can be a mechanism to exclude people from entering into a bond that involves more extensive mutual socio-economic obligations. Moreover, compared with patrilineal blood ties, milk kinship bonds are more hidden from the public domain, suggesting that they are established by the less powerful in society who may find in their mother's milk a crucial source of power. Male Shurfa pointed out the intricate kinship and

---

[34] See Mintz and Wolf (1967: 195) on the *compadrazgo* in Puerto Rico: 'There is evidence of landowners getting free labor out of their laborer brothers who have been made compadres. Contrariwise, laborers bound by compadrazgo to their employers are accustomed to rely on this bond to secure them certain small privileges, such as the use of equipment, counsel and help, small loans, and so on'.

affinal bonds within the village to illustrate the close relations between inhabitants and to evoke 'the community of Aduafil'. Drawa were thus excluded from this well-knit web of kin and affines. The 'community of Aduafil' was one preferably based on blood ties, while the community of Shurfa and Drawa which is created through colactation was mostly ignored.

Colactation links two families of unequal status and creates a durable and intimate bond. It removes from Drawa their outsider status but excludes them as marriage partners. It brings about a relationship that is alternative to kinship bonds based on blood. Not everyone liked to be reminded of the fact that with respect to the milk bond between Drawi and Sharif, it is through the body of the Drawia that the Drawa and Shurfa in the village are closely linked. For example, one Sharif denied the existence of milk bonds between his family and a Drawi family while I had heard from different sources that such a relationship did in fact exist. The practice of milk kinship is 'an exchange of sexual access for social access' (Long 1996: 65). In the village configuration of Shurfa and Drawa, it creates a balance between rapprochement and dissociation, inclusion and exclusion, and thus testifies to the double-bind between the two categories in the village.[35]

Conclusions

In exchange for access to land and water, the Shurfa offered Drawa security, stability and, in the past, physical protection. With a tenant looking after the land, Shurfa could refrain from agricultural labour in agreement with their high status as specialists of religious knowledge and practices. Additionally, the tenant and his family could fulfil many more odd jobs for his patron in and around the house. For the Drawa, sharecropping the land presented itself as the only

---

[35] We should, however, avoid a singular, functionalist explanation for the practice of colactation and milk kinship. People can enter milk kinship bonds for several reasons. Likewise, the meaning of milk kinship bonds can vary as well. In stressing the relationship between milk kinship and patron-client relations, one should in particular not underestimate the act of colactation that leads to the milk kinship bond. Chapter seven presents therefore an additional analysis of the existence of milk kinship bonds between Shurfa and Drawa that focuses on the healing power of mother's milk.

possibility to build up a durable subsistence in the oasis. The relationship that to a large extent still determines the relations between Shurfa and Drawa has been founded on the exchange of labour, agricultural goods, affection and mutual respect; the social inequality of the respective parties is inherent in the relationship.

The discussion of sharecropping pacts and milk kinship bonds exemplifies the permanent tension between practices that emphasize and continue interdependent relations and the wish to stay independent. Dependency, lack of autonomy, influences the status of Drawa as sharecroppers and tenants. Yet, the regular gift exchange streched out in time, proves the dependence of Shurfa on 'their' dependants. Most obvious example is the gift of mother's milk from Drawa to Shurfa. The latter like to point out the closeness and interdependencies between Shurfa, for example as blood relatives and irrigation associates. They are mostly silent on the dependent position, and the obligation to return, that the gift of breastmilk implies. This is in agreement with 'the myth of patronage' (Silverman 1977) that presents patrons as independent benefactors.

The exchange relations in the oasis community shall be taken up once again in the following chapter. Following Berque's note on the exchange of material for spiritual services in patron-client relationships (1938: 27), I hinted a few times in this chapter at the implications of Sharifian stature for the arrangements of reciprocal rights and obligations. In interviews held with members of 'holy families' (sada) and a 'Kurdish-speaking extremist shi'a marginal group' (Shabak) in Iraq, Amal Rassam 'was struck by the compatibility of their world views and the similarity of their idiom both "legitimising" their unequal socio-economic status in terms of their unequal religious prestige' (Rassam 1977: 162). It was said that the descendants of the Prophet were entitled to land and wealth because of their control over the divine force called *baraka*. The following chapter tries to show how an equal ideological underpinning of 'spiritual power' supports the exchange relationship between saints and servants in the Moroccan oasis community.

CHAPTER FIVE

SPIRITUAL SUBORDINATION
SUPERNATURAL EXCHANGES IN DEBATE

The relationship between ... *shorfa* ... and the laity is one of
spiritual subordination analogous to the relationship which exists
between God and the faithful, or between a father and his sons
(Jamous 1992: 180).

To decide that only socio-economic inequality characterizes the relations between the two population groups in the oasis community is
to disregard the significance of the hierarchical cultural principles
that inform and guide the inhabitants of the *qsar-s* in their daily life.
Hierarchy usually tends to be defined in negative terms, namely by
referring to what is lacking in a hierarchical relationship, that is,
social equality. Dumont, in *Homo Hierarchicus* (1980), should be cred-
ited for pointing out how in anthropological texts once 'equality is
accepted as the norm, any form of inequality appears to be the same
as any other because of their common deviation from the norm'
(1980: 251). Instead, Dumont argues for a perspective that considers
hierarchy as a positive ideology based on the symbolic opposition
and complimentarity of the extremes. Inspired by Dumont's study,
which continues to arouse fierce discussions and critique (cf. Appadurai
1986; Parish 1996), this chapter looks at the various interpretations
of the configuration of Shurfa and Drawa from the perspective of
the sacred/profane dichotomy. It singles out a discourse on spiritual
subordination and mutual exchanges between 'saint and servant' and
devotes special attention to one form of everyday resistance to the
religious authority and sacred status of the Sharifian population.
Leading thought is Berque's reflection on the reciprocal relationship
between client and patron in rural Morocco: 'There is not one economic collectivity in the Maghreb that does not rest upon this division of labour, which is a partition between the material and the
spiritual' (Berque 1938: 27).

Shurfa as cultural brokers

In Islamic rural society the translation of formal doctrines, as laid down in scripture, into preferential social patterns and cultural acts has generally been tied up with a specific location and category of people. In pre-independence Morocco, it was the intricate network of local rural sanctuaries with religious teachers *cum* possessors of *baraka* that constituted 'the main institutional mechanism for the mediation of Islam' (Geertz 1971: 51). This section shows how the descendants of the Prophet can for this reason be seen as cultural middlemen or 'brokers' (cf. Wolf 1956; Geertz 1960), transmitting the content of the 'great tradition' of Islam and the divine force called *baraka* to the laity.

Hierarchy and civilization

Villagers in the oasis argue that people are to be distinguished according to their cultural level (*mustawan*). Assessment of the cultural level starts from the birth status but may include the educational and professional career of a person. The level of a Sharif, for example, is based on his descent, religious knowledge and personal qualities. On the one hand, all humans are supposed to follow the cultural ideal that underlies the notion of *mustawan*, but on the other, differences exist according to age, ethnicity and gender. To each level belong certain models for behaviour, formulated in what is called the laws or rules (*qawānīn*, sing. *qānūn*). Shurfa are supposed to follow a set of stricter 'rules' than Drawa, particularly concerning the maintenance of the distinction between public and private domains and between the gender categories. An older Sharif should not participate in the festive parts of rites of passage because he should not mingle with younger men who are not of his level. A Sharif should not fulfil subordinate work in service of a second Sharif because both are of the same level. Above all, a Sharifa is expected to marry a man who holds the same civilizational standard. Sanctions, in the form of a loss of respect, are based on the premise that 'the highest positions are the most exposed'. Jurists designate with *qānūn* a law that is independent from the Shariah, the religious Islamic law, for example, a law that has been promulgated by the government (Hodgson 1974: 584). This distinction explains why opposition against 'the behavioural laws' that set Shurfa apart from Drawa, and thus against the hierarchical difference in general, discussed further on in this chapter, may be set in a religious discourse: Respectful behaviour toward the Shurfa belongs in that view to the field of the *qawānīn* and not to that of the scriptural Shariah.

The practical, and therefore diverse usage of the hierarchical notions appears from the following joke, related by a Sharif, and the comment of a Drawi that follows it.

> Once a Sharif and a Drawi were having a quarrel that turned into a fight in which the Drawi was killed. Infuriated by this murder, his fellow Drawa assembled in front of the entrance of the Sharif's village to demand revenge and repay in kind. For several minutes, the Shurfa gathered to decide what to do, then one of them left the meeting to go to the house of the Sharif who had killed the Drawi. He returned with a donkey and presented it to the assembled Drawa, saying the gift of one Sharifian donkey equals a murdered Drawi.

The joke translates the opposition of Sharif and Drawi into that of a horse and a donkey, with the authority and status of the Shurfa being symbolized by the nobility of the horse. The joke refers to the legal inequality of Drawa before independence but to Abdelhadi the harsh offense of the joke went beyond the juridical context: 'God has separated men and donkeys. He gave everybody, like men, women, chickens and donkeys, their own space. He [i.e., the teller of the joke] puts them together, that's devilish behaviour. He should not have told it because the level (*mustawan*) of men and donkeys is not alike'.

In the oasis, social hierarchy, formulated in terms like *mustawan* and *qawānīn*, is one forceful system of ideas and values structuring practices in the oasis. *Kalām* (or *kalma*) is another, interconnected concept used by villagers in everyday life which reflects a hierarchical world view that separates youngsters from older men, men from women, and Shurfa from Drawa. *Kalām* means 'word' or 'speech' but also 'influence' and 'authority'. A person whom is said to have 'the word' is an authoritative figure who may not say much, but when he does, he is listened to and eventually followed. The possession of *kalām* distinguishes men from women.[1] 'The word' also distinguishes Shurfa from Drawa, which puts Drawa on a par with women. It is said Shurfa represent the Arabic language. They are

---

[1] See for the concept of *kalām*, Eickelman (1976: 143–144).

said to speak a more refined Arabic than their fellow oasis inhabitants. The saying that Shurfa have *kalām* also refers to the authority
they embody as well as to the view that they represent a different
level of the hierarchical social order. Shurfa, more than members of
any other social category, are said to embody the strict rules of
behaviour that are implied in the hierarchical order. It is because
of their speech and authority that Shurfa may lay claim to be part
of the élite (*ḵāṣṣa*) as distinguished from the common people (cf.
Bourqia 1991a: 140). In agreement with this, it is argued, especially
by the Shurfa themselves, that they embody the cultural ideals from
which the behavioural rules or 'laws' derive their meaning. The ultimate example given by villagers concerns a Sharif who almost never
spoke, as talk only leads to gossip and furthermore distracts from a
concentration on God's word. Yet on the few occasions he did speak,
he was listened to. This Sharif and imam is best remembered by a
successful rain prayer during the drought of the 1980s. After his
death, following this last memorable event that proved his control
over *baraka*, villagers respected his last wish and buried him next to
the sanctuary among the sons of saint Mulay Adafal. The example
expresses the close relationship between public stature, being in control over one's word and 'the (sacred) Word', and the expression of
supernatural power.[2] Therefore the word is with the Shurfa.

The 'great tradition' of the Shurfa

> We commence with a prayer to our Prophet
>   Muhammad, praise to Him
> The supreme, divine flag
>   appears at every place
> Dafali is our saint
>   and we sympathize with him
> God's angels may testify
>   that we have always respected God
> I am content with there being only one God
>   I say to you, that is what I wish in life

---

[2] The rain ritual (*salat al-istisqa*) involves first a prayer ('God give us enough
rain . . . and bring life to your lands of death') and then turning one's *jallāba* inside-
out (cf. Charles Benjamin, personal communication; Champault 1969: 137). On the
relationship between rain prayer and death, see Rosen: '[I]t is believed that the
pious man who makes the request for God's benevolence on behalf of the community should die soon . . .' (1984: 64; cf. Abu Zahra 1997).

The above lines are the main parts of the *snisla*, a chant recited at two major rites of passage in the village, the part for the groom of the marriage ceremony, and the circumcision ritual. The celibates and young married men walk through the village one after the other. Those in front sing the first line, those at the rear respond. Accompaniment only comes from their own feet tapping rhythmically on the ground. Every line is repeated about twenty times, so that the whole performance may last for fifteen to twenty minutes. The ritual ends with the lines '*we have come to congratulate the Sharif on his son's feast/ may His goodness and peace shower upon him*' and a repetitious recitation of the family who organized the feast (*the community of Mulay so-and-so!*). In Moroccan Arabic a *snisla* is a zipper or a chain and relates to the Standard Arabic *silsila an-nasab* (chain of ancestors). *Snisla*, then, refers to the actual performance but also signifies the presentation of a new sprout on the genealogical tree of the Aduafil Shurfa. In a more general sense, the text expresses the pious ethos according to which the villagers choose to live their life and furthermore proudly stresses the closeness with 'the House of the Prophet' through the village saint Adafal. The text evokes the ancient tribal interlinkage of acquired and inherited merit (*hasab wa nasab*) that once determined one's nobility and is still used to circumscribe one's identity (cf. Pandolfo 1997: 104–131). How does the self-image evoked in the text relate to the oasis hierarchy and the status of Shurfa?

The inhabitants of Aduafil, except for the Drawa, define themselves first and foremost as Shurfa, descendants of the Prophet Muhammad[3] through the 16th-century saint Ahmad bin Muhammad Adafal.[4] The claim of the inhabitants is founded on two principles. First, on a genealogical principle, in particular the descent from the 16th-century saint Mulay Adafal and 'the House of the Prophet'. Second, the claim is based on a religious and intellectual bond with renowned teachers of religious knowledge. Both principles and sources of sainthood are symbolized in an ancient walking-stick of one and

---

[3] Descent is claimed via the daughter of the Prophet. This explains why one man stated that Shurfa are *wlad bint Muhammad* (sons of the daughter of Muhammad). The matrilinear link is sometimes emphasized by addressing one another with *ḳal* (mother's brother). Further on in the text, it will be shown how Najem Hazzabin reasons along similar matrilinear lines.

[4] The terms used by villagers are the Arabic *walīy*, *ṣāliḥ* and *šiḳ*, and the French *marabout*.

a half meters with a leather handle, that belonged to Mulay Adafal. It is kept by the muezzin and shown at one phase of the marriage ritual and the major calendrical Islamic rituals. At the outdoor prayers of the Great Feast and the Little Feast at the end of Ramadan, the stick signals the direction of prayer. Standing in front of the crowd, the imam recites specific passages from the Koran, while keeping his hand on the walking-stick. At the wedding ceremony, a basket filled with grain is offered to the married couple, with both the stick and Adafal's slate put on top of the basket. The stick is a powerful symbol of the genealogical link between the 16th-century saint and the present-day Shurfa and is itself imbued with *baraka*. This accounts also for walking-sticks of less famous Shurfa. When one of the oldest Shurfa of the village died, his son assured me he would preserve his father's walking-stick because, imbued as it was with *baraka*, it would favour the fate of his family members. As well as the father-son bond, the stick symbolizes the relationship between teacher and disciple. It is said that Mulay Adafal received the walking-stick from his teacher, the renowned Sidi Musa from Tazerwalt on his deathbed, as he was the disciple who was nearest to his heart. Finally, the stick is a symbol of authority. The transfer of the stick from father to son and from teacher to disciple is a delegation of (male) authority.

The most significant support of their claim to a Sharifian status is the genealogical certificate from the year 1565. Five other documents, signed by the Moroccan sultan, confirm the authenticity of the first document.[5] One Sharif compared the genealogical tree, or rather name list, of the first document to an ID. This man actually kept a copy of the last document in his wallet, next to his *carte d'identité*.

For years the documents have been kept in a metal case. At that time they had become obsolete. While the older documents were upheld by the promulgation of a certificate by Sultan Mohammad V in the 1930s, this did not happen with the newly installed King Hassan II. Villagers recalled that until the mid-1970s they never saw the written proof of their Sharifian status. In the oasis the documents were never shown to prove one's Sharifian origins nor were they used on special occasions. The inhabitants missed, in fact, the

---

[5] Four *dahir-s* are from the sultans Sidi Muhammad (1757–1790), Mulay Hassan (1873–1894), Mulay Abdelaziz (1894–1908) and Muhammad V (1927–1961); one I could not identify, probably from Mulay Slimane (1792–1822).

legal permission of the relevant authorities to hold the title of Sharif. This, however, changed when in the mid-1970s the Moroccan state decided to take the regional quarrel about sovereignty over the Western Sahara to the international court of justice in The Hague. The village was asked to hand in any documents that could be used as evidence in the argument concerning Morocco's borders. The document that is symbolizing the Sharifian lineage can thus only be effective through recognition of the bond between Shurfa and Sultan/King. The event in the 1970s re-established the bond between the village and the Moroccan Sharifian state, with the king as supreme Sharif in a religious hierarchy that extends beyond the local level (cf. Jamous 1981: 229–241). The villagers' documents were sent to Casablanca to be copied while the original certificate was framed. Since Shurfa from the neighbouring villages lack these kind of documents, the Aduafilis argue that their neighbours' claim to an honourable status as Shurfa cannot be certified, although the possibility should not be ruled out and the Aduafilis intermarry with the would-be Shurfa from nearby villages.

The walking-stick and the documents bear witness to the legitimacy of the Shurfa's claim to an honourable lineage and inherited merit. In the oasis, this claim to religious authority and superior status is to a large degree summarized in their ability to control and use efficaciously the divine force called *baraka*. Some people say *baraka* is at the disposal of Shurfa, others object to the idea that *baraka* can be possessed by someone. They suggest you cannot *have baraka*, but you can use it in practice, *evoke it*, so to speak, at certain times and places. Nevertheless most informants agree on the existence of the association of the divine force with the Shurfa, sometimes adding the provision that their way of life is in accord with their inborn qualities. To call on the Sharifian *baraka*, people from nearby villages, especially women, visit the shrine in the village. They stay at the tomb for a certain length of time, leaving a few dirhams in the tomb or handing a chicken to the muezzin. They attach a piece of cloth to the knocker of the entrance gate, which represents the wish or request of the visitor. Sometimes visitors spend the night in the tomb. Likewise the Shurfa visit families on request, for example, at feasts and important rites of passage they recite sections from the Koran. For pilgrims the shrine is one of many on their list. Even the Aduafilis themselves visit other ones, sometimes in a strict order (thus creating a network of interconnected shrines). At the feast of the birth of the Prophet, people from nearby villages are invited to join dinner in the courtyard of the shrine. To partake is to share in the hospitality and generosity of the Shurfa as well as to be blessed with the *baraka* attached to the shrine.

The village of Aduafil is a religious lodge (*zāwiya*) centred around the shrine of a saint that attracts devotees from the immediate surroundings. There are more shrines than lodges in Morocco, most shrines being solitary white domes in the countryside, while the religious lodges which have been developed around the remaining shrines have only a local appeal. The adherents of these latter variant of shrines were able to extend the meaning and function of their shrine and develop it into a peaceful enclave or market centre. A restricted number of lodges has attracted devotees nationwide and played a role in national politics. One of the best known examples in this major league of *zāwiya-s* is located only 60 kilometres away from Aduafil in Tamgrout. The lodge of Tamgrout was founded in the late 16th century and gained nationwide authority in the following century. The lodge has several annexes in the Ktawa Oasis (cf. Hammoudi 1980). The small-scale lodge of Aduafil, nominally attached to the *Darqāwa* religious brotherhood, is the more common format. Just like the larger ones, it is considered to be a sacred space and spiritual and intellectual centre for its devotees.

In pre-independence Morocco the religious lodges were juridical enclaves where excluded persons or hunted individuals could find refuge. In addition, the family that was attached to the centre functioned as arbitrator in tribal disputes. The 'Saints of the Atlas', figuring in Gellner's famous study (1969) were arbitrators for the different segments of the confederacy of the transhumant Ait 'Atta Berbers. There are indications that in the past the village of Aduafil fulfilled the same function, albeit on a much smaller scale, as the lodge figuring in Gellner's study. In chapter three this role was explained from the close bond between *Idrissī* Shurfa, like those of Aduafil, and the Ait 'Atta Confederacy.[6] At present, the juridical and scriptural tasks of the Shurfa have diminished but not disappeared completely.[7]

---

[6] Jacques-Meunié mentions the role of Sidi Salah in the southern most tip of the oasis: 'The descendants of Sidi Salah are consulted in case of disputes between tribes and their opinion is respected' (1947: 410). Today this sanctuary is still important and backed by the state (cf. Hammoudi 1997: 135).

[7] A few years ago the sanctuary was used to end a conflict that had caused the

In addition, until the beginning of the 1980s the village housed a small school attached to the mosque. Here, children from surrounding villages congregated to learn to read and write and memorize the Koran. Discipline was severe. The *fqīh* taught the older children, and they in turn aided the younger ones. The curriculum was aimed at the memorization and recitation of the Koran; when a pupil had managed to memorize the complete scripture he organized a Koran recitation for all villagers. According to villagers, competition from the public school (from the late 1960s on), the unwillingness of teachers to continue to work for free and unwillingness on the side of the parents to pay for the teachers, has led to the closure of the school. Still, a number of *fqīh-s* from surrounding villages have received their education in Aduafil.

For years the village has organized an annual saint's day. The Moroccan saint's day (*mausim*), of which its multifunctional character has been demonstrated by Reysoo (1991), is an annual feast organized in the surroundings of a shrine. It is primarily an occasion to visit the shrine, but children and adolescents may like the fair better. Part of every saint's day is the market. Additionally, at these saint's days people may have their children circumcised or even conclude marriages. In the oasis, the saint's day was another occasion to put the village and its inhabitants in the centre of attention. At present, villagers visit the *mausim-s* of Sidi Salah in the oasis and that of Tamgrout in the valley.

Maraboutism, that is, the North African local saint's cult put in a Frenchified concept, is usually considered to represent or belong to the 'little tradition', as Redfield coined the local peasant culture which was to be distinguished from the urban 'great tradition':

---

death of a man in a nearby village. The offender was confined in the prison of Marrakesh. After he had completed his sentence, the man let his family organize a large reunion feast to which all villagers were invited. The relatives of the victim, however, were not prepared to reconciliate and refused to cross the threshold of the offender's house. The offender took this as a threat and sought safety in the sanctuary of Aduafil. He returned to his village with the green cloth that lies on the tomb of the saint. The man spread the cloth on the threshold of his outer door and asked the victim's relatives to enter his home, and so they did. By placing the cloth on the threshold, the man had put himself under the protection of the Shurfa. A second refusal or even attack by the victim's relatives would not only humiliate the offender but would also be an affront to the honour of the Shurfa. By entering the sanctuary (*hurma*) of the Shurfa, the offender made a sanctionable demand (*wqaf ši 'ar*) whereby the Shurfa could not refuse to mediate in the conflict without risking loss of their honour (cf. for this *'ar*, Brown 1982: 250).

> In a civilization there is a great tradition of the reflective few, and
> there is a little tradition of the largely unreflective many. The great
> tradition is cultivated in schools or temples; the little tradition works
> itself out and keeps itself going in the lives of the unlettered in their
> village communities (. . .). The two traditions are interdependent. Great
> tradition and little tradition have long affected each other and con-
> tinue to do so (Redfield 1967: 41–42; cf. Eickelman 1981: 201–204).

In Redfield's original text on the great and little tradition, Von
Grunebaum provides the data for the Islamic 'cult of the saints' and
the ways in which 'the conflict, coexistence, and interaction of the
Islamic high culture and the local cultures can be described' (Redfield
1967: 48–49). Contemporary scholars mostly avoid usage of the terms
great and little tradition and instead choose to speak of a local, here
Moroccan, Islam (Eickelman 1976, 1981: 201–260; Jansen 1985). In
this way they intend to make clear that formal, textual doctrine is
interpreted in local practices in a more complex way than the previous dichotomy suggested (cf. Reysoo 1991: 204). Furthermore, as
Munson (1993: 83) states, '[a]nthropologists (. . .) often believe that
the late twentieth-century distinction between popular and orthodox
Islam existed throughout Moroccan history. That is not the case'.
Munson shows in his study the intertwinement of orthodox and popular Islam in Moroccan society. This implies that the urban elitist
adherents of the Salafi movement, which in the late 19th and early
20th century was allegedly opposed to maraboutism and strove for
the 'purification' of the faith and a scripturalist approach toward
practices, in fact supported local saints. They did so because, as one
adherent explicitly stated, 'without them, the sky would not give forth
rain, the earth would not produce plants, and misfortune would pour
down upon the people of the world' (1993: 87).[8] These nuances are
not necessarily in disagreement with Redfield, who should be cred-
ited for stressing the interdependence between the two levels and
pointing out the role of cultural brokers at the local level. By way
of the Koran school in the village, the provision of many Koran
recitators and their status as Shurfa, the villagers of Aduafil for a
long time have indeed fulfilled such a role as cultural brokers between
the formal doctrines of Islam and local practices.

I agree with the recent emphasis on the complex interdependence

---

[8] Munson explicitly reacts against the accounts of the Salafi by Geertz (1971)
and Gellner (1981: 207–213).

between textual doctrines and local practices but would like to make another point. On the basis of the genealogical bond of the inhabitants with a saint and the status of the village as lodge, fellow inhabitants of the oasis consider the Shurfa of Aduafil as embodying the material and spiritual civilization related to the Islamic faith and brought to Morocco by the first Sultan Idriss I (788–792), direct ancestor of the Aduafili Shurfa. One Sharif explained this linkage of the Shurfa with the Islamic *cum* Moroccan civilization in the following way:

> Idriss came to Morocco. At first, people did not respect him. They did not want him to live among the Berbers in the Zerhoun Mountains. These Berbers did not live in houses, but in tents and caves. They could neither read nor write. They did not speak very well [he demonstrates their gibberish talk, RE] and did not own carpets. In short, there was no civilization. Idriss' arrival was the commencement of the Moroccan civilization. Likewise, he introduced the language of God and the Koran. Later on, the Berbers came to respect Mulay Idriss who married with a woman from among them.

In this story, the Shurfa are by and large seen as representatives of the Moroccan civilization. Just like Mulay Idriss once brought the innocent rural Berbers into contact with Islamic civilization, Mulay Adafal is said to have brought Islam and Islamic civilization to the oasis. Shurfa are thus taken for the representatives of the 'great tradition' of Islamic civilization in the oasis society. As pointed out in chapter two, the connection between Moroccan civilization and the arrival of Sharif Idriss bin Abdallah is a general topos in the nationalist ideology.

The association of the descendants of the Prophet with the 'great tradition' is exemplified in the saying that they stand close to the (urban) civilization of Morocco (*ḥaḍāra* or *tamaddun*). People regularly evoke the imagined dichotomy of urban (*madanī*) and country (*ʿarūbī*) ways of doing and on the basis of this typecast each other as either city- or country-dweller. Living in either town or village does not determine a person's urban or rural identity alone. Descent and the pursuit of an urban lifestyle carry as much weight. An urban ethos is apparent in the whole of the country yet the idealization of 'traditional', *ʿarūbī* ways of living remains a persistent counterpoint.

After the introduction of Islamic civilization, a second contribution to Moroccan civilization, *ḥaḍāra*, came from the urban civilization that developed after the arrival of the Andalusian migrants as a consequence of the Catholic *reconquista* of Islamic Spain. In all the towns where Andalusian migrants settled (Fez, Rabat, Salé and Tetouan) a cultivated urban élite, predominantly tradespeople but also (state) bureaucrats and urban *fqīh*-s, developed a taste for poetry, music, the sciences, Islamic law and fine arts. The Andalusian towns earned the title of 'civilized', with the members of the élite considering themselves to be the pillars of the Moroccan *ḥaḍāra*. They prided themselves on their guardianship of high culture and 'distinguished themselves from others by their marriage partners (largely endogamous), religious (. . .) affiliations, dress, speech, and degree of women's seclusion' (Marcus 1983: 161–162; cf. Hayeur 1991). 'Urbanity' thus 'did not include the lower orders of society' (Ossman 1994: 23). *Ḥaḍāra* refers to a sedentary, Islamic social order. It is on the basis of their close involvement with this order that Shurfa claim to stand on a different civilizational level than their fellow villagers, that is, Drawa.

In general, Drawa and other oasis inhabitants accept that due to their distinct religious stature and closeness to the 'great tradition', the Shurfa have to abide by another, stricter, set of behavioural rules. However, even those Drawa who approve of the set of ideas concerning the Sharifian civilization remark that many Shurfa tend to forget their own rules of behaviour (*qawānīn*) while insisting on expressions of respect and different treatment from others. 'Real Sharifianism' resides in the heart, these Drawa say, adding that unfortunately at present not many Shurfa are equipped with such a heart. The Shurfa should bring their laws into practice, which means they should not steal or quarrel, but pray and not neglect their faith. Female Shurfa should not only wear their veil in the oasis but also in Casablanca— unlike Drawiat who have the right to go unveiled.

In the oasis, the position of Shurfa as cultural brokers between the great and little tradition is embodied in the former Koran school, regular ritual recitations and the practice of the lodge as a refuge. On saint's day and on the Prophet's birthday, by visiting the shrine, oasis inhabitants are able to come into contact with the supernatural power of the sanctuary. For those living outside the village, access to Sharifian *baraka* is possible by way of a small material gift. On saint's days, visitors can buy small objects such as candles and cloths that are said to be impregnated with *baraka* (cf. Reysoo 1991: 123–130). This exchange of grace for a material offer returns in the Sharifian practice of asking for donations, a share of the harvest, by visiting the villages of befriended tribal lineages. Alternately, land donations can be made to the lodge, which is understood to be a pious act. Together with religious merit (*ajr*), acquired after a pious deed, the practices with which one gains access to *baraka*, suggest 'the image of God as an accountant, who keeps record of *ajr* and *baraka* as receipts and expenditure' (Buitelaar 1991: 97). The small rural Shurfa have indeed been described as small independent entrepreneurs with the symbolic capital of Shurfa being exchanged for material donations. The Sharifian gift of *baraka* to their clientele, the local population, which is significantly called 'the bread' (*kubza*), always takes place in a hierarchical relationship, 'from saint to man, from chief to slave, from parent to child' (Bakker 1993: 211–213). The crucial principle here, although in practice not always working perfectly, notes Crapanzano (1973: 121; cf. El Mansour 1991: 75), is the exchange of wealth—via donations—for *baraka*. The resulting exchange relationship and division of labour between the Sharifian small entrepreneurs and their 'personnel' within the village shall be examined in the next two sections.

Division of labour in the sanctuary

To carry out the tasks that are linked to the functioning of the sanctuary and the mosque, a division of labour and therefore a necessary interdependence between Shurfa and Drawa are operative. This division of labour is key to the ideological underpinning of the social hierarchy, and the cultural identities of Shurfa and Drawa in the village.

The imam and the muezzin

Five times a day the muezzin's call for the obligatory prayers can be heard throughout the village. Notwithstanding the existence of the new minaret, the muezzin still summons people to prayer by standing on the roof of the mosque, just like in the days of the Prophet. This will end once the village council has collected enough money to buy a megaphone. Then, even when working in the fields outside the village, everybody will be informed of the time of prayer. According to Islamic law, a Muslim is allowed to pray wherever he wishes, provided he has a prayer-mat at his disposal or knows the

ground to be pure, but a communal prayer in the mosque is thought
to be more valuable. Most adult men try to visit the mosque as
often as possible, and thus make the mosque and the five prayers
the pivot of the daily schedule of their social contacts, work and
meals. The minaret of the village is the highest point in the oasis.
Driving through the hills surrounding the oasis, one easily sees the
minaret rising up above the green sea of palm trees, attesting to the
piety of the villagers.[9]

Inside the mosque, the daily prayer is led by the imam, in the
village called *fqīh*. At present, the function of imam is in the hands
of a Sharif from the Saint's Quarter. Before him the responsible
man was a Sharif from the Outside Quarter. In Islam an official
clergy does not exist; every adult male person can act as imam or
muezzin. The imam must be capable of leading men in their daily
prayers, as well as in the communal outdoor prayers at all the major
Islamic calendrical rituals. The imam also reads the Friday sermon.
Furthermore, he has to know the Koran by heart and be able to
participate in the Koran recitations (*silka-s*) that are organized on
the occasion of rites of passage such as birth, circumcision, marriage
and funeral.[10]

The person to fulfil the function of imam has to be of irreproach-
able standing. This implies that he has to know and follow the rules
of etiquette and civilized conduct (*adab*) and protect the honour of
his family. This demand for propriety includes the imam's family
members. Since the function demands moral as well as physical
purity, the imam has a high prestige in the village. For this reason,
a Drawi as an imam leading the prayers seems unthinkable in the
Sharifian village. Moreover, a Drawi would have to abstain from
tasks that interfere with the demand of moral and physical purity.
For years the nearby village of Ait Isful Berbers did have a Drawi
as imam. This man had studied in Aduafil and was the only Drawi
ever to live inside the *qsar* walls together with the Isfuli families. The

---

[9] In a recent overview of local adobe architecture the minaret of Aduafil is mentioned with much disapproval. The author complains that while the *qsar* has been
awarded with a concrete mosque and a minaret *de style urbain* 'that can be seen
from miles away', 'the path which connects this isolated village with the communal centre and with the rest of the country can only be followed with great difficulty'
(Mouline 1991: 99).

[10] A *silka* consists of the recitation of the Koran by twelve reciters. The twelve
men are consigned five of the sixty sections into which the Koran is divided.
Participation is rewarded with a meal and sometimes with a small sum of money.

prestige of the religious task of this Drawi overshadowed his humble origins.[11]

In Aduafil the function of muezzin is one of the religious tasks in the village that can be performed by Drawa as servants of the Shurfa. It is one of the humble, sometimes servile and menial tasks Drawa perform. Apart from a modest salary and irregular rewards, they first and foremost earn esteem and religious merit (*ajr*). The muezzin is responsible for the sanctuary. This means that he possesses the key with which he opens the door upon request of the female pilgrims who visit the sanctuary on Friday morning. They leave a small monetary gift on the tomb of Mulay Adafal or light a candle in the shrine. They might bring a chicken, or in exceptional cases a sheep, to have it sacrificed. The sheep is sacrificed by Hammed Hazzabin who divides the animal in as many parts as there are families in Aduafil, with special parts reserved for him and the muezzin.

The position of muezzin is associated with a subordinate status. The position originated in 7th-century Medina on the Arab peninsula. In the pre-Islamic Arab world the muezzin was already a familiar figure as the village crier, someone who walked through the streets yelling the news. Thus, in these early first years when the minaret had not been invented, the freed slave Bilal became the first Islamic muezzin. He walked through the street summoning people to prayer. It was only in the first century after the death of the Prophet Muhammad that '[t]he custom of calling from a raised position became general' (Pedersen 1969: 675). With this development not only the muezzin but also his status was raised: 'His work was not only to summon the people to divine service, but was itself a kind of religious service' (ibidem). At that point Bilal disappeared from the stage. Even so, the figure of the dark-skinned Bilal as muezzin of the Prophet remained attached to the call for prayer. It is worthwhile following Pâques' analysis of the imagined relationship between the Prophet and his muezzin in Morocco. The descendants of slaves in Morocco assembled in the *Gnawa* religious brotherhood consider Bilal as their patron saint. Also, other people associate the descendants of the slaves that were brought in from countries south of the Sahara, sometimes including the Haratin, with the Prophet's slave. Pâques argues that in the worldview of the descendants of slaves, the muezzin

---

[11] This practice is in agreement with Hart's statement that in 'Atta land '[t]he fqih is invariably an outsider to the community' (1984: 100).

is the 'voice' of the Prophet: 'More concrete it is said that he is the "saliva" (euphemism for semen), or fecundating sex, of the Prophet' (Pâques 1991: 53 *et passim*). Since the prayers constitute one of the five pillars of the Islamic faith, the 'fertile' call for prayer makes the muezzin a worker, a *kammās* ('one-fifther'), of God. Through his menial, or rather bodily, labour the muezzin is able to enlighten his fellow humans. Located between heaven and earth, the muezzin serves humans in the division of time and the ascent (*tl'a*) of their souls. The first dimension corresponds with other tasks fulfilled by Drawa that consist of the 'sacrilegious violence' (Bourdieu 1977: 127) of cutting and dividing (see chapter six). The second dimension also includes the heating of water and the burning of incense (see chapter seven); both tasks are fulfilled by Drawa as servants of the Shurfa. The muezzin is a servant raising his voice in public, just like the village crier, to inspire men to fulfil their religious duties. More-over, from his elevated position between heaven and earth, it is his task to mark the passing of day and of day into night. While the imam leads the prayer in the sacred environment of the mosque, the muezzin works on top of the mosque or on top of the minaret on the boundary of a profane and sacred domain.

In Aduafil until recently, the function of village crier and muezzin were united in the person of Salem Hazzabin. Before him the vil-lage has had two other Drawi muezzins. After the death of Salem most tasks were taken over by his son Hammed. Hammed, how-ever, because of his stammer, was unfit to fulfil the tasks of crier and muezzin. Thus, these tasks were split up and delegated to two other Drawa. In addition to this, the special task of summoning peo-ple to prayer with a long trumpet (*nafir*) during Ramadan was for a long time being performed by a Drawi. A few years ago this Drawi, Hammed's brother-in-law, refused to walk around with the trumpet any longer, probably because of some remark of his fundamentalist son Khalifa. Again, the qualification of the tasks as shameful and improper is most likely related to its asssociation with bodily activ-ities.[12] At present, the muezzin is a Sharif, but one who has a very low standing in the village. It is said he worked as a street-vendor

---

[12] See Pâques (1991: 58): '[W]hen one speaks of a *n'fir*, one always evokes an obscenity. In Casablanca it is called *zatot*, a word which designates any small object that moves a lot and, by extention, the monkey (which is a euphemism for the male genitals)' (cf. Chottin 1927).

in Casablanca, trying to sell prickly pears, shouting, *karmūs al-hindī . . . wa al-mūs min ʿandī!* ('prickly pears [for sale] . . . and I got the knife [to open the fruit]'). Already used to shouting in public, he seemed suitable to act as muezzin, so it is said. The gossip secularizes and debases the call for prayer of the present-day muezzin, comparing it to a market call or *al-klam dyal sūq* where the market, as shown by Kapchan (1996: 36–37), epitomizes all that is 'grotesque' and 'unruly' in Morocco. The low esteem of the village muezzin is exemplified in the criticism about his manner of proclaiming the hours for prayer in the month of Ramadan. One day he summoned at three o'clock, the following day a minute or two late, and the third day one minute before three o'clock. Especially during the month of fasting, people are focused upon the exact hour of sunset (cf. Buitelaar 1991: 134). It is crucial that the symbolic ordering of time according the five daily prayers is clear, leaving in particular no ambiguity as to whether one has broken the fast at the exact hour. During my fieldwork Ramadan took place in the spring. With the days growing longer, the muezzin should have added a minute or two every day. The heart of the reproach was that the muezzin did not follow a straight but a *zigzag* course. Where *zigzag* is associated with instinctive, as opposed to rational, behaviour (and therefore with feminine behaviour), the gossip and criticism relegate the call to prayer of the present-day muezzin to a bodily instead of a spiritual deed.

Spiritual subordination

A proper prayer procedure necessitates a variety of complementary servile tasks, of which the call to prayer by a muezzin is the most public one; equally important though are those of purifying the floor of the mosque, spreading the carpets, and heating the water for the ablutions. All these tasks are necessary preparations for the fulfillment of the religious duties of the villagers. This explains why they are considered by some to be religious acts in themselves. Just as with the muezzin, cleansing practices relating to the mosque reach back to the first years of Islam as an established religion, when Muhammad appointed a black servant to clean the mosque. In the larger mosques several servants (sometimes eunuchs; cf. Marmon 1995) were in charge of the purification of the buildings and the delivery of clean warm water for the Muslims to purify themselves.

Large mosques have their own personnel to take care of all these

tasks, but in a small village like Aduafil the tasks are the responsibility of one man. For a long time this has been someone from the
Hazzabin family. Until his death in the 1980s, Salem Hazzabin combined the work of muezzin, water-carrier, cleaner of the mosque as
well as several tasks related to the sanctuary. The commonality of
the practice of the accumulation of tasks relating to the mosque in
North Africa was already noted by Golvin (1960: 95) when he pointed
out how in the majority of North African mosques one person is
appointed as guardian: 'He is a kind of concierge and inspector of
the buildings' making sure that the domestics do their work in an
orderly fashion, receiving vistors to the sanctuary and taking care of
their gifts.

Intellectual capacities and education may influence whether a person becomes an imam or *fqīh*; yet, certain people are excluded from
certain tasks. Thus, while the function of imam demands an irre-
proachable standing and compliance to the rules of etiquette and
civilized conduct and is exclusively executed by Shurfa, these same
villagers mostly avoid performing tasks that tarnish their standing as
Shurfa and as men.

In the village, people do not always admit that menial tasks, possibly involving purification or contact with impurities, are carried out
by special men. Instead they stress the eligibility of all villagers and
the mutual interdependence of executors of the tasks. These were
some of the answers I received concerning the procedures of the last
rites.

> Question: 'Who digs the grave when someone has died?'
> Answer from the second *fqīh* of the village: 'Barka, Zdarni, Mumid,
> Hammed, Baqedur are the ones who dig the grave. Others cook the
> food while children take care of the livestock'.
> q: 'So, Drawa dig the grave?'
> a: 'Not necessarily'.
> q: 'But the names you give . . . [are all of Drawa]'.
> a: 'When someone has died, Hammed visits all the houses to say that
> Mulay so-and-so has died. People come out of their home and say to
> each other: "I am going to do this, you should do that". The *fqīh* and
> I sew the cotton for the dead person. [The muezzins of the two
> mosques] wash and prepare the body for burial'.

The following interlocutor was a Sharif whose father had recently died:

> Question: 'Who dug the grave?'
> Answer: (He bends forward and whispers in my ear) 'The Drawa'.

q: 'Why they?'
a: 'They want to do it. It earns them a lot of religious merit'.
q: 'Do the Shurfa not like to earn this religious merit?'
a: 'Listen, when a person has died, everybody takes care of something. Some cook, others recite'.
q: 'And the Drawa dig . . .'
a: 'They want to'.

When I asked Hammed Hazzabin, he responded that 'it would be shameful if people would see we let a Sharif dig graves'. A second gravedigger confirmed that a salary or financial gift was not involved in the task. Jansen (1987: 65), who gives an extensive description of the procedures involving the purification of the body in Algeria, observes that ideally the last rites should be executed by the relatives: 'Any relative of the same sex who is a pure and pious Muslim and knows how to perform the major ablution can do it. Yet, in practice, close kin avoid this obligation and prefer to call in a specialist'. In the village the same distanced stance toward the task and ritual handling of contact with the grave is evident. When asked, the eligibility of every person is stressed, but in practice the division of labour has been strictly fixed: The menial and servile tasks as well as those involving cleaning and purification are performed by Drawa, those involving recitation and representation by Shurfa. The remarks of villagers recognize the interdependence of tasks, albeit in a hierarchical way. Certain tasks are necessary, yet less valued and seen as unfit for certain people. In particular, tasks that include purification and contact with impure substances are avoided by Shurfa and considered inappropriate for them to do. In a simple binary scheme, the sacred Shurfa are associated with pure tasks in a pure environment (the mosque) vis-à-vis the profane Drawa who are there to take care of purification.

With the distinction of Shurfa and Drawa and the division of labour comes interdependence. At a funeral the person who has to dig the grave is as indispensable as the one who prepares the dinner for the guests and he who recites the Koran in commemoration of the person who has passed away. The religious impact of the tasks relating to the mosque and the Shurfa is clear, as they all involve the organization of religious services and activities dealing with the sanctuary, yet all the tasks—the call to prayer, taking care of the water for the ablutions, purifying the mosque, leading the prayer (done by a Sharif)—are necessary and complementary. Without

them, not one villager would be able to perform his daily prayers
in the mosque. Also agricultural activities, which do not directly
relate to the mosque or sanctuary are necessary in the sense that by
doing them, the Drawa set villagers free for other tasks, like recit-
ing the Koran on ritual occasions. The Drawa gain in religious merit
(*ajr*) and receive the grace (*baraka*) of the Shurfa.

Recognition of the differentiation and interdependence of tasks
does not exclude the existence of a differing evaluation of these same
tasks. In performing them, an ideological structure is operative which
expresses and reproduces symbolic dominance. This is illustrated by
the task of heating water for the ritual ablutions. This task is necessary and crucial for the functioning of the mosque. The gains consist of social respect and religious merit. At the same time, heating
water is a symbol of subordination. It is only done by Drawa, for
example at communal dinners and festivities. When villagers express
the pre-eminence of the sanctuary of Aduafil over that of another,
non-Sharifian, sanctuary in the oasis, named Sidi Salah, they state
that the founder of this latter sanctuary used to come down to the
village to heat water for the Shurfa. Through his assistance and the
fulfillment of the subordinate task of heating water, a transference
of Adafal's genealogical *baraka* (as a Sharif) to his maraboutic, non-
Sharifian, pupil Sidi Salah took place.[13] Thus, the acceptance of a
subordinate position opens the way to the transference of *baraka*.
This mechanism applies equally well to the relationship between
Shurfa and the Drawa in the present-day village, whereby submission or spiritual subordination opens the way to a coexistence with
the honourable Shurfa and the reception of *baraka*.

Hierarchical interdependence

The Shurfa stand at the apex of the social hierarchy. To maintain
recognition of their distinctive sacred status, they are dependent on
people for agricultural services and menial services in and around
the sanctuary. In the village, a group of Drawa takes care of these
tasks. How is this hierarchical interdependence between Shurfa and
Drawa, as 'saints and servants', conceptualized?

---

[13] Compare Crapanzano (1973: 38) for a similar case.

People without baraka

Najem is the fourth and youngest brother of the Hazzabin family. Living in the outskirts of Fez, he returns home regularly to earn some additional money picking dates. Since Najem is a relative outsider to the village, he was more willing to talk with me about the ins and outs of village life than other villagers. One day, I accompanied Najem on his daily walks to the palm trees to be harvested to discuss village matters with him. At lunch time, we elaborated on some of the issues I had raised during our walks in the fields. To clear up matters, Najem first objected against my usage of the ethnonyms Drawi and Hartani. Instead, he laid claim to a more honourable descent. Najem explained that his mother was named Belballi: 'She is a *marabta* from Tabelbala, just like Mumid [Najem's brother-in-law, RE]. So I am a marabout as well'.

I was not really surprised by Najem's claim to the status of a marabout.[14] Of all the Hazzabin brothers, Najem was the only one to have been educated at the local Koranic school near the mosque. In the last decade of the school, Najem belonged to a group of students who learned to memorize the Koran in the way as it has been done through the ages in the village. He was still able to recite the Koran and perform as a reciter and actually did so in Fez. In Aduafil he preferred to stay in the background. On earlier occasions I was confronted with Drawa who declared themselves descendants of a saint. The claims always applied to a local marabout, which made them difficult to prove or disprove. Through a natural disaster or because of violent conflicts with herdsmen, their ancestors were forced to flee to another region. In this way the ties with the sanctuary were lost, while the memories remained. In Najem's case the oasis of origin is called Tabelbala. This oasis, now in Algeria, used to be an important stopoff along one of the trade routes from Morocco to the region south of the Sahara. The oasis lies a few days' trip from the Ktawa Oasis. In chapter two it was argued that in the Ktawa Oasis descent is an important marker for the development of social identities, most usually patrilineal descent. On the basis of their patri-

---

[14] A marabout is a person, living or dead, who has a special relationship toward God and acts as mediator between God and humans (Eickelman 1976: 6). Some marabouts only have local fame, others have regional or even national importance. Descendants of a marabout are called marabouts as well.

lineal descent and lack of common patronymic—some of the other Drawi families had turned the *nisba* Belballi into their surname—the Aduafilis made the Hazzabins an exception in the village. They had arrived in Aduafil at a much later date and did not come from Tabelbala but from a northern oasis in the Dra Valley. In emphasizing his matrilineal descent, Najem tried to attach the Hazzabins to the Tabelbala branch and dispel the stigma of a restricted residence in the village.

Although difficult living conditions may have played a part in the motives of the Belballi ancestors to migrate to the Ktawa Oasis, Najem expressed the conviction that a religious motivation was the primary one. In his view, the Belballis were primarily the companions of Mulay Ahmad Adafal, the patron saint of the village. They were ʿawāmm. Najem explained this term in the following way: 'A man who comes to this village and starts to live with ("sits down with") a marabout is an ʿāmmī'. Travelling from Figuig to Ktawa, the father of Mulay Ahmad Adafal passed the oasis Tabelbala. One Drawi decided to accompany him. When they arrived in Ktawa, they agreed to stay to educate the people. They lived on the gifts of their fellow oasis inhabitants.

Najem's older brother Hammed had already told me at one of our first encounters at his house, he was an ʿāmmī. The denominations of the brothers can be connected to a geographically and temporally more widespread discourse on social distinctions. The word ʿāmmī belongs in Arabic to a family with a root form including words such as ʿāmm, which means that which is 'public, universal, prevalent, general, common', ʿāmmī (sing. 'common, man in the street'), ʿawāmm (plur. 'the common people') en ʿāmma (coll. 'generality, commonalty, the masses') (Wehr 1976). In early Islamic society this last word was paired with the term ḵāṣṣa to conceptualize a bipartite view on Arab society. In the first decennia of Islamic conversion and military conquest, the ḵāṣṣa versus the ʿāmma reflected the social changes in the urban society as a consequence of the military and religious conquest of non-Arab peoples. The Arab, Islamic 'free men' proclaimed themselves the élite of urban society, which automatically left the non-Arabs, unbelievers and slaves, to make up the category of the masses or common people. Later, when the élite had begun to incorporate non-Arabs into their circles, the terms came to refer mainly to a division along class lines. Included in all the contemporary texts on the two terms were prescriptions concerning proper conduct towards persons belonging to different social categories. For example, one author described 'the attitude which one should adopt according to whether one is in the presence of a member of the kāṣṣa understood as comprising people of merit and quality, or of the ʿāmma, a thousand times more numerous' (Beg 1969: 1098; cf. Marlow 1997: 101). The changing meaning of the conceptual pair of 'kāṣṣa wa al-ʿāmma' reflects the process of pacification and social differentiation and its interweaving with the development of a specific notion of self-restraint and civilized behaviour in the Arab world.

In texts on early modern *Moroccan* society, the ʿāmma was also contrasted with the kāṣṣa, the élite (Berque 1982: 255). In the 19th century 'all those who did not belong to the élite of the community: Peasants, craftsmen, shopkeepers and workers' belonged to the urban and rural ʿāmma (El Mansour 1990: 13; cf. Brown 1976: 9–10, 57). The élite encompassed the category of Shurfa, judicial and religious specialists, military officials, members of guilds and state officials. Persons belonging to these occupational categories were entitled to certain privileges of which the most important were exemption from tax, the right to receive gifts, and the right to appear in front of a private court of law. Again, in contemporary texts the social differentiation of élite and commoners was juxtaposed to a difference in cultural ideals (Brown 1982: 232).[15]

In the early modern history of southern Morocco the division between commoners and élite was also used. In the western part of southern Morocco, the élite consisted of Shurfa and Islamic scholars; then came the commoners (ʿāmma) 'who were divided into tribes, clans, and lineages'. Next came the Haratin: '[A]griculturalists and craftsmen, economically dependent on the commoners'. Last were the slaves (Abitbol 1988: 131–136). In the eastern part of southern Morocco, we find the same differentiation into commoners and élite and the exclusion of Haratin from both categories:

> At the basis of [the early modern oasis society] we find the *Ḥaratin* (. . .) Above the *Ḥaratin* we find the *ʿAwamm*. This light-skinned population,

---

[15] According to Clancy-Smith (1994: 23), in the time of the Ottoman Empire, the secular 'desert bourgeoisie' in the southern borderland of Algeria and Tunisia consisted of merchants, large landowners and state representatives. These 'people of distinction' or 'khassa' were distinguished from the workforce of 'khammas'.

composed of Arabs and Berbers and making up for the majority of
the oasis population, controls most of the lands on which they let *Haratin*
work in a system that comes close to that of Western servitude (Mezzine
1987: 268–269).

It appears that in the southern oases the crucial difference between
commoners and Haratin is the condition of dependence. Haratin were
not organized in descent groups and were furthermore dependent
on a landowning class for their existence—according to Mezzine in
a situation of social dependence that was not unlike that of European
servitude.

Members of the transhumant and nomadic Ait 'Atta Confederacy
came to denominate the white, free oasis dwellers as *common people*
to distinguish them from the *uncommon* Shurfa and Haratin. *'Awāmm*
were thus neither Shurfa nor Haratin, but a middle category consisting of light-skinned oasis dwellers. Also in an urban context the
word *'awāmm* was sometimes included in such a multipartite social
hierarchy (Brown 1976: 9–10) in which religious and ethnic criteria
were mixed.

While these ancient distinctions explain Najem's preference for the
status of *'āmmī*, as it implies a rise of status, references in literature
dealing with the contemporary period give indications to interpret
Najem's story in a slightly different way: First, it has been observed
that the concept *'āmmī* refers to a *religious* dichotomy between Shurfa
and non-Shurfa (cf. H. Geertz 1979: 346). *'Awāmm* are people who
are common because they fall short of noble and Sharifian descent.
Or, as indeed one local Sharif defined the term: "*'Awāmm* are people without *baraka*'. Yet they also are people who live close to religious specialists, for example, as servants bound to a sanctuary, as
Najem pointed out when he designated *'awāmm* as people who are
'sitting with Shurfa'. This is affirmed by Jacques-Meunié (1958: 247)
who writes that in a nearby valley the term *'awāmm* refers in general to the commoners who are distinguished from the religious specialists (Shurfa and marabouts), yet not to Haratin, as well as to
'affiliates of the lowest degree in a brotherhood'. This latter reference has to do with the hierarchical structure of the brotherhoods.
The *'āmma* are then those people who are outside of the small élite
of initiates. Berque (1938: 58) thus spoke for the north of the country of the distinction between 'clerics' or *'tholba'* and a group of
'uninitiated, or *'awāmm'*. The linkage between the present-day distinction of commoners and élites with the more ancient references

is the central value of independence. Where the Hartani is an isolated, dependent individual, without historical antecedents in the
community through family or landed property, the commoner is
defined by his independent condition, just like the name 'freeman'
(*Hurr*) implies he has been born and grown up in the community
(Filali 1984: 243; cf. Meillasoux 1991: 23). Najem and Hammed do
not lay claim to an equal status with the Shurfa. Instead, they emphasize the interdependent relationship between the sacred Shurfa and
the profane Drawa in the oasis and argue that the association and
closeness with the Shurfa is honourable. Taken the long-standing
association of Haratin with dependency, voluntarily accompanying
Mulay Adafal by the Drawa as commoners can be seen as an attempt
to dispel the stigma of dependence that inflicts Drawa in general
and the Hazzabins in particular. The claim of independence works,
however, only via the mutual interdependence of saints and servants.

Closeness

More can be said on the relationship of Shurfa and Drawa as conveyed in the claim on a commoner status. The claim of Najem and
his brother to a more respectable status than they are awarded on
the basis of their Drawi descent is based on a broadly accepted cultural notion, namely that of closeness. Closeness (*qarāba*) is one of the
'key symbols' in Moroccan culture (Eickelman 1976: 96; cf. Ortner
1973). Informants refer to the term regularly, stress its importance,
and use it in diverse contexts. It can be evoked when speaking of
the Islamic community (*umma*) (Buitelaar 1991: 73–75), neighbourhoods, households or extended families (Eickelman 1976: 95–102; cf.
Abu-Lughod 1986: 49–59). People agree on its centrality, but not
on its application and meaning. Those included in the category with
whom one is close, are contrasted with outsiders or strangers. Although
it is not part of the definition we normally give to the word stranger,
it was argued in chapter three that the Drawa of the village can be
considered as strangers who are near and distant at the same time
(Simmel 1950). Inside the sacred space of the village—sacred because
of the sanctuary and the Shurfa living there—the Drawa are the
only non-Shurfa, grouped together in one street. Drawa, however,
consider themselves to be close to the Shurfa, because of their permanent residence in the village. Their argument is built on the belief
in the *baraka* of the Shurfa. The belief that a Sharif is capable of

conferring *baraka* upon human beings is central to the practice of the Berber population in the oasis asking a Sharifian family to live within the walls of their villages. With regard to Aduafil as a village of Shurfa and the site of an important sanctuary, people consider the whole village territory as imbued with *baraka*. Such a sacred enclave encircled by profane space is in Arabic called a *ḥurma*. This word belongs to the same family of words as that for respect, *iḥtirām*, and indeed respect is what is demanded of visitors. By keeping distance, one shows respect for the sacredness of the village. Within the boundaries of the sacred village space itself other patterns of behaviour are required. Impure behaviour like smoking must be abandoned. One clear example of the exclusion of impurity from the village territory is the refusal to permit unbelievers entrance to the sanctuary, while in the past the Jews from the oasis villages further south either had to take off their shoes in passing the sanctuary, or go around it.

The sacred village space is not just an idea but a physical area confined by clear boundary markers. The earth of the enclave is a sacred substance. It is forbidden to sell land or water rights to outsiders because it is protected, inviolable land. The closed area of the sanctuary is saturated with the *baraka* of the Shurfa. Pilgrims rub themselves and their children with the soil near the sanctuary or take a handful home. Other oasis dwellers address a request to the head of the village to be buried *ad sanctos*, that is, close to the Shurfa. This practice of closeness is based on the belief that on Judgement Day, when the good people will be separated from the evil ones, those close to the Shurfa—who belong to the family of the Prophet and are known for their piety—will be included with the good ones. Inside the sacred village space (*ḥurma*) one can discern a graded sacredness. Aduafilis regard the Saint's Quarter (see figure 3 and 4) as the oldest and most sacred quarter. This quarter encloses the sanctuary, and its inhabitants descend from the oldest son of the patron saint. They are said to have the shortest genealogy to the saint. Their genealogical and spatial shortcuts bring them closer to the saint than the inhabitants of the two other quarters. It is this quarter which has been a forbidden domain for unbelievers for a long time. Moreover, it is the only quarter which is exclusively Sharifian— without Drawa. Inside the sacred village space of the village, the Drawa are the only outsiders to come near to the Shurfa and the sanctuary; in plain physical terms the Drawa are nearer to the Shurfa of Aduafil than any other social category. They are the only ones who profit permanently from the blessings of the Shurfa.

The notion of closeness is strengthened by the classical Islamic tradition in which the group of the Prophet's companions is circumscribed by the degree of closeness to Muhammad. The *muqarrab-s* (litt. 'those who are close'; i.e., intimates) include family members, first converts and close friends who have actually met the Prophet. The closeness between the Prophet and his companions forms a model for the relationship between Mulay Adafal and his companions. A reference to this specific configuration consisting of members of the Prophet's family and their servants was made by the nephew of Najem, Abdelhadi, when he spoke of the Drawa who maintain close relationships with Shurfa as 'their companions' (*aṣḥāb-hum*). Najem furthermore argued that in prophetic times slavery only occured because the Prophet was into trade, and money did not yet exist. He thus obtained slaves out of necessity, though he never addressed them as such. In fact, a voluntary relationship between master and servant prevailed.

The association of spatial nearness with 'proximity to the sacredness and blessings of the Shurfa' does not exhaust the possible meanings of the notion of closeness. This becomes clear when we return to Najem's words. In addition to his explanation of *ʿawāmm* as people who are 'near Shurfa', he explained that *ʿawāmm* are 'like their children' (*bhal wlad-hum*; 'their' referring to the Shurfa) in the same vein as the Shurfa themselves are the children of the Prophet (*wlad al-nabi*). His words do not refer to a common patrilineal descent with the Shurfa but should be interpreted along a different line. A usual practice in Morocco is to connect spatial closeness with social closeness. The group of people with whom a person is close (*qarīb*) ranges from neighbours, relatives, kin and patrons to clients. The idiom of descent and kinship is considered to be a powerful way of expressing the permanency of these ties (Eickelman 1976: 96). Thus, the Hazzabin children address the neighbours, Shurfa and Drawa alike, in kinship terms. Often adult neighbours treat each other as close relatives, for example, with invitations for family feasts. Yet the father-son relationship to which Najem referrred is also the classic model of an interdependent relation between dominant and subordinate (Dumont 1980: 36) and, in case of the village, compatible with patronage, an intricate ensemble of asymmetrical exchanges of goods and services between Shurfa and Drawa (see chapter four).

With regard to the Drawa as a group, the notion of closeness returns in their claim to a common history of migration and the same
date of arrival in the oasis. Once when I suggested that the Drawa
might have been latecomers to the oasis, I was immediately corrected
by one of them. It was important for me to understand that Shurfa
and Drawa had arrived in the Ktawa Oasis at the same time. Najem's
attempt to link the family history to that of the Belballis derives from
the same principle. Saying that Drawa are the sons of the Shurfa
means the use of the most forceful idiom, that of kinship, to express
the close, intimate bond between the two groups. Again, it should
be stressed that the bond is also a hierarchical one. One should pay
the same respect to a father as to the Shurfa.

The strong bond between Shurfa and Drawa was implicated in
an explanation which the Hazzabins gave of the visit of a Drawi
from an oasis further up the river. This man requested the head of
the village council of Aduafil to find him a Drawia as a wife for his
son. According to the Hazzabins, who were asked by the village
head whether they were interested, this stranger came to the village
of Aduafil because the respectability of the Aduafili Drawa is well-
known in the valley. Najem explained that because of their closeness with the Shurfa, Drawiat—the female Drawa—more or less
keep up the same standards of seclusion as the female Shurfa. This
claim is remarkable because Drawiat are allowed to leave the house
unveiled to fetch water and work in the fields. These are tasks which
marriageable and married Sharifat are not allowed to do. Najem
clearly interpreted the dominant values in the village to his own
advantage. Seclusion of women meant for him not wandering around
and seeing or even talking to men outside the close circle of kin.
According to Najem, the Drawa stand on a different civilizational
level to Haratin elsewhere and therefore keep up a different behavioural standard—and one somewhat similar to the Shurfa.

The coexistence with the Shurfa offers the Drawa a possibility to
redefine their position in the status hierarchy, in contradistinction to
the Haratin of neighbouring villages. The subordinate discourse concerning the figuration of 'saints and servants', with the Drawa as
'awāmm, seems irresistible to the Shurfa as it is based on generally
accepted key notions and hinges on the honourable and sacred status of the Shurfa. At the same time, it can be interpreted as a legitimation of the unequal socio-economic relations in the village, with

Drawa portrayed as mere servants of the Shurfa. This interpretation would correspond with Marchesin (1992: 37) who pointed out for Mauritania how in zāwiya-s the exploitation of landless individuals was covered up by denoting them as pupils (tilmīd-s) of the lodges. For Najem, this would imply that his interpretation of ʿawāmm as people that stand close to the Shurfa merely serves to highlight the rightful position of the Shurfa. There are some facts that would support such an interpretation. Thus, the urban privileges for the ḵāṣṣa reappear in the southern distinction between ʿawāmm and Shurfa. Until the independence of Morocco in 1956, the Shurfa successfully claimed exemption from specific taxes and the labour service (tiwīza) that was enforced by the local authorities. In the 1930s, the French authorities continued this service after having gained permanent control over the sedentary and nomadic population. The Shurfa refused to work with the argument that the sultan was their equal (as he is also of Sharifian descent). They asked for respect to their sacred status and applied for exemption from the sultan. This was a common practice for Shurfa, and through an official declaration by Sultan Mohammad V the exemption from forced labour services was granted to them. Instead, the ʿawāmm had to perform these services.[16] Saints also sent their servants twice a year, after the grain and after the date harvest, to collect the gifts of befriended tribes to the sanctuary (Jacques-Meunié 1947: 366).

Further research should uncover the intellectual roots of the discourse that was introduced in this section by way of Najem's words, as well as its diffusion in the region.[17] Yet, I believe it would be a mistake to deny the authenticity of the performative attempt to shake off the stigma of a Hartani identity. Although Shurfa did not object to the claim of Drawa being ʿawāmm, it was never brought up by them. The Shurfa always denoted people like Najem as Drawa. More importantly, closeness and the status of Drawa as ʿawāmm also underlie the Drawi claim to possess baraka (and Najem to be a marabout). This is the outstanding characteristic of the Aduafili Drawa

---

[16] For the Shurfa of Ouezzane see Berque (1938: 29) and El Mansour (1991: 79).

[17] It is striking that the same discourse can be found in the oasis Tabelbala, where the roots of the Drawa are said to lie: 'At last, very close to the merabtin, one should note the existence of those who call themselves "in the middle of or among the lords" (bin es-siyed), orginally white Arab or Berber' (Champault 1969: 371; compare Gaborieau 1983 on Islamic 'servants of saints' in Nepal).

compared with Haratin from outside the village and totally at odds
with the opinions of Shurfa. This conclusion of Drawa is remarkable when we realize that Shurfa define *'awāmm* as 'people without
baraka', and that even Drawa accept the *baraka* of the Shurfa (as
their closeness to the Shurfa is built on it). The claim hardly fits
into the 'relatively autonomous realm of discursive freedom' (Scott
1990: 157) which the public discourse on the status of the Shurfa
offers. It seems to be the ultimate consequence of the application of
the notions of spiritual subordination and closeness which are the
cornerstones in the designation of the Drawa of the village as *'awāmm.*
In exchange for their assistance and subordinate tasks, the Drawa
are able to live close to Shurfa who are different because of their
control over the divine force called *baraka*. The Drawi *'awāmm* earn
respect and something of the *baraka* for which people from other villagers have to visit the village and present a donation.[18]

Contested honorifics

> The struggle between the champions of the older pattern and
> those of the new was bitter and intense, and it has not ended
> yet (Geertz 1971: 71).

If I am correct that in the village the destinies of Shurfa and Drawa
are interconnected, 'as two bandwagons tied together',[19] the question arises of how the erosion of the Sharifian sacred status, their
role as cultural brokers, and the related religious and cultural discourse they represent in contemporary Morocco affects the identity
of the Drawa. I will consider the contestation of the status of the
Shurfa, with the interlinkage of Sharif and Drawi kept in mind.

Profanation of the Shurfa

On the basis of their activities, the possession of certain attributes,
and the presence of the shrine, the Shurfa of the village have since
the 16th century acted as religious entrepreneurs and successfully
sanctified their individual personae and the space where they live.

---

[18] Compare Marmon (1995: 45) for similar notions concerning the impact of
closeness to the Prophet for the transference of *baraka* to servants.
[19] James Scott, personal communication 1995.

They competed against contesters such as those of nearby Sharifian shrines and allied with more powerful ones, like the Moroccan sultan, to find support for their claims. They were able to exchange their intellectual capacities and control over the supernatural grace called *baraka* for material donations and respect. In contemporary Morocco, the descendants of the Prophet are still approached with respect. Since the 1950s, however, state policy has increasingly put pressure on their privileged status. First and foremost, through monopolization of education, arbitration and religious authorization, the state has deprived local specialists of their functions and, in the person of King Hassan II, appropriated religion as the ultimate source of legitimation (Tozy 1987). These developments have led to a profanation of the Shurfa, for example, through the refusal to accept their exemption from collective labour and taxes. The king, however, has continued to make use of his Sharifian descent:

> As you know, I am Commander of the Faithful. I received this title when I was born, without having asked or desired for. It means that I am a descendant of the Prophet. (. . .) This title imposes much humility and at the same time certain responsibilites (cited in Burgat 1995: 185).

All the same the interconnected developments of the spread of state education and growing access to international media have introduced religious discourses from elsewhere that threaten the state as monopolist of the means of orientation. Reflections of this nationwide process at the local level can be seen in the Ktawa Oasis.

In the curriculum of the religious education at school and university, the belief in local saints is portrayed as 'traditional', I was told. In the oasis, youngsters and migrants, including Shurfa, explained to me that visits to the shrine are a form of superstition. Those who strive for a 'modern' Morocco, with Europe as main example, as well as adherents of what we may call fundamentalist views, are opposed to the belief in saintly *baraka*. They argue that the ageing Shurfa do not understand the Koran, while their followers are said to create a mirror-image of God (*širk*) and follow a polytheistic creed. In the village, a visible expression of the religious debate is the discussion on the legitimate way to perform the prayer that is said five times a day. In the standing position, what should be done with the hands, along the body or crossed over the chest? Younger people, informed by practices introduced in the northern towns, opted for the latter position, arguing that this is the original position intended by the Prophet though only recently introduced in Morocco; the elderly men stuck to the first option, the one they learned as a child. Thus, of the public prayers I witnessed, the prayer was not performed by all men in the same fashion. Similar confrontations return in the celebration of circumcision—is a visit to the shrine an essential part of the ritual?—and marriage.

With respect to the profanation of education, mention was made of the disappearance of the Koran school in the village because of a lack of willingness of parents and teachers to invest time and money in it. As part of the national schools program set up after independence, a public primary school has been built in the village for the children of Aduafil and nearby villages. Young villagers, also Sharifian, make a distinction between the interpretation of texts as taught at this public school and recitation without understanding at the ancient Koran school (cf. Eickelman 1992). The Shurfa of the village do maintain something of their didactic role as two of the teachers at the primary school are from the village.

Profanation in daily life in the oasis village can most clearly be seen in the discussion on the use of honorifics to address the Shurfa. In Moroccan society, Shurfa are addressed with the honorific *mulay* ('my lord') or, in specific cases, *sidi* ('sir', also *si*) and Sharifat with *lalla*. When you approach a person you do not know, for example in a shop or in the street, you use the phrase 'Sidi Muhammad'. Since Muhammad is the only name for which it is inappropriate to use *mulay*, addressing a stranger with Sidi Muhammad avoids the impoliteness of not addressing a Sharif in the correct manner and giving inappropriate honours to a non-Sharif.

In the village, people are very careful about the use of honorifics. When I referred to my neighbour as *Sidi* Omar instead of *Mulay* Omar, a Drawi pointed this out immediately as impolite. Similarly, as an incident from the first weeks of my fieldwork illustrates, an improper use of the term is very much disliked. In those first weeks I tried to learn all the names of the villagers I met. During the daily meeting in front of one of the three village shops, a young Sharif helped me by naming all those present. 'Mulay Habib, Mulay Ali, Mulay Aziz . . .'. When he had arrived at the last person, I jokingly added one more name, that of the only Drawi present: 'Mulay Abdelhadi'. This infuriated the Sharif: 'You mean Mulay . . .! Why do you call him *mulay*? Is he a Sharif?' He became even more infuriated when I dared to write down the abusive word he used (instead of Abdelhadi's name). Clearly I had touched upon a sensitive issue. Variables like age, wealth and reputation affect the public respect a person is awarded, yet it still is the permanent attribute of Sharifian or Drawi birth that requires at least a minimal differentiation in respect awarded (cf. Silverman 1966: 906). Nevertheless, also these small testimonies of difference in status are under fire from several directions. With some nostalgia, older Shurfa remembered how Drawa used to kiss their hands, just like children kiss the hand of their father out of respect. At present, young and old people jokingly kiss the outstretched hand of the oldest and somewhat demented Sharif in the village. They say that otherwise he would get angry for the lack of deference toward him. Even so, I noticed on several occasions how older Shurfa with a prominent reputation were kissed by Drawa with a serious intention, although this was denied by villagers. This enduring act of awarded respect applied especially to the head of the village.

The same process of erosion of respectful behaviour toward Shurfa that is indicated by the reduction in greeting practice seems to be acting on the honorific titles. It is in fact a simple and direct way to contest the status of Shurfa. Already in 1955 captain Moureau observed how parents of young revolting Haratin 'taught them to say sidi and lalla to men and women of the white race'. Only by fleeing to Casablanca these youngsters could get away from this obligation (Moureau 1955: 8). The opposition of Drawa is indirectly shown by way of a joke related by a Sharif.

> A Sharif and a Drawi are having a quarrel. At one point, the Drawi announces to the Sharif that practices expressing differences among human beings have to be abolished: 'Everybody is equal, so from this day on everybody has to be addressed with the honorific mulay'. So the Drawi goes home, where he tells his relatives about his decision, and they agree. The next morning his young son wakes up and asks his mother: 'Mulay mama, where is Mulay papa?' His mother replies: 'Mulay son, Mulay papa has put the Mulay baskets on the Mulay donkey, filled them with the Mulay manure, and went to the Mulay field'.

As the joke refers to the claims of Drawa to a fair treatment, the commentary implied in the joke is obvious. The Drawi's ideal of equality is based on his structural inability to differentiate between humans and animals and between different categories of humans (of age and gender). Just referring to the pun was sufficient to make

Shurfa laugh again over Drawa being portrayed as donkeys (*Mulay donkey*). In this sense the joke also touches on a fundamental characteristic of the set of cultural ideals, namely the ability to recognize differences and act according to them. The joke states that an attack upon the use of honorifics is in fact one upon shared cultural ideals. Part of the cultural ideals is the required stance to distance yourself from those people to be respected. One way to express the respected distance is the use of honorifics; not using the honorifics desacralises the Shurfa. The following case exemplifies the denial of the use of honorifics as an everyday form of resistance (cf. Scott 1990: 196).

The Drawi Ibrahim, the second son of Hammed Hazzabin, dislikes the use of *mulay*. When I met him for the first time in a noisy neighbourhood café in a quarter of Casablanca, we were talking about his family when I mentioned the words 'Sharif' and 'Drawi'. After a short silence, Ibrahim corrected me. He explained that the words Sharif and Drawi carried no meaning whatsoever to him. There were just human beings, equal before God.

Ibrahim no longer lived in his natal village. He had left it as a teenager when Hammed sent him to his oldest brother Ali in Casablanca. His brother's sons had all married and left Casablanca to find a job somewhere else. So Ibrahim came to *Casa* to complement the household of his uncle and eventually marry his uncle's (father's brother) daughter. The marriage took place during my stay. Ibrahim had turned into a real *Beidawi*, an inhabitant of *Dar al-Beida* (Casablanca), who detests the difficult, burdensome oasis life. He only returned 'home' to visit his parents, but during the entire period of fieldwork he did not come once. His marriage took place in Casablanca, without the extensive and expensive collective dinners that are obligatory in the village. Although he almost never visits the village, Ibrahim regularly sees Aduafilis who visit relatives or friends in Casablanca. Ali's one-level apartment is situated in one of the vast neighbourhoods on the confines of Casablanca. The large date market indicates that he is not the only migrant from the south to have found a home in this part of town. In this metropolis of officially four million inhabitants, people from the Dra seem to have created their own village with their own bus company (once a day to the Dra), public shower and meeting point. Every Sunday, Aduafilis meet at a square only twenty meters away from Ali's home.

Mulay Mustafa is one of the Shurfa born in the village, but now living in the same neighbourhood. He is related to the Sharifa who owns the land and date palms that Ibrahim's father Hammed share-crops. Her house near Ali's house was part of the quarrel between Mustafa and Ibrahim, because both wanted and were entitled to live in it. There was also a more long-standing issue that bothered them. Their quarrel took place in the public neighbourhood shower. One day Ibrahim met some friends there, with whom he was talking when Mulay Mustafa came in. Of course they shook hands, Mustafa greeted everybody present, including Ibrahim. Ibrahim refused to use the honorific *mulay* in addressing Mustafa. Mulay Mustafa asked for an explanation for this, which triggered off their quarrel. Ibrahim's explanation of his behaviour was simple: 'Did one say *mulay* to the Prophet Muhammad or to Aisha? Or does one say *mulay* to the king [although he is a Sharif as well, RE]?' As already stated, in his view there were just human beings, all equal before God. It is impossible to pay respect to people, just because they are born as members of a certain family. Only through his deeds can a person earn respect, but then again, a human does not know the hidden life of his fellow humans: Who knows about the secret behaviour of a Sharif? For this reason, only God is able to judge human beings.

Mulay Mustafa was interested in the same issues as Ibrahim. He acknowledged that it was necessary to reflect upon some aspects of the Islamic faith as practised in the valley. But he suggested that those fundamentalists (like Ibrahim) who argue in favour of practices regarding dress, table manners, praying, et cetera of the Prophet or his companions should instead follow the example of members of 'the House of the Prophet', i.e., the Shurfa. The present-day Shurfa are the living representatives of the Prophet. It is furthermore explicitly stated in the Koran that one should express respect for 'the House of the Prophet'. It was this reference to the Koran which made Ibrahim cry out that one never knows about the secret life of another person and therefore might express respect toward a person inappropriately. Of course Mulay Mustafa knew all this. From my conversations with him, it became clear he struggled with the acceptance of social equality versus the separate status of the Shurfa: 'O.K. people are equal before God and in heaven, but on earth "we" Shurfa are different. Moreover, we are the "nephews" of King Hassan II'.

The dispute between Ibrahim and Mustafa demonstrates that the small acts of paying respect are a sensitive issue. The Shurfa have lost their monopoly on the transmission of the Islamic and cultural discourse and now find competing 'brokers' beside them. A second case of the problematic use of Sharifian honorifics presented by Rabinow (1975) exemplifies this process. In 1967 a small revolt took place against the Shurfa of Sidi Lahcen Lyussi in the Middle Atlas Mountains. Young teachers and students, working outside the village but returning to the village during the summer, secretly arranged a meeting to discuss and adopt a proposal to abolish the honorific *sidi*: 'The children of the men present were to deny the recognition of the "specialness" of the wlad siyyed [sons of the saint, RE] by refusing to call them "sidi". Further, they were not even to play with the children of the wlad siyyed' (Rabinow 1975: 86–87). The revolt failed because of the resistance of their parents and the threat of a state official. In Rabinow's description, an articulation of polarities can be found that appears in the oasis as well: Urban youngsters revolt against the old rural 'traditions', as they call it. The Shurfa, as the specialists of knowledge and orientation, stand against the new teachers and students. In addition in Rabinow's report the government official opposes the local population. A crucial opposition is that between literate students and teachers versus illiterate and traditionally literate (that is, focused on memorization) parents and the elderly in general. Both sides in the conflict seem to agree on the importance of a proper use of names and honorifics, but they disagree on whether Shurfa are entitled to the respect that is implied in the use of honorifics.

Gellner has criticised Rabinow for paying insufficient attention to the national and international context of the 'village-pump battle' (1981: 209). Perhaps such an approach could tell us whether the educated organizers of the secret meeting copied their demands from the most important historical example, namely the decision of the French revolutionary constitutional assembly to abolish all hereditary, aristocratic titles (June 19, 1790). In fact, the members of this historical meeting considered all 'the insignia of social superiority' incompatible with the ideal of fraternal brotherhood: 'Henceforth no citizen was to bear a name that signified his domination or possession of a *place*. His sole inherited badge of identity was to be the family name of his father' (Schama 1989: 478). Probably indirectly and unconsciously—by reading the books of internationally known authors—the young students and teachers were influenced by European texts. Tozy (1990: 97) wrote of the Islamists' texts in Morocco that

instead of references to religious doctrinary texts '. . . one can sense
the effort to utilise logical reasoning and the frequent invocation of
concepts like equilibrium, human nature, liberty, et cetera'.[20]

To make sense of the events in the public shower of Casablanca
(the quarrel of Ibrahim and Mustafa) and the village on which
Rabinow reports, we have to broaden our perspective. At least Mulay
Mustafa learned of the event that it is hard to be recognized as a
saint in the city. Ibrahim knew him to be a Sharif, but other people might not. From the point of view of Mustafa, Ibrahim's refusal
did hurt because his friends might not know that he is in fact a
Sharif. Shurfa had tried to solve this problem by paying civil servants to have them print *mulay* in front of their first name on the
ID. Mulay Mustafa also kept a copy of a declaration of the Sharifian
status of the Aduafilis by the former Sultan Muhammad V in his
wallet. He was not the only one to print *mulay* on his ID for urban
occasions. The local teacher had done it for himself and his oldest
son, but by the time his youngest son was born, measures had been
taken by the state to stop the practice. The same practice had existed
with regard to the honorific for someone who has made the pilgrimage to Mekka. Locally, these pilgrims are named hajj or hajja
(fem.), sometimes as a substitute for their personal names. Some people use the honorific as part of their name, printing it on their shop
window, while sons inherit the title from their parents (for example,
someone naming himself Ali hajj Mustafa). In 1985 a law was passed
that forbade civil servants to accept the use of an honorific (*mulay*,
lalla, hajj, *fqīh*) placed before a first name (Agnouche 1992: 282).
The objective of this measure was to accomplish social and religious
equality, while exempting the king, as supreme Sharif at the apex
of the religious hierarchy.

Contesting the importance of Sharifian descent as a determinant
of one's identity is nothing new; 'since the very earliest period of
Islam a tension [exists] between the veneration of these honored descendants of the Prophet and the belief in the equality of all Muslims
as articulated in the famous Quranic verse [49: 13]: "The most right-
eous among you is the most honored before God"' (Munson, Jr.

---

[20] Equally striking is Munson's remark that Morocco's best-known fundamentalist Yasin 'speaks of the "dependence" of secular Moroccan intellectuals on Western
thought, while his choice of words reflects his own dependence on Western dependency theory' (Munson, Jr. 1993: 170).

1993: 11).[21] This verse figures as counterpoint to the Koranic verse
33: 33 that can be read as a legitimation of the privileged position
of the descendants of the Prophet; it is indeed this verse to which
Mulay Mustafa referred when he demanded respect from Ibrahim.
The verse speaks of the privileged status of those who belong to 'the
household of the Prophet', 'for God desireth only to remove from
you the abomination of vanity, since ye are the household of the
Prophet, and to purify you by a perfect purification'. One crucial
problem in the interpretation has been to decide if the prescription includes only contemporary members of the Prophet's family
or also his descendants (cf. Agnouche 1992: 276). More general,
commentators disagreed as to whether social equality is an ideal to
pursue on earth or rather something attainable only in the afterlife
(Marlow 1997: 97).

Criticism of the saint's cult can already be found in the 9th century (idem, 84). Writing on Morocco, Berque (1982: 232–233) even
suggested complementing Lévi-Provençal's *Les historiens des Chorfa* (1922)
with a repertory on *Les opposants des Chorfa*. Yet, according to Munson,
fundamental criticism of the saint's cult and 'outright condemnation'
only started in the early 20th century in connection with the growth
of the Salafi religious reform movement. Originating in 19th-century
Egypt, this movement aimed to follow *as-aslāf*, the ancestors, and
thus to return to the original prescriptions of the faith to purify
Islamic law from post-Koranic, allegorical interpretations. Adherents
opted for a scripturalist, rationalist, 'schoolmaster's Islam' (Geertz
1971: 71), in a later phase of the movement objecting mostly against
'hereditary maraboutism' and the 'sherifian principle'. Moroccan religious scholars and intellectuals did so by founding Islamic schools
throughout the country (Abun-Nasr 1987: 383). Sultan Muhammad
V, father of King Hassan II, shared the Salafi ideas when these
became integrated in a nationalist discourse. At the end of the French
Protectorate, Montagne (1953: 217) signalled 'the struggle of the
palace against the brotherhoods and the saints . . .'. As early as 1949
a law was proclaimed which made it obligatory to hand over a notar-
ial act to claim right on a Sharifian, in particular *ʿAlawī*, surname

---

[21] The full text of the verse in the English edition I have consulted is as follows:
*O people, we have created you from a male and a female and we have made you into confed-
eracies and tribes so that you may come to know one another. The noblest among you in the eyes
of God is the most pious, for God is omniscient and well-informed* (Koran 49: 13; translation Sale).

and honorific (Chafi 1989: 8). It was, however, after independence, that Sharifianism became a major point of discussion at the level of the state.[22] The Sharifian privileges seemed to be doomed to oblivion, when King Hassan II successfully blocked possible dynastic ambitions of Sharifian groups of more than local importance. In reaction, the Shurfa established voluntary associations to promote their interests in the national state (Agnouche 1992: 280).

It remains to be said that downright rejection of Sharifianism is hard to find, and an ambiguous attitude characterizes even the severest critics. Thus, the saint's cult and Sharifianism were never repudiated by all Salafi adherents. Some of them even took great pride in their own Sharifian descent. Moreover, socio-political criticism of the state has often been translated into a dispute *between* Sharifian lineages, i.e., *Idrissī* criticism of the *'Alawī* state (idem, 279). The restructuring of the religious sphere by the Moroccan state after independence involved the absorption of competitive religious forces and the creation of a new, unified religious hierarchy, with the king as Sharif and Commander of the Faithful on top (Tozy 1987). Part of this development has been the establishment of a new council of religious leaders, with a Sharif from the Dra Valley (Naciri lodge in Tamgrout) appointed as head of the council.

A new impetus to the opposition against the dominant social and cultural order developed in the 1970s under the cloak of *Islamist* or 'fundamentalist' ideas. Here profanation took place by locating sacredness outside the domain of Shurfa.

First names and fundamentalism

> In the towns extremist parties give Haratin the illusion to be part of the avant-garde of a novel ideology, symbol of a profound evolution (Moureau 1955: 15).

---

[22] Compare the following note on the former People's Democratic Republic of Yemen in 1959: In public people show respect for the descendants of the Prophet. In private they loathe them: ' "We kiss their hands now (. . .) but just wait till tomorrow". [The speaker] was a Nasserist, a word that to the British and sherifian authorities meant subversion, communism . . .' (Gilsenan 1982: 9–10). In the former Yemen Arab Republic the revolution of 1962 brought a new government to power: 'On assuming power, the republican government (. . .) declared the abolition of social divisions based on hereditary and religious denomination' (Vom Bruck 1998: 153). Main target was the ruling élite of descendants of the Prophet (*sāda*). More recently, Islamists have rallied against the persistence of social distinctions. Or as one tribesman said: 'We want the *sāda* out of our minds' (idem, 163).

Ibrahim acted not only against the use of honorifics, but also against his personal name. Ibrahim's parents had named him Fatih, but he had recently changed it to Ibrahim. To understand the significance of this step, one should realize that the domain of personal naming patterns forms a significant system of classification that determines the social identity of the Drawa. As a whole it refers to other domains of naming systems and ways of addressing individual human beings, such as family names and honorifics (Geertz 1973: 360–411). In addition, it refers to symbol systems outside the immediate domain of naming patterns. In the oasis, the meaningful aspect of a personal name is recognized and worked upon. The naming of a newborn child is part of an elaborate family ritual on the seventh day after birth. Family members come together to choose a name, or draw branches, each connected to one favoured name. Although in this way sometimes chance determines the name of a newborn child, there are certain discernible patterns in name-giving. One such regularity is the naming of a first male child after the Prophet. This practice explains the high frequency of Muhammads in Moroccan name lists (H. Geertz 1979: 342). Originally, Hammed Hazzabin was also named Muhammad. Villagers nevertheless always call him by his usual name Hammed. When I asked a Sharif why they did so, he answered bluntly without further explanation: 'Because he's a Drawi', for whom, I add, a sacred name would be misplaced. Another distortion of the original name Muhammad for Drawa is Mumid (as Hammed's brother-in-law is named).

In Moroccan society personal names reveal one's Islamic identity. Names are chosen from a vast but fixed repertoire that consists of names from the Koran or from the early history of Islam. An important corpus consists of the list of the 99 names of God that describe Him in all His dimensions (cf. Daniel 1988). The Prophet's name carries an exceptional symbolic meaning in Moroccan society. It is the ultimate Islamic name, bringing blessings and respect to its bearer. It is only to be pronounced by putting the honorific *sidi* in front of it. While the names in the village have been restricted to a few of these 'Islamic names', nowadays Egyptian soaps offer villagers the opportunity to extend the repertoire. Innovating minds thus select their children's names from radio and television. When Abdelmzid, one of the sons of Hammed Hazzabin, and his wife, a daughter of Najem and Mina, produced their first child, they named her Khaltum, which at the time was an unusual name in the oasis. However, the local schoolteacher had already named his daughter Khaltum. 'Then in the early days', one of the Hazzabins told me, 'he would have asked to pick another name. They don't like it when our daughter carries the same name as his daughter'. Indeed, names of male Shurfa and Drawa do not correspond: Drawa are named Salem (versus Abdessalam), Redouan, Salah, or Sadiq. When a Drawi birth name does correspond with a Sharifian name, it is moulded into one that differs considerably, or vice versa. Thus, although certain names are restricted to Drawa, it is the binary opposition within the village that really matters.

Fatih's name-change was made possible through his father's negligence. Hammed never registered his first son. Only when his fourth son was born, did Hammed register a son named Fatih. In the village, however, this fourth son was called Abdellatif. Later on, the first son and *real* Fatih changed his name into Ibrahim. Ibrahim did so because he considered Fatih to be a black name, only carried by slaves and Haratin. The name-change, by which he laid aside his Drawi identity, then can be seen as a rite of passage,—significantly taking place in Casablanca—which emphasizes his personal conquest of mind over matter.

Relating his version of the quarrel, Mulay Mustafa told me that, because he was aware of the importance Fatih attached to being addressed with his new name, he did in fact say Ibrahim to him. 'Why then would not Ibrahim address me the correct way?' Ibrahim's objections to the use of honorifics and his 'rebirth' can be explained by his interest in the ideas of several Moroccan and foreign Islamic fundamentalists. In Rabat he had been to a meeting with Abdessalam Yasin, Morocco's best-known *Islamist*, and at his home I was shown a video of an election meeting of the Algerian Islamic Salvation Front (FIS). In his objection to the use of the Sharifian honorific, Fatih alias Ibrahim did not protest against articles of the Islamic faith as such, but against specific interpretations of these articles. He furthermore argued against practices and rules (*qawānīn*) that keep the differences alive and suggested the Shariah should be superior to these local laws. In the village his nephew Khalifa had followed the same path. Both Drawa had grown a beard, the international symbol of *Islamist* adherence *par excellence*. *Islamists* who wear a beard just like in the days of the Prophet do this at the cost of the authority of older men. Thus, when referring to an older man (*šibanī*), one lenghtens the 'a' while striking vertically with one's hand along the chin (to suggest a long beard), *šibaaanī*. The fundamentalists are collectively

known as 'the beards'. In the oasis, a man told me that because the
Moroccan authorities dislike the *Islamists*, they once publicly shaved
the beard of a young fundamentalist by force—and without soap,
he added (not unlike the public plucking of beards in colonial times,
a practice preceding the Protectorate period; cf. Hammoudi 1997:
50, 131). Both Khalifa and Ibrahim are not afraid to contest well-
accepted divisions of ethnicity and age, disputing 'traditional ways'
of religious expression and instead putting themselves forward as the
ideal model to follow. The abandonment of Ibrahim's previous Hartani
identity through his name-change and his refusal to accept the status differential of Shurfa through the use of honorifics are thus interconnected.

Nevertheless, the Sharif Mustafa did seem to have a point when
he said that 'going back' to the origins of Islam should include respect
for the Shurfa. Ibrahim used *Islamist* ideas to argue for a radical
change in the direction of social equality; Mustafa pleaded for the
conservation of respect toward the Shurfa. Most remarkable is that,
as we saw in the previous section, Najem presents the hierarchical
village configuration and the subordinate status of Drawa as legitimate and honourable because it reflects the relationship between the
Prophet and his companions, while the plea for social equality of
his nephew Ibrahim hinges equally on a 'return' to prophetic times.

All these opposing interpretations of belief in the need to return
'back to basics' become even more complicated when we return to
the ideas of Ibrahim's inspiration. Abdessalam Yasin is considered
Morocco's most radical fundamentalist, arguing for a total religious
and political revolution. A public letter named '*Islam or the Deluge*',
sent to King Hassan II in 1974, is considered to be one of the most
radical critiques on a religious leader and head of the Moroccan
state ever. The letter asks for a response from the king and states:

> Whatever may be the response, my dear nephew of the Prophet, you
> cannot forbid the Word of Truth and Justice that I proclaim (cited in
> Burgat 1995: 183).

By referring to the king as nephew of the Prophet, Yasin seems to
emphasize his own Sharifian status as much as his critical prede-
cessors. In an interview conducted by Munson, Yasin was asked
about 'how he reconciled his references to Sharifian descent in his
epistle with the egalitarianism he usually stresses'. Yasin answered
that he had done so only for pragmatic reasons. Munson (1993: 168)

comments that 'one gets the sense that Yasin takes great pride in his (alleged) sharifian ancestry, as do many other educated Moroccans who claim to scoff at the traditional veneration of the descendants of the Prophet'. The veneration of saints thus is repudiated by educated Moroccans, who relegate it to '(little) traditions', but membership of 'the House of the Prophet' continues to be a source of pride and respect. As far as grievances of Sharifian status are concerned, Drawa such as Ibrahim and Khalifa can thus only find partial consolation in *Islamism*.

Conclusions

Awareness of the existence and force of an ideology of hierarchy and subordination to the supreme status of Shurfa in Moroccan society is of crucial importance for an understanding of the coexistence of Shurfa and Drawa in the village, as well as for an understanding of alternative viewpoints. Central is the 'spiritual subordination' of laymen to the sacred Shurfa which is a reflection of the hierarchical relationship between father and son. The numinous force *baraka* is a superior currency that is transmitted in a submissive relationship between saint and servant (cf. Jamous 1992: 180; Bakker 1993: 211–213). In Hammoudi's *Master and Disciple* (1997), this juxtaposition of exchange and spiritual subordination has been raised from the local to the national level, serving as one of the 'cultural foundations' of the Moroccan authoritarian political system. The result is an argument that is strikingly similar to the one presented here. Hammoudi notes that 'closeness, service, and gift exchange constitute the vehicles which motivate the interactions within and around the royal palace' (1997: 81) as well as at the level of notables whereby '[m]any take advantage of their sharifian or maraboutic descent' (idem, 39–40). This national service system includes friendship, alliance, but above all, subordination and feminization on the part of the servants. As far as this latter dimension is concerned, gender classification indeed informs the status inequality between Shurfa and Drawa. Lack of autonomy and servility, emphasis on bodily labour and instinctive behaviour (as the muezzin was accused of) all influence the gender identity of Drawa. In the following chapter this theme will be taken up in an examination of the essential contributions of Drawa as mediators in the oasis community.

CHAPTER SIX

CIVILIZED CONDUCT
SOCIAL MEDIATION IN THE VILLAGE

> The servant of God must not overstep borders (Moroccan proverb; Westermarck 1930: 252).

Cultural ideals inform humans about what correct behaviour entails and dispose them to act accordingly. These ideals find expression partly in what we usually call the rules of etiquette, which deal with the correct ways to establish and maintain contact between humans. Via 'social restraint to self-restraint' (Elias 1997 ii: 324) and ultimately self-control later in life, humans are expected to learn, follow and internalize the cultural ideals of a particular society. The demands, however, are not necessarily identical for all men. Where hierarchy is accepted as the basis of society, variations are likely to exist for the different status groups. A high standard of compliance with the rules of civilized conduct is then taken as the differentiating marker and proof of moral superiority of the élite. Moreover, if there is a strong recognition that certain deeds are only permissible behind the scenes of everyday life or undertaken by way of circumspect rapprochements, and members of certain categories of people are not supposed to come into contact with one another in a direct fashion, then people are necessary who are prepared to encroach on the rules. This is the niche where mediators as 'professional norm breakers' can be successful, usually having to accept the reproach of being uncivilized. This chapter examines how Drawa act as social mediators and servants between the social categories of gender and age. How does the fulfillment of their mediating activities position Drawa in the field of ideas and practices of civilized conduct (*adab*)? Moreover, how do they forge a positive identity out of the contrasting demands of work and prevalent cultural ideals?

Community tasks

The tasks that Drawa perform in the village position them outside of village territory, possibly at night, and into contact with outsiders. A further general characteristic is that these tasks bring them into the private domains of family and home. Tasks fulfilled by Drawa include that of field-guard, porter of the *qsar*, 'invitor', village crier, marriage broker and matchmaker, doorman at communal dinners, messenger of the village council and unofficial messenger who informs people in a more confidential way than the village crier in cases of birth or death,[1] organizer of collective work on the irrigation ditches and controller of the division of water rights, and informal mediator. Finally, there are a number of tasks for women such as midwifery, application of specialized knowledge in matters of virginity and sexuality, and assistance at marriage. All these tasks are executed by Drawa. The range of tasks fits nicely with the local school teacher's portrayal of the Drawa as people working 'in service of the community'. Some tasks are exclusively performed by members of one family, the Hazzabins, others are done as part of the duties of Drawi clients toward their Sharifian patrons. Here, Drawa appear to be like ritual specialists at the service of one or a restricted number of Sharifian families. In the village, the fulfillment of these tasks is part of the regular exchange of goods and services between Shurfa and Drawa.

The exclusive fulfillment of these tasks by Drawa is not coincidental but typical for the division of labour in the valley. Moreover, a similar division of labour can be found in the Tunisian oases with the social marginals called *Šwašīn* taking care of, in the words of Bédoucha, 'tasks that are essential to life in the village': They are responsible for water rights, public announcements and private messages, and the division of meat (1984: 96; 1987: 255). The social marginal as jack-of-all-trades seems to be a general figure in North African rural communities. Pâques (1964: 33) speaks of 'that alien mediating figure' in the Libyan oasis society who acts as policeman, messenger, butcher, circumciser, and executor of other activities that are 'contemptible in the eyes of everbody'. People are dependent on

---

[1] Like the proverb goes: 'A crier, and his donkey is gone way from him' (Westermarck 1930: 299). A crier is only to be called at occasions that involve all villagers. Otherwise, a messenger informs people individually.

these kind of 'social marginals' for the fulfillment of many services that are shunned by the majority. Why do these tasks constitute such an appropriate niche for Drawa and Šwašīn alike? To answer this question, I shall first consider the similarities between the various tasks.

Distribution

Some of the tasks involving the distribution of goods and services within the village are directed toward a smooth flow of exchanges between Sharifian families with respect to marriage partners, food and signs of respect (by way of invitations). In particular, Drawa take care of the division of irrigation water, the distribution of state flour that is sold below market prices, and the assignment of work related to the maintenance of the irrigation system. Surface water is the most important source of irrigation for the fields and date palms. Since the early 1970s, decisions regarding the date and duration of the flow of water through the canals are made in the provincial capital. Once the water arrives in the village, an internal ratio of distribution becomes operative. It is up to Hammed Hazzabin in his function as irrigation overseer (ʿālim) to decide where to start in the distribution cycle and where to end. This implies he has to know where the irrigation cycle ended the last time. Additionally, Hammed is one of the few persons in the village who knows the ratio of distribution among the separate households by heart.

Distribution is also at the centre of a second more or less informal task. A few times a year villagers have the possibility to buy a sack of flour from the state for a substantially lower price than the market value. When the village has been allocated ten sacks of flour, not every family will be able to share in the distribution. A family consisting of five persons has a right to 25 kilos, a family of ten may claim 50 kilos (that is, one sack). It is up to Hammed Hazzabin to decide whose turn it is to share in the distribution this time, to collect the money to buy the sacks in the oasis centre (also done by another Drawi from the village), and eventually to bring families together who may share one sack. Seldom does one of the phases pass without problems. Regularly, there are quarrels over the collected money, the quality of the flour and supposed illegalities in the distribution of the sacks among villagers. The work of Hammed here is not unlike that of the *kabbar* (informer-negotiator), 'a black man who divides (...) the grain on the market' (Pâques 1991: 167). As slaughterer and butcher of the sanctuary, Hammed distributes meat among village households. As sharecropper he divides the harvest among the rightful shareholders (owner of the land, tenant, field-guard, day labourers) at the end of every harvest day.[2]

A comparable task concerns the maintenance of the irrigation canals. This may be an inter-village canal, in which case Hammed is called upon by the local irrigation overseer to 'invite' an agreed-upon number of villagers to execute the reparations. When it concerns an internal ditch, villagers have to agree among themselves whether the reparations are the duty of all villagers or only of those families who own plots next to the canal. This may lead to fierce discussions. For example, a villager might oppose the decision that only a restricted number of villagers has been invited to repair an irrigation ditch (because only they own land irrigated by the ditch), with the argument that as the collective herd grazes on one of the plots every day, all the men in the village should aid in the reparations. Although it is not always clear whether Hammed decides upon these matters alone, as messenger of the village council he always is at the centre of these kind of decision-making processes, that is, village quarrels.

Inside knowledge

The fulfillment of community tasks demands confidential knowledge concerning the people in the village as well as the readiness to correct people and address them in a direct fashion, for example, at home. In his function as messenger of the village council, Hammed collects the fines imposed upon villagers for violation of village rules, such as stealing dates or letting your donkey walk around on someone's land. The people whom Hammed contacts must accept him as collector, trust him when they confide in him, and abstain from being offended by him personally. For both parties, Hammed is best seen as 'service specialist' faced, in Goffman's terms, with the secrets of public performances that take place 'back-stage'. Discretion is a crucial attribute of the service specialist (Goffman 1959: 153–54).

---

[2] Pâques (1991: 46) argues that the (dark-skinned) blacksmith, sacrificer and distributor are symbolically linked in the cosmology of the *Gnawa*. The blacksmith constructs the metal measure box for the ritual gifts of Ramadan as well as the plough needed for the cultivation of the grain that is distributed.

This dimension of the community tasks can be inferred from the following detailed description of the task of field-guard.

Now and then, Hammed has acted as date palm field-guard ($r\bar{a}\mathfrak{i}$) during the harvest period, just as his father had done before him. Some years ago Hammed resigned from the function. In 1993, he told me that it is not a good job, while expressing his discontent at being reminded of his past as a guard. At the time there were two members of the Ait 'Atta Confederacy appointed as field-guards. Only one year later Hammed was again called upon by the village council to act as guard. A description of the work of the two Berber field-guards below, taken from my notes, reveals the family resemblances between the already mentioned tasks of Hammed and the $r\bar{a}\mathfrak{i}$ guardianship.

In the beginning of August, two families arrived in the village. Unlike other strangers who have visited the village during my stay, these visitors remained in the community for quite some time. The male heads of the two households were field-guards of the date palms. The village council who had assigned the guards granted them a field at the edge of the village territory to pitch their tents. From August until January they walked around the gardens to guard the villagers' palms. They questioned every stranger taking a promenade in the gardens, even asking for his ID. They paid attention to children, men and women from the village who acted suspiciously near palms that were not their own. They notified the village head of any thefts of dates.

Before 1956 the function of $r\bar{a}\mathfrak{i}$-s was filled by transhumant herdsmen who once a year made their camp in the oasis. At that time the protection of the Ait Isfulis against robbery by other herding groups was more or less imposed upon the sedentary population (Niclausse 1954; Azam 1946). With the arrival of the French administrative and military force, the task of the $r\bar{a}\mathfrak{i}$-s changed dramatically. Most importantly, the imposition of protection pacts upon the sedentary population weakened and eventually disappeared. The $r\bar{a}\mathfrak{i}$-s came to be hired, not so much for the protection of the palm groves against outside predators, as against the threat of thievery from inside the village. Thus, once the region was pacified, the $r\bar{a}\mathfrak{i}$-s turned into a kind of oasis field-guard. The threat of thievery from inside is recognized by most villagers. Men point to the children in the village who during the pre-harvest period have to gather the fallen dates. For them it is quite simple to increase the daily yield by climbing up the trees and picking more dates.

The contemporary Berber field-guards, belonging to the Ait 'Atta Confederacy, have an ambiguous status in the village. Villagers define them as outsiders, pointing to their striking appearance—facial traits and black turbans—and behaviour. Furthermore, the guards live in tents at the edge of the village territory. Villagers mock them because of their sometimes hesitant Arabic and scorn them because they smoke in public on the village square. At the same time, however, it is obvious the Aduafilis depend on the field-guards for the protection of their property, while the guards themselves can only fulfil their task with a profound knowledge of all village families. It is the juxtaposition of their outsiderhood and inside knowledge as well as their lack of 'proper conduct' that is at the basis of their function. The following conflict in the village illustrates this point.

In the middle of the harvest period, some villagers had seen some women from the village stealing dates. They did not want to inform the village head themselves and instead accused the field-guards of neglecting their duty. One man of the ancient village that is now incorporated into Aduafil was especially infuriated. He argued convincingly that as Aduafilis take care of the assignment of guards, it is also their responsibility to look after their functioning. According to the man it was only because the villagers of Aduafil do not trust one another that they are forced to hire outsiders to guard their property against their own fellow villagers. This, indeed, was a serious point. Until a few years ago, the village had relied on its own guards, and it was only recently that the council had turned again to members of the Ait 'Atta Confederacy for field-guards. After the death of Salem Hazzabin, his son Hammed and the phlebotomist of the village had been guard for some years. This did not turn out to be a success; villagers considered the guardianship of the phlebotomist too strict and that of Hammed too lenient. As one villager remarked: 'People agree that the guards are necessary, but at the same time they are used to the practice of "zigzag"; they are not familiar with someone who acts straight (that is, making no exceptions to the rules), like you do in Europe'. Thus, while people complained about the *dimuqrāṭiya* the phlebotomist tried to impose, they were afraid that Hammed's lenience would be to their disadvantage.

The difficult position of the present-day field-guards became clear when they were asked to explain their lack of attention at an informal gathering on the village square. First, they denied in public having seen anyone stealing dates. Later on, one man confessed that he had indeed seen some women in the gardens picking dates but unfortunately had not recognized them. Villagers advised him and his colleague to follow the women to the village next time and then ask someone to name the family they belonged to. The two men agreed. In private, however, the *rāʕ* confessed he had not only seen everything but also knew the women by their family name. The true reason for his fault, he continued, was that because they were female Shurfa, he was ashamed to speak to them. In a normal situation this would indeed have been highly inappropriate. However, for the field-guards it lies within the definition of their task to set this rule aside.[3]

'It is plain that the specialist whose work requires him to take a backstage view of other people's performances will be an embarrassment to them', wrote Goffman (1959: 156). Hammed's shame at being reminded of his task as field-guard had to do with this latter aspect. Unlike the other services mentioned in this chapter, that of the field-guards is rewarded with a substantial material gain (1/32 share of the harvest). Where execution of the guardianship leads to improper deeds, a material reward is inappropriate. In defining the tasks for the community as a favour or aid instead of as work for which one should be paid, their improper aspects are mitigated. Moreover, tasks performed by social marginals like Hammed are often directed at the durability of bonds between performer and recipient. Having to ask for a material reward would endanger the long-term bond that gains significance through regular gifts and services throughout the year. Nevertheless, as we have seen, the year after I had left the village, Hammed and another Berber field-guard from outside the oasis were asked to act as field-guards again. They had even raised their share to 1/25 of the harvest. The guardianship might be a difficult job for a villager to pursue, nevertheless it is a profitable 'inside job'.

Tasks in the private sphere

In addition to public distribution and the management of intimate knowledge, a third feature of the communal tasks is that they bring

---

[3] See the following article of the customary law of a nearby village: When a woman enters the garden, the *rāʕ* has to ask her to leave and, when she refuses, he has to take notice of this; he is, however, not allowed to slap her. She will in any case have to pay two reals (Niclausse 1954: annexe 8).

their executors, usually Drawa, into the houses of Sharifian families, or even into contact with female Shurfa. Mina, belonging to the Hazzabin family, is the midwife of Aduafil. She succeeded her husband's mother in this role. Her work as a midwife is restricted to the village, in contrast to her mother-in-law whose work covered nearby villages as well. Women give birth in their own house, or that of the husband's family. They stay there for seven days after the delivery. They then might go to their father's home until the 40th day, after which they return home. Mina usually takes care of the mother and child in the first week after the delivery. Her reward consists of the head and hide of the sheep that is sacrificed on the seventh day as part of the name-giving ritual. This ritual gift even took place when her own grandchild was born. Mina and her daughters also act as housekeepers in Sharifian homes in case of sickness.

Another task of Mina is that of matchmaker (*ḵāṭiba*). On request, she inquires after the possibility of a marriage between members of two families in the village. In this case her task is that of a messenger. Her role might be more substantial when she actually looks for a marriage partner outside of the village. Then, to avoid the shame of an open rejection, it is only when the two parties agree on a marriage that the parents get into direct contact. The matchmaker, as has been observed by Jamous (1981: 251–252; cf. H. Geertz 1979: 363–370; Bailey 1969: 170), acts as an interpreter, translating the covert allusions concerning preferred marriage partners and the amount of the brideprice, set by parents, into a concrete proposal. From the first cautious explorations until the final negotiations, the matchmaker or marriage broker acts on the edge of the family privacy, public knowledge and the honour of both families involved. Men gain honour or have to accept defeat according to the outcome of the negotiations. Not only the highest outcome counts. Villagers see to it that the couple is a respectable one, with its members of the same level (*mustawan*) and age. Thus, one man of whom it was said he had 'sold' his young daughter to the richest man in the village was scorned for this by all villagers. A family member of this man who had acted as second imam was no longer accepted because of the dishonourable deed of his family.

Finally, there are the tasks of the ushers (*wazīr* and *wazīra*). During the actual marriage ceremony, the usher is the assistant and aid of the groom in the week after the marriage. If the groom is like a king for the period of the wedding ceremonial, then the usher is like his minister. 'The *wazīr* moves and stands still with the groom', as someone put it. He lives in the house of the groom and takes care of all serving tasks, because the groom either is not allowed to leave the house or because he has been exempted from a number of tasks. The usher serves food, prepares tea, and boils water to wash. In return, he receives either the cotton cloth worn by the groom during the rituals or his *jallāba*. The bride has her own female usher. Starting a couple of days before the wedding night, she serves the bride. Jansen (1987: 137–138) noted how a 'good *wazīra* stands up for her ward; she will ask the groom to be careful; and she will help the bride, when necessary, with home remedies against the pain of defloration'. In the village, the female usher receives the black cloth (*gunʿa*) and sandals of the bride. As a rule, *wazīr* and *wazīra* are Drawa. Two of Hammed's sons and his daughter have already performed these tasks more than once. During my stay, Abdellatif was asked to act as *wazīr*. His father, however, did not want to let him go with the argument that his son was too old and would be ashamed. Mina, the midwife, has been *wazīra* many times, which is not unusual. In general, the *wazīra* is much older than the *wazīr*. Both *wazīr* and *wazīra* are allowed to enter the most intimate space of the house at the most delicate moments. This is why there should be no shame between the marrying couple and their ushers. They at least are aware of difficulties during the defloration of the bride and are supposed to help when necessary. The serving couple also acts when the man is unable to penetrate the bride, out of nervousness or because a rival has used a magic spell to make him impotent. In agreement with the *ʿārīfa*, 'an old [Drawi] woman' who checks the virginity and consequently defloration of the bride, the serving couple either might ask a Drawi *fqīh* from a nearby village 'to write something from the Koran' to help the young husband with his marital plight or perform an act that counteracts the magic spell. After the first week of the marriage, the family of the groom visits the family of the bride, accompanied by the *wazīr*. He carries the bag with almonds and other edible presents and hands it over to the mother of the bride.

Monopolization

The above mentioned tasks bring Drawa out into the streets, outside of the village, and sometimes into contact with strangers. One is reminded here of the tasks performed by Drawa when they migrate. In accordance with their tasks in the oasis villages, Drawa became milk- and water-carriers, street vendors, and coachmen on the streets of the northern towns. In the oasis, these kind of tasks are shunned by Shurfa, as they are shunned by the Berber-speaking inhabitants of the village nearby.[4] There, as well, these tasks are performed by Drawa. Likewise, the economic and social marginality of the executors whose work has to do with irrigation is more of a general feature in southern Morocco. While the function of inter-village irrigation overseer enjoys overall esteem, being fulfilled by landowners belonging to the social category of *Aḥrār*, the function of intra-village 'irrigation invitor' and guardian (*'ālim*) is in general performed by a Hartani who most often does not own any water rights or landed property and 'who is known for his uprightness and is accepted by all' (Hammoudi 1985: 46; Ouhajou n.d.: 99).

Simmel denoted objectivity as one of the central traits of 'the stranger' (1950: 402–408), whose existence was defined as the outcome of 'a particular structure composed of distance and nearness, indifference and involvement'. Since the stranger is by definition 'not radically committed to the unique ingredients and peculiar tendencies of the group', he 'approaches them with the specific attitude of "objectivity"' or rather neutrality. With regard to the Drawa, whose attribute of protracted strangeness I have dealt with in chapter three, these 'unique ingredients and peculiar tendencies' come down to their social and economic marginal status in the village community: They do not possess a substantial amount of water rights nor tracts of land. They are not part of the descent group on which the village *cum* sanctuary has been based, nor hold kinship or affinal ties with those who do, the Shurfa. In addition, because of their low status, they might be commanded by people from outside the village (e.g., the inter-village irrigation overseer who is a *Ḥurr*) and can deal with Shurfa of all ages without loss of respect. The juxtaposition of a marginal status with neutrality and intimate knowledge determines the eligibility of Drawa and constitutes their main source of power.

It seems that because of the similarity of tasks, Drawa are able to develop a monopoly on their fulfillment. The family that personifies

---

[4] The Berber-speaking field-guards in the present village are from outside the Ktawa Oasis.

the features of the Drawi as stranger in the most outstanding way, the Hazzabin family, has monopolized almost all of the central tasks in the village. For most villagers it is indisputable that Hammed Hazzabin and his family members function as the pivot on which village life hinges. He is the one person in the village who keeps account of village affairs. This important role of Hammed, and of his household, was inherited from his father Salem Hazzabin. Salem, even more than Hammed, was considered to be the overall dominating figure in the village. Some villagers compare him favourably with his son who, because of his stammer, is not always capable of bringing his message across. It obliged Hammed to turn over the functions of muezzin and of village crier (performed by another Drawi) to other villagers. Nonetheless, there were sufficient duties left to him. Hammed is still the unofficial messenger, the organizer of collective work and controller of the division of water rights, barber, slaughterer and butcher of the village. On request, he performs sacrifices for families and visitors to the village shrine. In addition, Hammed and his family members perform a number of tasks as part of major life crisis rituals in the village. The family has been able to keep tasks united in one hand and within the family over generations. Some tasks are inherited from father to son: Hammed has inherited the task of village barber from his father. His son Abdelhadi has already taken over some of Hammed's clients. This is not that difficult, as the barber only has to master one haircut, that of the older men in the village who prefer their heads to be bald. Likewise, the female tasks of midwife and matchmaker have met in the same person for more than one generation. The successful accumulation of these tasks in one family means that they have been able to profit from their anomalous status in the village. It furthermore signals the common features and enduring consequences for the reputation of the performers of these tasks. The tasks involve transgression of clearly demarcated social boundaries—'the usual barriers of prudery and seclusion' (Barth 1960: 123–24)—and involvement in the private spheres of family and home. The family resemblances between the tasks (cf. Blok 1981: 108) explain why they have become the responsibility of one man or woman. Fulfillment of the communal tasks bring its executors onto the streets and into the private spheres of the Sharifian homes. The tasks all involve the mediation between categories of people:

- between villagers and outsiders
- between village families
- between men and women
- between youngsters and elders

Execution of the tasks contributes to the ambivalent position of Drawa in the village: Proper fulfillment hinges on the combination of outsiderhood and intimacy. An executor should be trustworthy and neutral, yet willing to transgress social boundaries where others are not allowed to. Additionally, some of these tasks contain a serving component which emphasizes the subordinate status of Drawa. Thus, while Mina's performance of the tasks is related to her status as a woman without a man, being marginal with respect to the social norm of married life and consequently economically marginal and forced to work in the service of others (cf. Jansen 1987; see for bachelors as mediators, chapter three, note 22 and Armstrong 1967), her tasks are also related to the marginal status of Drawa in general.

To some extent, it might be said that in fulfilling their tasks, Drawa gain in power but lose in reputation. To make this point clear, I shall take a closer look at the complex of ideas of civilized conduct that informs and guides Shurfa and Drawa in their daily activities. With respect to the afore mentioned categories, a central theme is the maintenance of the boundaries between the public and private domain.

Honour and civilization

Adab, the *emic* term by which some of the cultural ideals can be summarized, constitutes the complement to the already discussed complex of ideas summarized in the concept *ḥaḍāra* (see chapter five). Where *ḥaḍāra* mainly refers to civilization in the English meaning of material and immaterial development, *adab* comes closer to a combination of the French *civilité*—external polite behaviour (etiquette)—and the German *Kultur*—an internal intellectual quality (cf. Elias 1997 i: 95–131). *Adab* is an individual virtue related to etiquette, ethics and education. It combines religious knowledge, intellectual refinement and propriety in daily life, translating cultural ideals into a prescribed mode of living. As such, it will be shown that living in agreement with the rules of *adab* attests to the social superiority of the Shurfa.

A straight course versus zigzag

The meaning of *adab* is indissolubly tied to an extensive complex of religious practices that has gained importance from the early history of Islam (cf. Hodgson 1974: 444–472) and extends beyond the boundaries of our singular Moroccan oasis community. In one tradition, *adab* refers to intellectual refinement and knowledge of literature and poetry, as well as the corpus itself. In a second tradition, *adab* became a crucial ingredient in Sufi doctrines. In this latter development, the deeds of the Prophet were taken as the ultimate model for the ideal way of behaviour, expressed in compendia on prescribed rules for dress, table manners, invitations, et cetera (Böwering 1984: 67). Common to all interpretations of *adab* is the synthesis of personal advancement and codes of behaviour. *Adab* alludes in particular to a process of learning to differentiate. *Adab*, then, is about the 'proper discrimination of correct order, behavior, and taste' (Metcalf 1984: 2). It is revealed by 'the respect or deference one properly formed and trained shows to those who deserve it' (idem, 3). Another keyword in the tradition of *adab* is poise. The ideal person is he who partakes in societal affairs with autonomy, deliberation, and patience. A vigorous performance is welcomed but more important is the avoidance of passions taking control over one's senses. In social life, poise also means independence, not being bound by others, and capable of making independent decisions. In early modern Arab history, knowing how to comply with the rules of *adab* has always distinguished the urban élite, consisting of civil servants and religious authorities, of urban commoners. Taken to the countryside, the Shurfa came to personify the urban *adab* standard.

In the village interpretation of *adab* the classic ideal returns. For villagers *adab* stands for civilized conduct or etiquette. They refer to it when discussing instructions in proper public conduct, for example, regarding rules on how to sit, drink and eat when invited for dinner. As part of their upbringing, children are supposed to learn the rules of *adab*. The implication of growing older is that one has to follow in a progressive fashion the Islamic articles of faith and complementary prescriptions of civilized behaviour in daily life. This involves learning to differentiate and to act along the social boundaries of gender and age, and to learn the difference between inside and outside, ours and theirs, in the conviction that this is the correct way to command and pay respect.

The recognition of separate spatial and temporal domains for human activities is expressed in the viewpoint that certain deeds are only permissible behind the scenes of everyday life and reserved for the evening and night: This refers to the expression of passionate behaviour and the indulgence in explicit physical activities or pleasures (smoking, dancing, singing, yelling). The centrality of the maintenance of the distinction between a public and private domain by way of appropriate behaviour is probably a cross-cultural dimension of cultural ideals.

Adab requires a person to have his passions or 'instinctive desires' (Dwyer 1978: 174) under control. According to villagers, human beings consist of a rational and a passionate part (*'aql* versus *nafs*). *'Aql*, reason, has been defined as 'adroitness or cleverness' and the 'knowledge of and capacity to manipulate the shared code of conduct called the *qa'ida*, "the way things are done"' (Eickelman 1976: 130). A man needs reason to know what is appropriate in social affairs. Once, a villager wore rumpled old clothes at the Great Feast, while at the same Islamic feast his brother was dressed in new festive clothes. Surprisingly, it was the latter whom was said to lack reason. This was because he showed happiness at the first Islamic feast after the death of their father. It was his brother who knew the appropriate way to express his emotions. The example shows that for a proper social functioning, men cannot act without either *'aql* or *nafs*. Although the rational part is valued more positively, both are necessary. Just as the coexistence of men and women may lead to collisions, villagers state that incidents caused by the contrast of reason and passion belong to the inevitable facts of life. Life consists of acting out this double-bind.

The ideal aim in life is to maintain a just equilibrium of reason and passion in one's behaviour. This can mean a dominance of the rational part over the passionate one. To some extent this is a natural process: Ageing involves increasing the importance of the rational part, although this is not attained without difficulties. Children act from their passions mostly, but remain innocent of their deeds because they lack reason. In contrast, adults are supposed to have reason, but may not use it, or use it in an absolute manner. Thus, for them it is more demanding to remain morally pure. Gender and descent also can make a difference in the stability of the desired equilibrium. My male informants consider that women find it more difficult to keep the two in balance as they have less reason than men and consequently are thought to fall prey to their passions more easily than men. Different standards for the various categories of people thus exist regarding compliance with the rules of civilized conduct.

In the village a virtuous performance, i.e., one that expresses reason and self-control, is embodied in the expression that humans should walk along a straight course with a clear goal (*ġaraḍ*) in mind. The opposite is symbolized by a zigzag road, shown by waving one's hand from left to right. The importance of a straight course for a *fqīh* was shown to me by a neighbour in the village who drew the following forked road in the sand in front of him (figure 9: A straight course):

'When a *fqīh* starts his career, he reads and studies a lot. Then he comes at this crossroad. He has to decide which road to take. The straight road is the right one. The left road is the road of evil. It is the devil's road (*al-ṭarīq dyal šaiṭān*), the forbidden one. It will bring him into contact with the ghosts (jinns). He will write amulets with bad intentions and consequences'.

A straight course is equally important for a muezzin. Thus, the present-day muezzin was reproached for not following a straight course in the proclamation of the hours for prayer. The heart of the reproach of zigzag was that he acted without a clear goal in mind. The same lack of goal was attributed to the inhabitants of the nearby village of Berber-speaking Ait Isful. They are said to follow a zigzag course when performing the traditional Berber wedding dance (*aḥidūs*) that mixes men and women and gives free rein to the release of their passions. Those who should be separated, men and women, are intermingled. It is significant then that among men the gesture of the zigzag is a symbol for women (in some regions the zigzag pattern is a common tatoo on female chins), and particularly hints at illicit sexual relations (Boughali 1987: 113). For a man being accused of zigzag behaviour is to be charged with a feminine feature and with an uncontrolled release of passions. Women are said to act less responsibly. One man showed this by taking a number of odd objects from the table and putting one on top of the other. Without him holding the objects, the tower would collapse immediately. He commented that this is the way women build. An idea rises up in their mind, and they act on it without thinking of the consequences. For example, out of compassion a woman might too easily agree on nursing a girlfriend's child without realizing the complications of the enduring milk kinship bond that grows out of this. Shurfa judged the Drawa in the same manner. Both women and Drawa are said to lack or fall short of ʿaql and foresight.[5]

The cultural ideals and rules of conduct are to some extent formulated in a religious vocabulary. One day, I was standing with a group of mainly Sharifian villagers when a young man named Khalifa passed us, making a sound as if he had broken wind. Immediately, the assembled men became angry and questioned his knowledge of adab. They did so especially because Khalifa, a Drawi, was a newly wed Islamic fundamentalist who himself often questioned the religious knowledge and piety of his Sharifian fellow villagers. One man said: 'You may wear a beard and say all day "God is great" but that doesn't mean a thing when you don't have any sense of adab'. Khalifa was reproached for the fact that on the one hand he acted like a pious man, rapping persons on the knuckles when they failed to visit the mosque, while on the other he returned to his former way of living, that is, making fun of people, scolding, fighting, smoking and drinking. Furthermore, since Khalifa was still in his twenties, villagers argued that he had set too high a goal for himself. The path he had set for himself was too strict and meant that he could not develop any further. It was the path of an older man who could not be seduced by playing card, smoking, drinking, laxness in prayer, and whose former deeds might be forgiven through a pilgrimage to Mecca. As a consequence, Khalifa distanced himself from his age group. That was another blameworthy deed.

---

[5] For contrasting female views on the ʿaql of men and women, see Dwyer (1978: 67, 152).

Villagers, in explaining the ins-and-outs of village life, regularly came up with the Koran as the ultimate source of authority. Women's lack of *ʿaql* and patience,[6] the interdiction for them to recite the Koran and to slaughter, and the rules of *adab* could all be sustained by the claim that it was written in the Koran. The central quality of the Koran as explanatory device corresponds with data on Marrakshi women, provided by Buitelaar (1993). Her informants frequently used the phrase 'it is written in the Koran' to legitimize or condemn certain deeds, though they were rarely able to specify the exact location, nor did they differentiate between the Koran and the Hadiths. The Koran functioned as a summarizing symbol for the assessment of civilized, i.e., Islamic, conduct. Aduafilis didn't leave it at a singular statement of *maktūb* ('it is written'). Often they were able to name the *sura* or even recite the verse at issue. One villager denoted the Koran *al-furqān*, that is, the distinguishing device: If *adab* involves learning to differentiate, then it is the Koran which specifies to humans how to distinguish between *ḥalāl* (lawful) and *ḥarām* (unlawful and impure).[7]

Honouring the forbidden domains

The connection between cultural ideals and Islam, as well as the brief descriptions of the sexual ideology, come close to the protracted Western stereotype of Islam covering every aspect of daily life. I would instead argue that the references to Islamic articles of faith and the rules of *adab* constitute the cultural repertoire, consisting of temporal and religious values, in which the prestige differential between Shurfa and Drawa is expressed. Prestige or honour denotes the incorporation of the complex of ideal models for behaviour in an individual or group of people ('social honour'). It furthermore denotes the demand for a deferential approach by others, as, for example, shown in the maintenance of social distance. The studies of Jamous

---

[6] 'Patience belongs to men, it does not belong to women nor to boys' (Moroccan proverb; Westermarck 1930: 240).

[7] *Al-furqān* is mentioned in the Koran seven times. Although according to Watt (1988: 139–141), it probably originated in a Jewish-Aramaic or Syrian term for salvation (*purqana*), the Arab root verb *faraqa* ('to separate') certainly influenced its meaning. In the Koran *al-furqāna* expresses the divine consent and final separation of believers and unbelievers.

(1981) and Marcus (1987) on northern Morocco, make clear that ideas and values on social honour centre in particular around the construction of land, family and women as 'forbidden domains'. An honourable man strives for the inviolability of his person, family and his property at the danger of losing his honour (*'ird*). In the village, these ideas must be understood from the viewpoint of the hierarchical interdependence between Shurfa and Drawa, and of the place of the Shurfa in the oasis society as a whole. Respect for the Shurfa always has been based on their ascendancy, liturgical and ritual roles, and peaceful appearance. For Shurfa, consolidation of their economic and cultural and social capital was accomplished through gifts and sacrifices of oasis inhabitants to the *zāwiya*. In addition to their ascribed honourable status (*šaraf*) owing to their noble descent, the Shurfa command respect from non-Shurfa through a strict compliance with the behavioural rules of cultural ideals. They maintain a superior prestigious status through self-restraint, social cohesion (cf. Elias 1994: xxii), and by having others perform work which, if done by Shurfa, might lead to a violation of their social honour. Thus, although to all villagers the attainment of prestige is connected with compliance with the behavioural laws (*qawānīn*), in particular concerning the maintenance of a public and private domain, this demand applies with greater force to Shurfa.

Since the cultural ideals are bound up with a sexual ideology that provides models for inter- and intra-gender behaviour (cf. Brandes 1987: 132), the difference in *adab* rules for Sharifat vis-à-vis Drawiat offers a clue to estimate the differential demands to stick to the 'laws'. Consider, for example, the separation of spatial domains along gender and age in the village. The centre of public life in the village is the area in front of the Friday Mosque and the sanctuary. Along the major irrigation channel, usually older (married) men gather to wait for prayer time or for their turn to irrigate their fields, while keeping an eye on the gate of the irrigation canals to prevent someone opening or closing it too early. Some twenty meters away from the older men sit the younger men. Both young and older men face the unpaved road, parallel to the canal, and the mosque. The last category of villagers using the central public space is comprised of children and Drawiat who have to pass the men to go to the well of the mosque. From the nearby village of the Berber-speaking Ait 'Atta, young men and women also come to the well to fill their

plastic buckets with water. Sharifian married women never leave
their house to go to the well. Outside of their home, if they wish
to visit another quarter, they try to stay within the walls of the quarters. Their 'territory' is the space in between the privacy of their
homes and the public space of the village square, the *residential exte-
rior* of the covered *qsar* streets. Here, sitting on the threshold of their
houses, they meet other women, just like the men do on the public square outside the *qsar*. The reader might remember from chapter three that Drawi houses are located next to the gates of the
quarters. This means that Drawiat sit in the most public spot of
the *qsar* streets. Just as the village square is a forbidden domain for
the Sharifian women, the men cannot enter the streets of the village quarters other than their own without making preparations. For
me, the Drawi street was the only one I could enter after a few
weeks without permission or having someone in front of me warn-
ing the women to go inside and close their doors.

The use of the village space reflects and strengthens the notion
that Sharifiat are a forbidden domain for outsiders. This is well
known in the village. Most men are aware of life in Casablanca and
compare, for example, the way they go about with women over
there with the restrictions in the village. 'You know I have seen
women from the village in Casablanca, that I never was able to see
in Aduafil', a young Sharif once said. The difference in public appearance between female Shurfa and Drawa is as striking as the difference
between town and village life. Likewise in Casablanca, as Ossman
(1994: 48) recalls, '[t]he "modern" girls and boys never cease to describe their differences with the past or other regions of the country'. The Casablanca girls say that especially in 'the south, women
didn't or don't do things like we do'. The 'things they do' relate to
meeting boys and flirting with them. For a male outsider, the rules
of *adab* among women in the village could most clearly be seen in
the dress codes. Young girls start to cover their hair with a small
wrap when they are about eight. An unmarried girl in her puberal
period wears a larger black cloth of 4–8 meters that covers head
and shoulders (*gunʿa*). Then the roads of Drawiat and Sharifat part.
While married Drawiat keep on wearing the same black cloth, married Sharifat will change to white clothes in public and furthermore
wear a veil. Outside they are covered completely, holding the different
ends of the white cloth (*kisāʾ*) closed above their heads. Drawiat work
in the fields, gathering daily fodder and amassing dates. Sharifat

abstain from activities that bring them onto a public stage. They are expected not to come into contact with male outsiders, denoting all men who do not belong to the household or patrilineal family. During my visits to village families, Sharifat always remained separated from me and my male host. Drawiat often dined in the same room, although we never ate from the same plate. In the field Shurfa address Drawiat without any problem. Jokingly, one Sharif said that all Sharifat do is eat and make love, while in comparison Drawiat at least work in the fields. The serious undertone of the remark reflects pride in the honourable status of the Sharifat as a separate forbidden domain.

Adab and Drawi mediation

Drawa face difficulties living up to the rules of *adab*. In the fulfillment of their tasks, they have to enter homes and invite people without difficulty, in short, act as social mediators. With respect to the status of similar marginal figures, Jamous (1992: 170) notes for northern Morocco that 'such people can enter the fields of a man of honor, or go into his house while he is away and see his wife and talk to her, without being deemed to have issued a challenge to honor. The act of transgression [that is, violate the forbidden domains and contest the honour of a man, RE] can be performed only by a man of honor and not by someone who is marginal'. The attribute of a 'non-person status'—defined as 'someone who isn't there' or for whom 'no impression need be maintained' (Goffman 1959: 151)— may apply to Drawa as well. Drawa are necessary for upholding the honour of Shurfa. Bourdieu noted for the honour complex in Algeria that '[t]here is nothing worse than to pass unnoticed, like a shadow. Thus, not to greet someone, is to treat him like an object, like an animal or a woman' (Bourdieu 1965: 199). It are, however, social invisibility and the attribution of feminine qualities that make the fulfillment of tasks by Drawa possible. They are not supposed to pose a threat to Sharifian men and as mediators are bound to make compromises. As such, Drawa help in the maintenance of the forbidden domains of Shurfa even if this represents them as unmanly. This is the double-bind Drawa and Shurfa have to deal with. The following incident involving possible 'zigzag behaviour' exemplifies this aspect of the Drawi-Sharif interdependence.

During the Islamic month of fasting, my Sharifian neighbour's

daughter Latifa asked a young man named Rashid to buy her something in the oasis centre. In itself this is quite normal as men do all
the shopping and women never visit the market. Latifa turned to
Rashid because she didn't trust her brother Hassan with the money
as he never returns with what she asked for. So she gave the money
to her girlfriend, who gave it to her brother Rashid. Unfortunately,
there was not enough money. Even more unfortunately, instead of
following the same indirect way, Latifa addressed Rashid (her girlfriend's brother) herself while herding the cow. Usually, Sharifat when
not yet married are allowed to do these kind of tasks on the walled
fields close to the village. However, villagers considered Latifa, who
was 24, to be too old to work in the field. Villagers called Latifa
pitiful because so far no one had been found to marry her. A third
person witnessed the meeting of Latifa and Rashid. This man informed
Latifa's brother Hassan about it. Hassan decided to take action. He
did not contact Rashid himself, but instead went to Hammed whom
he told about the verbal contact between Latifa and Rashid. In a
short though dramatic conversation witnessed by the village men
from a distance, Hammed and Rashid agreed that Rashid and Latifa
would never meet again. It was concluded by all that Hammed's
intervention had succeeded in avoiding a major quarrel between the
two families.

Even though the contact had been quite innocent, it was said that
Rashid had cried because of the unjustified accusations of intimate
contact between him and Latifa. Villagers agreed upon the fact that
the two had been asked to explain their transgression of the strict
rule that Sharifian non-family members of different gender do not
speak with each other in public. Neither Latifa nor Rashid were
married, and their contact could lead to 'future problems', dealing
with Latifa's assumed virginity. Khalifa, the witness of their meeting, explained his squeamish behaviour to me by arguing that especially in the month of fasting humans should abstain from passioned
behaviour. It is especially then that a Muslim should repress his passions and instead express virtues like patience and rationality. As
noted above, it was not the first nor the last time that Khalifa pointed
out the unorthodox behaviour of his fellow villagers. The family of
Latifa was blamed by Hammed for letting her do tasks that could
bring her in such a position. Instead, it would be better to teach her
the necessary household tasks for a married Sharifian woman. Her
brother was praised because in his anger he remained calm and first

tried to solve the transgression by asking Hammed to intervene. In short, the Latifa situation illuminates what happens if 'a socially validated script (. . .) for acting out relationships between men and women in situations outside of marriage and the family' is missing (Ossman 1994: 47). In the village every contact between a man and a woman carries with it the danger of a bad outcome. This applies especially to Shurfa and to a lesser extent to Drawa.

A second striking aspect of the incident is the role of the Drawi Hammed as intermediary. His son Abdelhadi had once called him 'the village lawyer' (muḥami), since he always discusses and settles small village disputes in which state officials will never intervene. Although he indeed did so several times during my stay, as long as his illiteracy was not an objection, in this particular case Hammed intervened between two families with whom he maintains close relationships. Hammed had been a tenant of the young man's family for several years. After the death of the father of the family, he had helped to divide the inheritance among the three remaining sons. The close and intimate relationships of Hammed and his wife with members of this family continued after the tenancy had ended. Latifa's family had hired Hammed as their sharecropper. Moreover, milk kinship bonds had forged enduring ties between the two families.

Just like the field-guards, Hammed knows in his role of mediator the rules of etiquette involving inter-gender contact by heart. More than once, Hammed and his sons complained about the behaviour of present-day Shurfa: They are greedy instead of generous, lax in their pious behaviour, and the Sharifian women have lost their shame (especially those in Casablanca). In short, they say that the Shurfa demand respect because of their descent but in the meantime have lost their Sharifian heart.

In the use of a mediator, a person is 'caught between his great desire to keep his own affairs secret and his unwillingness to face issues in their naked form', that is, take care of them on his own (Geertz 1976: 245). This, of course, makes the task of mediator a delicate one. Moreover, as the examples of Hammed and of the field-guard make clear, the mediator has to know the rules when others trespass them. They are regarded with suspicion, precisely because as mediators they look for compromises: 'He must always, therefore, be regarded with suspicion and contempt by those who have made an ideological commitment to their own cause' (Bailey 1969: 168; cf. Goffman 1959: 149). Once a landowner who had a

conflict with another landowner said about Hammed acting as mediator that he always knows best to name right and wrong when others
are involved, but at the same time he is the greatest thief stealing
behind the back of his patrons. Likewise, we saw how Hammed as
field-guard was accused of lenience and zigzag. It seems to be the
fate of the mediator to be accused of moral equivocalness, while he
alone knows who in fact is transgressing the rules of *adab*.

The status of serving

The evaluation of what is acceptable, civilized, behaviour differs for
different categories of people. This becomes clear from a discussion
of the tasks at the numerous feasts held on the occasion of a marriage or circumcision. Particularly striking are the serving tasks of
Drawa at these happenings.

Serving as topic for discussion

The status of Drawa is closely related to their task as servants. In
her research on women and social stratification in southern Morocco,
Maher emphasizes the servitude of Drawa: 'They tend to serve wherever they happen to be' and 'tend to take undignified roles' of which
the servant is one (Maher 1974: 25). Literally from my first day in
the village, contacts with villagers offered confirmations of the view
that serving epitomizes the social relations between Drawa and Shurfa
and, in particular, that the subordinate status of the Drawa in the
village was attached to a notion of servitude and servility. Sharifian
villagers, in their attempts to mark the boundaries between us and
them, made clear that serving played an important role in this boundary marking process. At all the initial encounters with villagers, serving was a topic for discussion or became an issue through other
means. For example on the third day I was invited at a collective
dinner in celebration of a birth. I was placed on a carpet in one of
the corners of an open field in the midst of which some men were
busy with boiling water and filling kettles with it.[8] I was surrounded

---

[8] See a description of a visit to the religious lodge of Tamgrout in the Dra Valley
by Epton (1958: 163): 'It was a holiday, and the men of Tamgrout were lounging

by a few young men who were curious about the reasons for my stay. They explained to me they were Shurfa. When one of the men from the centre field approached us, the Sharif next to me whispered that the men in the middle were 'Africans', who were here to serve the Shurfa.

The next day my Sharifian neighbour invited me for tea, and again I met some of the young Shurfa. This time they were making fun of a young dark-skinned man, who was walking up and down fulfilling the same tasks that I had seen being done by the Drawa the evening before. After the tea I went home and wrote down what I had seen and heard, including their statement that this young man was a Drawi serving in the house of my neighbour. Several days later I realized that they had been teasing me. The young man was the son of my Sharifian neighbour and was just serving in his own house. He was a Sharif and not a Drawi at all. The joke consisted of the association of the dark skin of this son with his serving activities. Clearly, the stereotypic view was that serving and being black meant being a Drawi. A Drawi can also make such an explicit reference to the connection, albeit turned around. Once someone had just begun to make a round with a kettle for people to wash their hands before dinner, when Hammed's son Abdellatif approached him and asked for the kettle. To the seated guests he remarked jokingly: 'I should do this, as I'm the Drawi here'. Jokes like these make clear that the connection between certain services, especially attending at dinners and large gatherings, and the Drawi status is an openly debated and contested issue. Hammed's oldest son Ibrahim, living in Casablanca, objected against any anachronistic criterion for assessing human beings. He pointed at his brother Abdelmzid, who had refused to serve his fellow villagers any longer. Also, the Sharifian teacher of the local primary school who was born in the village spoke out against a necessary connection between serving and Drawa. He indicated that the cleavage between Drawa and Shurfa was becoming more and more something of the past: 'The older people still like to have Drawa to serve them, but there's not any passage in the Koran that says that as descendant of the Prophet you have

---

among the sand dunes at the foot of their salmon-pink kasbahs brewing tea and playing casual, meandering tunes upon flutes and drums. Every one of the grave copper kettles set upon a tall tripod had its individual attendant kneeling reverently before it, bellows in hand'.

to be served'. However, other Drawa, including Ibrahim's father Hammed, his brother Abdellatif and his uncle Najem, accepted their role as servants in the village. They considered serving their Sharifian fellow villagers to be an honourable activity, in congruence with the acceptance of the hierarchical interdependent relationships between Shurfa and Drawa.

Serving at public gatherings

A common type of public gathering in the oasis consists of a collective meal and the recitation of one or several religious texts. These *zarda-s* are organized on the occasion of all the major life crisis rituals, where food is provided for by one household or family. Through the village crier, they let villagers know whether every man at the age of fasting is invited for the meals or only one member of every household. Another type of gathering takes place when a respected village outsider or former resident of the village visits Aduafil for a number of days. In successive order, villagers are then called upon to provide for a collective meal. Although one participates on a voluntary basis, Shurfa especially feel morally and socially obliged to take part. It would be shameful not to do so. Hospitality, Jamous has pointed out for the Iqar'iyen in the north, is part of the system of honour. It is not only an obligation for the host but an actual challenge to other partners of the exchange system, so '[t]he whole iqar'iyen confederacy is pervaded by these reciprocal invitations manifested in time' (1981: 72). In the village, passers-by are always vigorously invited: 'Come on, let us drink some tea (or: join lunch, dinner)'. Although the invitation will be repeated several times, it is never accepted. Villagers agree this is the right thing to do and furthermore differentiates 'those who know' from foreigners. I almost always accepted invitations, based on the hope that the dinner would provide an occasion for asking questions. This led sometimes to an embarrassing situation when the 'invitor' had only meant to make a polite gesture instead of a real invitation.

Through the display of hospitality, a host expresses his poise and autonomous position. It is one way to earn respect. Drawa usually do not take part, because if they participate in the '*zarda* exchange system', Shurfa would arrive in a dependent and consequently subordinate position. At the same time, social pressure forces Shurfa to participate. Thus, while in Aduafil a Drawi can argue convincingly he is too poor to offer a meal, it is agreed upon that the same argument does not hold for an equally poor Sharif; for him a collective breakfast might be the least to demonstrate his hospitality toward and respect for the guest. Expenses are somewhat limited because for these meals usually only a restricted number of invitations are sent out. In that case they ask a Drawi to invite all the respective persons. Seldom do Shurfa invite their guests themselves. This practice was already mentioned in the 1920s by Brunot, when he observed that 'making use of an intermediary when one has a specific demand is considered as a sign of a proper education' (Brunot 1926: 25). Thus, in explaining the procedure of a collective meal, one Sharif told me quite innocently that one starts with asking 'a black man' to invite the guests.

Drawa also help their patrons to organize the dinner, for example, through an assessment of the food that is necessary. Hammed Hazzabin is generally considered to be the expert on this issue. Without him, one Sharif told me, no feast could be held. Drawiat, women and daughters of the men, prepare the meal, if necessary (at weddings) several times a day, a week long. Food preparation, rolling couscous, baking bread are physically intensive and laborious tasks (cf. Jansen 1987: 207; Maher 1974: 49–52). For large feasts the host family might construct an additional furnace for bread. This is done with the aid of an older Drawia who knows how to build a safe mud-brick furnace. During the actual feast, Drawi men commute between the separate groups of women, men and children, serving plates. The Drawa constitute the service personnel, acting as servant and working backstage.

During a meal six or seven guests sit around a small low table that will be removed by a servant the moment the meal has finished. The guests eat with one hand from the same plate of couscous and one of them will divide the chunk of meat in the centre of the plate. One only eats from one part of the plate and gives fellow-guests ample opportunity to eat their part. For example, one should not eat through the pile of couscous to make the vegetables on top of the pile fall right in front of his part of the plate.

The prestige of the dinner rises with the amount and quality of the food presented. A real treat then is the presentation of liver pikes (*bulfaf*, prepared by Drawi men and youngsters). A Drawi brings them round and lets everyone take one or two pieces of roasted liver. *Bulfaf* is typically the type of food that can be presented to the special guests only, excluding the women and most adult men. The Drawi also distributes tea, cookies and nuts. The village crier may be asked to announce that all present are invited for breakfast the next morning.

The quality of a collective meal increases also with the presence of a *fqīh*, who at least recites a short prayer to thank the host for his hospitality, and may even recite a section of the Koran. Male villagers regard recitation to be the differentiating characteristic of a male gathering as opposed to a female gathering (which may be held at the same time). Sometimes more than one reciter demonstrates his qualities. Another type of religious texts, those by Ibn al-Malik, are recited by all those present, including children. Because recitation starts without an announcement, other guests might have to cease talking in the middle of a sentence. During recitations, the servants, that is older male children and unmarried men of the house as well as loyal Drawa, are the only persons who walk around to pour boiled water into the teapots or distribute tea or water to the guests. They do so in spite of the noise they cause. One Drawi sometimes walks around with a palm branch to hit restless or quarrelling children, if necessary.

The grouping of the guests over the various tables follows a strict hierarchical order with the village head, *fqīh-s* and important guests from outside the village at the apex (cf. Gerholm 1977: 176–180). They sit in the most attractive chamber with thick rugs at the most agreeable spot (the coolest in summer and warmest in winter); they are served the nicest crockery, the best table (one that doesn't wobble), perhaps even with a tablecloth. The second and third categories consist of family heads and married men. Next are the young unmarried men. Last is the group of male children.

An older Drawi, usually someone who has a confidential relationship with the inviting family, sits on the threshold of the house to act as doorman. A second Drawi stands outside to boil water in a large jar (to be poured into the smaller kettles inside). They and other servants, usually young members of the family of the host and sons of the older Drawa, assist to serve the guests. Thus, while older Shurfa never help with serving, Drawa serve at every age. Furthermore, they are often not able to eat with the guests because of their work such as going round with drinking water, boiling water for tea, or keeping the younger kids silent and helping with the division of the meat. Often servants eat together after the others have finished, sometimes with the children when they also have to wait for the adults finishing their meal. I observed often how Drawa, even when not assigned an official task, rose to help of their own accord. Otherwise, they would be asked to help the host. In any case they are seldom normal guests. Some tasks are never done by other family members of the host and solely by Drawa. This accounts especially for heating water and going round with a kettle before and after dinner to let everybody wash his hands, a task that otherwise children would do.

An important quality of *zarda-s* is that they offer an opportunity to guest, host and servant to demonstrate their cultivated conduct and knowledge of etiquette. Basically, all village *zarda-s* are structured in the same order. But, just like the Balinese cockfights described by Geertz (1973), it is not from their structure, but from the *deep play* of the actors involved that meaning can be gained.[9] Villagers measure the quality of a *zarda* through the quantity and quality of food, guests, and recitation of the Koran. The food is discussed and evaluated, with the economic position of the host in mind. During dinner, participants can express their knowledge of table manners, and *adab* in general, by showing poise in eating and drinking, and hospitality (cf. Jansen 1995: 91–92). The following local joke on table manners comments on this dimension of the cultural ideals.

> A man has been invited for dinner by another man. When the plate is served, the host asks the guest about his father's health. The guest tells him his father has died, whereupon the host asks him how he died. In a long story, the guest relates how his father once was a strong man, until he suddenly became sick and eventually died. When he has finished his story, he notices that in the meantime the host has eaten the entire plate and left nothing for him. The guest understands the host's trick, and broods on revenge. As is quite normal, he invites the host to a dinner in turn. When this time dinner is served, the man, now in the role of host, asks his guest the same question: How had his father died? The guest answers in a succint style: 'He became sick, he died; and eat your dinner' (*mraḍ, mat wa kul ʿašaʾek*).

The joke exemplifies the first hosts lack of compliance with a crucial *adab* rule, showing hospitality. The guest, however, is not blameless as he should have focused his attention on the food. Too much

---

[9] Compare Herzfeld's depiction of the dinners with an abundance of food and drinks on the Greek island of Crete as an 'idiom of contest' in which men display their hospitality and social excellence (1985: 135).

talking during dinner is considered bad mannered. Lastly, the joke shows the *ʿaql* of the first host, who in his response during the second dinner acts with foresight. The required civilized behaviour around the tables contrasts with the heated debates that go on in the adjacent room where food is prepared. There I witnessed quarrels over the distribution of liver pikes and the quality of the food. To clarify the nature of a typical *zarda*, it can be compared with the *walima* of the teenagers and unmarried men. The following example shows how these small collective dinners present us with a reversed version of the *zarda*, though they are structurally the same.

In honour of the temporary return of some men studying abroad, five young men decide to organize a *walima* one day in December. By lot, one boy was chosen to take care of the first meal. This means he has to buy either vermicelli (to be served with tomato sauce and crumbled hard-boiled eggs) or *barkūkš* in the village shop, ask the women of the house to prepare the food, and welcome the guests with tea and either biscuits or peanuts. Around half past four, all those invited assemble in front of the *qsar* entrance and walk together to the house where the *walima* will be held. Upon arrival, they look for a place to sit, while some just flop to the ground. One boy puts a cassette in the recorder and soon Moroccan pop music sounds from the speakers. In the meantime another boy has prepared tea. Some refuse a glass, others drink from two glasses at the same time. One or two start smoking kif. Then the bowl with vermicelli is served. As quickly as possible the bowl is emptied, after which everyone leaves without delay, just in time to make the *maġrīb* prayer for those who want to. Next day the same programme is followed. Only this time some young men who were not invited to the first meal, got wind of the *walima*. To lead them astray as to where the meal will be held, the participants try to follow a secret route through the *qsar*. Unfortunately, when they arrive at the house, the uninvited guests are already there, awaiting them with a smile on their face.

Walima-s are one of the rare occasions for young men to gather outside the public space of the village square. They value the collective meals primarily for this reason, though in front of the anthropologist an additional religious meaning was presented: 'At this *walima* poor and rich people come together, to be fraternised. This is what we call the *umma*, the Islamic community'. It is true that at *walima-s* Drawa don't serve Shurfa like they do at the adult gatherings. In the succession of meals and the limited invitations the *walima* copies the model of the adult *zarda*, especially the one that is held for respected outsiders who are visiting the village for a few days. But the loose behaviour and lack of poise, not sitting in the correct position, drinking from two cups, music instead of recitation, even smoking makes the *walima* more look like a parody of the *zarda*. At a *zarda* it would be shameless to enter uninvited. Thus, while the *walima* copies the structure of an adult gathering, it is in its 'uncivilized' content and emphasis on equality a far cry from the original *zarda* in which the status differential between Shurfa and Drawa is played out.

Serving as gendered activity

Two aspects of the status dimensions of serving, and already hinted at a few times, are that of gender and age. Most striking at the collective dinners is the crucial role of Drawa who at the same time remain socially invisible. That is, they, and only they, are allowed or forced to cross or permeate the agreed-upon social boundaries and rules of conduct, that is, enter the women's spaces, sit with children and run around during recitation. Borrowing the dramaturgical terminology of Goffman, one might say that the serving tasks of Drawa and their constant movement between front and backstage at parties is part of the 'show' that patron and client perform. As part of the display of civilized conduct, a *zarda* expresses and reconfirms ties of loyalty and hierarchy between those present. I regard this as one of the main reasons for Shurfa clinging to the practice of Drawa serving them. Among Shurfa, the positioning of guests is already an indicator of their social status. Furthermore, some Shurfa stress their honourable status and presence as males at special occasions by wearing a snow-white *jallāba* and turban and dagger. They also visit *zarda-s* in other villages riding a horse or mule (in contrast to a donkey which situates the rider in a low position).[10] Vis-à-vis guests, the assistance of Drawa reconfirms the status of the Sharifian host and guests, while at the same time it gives new meaning to the bond between patron and client.

---

[10] This is not unlike the *supreme Sharif,* i.e., the king of Morocco, who visits his subjects, surrounded by his servants. According to Le Roy Ladurie (1979: 81), the same role was assigned to the horse when it was introduced into the rural civilization of Europe: '*the "noble beast" was associated with a new social distinction*: in its way it marked the appearance of a group of aristocrats, living off contributions levied from the peasants, and of course riding on horseback . . .' (italics added).

Serving, when inside the homes of Shurfa, touches upon the cultural ideal of increasing poise and autonomy. Once a Drawi related with disapproval the story of a Sharif who, when ordered by his Sharifian friend to wash his car, did so immediately. The Drawi commented that serving and especially being commanded was below the level (*mustawan*) of a Sharif, certainly when a Sharif of equal status is involved. Yet Drawa as well pay the price of low prestige when working in the service of other men. Here the ever-recurring image of the Drawi as a donkey returns. Not only is the donkey stupid (i.e. lacking *'aql*), he is also a servile animal. There is a local saying that illuminates this aspect of the Sharifi-Drawi relationship: When collective agricultural work has to be done, Drawa work for themselves, while Shurfa send their donkeys (Ouhajou n.d.: 98). The Shurfa's donkeys are their Drawi clients. Indeed, when called up for collective labour on the irrigation ditches, Shurfa seldom go themselves, in particular when it is outside of their village and they have to work together with inhabitants from nearby villages, possibly receiving orders from them.

Serving affects a man's status and is consequently limited to a certain phase in life. A Sharifian male starts as a *wuld*, a young boy. A *wuld* is ordered to do all kinds of services. He may be asked to fetch water, serve at dinner and gather fallen dates. A *wuld* is mainly expected to obey his parents and older siblings. Next in line comes the *'azab*, an unmarried adolescent. He already is expected to show his knowledge of *adab* in a more intricate manner. He should avoid 'intimate contact' with Sharifat, as the Latifa situation showed, and pray now and then, especially at major calendrical rituals. In addressing these youngsters, the honorific *mulay* is already used. A married man with children is a *rajul*. He has a large responsibility towards the respectability of his family. Ideally, he not only pays respect to his peers but also commands respect from them. A married man also has certain privileges. In general, he does not serve or fetch water, although when still young and living at home, he remains under the tutelage of his older brothers and father. An elderly man is a *šibanī*, wearing the proverbial white beard.

The assistance of youngsters and young men at the communal meals expresses the 'agnatic solidarity' between family members. They do serve and are commanded but they also know that one day they shall be head of a family, able to invite guests and command servants of their own accord. At the communal meals, the older Drawa are placed at the same level as these not-yet autonomous men. The older Drawa have, of course, sons to command, but outside the domestic sphere they are the ones who are commanded at will, even when having attained an advanced age. These serving Drawa are men but lack some of the means to act like one. They are, as Herzfeld (1985: 4, 46) put it, not good at being a man: As dependants, they are commanded and at the service of others. They are able to express hospitality toward guests only in their capacity as servant, do not join in the *deep play* of communal meals (with exception of festive occasions like a marriage) and do not participate in the competitive display of civilized conduct of guests. The Drawi servants are there but are ignored nevertheless. They move between the spaces of men and women yet do not exactly cross genders. They are rather stuck in-between, similar to the category of subservient men in Yemen, who face 'the projection of female attributes' by people of higher status (Vom Bruck 1996: 148). Likewise in Algeria women without men who act as social and cultural mediators may be assigned with, or appropriate, male attributes (of posture and movement; cf. Jansen 1987: 175–189).[11] It appears that social hierarchy and gender are closely linked cultural domains— with autonomy and independence as common ideals—in circumscribing the social marginality of Drawa.

Respect and religious merit

The public dinners (*zarda-s*) express in an evocative way the status differential between Shurfa and Drawa and by way of their serving tasks, the Drawa accept and reproduce this status differential. Because of their seeming non-compliance with the 'laws' of civilized conduct, the Drawa live up to the dominant discourse that deprives them of the same status as the Shurfa. However, here again (see chapter five) we find a set of ideas that reestablishes their status. This set is not so much a hidden deviant discourse as presented by Scott in a number of publications (1985, 1990) as it is an ensemble of alternative interpretations of key notions; it is, then, more like a 'discourse of dignity and self-assertion within the public transcript' (Scott 1990:

---

[11] Extreme example of the ambivalent status of servants, born as men but not able to act masculine in every respect, is that of eunuchs, 'nongendered individuals who both defined and crossed highly charged boundaries' (Marmon 1995: ix).

137), here hinging on the exchange relationships between Shurfa and Drawa. As noted in the previous chapter, living in a village of Shurfa offers Drawa the possibility to take a more positive view of their status compared to Drawa in the surrounding villages, namely as common people (*ʿawāmm*) or servants of the saints. Serving is part of this view.

Most tasks fulfilled by Drawa are without direct monetary reward, though a ritual gift in kind might be involved. Once, when I enquired after the recompense for the serving tasks of a Drawi, another Drawi said: 'Look, he drinks tea and buttermilk, and eats dates for free, is that not enough?' In a more indirect way, via the annual contributions after the harvest from patron and other fellow villagers, the Drawa are materially compensated for their communal activities. However, villagers including the Drawa themselves, mostly refer to the immaterial rewards: Respect for the Shurfa (*iḥtirām*), religious merit (*ajr sidi nabi*), and 'the charity of one's parents' (*ʿllah raḥma al-wālidīn*) are mentioned when asked about their motives for carrying out their numerous community tasks.

Since, as we have seen, respect for the Shurfa is closely related to sacredness (*ḥurma*) and purity (*tiḥram*), Drawa comply with the different set of behavioural rules by which Shurfa have to abide and accept that Shurfa should abstain from activities that would diminish their respectability. For Shurfa these rules hold that they should abstain from activities for which it would be necessary to transgress any of the agreed-upon social or cultural boundaries, at the risk of an infringement of their sacred and honourable status.

Through their tasks, Drawa reconfirm the social cleavage within the village and reproduce the sacred realm of the Shurfa. At the same time, the tasks testify to the mutual interdependence between Shurfa and Drawa. For people like Najem and Hammed, the satisfaction in fulfilling the kind of services Drawa are expected to do is related to this mutual interdependence. When referring to their services, Drawa use the verb 'to serve' (*sakira*) when it concerns paid work. 'To serve' is related to the word used for statute or corvée labour (*sukra*). Likewise *rajl al-sukra* are bondsmen (Wehr 1976: 401). Drawa state that they serve only out of goodness (*ġir b-l kir*) and not out of necessity or command ('like in the old days'). Thus, one Drawi said that *ʿAbīd*, as opposed to Drawa, are those people who have 'to serve in the house of the Shurfa, just like the slaves of the king', while Drawa 'aid' the Shurfa. In this view, Drawa keep their independence, making a decision whether to help someone of their own accord. Furthermore, and this is an important point, Drawa stress that the aid is their part of an equal exchange of services between Shurfa and Drawa.

For Drawa the tasks and other good deeds involving their fellow villagers offer the possibility to regain esteem and religious merit. For example, Hammed's pivotal role in village life was recognized by all villagers and publicly stated at a meeting where the imam of the village recited the Fatiha, the sevenline verse with which the Koran opens. The text of the Fatiha has the character of a prayer and is used as such. The significance of the prayer is increased when it is recited by a religious authority (an imam or Sharif, who can also be an imam) and secondly when this is done in large gatherings. In Morocco the Fatiha is part of a larger ritual. The Koranic verse is then extended with more specific wishes and blessings in favour of certain persons. People practise the shortened form at the end of a meal. The participants hold their hands as if holding a book and respond to the blessings by saying *amin*. When Hammed had the honour of being blessed, the imam, after the usual words of thankfulness for the dinner, blessed him and his family with the *baraka* of Mulay Adafal for his work in the village. Being 'in the middle of the village community' (*wasṭ al-qabīla*), the Aduafili Shurfa could not do without him. Those present, among them the first and second imam and the head of the village, nodded their head in agreement and quietly praised Hammed.

In a more general way, Aduafilis repeatedly refer to a notion of religious merit, to explain and evaluate their actions or that of their fellow villagers, by using the word *ajr*. Buitelaar (1991), who gives a comprehensive account of *ajr* as a key notion in Moroccan culture, defines it as 'spiritual reward for pious acts' (1991: 93). She argues convincingly that the notion reflects a rather calculating way of dealing with the divine. When I asked a Drawi if he worked as a gravedigger for free, he answered that no money is involved but rather the *arzāq Allah*, the 'fortune of God'. Someone else told me "*llāh kallas*', God pays when you do something gratis. Earning money and *ajr* are incongruous. When you work during Ramadan, you don't get paid, as you already earn *ajr*. However, prosperity and religious blessings must, just like material gifts, be reciprocated by other acts. This can most clearly be seen in the pattern of alms giving. When I asked a Sharif why an old woman handed over a piece of land to the village of Aduafil, he answered she gave it as a gift (*sadaqa*) with which she would gain a lot of *ajr*, especially because the land would be used to enlarge the cemetery. A calculating mind can refuse to act because it is not rewarding. A man who refused to give alms to some young men during the date harvest defended himself by saying that 'there's no *ajr* in it' because young, strong men can work as day labourers instead of asking for free dates. Another man stated that giving alms to rich people doesn't award you any religious merit. *Ajr* is mentioned when it concerns an explicit religious deed, especially when you perform it in an extraordinary way (fasting, alms giving, additional prayers), but it returns in the daily activities of villagers. It applies in particular to collective activities within the sphere of the village. Thus, many activities of Drawa are explained by referring to the concept of *ajr*. I already mentioned the gravedigger who worked for free, but also Abdelhadi and his father Hammed, who are both village barbers say they work for *ajr* and do not get paid. A Drawia explained the refusal of a Drawi to do a certain task normally done by Drawa by saying that apparently 'he doesn't want *ajr*'.

The religious merit of serving at ordinary meals seems less easy to pin down. Clearly, it marks the Drawa as submissive. Drawa, however, make a difference between serving in the sense of being commanded (*sakira*) and serving in the sense of helping. The first is done out of necessity (lack of money), the last is done for pious and *adab* reasons. Najem Hazzabin argued in favour of serving when I asked him for his opinion on the topic. He referred to *ajr* and gave the following anecdote of the Prophet as illustration:

> The Prophet organized a dinner to which he invited several people. Before the first guests arrive, he agrees with his servants to change places. They can sit down while he serves the guests. Then the guests arrive, some of whom have never seen the Prophet. One of them asks someone next to him which of the men present is the Prophet. This man, who is the Prophet's servant, answers: 'He who serves us, is our master'.

According to Najem the anecdote is a Hadith, an officially authorized tradition on the deeds and sayings of Muhammad. It expresses the religious merit for serving and states that serving is not something to be ashamed of. Najem's claim that the story is a Hadith could not be confirmed by a check of the Hadith concordances. The last line of his story, however, does appear in Westermarck's list of Moroccan proverbs: 'A good host entertains his guest as though he were their servant, in accordance with the traditional saying: "the lord of the people is their servant"' (1930: 207).

Earlier on, we saw how a more public recognition can also follow by way of a Fatiha, when Hammed Hazzabin had the honour of being blessed by the imam. Thus, Drawa explain their serving tasks as an expression of their autonomous will and poise. Both are crucial ingredients of the set of cultural ideals.

The notion of *ajr* confirms the idea that religion provides guidelines on how to behave in daily life. It is one element of the religious worldview in which the tasks and the status of the Drawa can be seen. It makes them a member of a religious community and necessary members of the village community. It gives them self-esteem and prestige. As Jansen (1987: 157) has demonstrated, religious merit (instead of cash money) strengthens the durability and multistrandedness of bonds between humans. In accordance with her analysis, one may wonder why it is shameful for a gravedigger to ask for money while the imam and the muezzin do obtain some recompense from the state. This discrepancy reinforces the accuracy of the hypothesis that for Drawa the discourse on religious merit is to a large extent an alternative, subordinate discourse to earn respect. Or, as Abu-Lughod (1986: 104–105) notes on the Bedouin in Egypt: 'Those who are coerced into obeying are scorned, but those who voluntarily defer are honorable. (. . .) Voluntary deference is therefore the honorable mode of dependency'. The subordinate discourse is not contrary to the hegemonic set of cultural ideals but in a sense complements it: The Drawi discourse on help and religious reward accepts the prestige differential and its criteria of independence, poise, and the expression of respect to those who are worth it in exchange for religious esteem and respect. It seems that the cultural ideals are not interpreted unequivocally; therefore, divergent views on what *adab* entails, how to follow its codes and who does so correctly remains a distinct possibility.

Conclusions

The fulfillment of tasks by Drawa structures and reinforces their marginal position in the village. They trangress the boundaries between the public and private domains, and male and female domains. Carrying out the community tasks is embedded in the oasis hierarchy and the durable and multifarious exchange relationships between patrons and clients. Compliance with the complex of ideas and practices of civilized conduct and the command of a deferential attitude by others that is expressed in the maintenance of social distance are initial criteria by which people measure the public prestige differential. Male Drawa do not live up to these demands and seem to stand outside of the challenging acts of honour between men. The outcome of their dependency (being commanded by others) and lack of social recognition is an unmanly, *feminized*, stature.

Dependence and being commanded versus independence and command are central criteria by which prestige is measured. We saw in chapter four how the lack of independence of the sharecropper and his family determines his low status. In the present chapter, the serving tasks of Drawa exemplify their low status. However, in the acceptance of hierarchical interdependence between Shurfa and Drawa, the executors of the sometimes poorly rewarded and servile tasks find ways to gain public esteem and self-esteem. Furthermore, the activities of Drawa as distributors and confidants bring them in a powerful position toward Shurfa.

The activities of Drawa as social brokers, moving between segregated social domains, is tied up with cultural mediation. This is a more general feature of social marginals in the Middle East (Bédoucha 1984; Casajus 1987; Jansen 1987). In the strongly hierarchized Yemenite society, as observed in the late 1960s, a category of specialized servants (*Subyan*, 'houseservants') was also occupied with ceremonial services and involved in all major rites of passage between birth and death (Bujra 1971: 43–44). In an examination of similar activities being fulfilled by Drawa, the following chapter aims to show how the mediation between cultural categories which these activities involve relates to the wider configuration of saints and servants.

CHAPTER SEVEN

BODY AND SOUL
CULTURAL MEDIATION IN THE OASIS

> [T]he necessities of practice demand the reunion of things which
> practical logic has sundered ... (Bourdieu 1977: 124).

The reproach of a lack of civility is a universal device to express
the otherness of people. Cultural ideals circumscribe man's relationship with the natural world, his fellow humans, and his organic
functions and affections. When people like the Drawa in the oasis
are perceived as ill-bred and impure, it is with respect to this 'triad
of basic controls' (Elias 1971: 176) that they supposedly fail to live
up to hegemonic ideals, unlike those at the apex of the social hierarchy who are recognized as well-mannered, cultivated and, ultimately, pure. While the usage of such a cultural idiom serves to
underline and legitimize power differentials (Elias 1994: xxvii), it may
relate to differences in actual behaviour. Cultural standards thus do
not just express and reinforce social differences but create interdependent relationships between people. Following the assertion that
'the execution of impure tasks by some is necessary to the maintenance of purity for others'—both sides being equally necessary, yet
unequal (Dumont 1980: 55)—the present chapter examines this complementary relationship for the Shurfa and Drawa in the village. In
chapter five, the Shurfa were denoted as 'cultural brokers' between the great and little tradition of Islam. Social marginals like
the Drawa in the village, although not dealing with two distinctive
cultural traditions, can become cultural brokers as well. In their role
as 'specialists in impurity' (idem, 47) Drawa mediate between cultural categories, assist in subsequent transitional processes and act as
access point for specific specialized knowledge. How do the mediating activities of these brokers correlate to the better-known activities
of Shurfa?

Purification

Practical knowledge regarding purity and pollution are part of the constellation of mental dispositions toward man's body and soul, toward other humans and toward the natural world that I have coined the cultural ideals. Civilization is then defined as the appropriate regulation of human organic functions, the avoidance of impurities and, in case of defilement, stringent purification. On the close relationship between the conceptions of purity-and-pollution and the cultural ideals in the Maghreb, Jansen notes that,

> [t]he essence of civilization is seen as this control over impurity, which is a control over the physical processes of the body. The ability to regulate physical needs, to control one's body and to purify, differentiates humans from animals. An impure person is nearly dehumanized (Jansen 1987: 53; cf. Dumont 1980: 60–61).

Physical purity, that is, control over the organic functions, and moral purity are linked, as could be inferred from the strong objection against the expression of passionate behaviour in the Islamic month of fasting.[1] Moreover, certain conditions, bodily activities and organic functions can be considered as dehumanizing. The 'social constraint towards self-constraint' (Elias 1997 ii: 323) finds expression in the elaborate refinement of behavioural legislative rules in Islamic law on the appropriate steps to take in case of pollution. Pollution (*ḥadaṯ*) occurs in case of contact with or emission of impure bodily substances. A 'major pollution' (*janāba*) occurs mainly with sexual intercourse, menstruation and giving birth, a 'minor pollution' (*ḥadaṯ as-sabīlīn*) with attending the call of nature and sleep. In both instances, purification can be accomplished by way of a major or minor ritual ablution (*wuḍūʾ* and *ġusl*). An impurity that cannot be reversed occurs with the consumption of prohibited food such as liquor, blood, swine and improperly slaughtered meat. Hides can be made pure after tanning.[2] The codification of purity rules in Islamic law has the effect of objectifying the dispositions of villagers. These 'legisla-

---

[1] Compare the following note by Buitelaar (1991: 85): 'The link that people make between the purifying quality of fasting and its alleged effect of upgrading society, aptly illustrates Douglas' contention that pollution beliefs and moral codes are closely connected'.

[2] Cf. Juynboll (*djanāba*), Bousquet (*ḥadaṯ*) en Wensinck (*nadjis*) in *The Encyclopaedia of Islam* (new ed.).

tive rules' however, do not cover the practical knowledge of the villagers, which often go beyond spheres dealt with in law texts. Moreover, people may make a simpler differentiation between what is permitted (*halāl*) and what is forbidden (*harām*). Both terms may apply either to bodily functions or to other deeds. To blow on one's hot tea can be called *harām* because of the impurity of human breath but it is equally *harām* to pour tea into the teacups on a plate by starting from the left instead of the right.[3] These examples direct attention to Douglas' argument that ideas concerning pollution through bodily functions and contact with organic substances are only one aspect, though an important one, of a wider system of symbolic classification. In the pioneering work of Van Gennep (1960), Durkheim and Mauss (1963), Leach (1964, 1978) and Douglas (1966, 1975), it has been argued that humans strive for a systematic ordering of their sensory perceptions. The avoidance of dirt, defined as 'matter out of place' and out of the perceived order, must be seen in this light.

> Dirt avoidance is a process of tidying up, ensuring that the order in external physical events conforms to the structure of ideas. Pollution rules can thus be seen as an extension of the perceptual process: in so far as they impose order on experience, they support clarification of forms and thus reduce dissonance (Douglas 1975: 53).

Purity is a state of cultural order; pollution occurs where the basic categories of the perceived order are confused or blurred. The pollutant aspects of organic functions and bodily fluids are only one extreme variant of a general human need to treat all 'margins or ill-defined states' with special attention and make these the object of avoidance rules (i.e., taboo; cf. Leach 1964). Anomaly can, however, also be employed in a positive way. Purification is the removal of disorder and the creation of order. In this transitional process, mediating concepts as well as mediators, are needed to establish the transition from a former state to the next one. Organic substances are thus often the object of taboo but can also be used to move from an ill (impure) to a healthy (purified) state. Where instead purity remains untouched and isolated, a sterile state is the result. It is from the transitional processes between cultural categories, when 'the system of classification hesitates', as Bourdieu puts it, or is reversed, that

---

[3] 'It is recommended after the Prophet to commence every act of nature from the right in honour to its maker' (Brunot 1926: 19).

life comes forth. Drawa as cultural brokers contribute significantly to these transitional, fertile, ritual processes.

Practical knowledge regarding purity, pollution and purification also is important for circumscription of the boundaries between social categories. Abstinence from pollutant activities and knowledge of the means of purification then become symbols of distinction and a source of power. Shurfa personify the cultural ideals and therefore have to live up to the demand to remain morally pure more stringently than common people. The pure condition of those who belong to 'the House of the Prophet', descendants of the perfect human, 'the archetypical role model' (Lahlou 1986: 22), is expressed in their white clothes and public expression of civilized conduct. The control over *baraka* by Shurfa is based on their noble ascendancy but also hinges on their moral and physical purity as *baraka* 'is extremely sensitive to outside pollution' (Westermarck 1926 ii: 196). The village ground of Aduafil is defined as a *ḥurma*, a sacred, pure space because of the shrine and the Sharifian inhabitants living there. In the past, impure persons, unbelievers such as the Jewish population, were not allowed to pass through without special precautions. At present, it is not permitted to smoke in the village. Another sign of the sacredness of the village territory is that the plant henna, the raw material for the popular reddish dye, cannot be grown there. Henna, as we will see, is attributed with special qualities and can be cultivated without difficulty in nearby villages. The interconnection of physical and moral purity thus returns in a particular acute fashion in the sacred status of the Shurfa.

From the perspective of the Shurfa, the Drawa live in the village to take care of pollutant and purificatory activities, just like outside the village, occupations that involve contact with organic materials are executed by Drawa. Earlier on, Pascon was quoted on 'the quasi-impurity' of working with iron, fire and pottery in Moroccan society (1979: 113). Drawa are, indeed, traditionally known as blacksmiths, cauterizers, agriculturalists and potters. I would, however, add that the impure nature of these tasks is not so much inherent in the organic substances but has to do with the act of changing natural substances into cultural artifacts (see below).

In the village, the task of the butcher is an example of the occupations fulfilled by Drawa that involve the handling of organic material. Hammed Hazzabin and a second Drawi, also named Hammed, are the butchers of the village. The slaughter of sheep, goat or cattle is another specialty of Drawa. Slaughter takes place particularly in association with dinners organized by families in the village on the occasion of a birth, circumcision or marriage. Also on the day of the Great Feast, when every household head in the country sacrifices a ram to commemorate Ibrahim's (i.e., the Biblical Abraham) near-sacrifice of his son, numerous Sharifian men leave the actual sacrifice to the Drawi specialists or their clients. Every slaughter (_dabīḥa_) has to follow religious prescriptions and in fact is a religious deed in itself. _Dabīḥa_ is a sacrifice, only to be performed by adult men, capable of praying and in possession of *'aql*. Women are not allowed to slaughter; yet many men in the village are not capable of performing a sacrifice either.[4] When asked why they do not know how to fulfil the *ajr*-gaining task of sacrifice, Shurfa responded they have just never learned how to slaughter properly. Others made clear that because they never have tried, they were just as averse to the blood and dirt that comes with slaughtering as I was. 'They are afraid of the blood', one Drawi said, and 'they do not want their white *jallāba* to be stained with blood'.[5] Furthermore, the slaughter and the preparation of the meat is a strenuous activity, requiring strength and skill. The butcher's work brings him into contact with organic materials, somewhat similar to the Drawa who work as tanners in the towns. Additionally, central in the butcher's work is the sacrifice, that is, a mediating activity between life and death, an aspect to which I shall return below. Here let me point out that the tasks of the Drawa do not just involve contact with impure materials, but are aimed at active purification. Three ways of purification can be distinguished, by means of cleansing, alteration of the body and by means of natural substances.

Purification by means of cleansing

This category includes the handling of refuse or organic substances and the purification with water. At festive occasions, Drawa make a round with a kettle of water to clean the hands of guests before and

---

[4] See for the celebration of the Great Feast in Morocco, Combs-Schilling (1989; cf. Munson, Jr. 1993 for a critique; cf. Rachik (1990).

[5] See Bourdieu (1977: 133) on Kabyle society: The slaughter of an ox is entrusted to a smith or a black man, that is, a 'scapegoat whose rôle is to "take away ill fortune"'.

after dinner. In their work as ushers of the groom and bride (*wazīr* and *wazīra*) they also take care of heating water and aiding in cleansing. In the village, when someone has died, the muezzin (not necessarily a Drawi) washes and dresses the corpse according to Islamic prescription. In the case of a woman, the Drawi midwife takes care of this task. Cobbling is another occupation in which one deals with cleansing. In Islamic thought, the appreciation for cobbling differs. It means dealing with prepared leather and not with the purification of dead material, yet does involve cleansing shoes from dirt and soil. It is done in the urban streets (just like, for example, water-carrying), it carries little esteem, and it was once reserved for Drawa.

Purification by means of alteration of the body

Circumcision alters and purifies the body. It also transforms a natural body into a civilized one with consequences for the way a man deals with the supernatural world, his fellow humans and his inner self. Circumcision is the second of the three rites of passage boys go through on the ideal path of life towards adult, virile men (the other two are birth and marriage). As a religious act, circumcision is based on the traditions of the Prophet Muhammad. In Moroccan practice it is strongly recommended. Circumcision is a purifying act as is shown in the colloquial term for it, *ṭahūr*, from *ṭahara*, 'to purify'. The boy passes into a state in which he may partake in sexual intercourse and religious practices like prayer, fast, and sacrifice (Reysoo 1991: 102–107). In the village, circumcision is usually undergone collectively and carried out by a Drawi barber from a nearby village.

Usually one or two parents hire the circumciser, buy the prescribed ritual clothes for the boy and arrange a collective meal, while the other parents just join in on the day of circumcision, in this way saving the expenditure of the offering of a sheep. People from nearby villages may have their child circumcised in the village of the Shurfa, near the shrine of Mulay Adafal for a similar reason as Reysoo (1991: 98) notes with respect to an annual saint's day in the north of the country, namely because of the transfer of accumulated *baraka* at the specific time and place onto the boy and his family. However, the actual circumcision is performed by dark-skinned servants and not by the descendants of the saint. These servants are the only men to enter the sacred circumcision area and are the ones who do the actual cutting.

In the village, a day before the ceremony a Koran recitation is held at the house of one of the boys. The boys, ranging from two to six years old, are dressed to the accompaniment of the recitations asking for protection of the boys. They are dressed in new white clothes, a green vest with golden stitches, and a green fez. Around his ankle, the boy wears a string with a small bag containing herbs, an ancient Moroccan coin and a cowrie 'from the Sudan'. Before the recitation (*silka*) their hands and feet have already been dyed with henna, normally something only women do. Hammed shaves a strip of hair just above the ears of the boys. After the recitation, they are carried home by their respective brothers. On the day of the circumcision, a sister or niece carries the boy on her back. They first visit the shrine where the boy receives a mixture of henna and a *mélange* of herbs (*ḳuad*) on his hands, and then go to the place of circumcision. Nowadays, the Drawi who performs the circumcision comes from another village in the oasis, while in the past it was done by Hammed's father Salem and the (Sharifian) phlebotomist (*ḥajjām*). The circumcision takes place on the village square. The stone serves as a seat for the circumciser. Two white sheets create a separate ritual space (*ḥurma*) and keep curious villagers at a distance (in agreement with the tents used at large collective circumcisions). The circumciser sprinkles salt and the seeds of the plant *ḥarmal* on the spot where blood will drop. He then circumcises the little boy. A Drawi lifts the boy up and returns him to his sister, while a Drawia gives the boy a white bandage around his head steeped in a mixture of water, saffron and henna. He is, then, carried back home. This all happens in a hectic atmosphere with small girls and women assembled in front of the circumcision area.

Unlike circumcision, shaving only temporarily changes and purifies human bodies. On request, Hammed and his son Abdelhadi shave heads, especially of the older men in the village. Shaving returns as a purificatory practice in a number of rites of passage, and the circumciser and barber may be the same person. Shaving as part of a ritual marks the separate status of the 'liminar' (Turner 1974: 232) and is furthermore meant as an act of purification, just like the barber's wife uses henna and other substances to protect and purify the liminars. Westermarck states that the shaving of a newborn child is done by someone who is lucky (1926 ii: 409). Rachik (1990: 134–35) notes that in the High Atlas region a baby's first haircut is aimed

at sanctification of the child and his integration into the human
world. Shaving is also part of the marriage ceremony, when the barber cuts a strip of hair off the groom, in the same manner as was
done at his circumcision feast.

Purification by means of natural substances

The treatment of liminars during the rites of passage with purificatory
substances is particularly a task for Drawa. One of the most frequently
used substances is the reddish dye henna. It has not just cosmetic
value but interconnects bodily and spiritual purification. Henna purifies a human being and protects him or her against any possible danger but can also attract danger. It has thus an ambiguous quality, the
same as blood which it resembles in colour. In this respect, a number of ethnologists have pointed to the use of henna as a symbolic
metonym of blood. For instance, Combs-Schilling (1989: 197) argued
that the henna ceremony has to be interpreted as a ritual expression of the blood that will be spilled in the night of the defloration.
Henna not only wards off danger. When henna is prepared it is
powerful but when it is cultivated and dried, it is polluting: It is
therefore not allowed to grow henna on the village territory as it
would endanger the lives of the villagers.[6] *Ḥarmal* (African rue) is
another herb that has a special place in prophylactic practices. It is
sprinkled on the ground before circumcision takes place. It is a sacred
plant that wards off attacks of the evil spirits (jinns) and is used as
an ingredient in fertility *mélanges* (Jansen 1987: 142).

For example rose petals (*werd*), myrrh (*rihan*), lavender (*ḳazāma*),
cinnamon (*qirfa*), *sargīna* (the root of the Saharan plant *Corrigiola tele-
phiifolia*), *ṭarra* (*Cyperus longus*, a kind of aromatic tuber), together with
the unidentified ingredient *sinabin* are ingredients of *ḳuad*.[7] They are
ground and mixed with water and saffron. *Ḳuad* appears in several
phases of the rites of passage. *Baḳūr* is a generic name for different
kinds of aromatic burning incenses used to purify rooms, clothes,

---

[6] This corresponds to Douglas' assertion that it is only in the final stage of decay
that 'anomalies acquire positive power' (cited in Ohnuki-Tierney 1981: 125). See
in this respect Kapchan (1996: 159): 'Even substantially, henna is ambiguous; when
applied it is a viscous paste, neither liquid nor solid'.

[7] However, the composition of the *mélanges* may differ from one person to another.
The ingredients were identified with the help of Salmon (1906), Venzlaff (1977) and
Bellakhdar (1978).

and people at all rituals. These substances are especially used by Drawa who assist at the rituals.

Some of these substances are associated with the superhuman creatures called jinns. *Sargīna* is supposed to act powerfully against supernatural diseases inflicted by the jinns. *Qatrān* (tar, used in combination with *African Pyrethrum*) and *harmal* are associated with specific jinns (Crapanzano 1973: 146); in general, jinns can be recognized by their particular attraction to specific incenses. In the next section this connection between purification and the world of the jinns will be considered.

The subterranean world

Practical knowledge regarding purification and defilement is part of the prevailing cosmology, in particular concerning the belief in a superhuman world of jinns. In the village, as in the rest of Morocco, transitional processes which lead from one cultural category to the next one are symbolized in the belief in the other or subterranean world of the jinns (cf. Westermarck 1926; Crapanzano 1973; Lahlou 1986); thus, villagers will inevitably refer to the beings that symbolize a moment or place without order, when finding themselves in an ambiguous state. Drawa, in their roles as specialists of social and cultural mediation, are associated with this subterranean world; they stand with one leg in this world and one in the netherworld.

In the Islamic creation myth, jinns are male, female or hermaphroditic creatures situated between humans and angels. They are as diverse as humans, but cannot be seen by them. Where angels are created out of light (*nūr*), jinns are made out of fire (*nār*). This wordplay determines their status: They seem to be normal beings, but in fact symbolize a human counterworld. When disturbed in their natural habitat, jinns are capable of harming humans. Jinns are literally 'the covered or hidden ones' and the majority of jinns indeed live underground, which gave them the euphemistic name of 'inhabitants of the earth' (*mwalin al-arḍ*). Their world is 'subterranean', in contrast to the supernatural world of God and his angels. Although jinns are non-human, they do feel attracted to them: Another euphemism labels them 'those other people'. They live in proximity to humans, but humans, when they stick to a straight course and take the right precautions, will not have to fear them. There is a risk of offending a jinn when one commits an act that involves the disturbance of the social, spatial or temporal order or brings one into contact with impure substances. For example, someone may throw away dirty bathwater into a dried-up irrigation canal and splash the jinns that inhabit the spot. When done at night, an additional risk is involved. The jinns are attracted by human dirt, blood, and fire and can be found in bathhouses and showers, near fire, and slaughter places. You should fear them, as one villager said, 'when you do something dirty' like urinating on the wrong spot or in the wrong direction (direction of prayer). Additionally, in any transitional undertaking, that is, rite of passage, a human is vulnerable to an attack by jinns.

The fear of jinns for light, salt, iron and steel, coins, and charcoal is an indication that their world is taken as a symbolic counterworld to the human world. Its existence defines the boundaries between, on the one hand, the civilized and pure world of humans and, on the other, the uncivilized and impure, non-human world. These binary oppositions of nature versus culture and defilement versus purity, return in an additional range of binary oppositions—day: night; right: left; human speech: non-human sound; salted food: unsalted food—which connect the belief in jinns with the prevailing *habitus* of proper behaviour. The distinctive elements of these oppositions should not be confused. For example, whistling in general is considered to be an unwise act. It is an inhuman sound and attracts jinns. When done at home it combines the habitat of humans with an inhuman sound. The same accounts for the bark of a dog inside a *qsar* house. In the dark, when humans are already displaced and 'out of time', whistling reinforces the risk of attracting jinns, unlike the recitation of the Koran which keeps them at bay. The Koran here functions as an actual device (*al-furqān*) to distinguish men from nature. Particularly with the blurring of boundaries between cultural categories, like sparkles (in between light and dark), intermediary moments of place and time, and persons in an intermediate state (pregnant women, newborn children, bride and groom, et cetera), threat of jinns arises and precautions are necessary. When following a straight course, humans do not have to fear jinns. The cultural ideals of the oasis society thus find expression in the interconnection of physical and moral purity with the cosmology of the jinns. Figure 10 presents the relationship between the social division of Haratin and Shurfa and the cosmological division of the supernatural and subterranean world:

God (culture)
  (angels)
  |
  |
  Shurfa; in control of numinous force
commoners (human civilization)
  Haratin/Drawa; in control of numinous force
  |
  |
  jinns
  (human nature)

Figure 10: Cosmology

God's angels, of whom every person has one on each shoulder, are perfect. Unlike jinns and humans, they do not know sexual drives (Lahlou 1986: 46). Perfection, as we will see, is thus also infertile.

Elements, substances, creatures, and moments of time and place that are in the well-known words of Victor Turner 'betwixt-and-between all fixed points of classification' (1974: 232) are ascribed with a particular positive or negative force. Drawa, who have been portrayed as living in a permanent marginal state, appear to be equally attributed with a numinous force. Moreover, it is widely known that Drawa have a special relationship with the jinns: They are able to withstand the jinns and protect their fellow-humans from them. The jinns may be represented by Drawa (Maher 1974: 25). Among the Berber-speaking Ait 'Atta there is a taboo on the utterance of the word Hartani or on meeting one in the intermediary period in the morning before breakfast (Hart 1984: 110), probably because of an association with the world of the jinns. The same accounts for the cat, the animal to which body a jinn may transform.

The association of Drawa with jinns can be seen in their occupations involving transforming and 'separating, cutting, and dividing things which nature (. . .) has united' into cultural artifacts.[8] In these occupations, Drawa act as cultural brokers, mediating between nature and culture, dealing with the four elements (soil, water, fire, and air) to create cultural artifacts. Each of the four elements is known for its particular jinns. People distinguish water jinns (in wells and sources), earth jinns (numerous and particularly attracted by blood), fire jinns

---

[8] The phrase comes from Bourdieu (1977: 133).

(eating your breath and disliking the dousing of a fire), and wind
jinns (at the service of sorcerers) (cf. Lahlou 1986: 58–59). A typical
Drawi task is to work the bellows to make a fire for cooking water
at large communal dinners. Normally, it is an older Drawi who sits
outside all night to keep the fire going. Although this is quite a bor-
ing task, he at least avoids the burden of running around as in his
younger days. Similarly, Pâques (1991: 162) notes on the fire in the
urban bathhouses: 'To kindle and maintain the fire in the *hammām*
was work reserved for the black slaves, "the men of the burning
coals"'. Since jinns are attracted by the fire, the work is not without danger to men. The handling of the bellow and the maintenance
of fire return in the work of the blacksmith. In the village there is
not one practising blacksmith, but in the oasis and in southern
Morocco as a whole, blacksmiths are Haratin. As one man told me,
it is not unusual to find in the High Atlas Mountains an all-ʿAttawi
village with one Hartani blacksmith living amidst them. Lastly, there
are the occupations that involve working the earth and soil to create cultural artifacts. The Drawi potters in the oasis, making unglazed
earthenware, resemble Drawi grave- and well-diggers in their close
contact with the earth. When a house is built or a hole dug (for a
grave or a well) a sacrifice is made against a possible attack of the
jinns. In the death rites, the muezzin (Drawi or Sharif) takes care
of the corpse, while a male Drawi looks after the grave. Before he
starts to dig, salt is sprinkled on the ground to purify it and ward
off the evil sprits lurking in the ground.

Because of these occupations, Drawa may inspire fear and awe
for their proximity to jinns. Even so, they are attributed with the
quality of protecting others from the jinns. This belief explains why
when circumcising the young boys in the village (done by a Drawi),
the first boy to be circumcised is always a Drawi. Boys at the moment
of circumcision are powerless before the dangers of the jinns—who
are attracted by the blood that will be spilled. Therefore, protective
measures are needed. One way to keep the jinns at bay is with
harmal and salt used by the circumciser. Salt is considered to be a
human substance[9] and is very much disliked by the jinns. Letting a

---

[9] See Rachik (1990: 64): 'The absence of salt, which defines two types of food,
was the symbol, the criterium of an ontological distinction between two classes of
beings, humans (*lins*) vis-à-vis *jinns*'. Salt purifies, mediates and binds people (for
example when enemies eat from the same plate).

Drawi go first is another protective measure. Likewise, bride and groom are accompanied by Drawa, especially when the bride moves from her parental home to that of her future husband. The capacity of Drawa to accompany people who may come into contact with the subterranean world of the jinns can furthermore be seen in the calendrical ritual of the Islamic Fast.

Ramadan is the Islamic month of fasting. From sunrise to sunset every Muslim abstains from eating and drinking. After the *maġrīb* prayer (when the sun has set), the fast is broken with a few dates and a bowl of soup. During this month, ordinary social life is turned upside-down: Breakfast is eaten at the close of the day and the last dinner before sunrise in the middle of the night. In the evening adults visit relatives and friends, and children play card games they never play during the rest of the year. Furthermore, '[f]or one month, people act as if they could create "Paradise on earth"' (Buitelaar 1991: 131). For the period of one month, a sacred time reigns with every impure activity being abandoned. Until recently, the start of Ramadan was announced by a Drawi who blew a horn (*nafir*) while walking through the village at *maġrīb* prayer. This Marrakshi practice (Chottin 1927) was brought to the village by a Sharif who had lived in the northern town for many years. The practice marks the beginning of a liminal period, the Ramadan Fast;[10] the involvement of a Drawi is another way to express the transitional nature of the moment.

In the village, as elsewhere in Morocco, it is believed that part of the sacred and pure quality of Ramadan is the absence of any danger from the spirits of the earth. They are 'locked up' for the main part of the month and return in the night of the 27th day of Ramadan. In orthodox Islam, the 27th night is considered the one in which the Koran was sent down to the Prophet. To commemorate this crucial event in Islamic doctrine, in the village, as in the whole of the country, men stay up all night to pray in the mosque. Girls and boys organize festive parties. It is said that the prayers of 'the 27th' are more valuable than those of a thousand other nights; yet, the sacred 27th night is dangerous as well. To ward off the danger of the jinns, young women walk through the village with incense to purify the houses and *qsar* streets, because, in the words of Buitelaar

---

[10] In Buitelaar's study on the celebration of Ramadan (1991: 134–35), this point is discussed more extensively.

(1991: 54), '[o]ne never knows in what mood the whimsical spirits will be, so precautions must be taken to avoid irritating them while they are trying to settle down again'. On the basis of what has been said about the association of Drawa with the spirits of the subterranean world, it may come as no surprise that members of the Hazzabin family fulfil an important task in this transitional night. The women of the family prepare a few buckets of sauce and many loafs of bread, which are taken by the male members of the family to the praying men in the mosque. Hammed Hazzabin stated that the preparation is a duty he inherited from his father Salem.[11] Yet, the association between the gift of food, the 27th day, and social marginality is more than a coincidence. Bédoucha (1987: 255) mentions in her study how the Tunisian Haratin, called *Šwašīn*, were assigned a similar task. Just like in Aduafil, it is the Šušana town crier who brings food to the mosque on the 27th night of Ramadan. I believe the practice has to do with the transitional nature of the 27th day of Ramadan, as symbolized in the return of the jinns. In normal life, the night time belongs to the jinns. Humans should not cook or eat during this time of day. However, during the liminal topsy-turvy world of Ramadan, humans do exactly this. Luckily, because of the absence of the jinns, they do not have to fear for repercussions. The 27th night is the turning point, a liminal moment within the liminal month itself, the moment when the jinns return. It is appropriate, then, that Drawa, who are associated with the jinns, prepare the dinner on this night. Their participation in the beginning and at the turning point of Ramadan protects villagers against the jinns and amplifies the meaning that is conveyed in this crucial moment of the Islamic month of fasting. Their material activities help to bring the villagers into a spiritual state. In the next section, we will see that similar functions lie at the heart of the participation of Drawa in other rites of passage.

---

[11] According to villagers, the duty in the 27th night is a survival from an extensive system of food exchange that once included the whole village and every day of Ramadan. On some of the other days, Sharifian families still prepare dinner. On the Little Feast that celebrates the end of the fast, one Sharifian family invites villagers for breakfast with bread and honey.

The cycle of life

> It is indeed a cosmic conception that relates the stages of human existence . . . to the great rhythms of the universe (Van Gennep 1960: 194).

From the previous two sections, it appears that distinction of the elements that constitute major symbolic oppositions like impure: pure and nature: culture may be the cultural ideal. However, as Bourdieu (1977: 124) has noted, 'the necessities of practice demand the reunion of things': Unavoidable transgressions form the foundation of life. Pandolfo (1989: 17) in an article on 'space and bodies' in southern Morocco argues in a similar vein: 'Presence, life, seems always to be in transit between the wet and the dry, the black and the white' to fill that which is empty, to elevate what is down and to bring inside what is outside. This is the cycle of life that flows like water in the irrigation canals. The symbolic oppositions of white: black; Shurfa: Haratin/Drawa; pure: impure in fact constitute a generative scheme of 'becoming': A pure (white, Sharifian) condition is dry, without life, barren and infertile. It needs the input of Drawa who are in control of the white substances semen, pollen of date palms, water and, I would add, mother's milk (cf. Delaney 1991). These are the fecundating substances that bring forth life: 'Without the movement of black people going up to bring the "seeds" down, fertilizing and enworlding the white principle, the inseminating capacity of the white people would remain barren' (Pandolfo 1989: 16).

These notions, going beyond a static structuralist perspective, help to clarify the interdependent tasks of Shurfa and Drawa in major rites of passage. At all those occasions where Shurfa contribute to a positive outcome by their graceful presence—being in control of *baraka*—and the recitation of the Koran, Drawa do their own particular bit: They accompany, protect and aid those individuals who undergo a dramatic change of status or phase in life and join them in the experience of the ritual in which the status reversal has been most dramatically laid out.

Life crisis rituals

Haratin or Drawa participate in rituals surrounding the birth and first vulnerable days of newborn babies. They fulfil a pivotal role in the circumcision and marriage rituals and the last rites. When a woman gives birth, Mina Hazzabin helps with the delivery and takes care of the mother and child in the first seven days. On the seventh day, the child receives a name. Usually this happens during a small party in a familial atmosphere. In particular, when it concerns a first child, one may decide to organize a collective dinner with Koran recitation (*silka*). Hammed Hazzabin is then asked to sacrifice a sheep or goat for which he receives the head of the offering, if it is not already promised to the midwife (his sister-in-law). On the 40th day after a delivery, Hammed shaves the newborn child for the first time. First, the women of the family visit the village shrine with the child. There, they mix a bit of water with saffron and wet the head of the child with it after which Hammed shaves it. Sometimes a small tuft of hair in the middle is left untouched as a remedy against illnesses. Nowadays, it is removed after some months or one year, whereas in the past it might have stayed for years. After the shaving a bit of henna and a *mélange* of herbs (*kuad*) is put on the head. In exchange, Hammed receives some eggs and sugar and additionally joins in the family meal with, as a rule, the head and stomach of a sheep. During a child's first year of life, the mother visits an old Drawia in a nearby *qsar* to have her child treated prophylactically with cauterization (see below).

Marriage is the second example of the accompanying role of Drawa in transitional rituals in the cycle of life. The first step to conclude a marriage in the village is done by going to the administrative centre of the oasis and having two notaries draw up a marriage certificate. This is usually done without much ado.[12] The next step in the case of a first marriage, the actual consummation, is surrounded by an elaborate set of activities, fixed in time and place and aimed at an evocative performance of the change of status the participants go through. The marriage rituals and festivities begin with a public announcement by the village crier.

The marriage rituals follow a tripartite scheme of separation from a former status, liminality with regard to established social categories, and reintegration into a higher status (cf. Van Gennep 1960; Turner 1974: 231–232). Drawa as structural marginals play pivotal roles in

---

[12] Although the draft of the marriage contract is not surrounded by specific rituals, it is of course very important to parents and the couple involved, and likewise the subject of intensive negotiations.

the course of events. In agreement with observations of two anthropologists who have written extensively on the Moroccan first marriage rituals (Jamous 1981; Combs-Schilling 1989; cf. Laoust 1993;
Westermarck 1914), I concede that the male rituals express in an
intensified way the forthcoming role of the groom as a married
man; thus, during the liminal phase, the groom is already portrayed
as an honourable, powerful male. 'The ritual must inculcate within
the young man the model of adulthood he must embody' (Combs-
Schilling 1989: 191).[13] This is most aptly done by transforming the
groom for the period of the marriage rituals into the sultan (*mulay
as-sulṭān*), the highest authority in the country.

In the village this takes place on the Tuesday of the marriage
rituals. First, on the Monday, a ritual called the *kabb* takes place; gifts
from villagers are noted down by the imam and later in the day
brought to the house of the groom. The gifts normally consist of large
quantities of sugar, flour and oil. The day receives its name from a
ritual in which a Drawi used 'to pour' almonds from the second
floor upon the guests present. Nowadays, almonds are more decently
divided. A Drawi walks around with almonds in his *jallāba*, held up
as a sack, giving everybody present five or six unshelled almonds.

On Tuesday, one day before the groom will actually meet and
deflower his bride, a ceremony is held at his house (or in a nearby
open field) that transforms the groom into the *mulay as-sulṭān*. The
groom stands in front of the older men of the village who recite sections of the Koran. Then, while they pray for his divine protection,
he gets dressed, with a black woollen cloak and a hood covering his
head and face. A sword, hung around his shoulders, completes the
costume. At this stage the groom is about to leave his status as unmarried man behind, while not yet having attained the forthcoming
married status.

The liminal status of the groom, that is, his withdrawal from normal social life, is emphasized by the covering of his face and the
interdiction to speak. Also, the point of time of the ritual is liminal.
It starts at *maġrīb* when the sun is about to go down, and day passes
into night, and ends when the sun has sunk completely. Then, a

---

[13] Combs-Schilling (1989: 190) has argued that this interpretation should be taken
as a deviation from Turner's analysis of rites of passage, in particular where he
states that '"the passenger" or "liminar" (. . .) passes through a symbolic domain that
has few or none of the attributes of his past or coming state' (Turner 1974: 232).

Drawi (usually Barka Hazzabin, or when more than one groom is involved, assisted by his sons) takes the groom on his back and runs as fast as he can to the location where the groom, as *sulṭān*, is going to receive the henna that will protect him during the following days.[14] As a rule, the march of the Drawi with the groom on his back should be done alone; male children however, try to break this rule. Adults present at the dressing ceremony have to stop them from following the groom. When he arrives at the village square, the Drawi hands the groom over to one or two Drawiat (among them Hammed's wife Aisha) who take charge of the henna ceremony. The ceremony involves dyeing the hands and feet of the groom. It is furthermore said that the groom receives some advice concerning the defloration of the bride. On this day the work of the male usher (*wazīr*) starts. The location of the henna ceremony is separated by an irrigation canal from the place where, at the same time, the men congregate to make music, perform a stamping-foot dance called *snisla* and possibly sing praises. A Drawi, normally Hammed, stands armed with a stick on the canal bridge to guard the women from being disturbed by children. After dinner, musical festivities continue in a field nearby. Late in the night just before dawn a Drawi and a Drawia accompany the bride to the groom's house. In the morning, women's ululations celebrate the successful defloration of the bride. Subsequently, small portions of food are sent out to related and befriended households.

The marriage ceremony is drawn from the same ritual repertoire as the circumcision. In both, the liminar is not allowed to touch the ground, but is carried or made to sit on a mat. He is temporarily transferred to the women, away from the male group, into which he will be reintegrated at the end of the rituals. Second, in both ceremonies, purification of the individuals taking part in the rituals is done by shaving their head and applying henna and a mixture

---

[14] The only other similar practice I found in Westermarck (1914: 109) is part of the male marriage ceremony of the Ait Warain Berbers: 'The Sultan and his vizier hide themselves in some place outside the village (. . .). The bachelors go to search for him; when he is found the vizier takes him on his back and runs away with him . . .'. Next, the henna ceremony follows. Then, '[the groom] is hastily carried away on the back of the vizier . . .'. Likewise, the bridal marriage ceremonies, as they have been described by Westermarck, may also include the carriage of the bride by her *wazīra* (for example: idem, 145). Most similiar is the following practice from Tangier: 'In the evening [of the day the bride has been to the public bath, RE] (. . .) the girl (. . .) is carried by a black woman (*ḫâdĕm*), called the *nggāfa*, to the room in the house where she is now going to be painted with henna' (idem, 141).

of herbs. Third, these are the only two ceremonies where the *snisla* is performed. By doing so, with the aid of lyrics and rhythmic foot-stamping, a new (male) sprout on the genealogical tree of the founder of the village is celebrated. Lastly, the most obvious connection is one of terminology. 'To circumcise', *katana*, comes from the same root as the word for bridegroom and son-in-law, *katan*. The circumcision ritual anticipates the future role of the boy as married man, just like the marriage ritual foresees the groom in his role as head of a house-hold (and in both, as a Muslim; cf. Reysoo 1985: 15).

Through different means, the transgressive phases of the ritual firstly stress the liminal character of persons undergoing the ritual, and secondly protect and strengthen them on their ritual and future lifepath. With respect to liminal time, the ritual moment of *maġrīb* occurs when day turns into night and night into day. With respect to liminal space, one location has an interesting function in the rit-uals, the so-called 'eye of the house' (*'ain d-dār*). This is the quadrangular open space in the middle of a *qṣar* building. It is a hole from top to bottom through which sunlight enters the house and smoke may leave it. Four pillars mark the boundaries of the 'eye'. Through the eye, light enters the house, symbolizing God, though evil things may also enter. Because something bad may befall you, villagers do not like to sit in the eye. Hammed once even suggested that Islamic law forbids sitting in the quadrangular eye. At the same time, it is an important ritual spot. It is the place where the sheep of the Great Feast is sacrificed and put on display and where dancing takes place at marriages and circumcisions. Thus, on the very first day of my stay, Hammed, when showing me his house, stopped at the eye and started to clap hands, evoking marriage music and villagers danc-ing. It is also the place where women rain their ululations down upon the men, for example, on the first marriage day when men sew the marriage clothes, and where in the past on the day of *kabb* a Drawi dropped almonds down upon the villagers. Both ululations and almonds are known for their fertile quality, and together with music and light, the ambiguous location of the eye is the place from where they reach humans.

By definition, a person undergoing the ritual maintains an ambigu-ous status throughout the ritual process. Being out of time and with-out clear-cut status, he or she is sensitive to outside influences and pollution. The role of Drawa corresponds with what already has been said about their intermediary and order-keeping qualities. They

intermediate between men and women and keep children calm and
at a distance. Most striking is the Drawi as carrier of the groom;
'carrying and being carried is one of the practices which is found
more or less universally in various ceremonies through which a person
passes in the course of a lifetime' (Van Gennep 1960: 185). Here,
the carriage corresponds to the offensive association of Drawa with
donkeys (Drawa being the donkeys of the Shurfa). More importantly,
it is Drawa who carry the person undergoing the rite of passage
over the threshold of the house, at the moment when day turns into
night, from the male group to the female group. Again, a Drawia
gives him the henna that will protect him from the danger he faces
as a liminar. Drawa take on a stereotypic role in the rituals: They
protect the Shurfa from the dangers of impurity and, if necessary,
purify them.

Fertility

> [U]ncleanness, though chiefly of an injurious nature, may in
> certain circumstances be a cause of good. It is like a poison which
> sometimes, taken in small doses, acts as a remedy (Westermarck
> 1926 i: 260).

The second dimension of the contributions of Drawa to the cycle
of life is their transmission of a positive, fertile quality to those passing through the ritual. Both marriage and circumcision can be seen
as fertility rituals. It is common knowledge, and a popular topic for
youngsters to discuss with me, that only circumcised men are capable of proper sexual intercourse. In general, it has been argued that
Moroccan marriage rituals can be seen as fertility rites (Jamous 1981:
258). According to Combs-Schilling (1989) the sword which is hung
around the shoulders of the groom is an authority symbol and phal-
lus symbol at the same time. Besides the fertile female ululations at
the rites of passage, the specific 'fertile' contribution of Drawa can
be seen in the *kabb* ritual and their musical contribution to the rituals (see below). In all these instances Drawa 'fill'—literally in the
case of the *kabb* ritual—the ritual that would remain 'empty' and
sterile without their contributions. Drawa play a central role in rituals in which fertility is a significant element and transmit an indispensable fertile power. It is said that the Hartani specialism of the
pollination of date palms resembles human fertilization. People do
in fact refer to the whole process of date palm cultivation—from

pollination to the cutting of dates—as a cycle of life and death, using the same verb to speak of human and date palm fertilization (*dakkar*). In the rituals, the supernatural power of the light-skinned Shurfa, that is their *baraka*, would remain sterile and dry 'like a dead plant' (Chebel 1984: 33) without the inseminating capacities of the dark-skinned Drawa.

The fertile quality of Haratin is visible at a kind of masquerade held on the day of *'ašūrā'*, the tenth day of the first month of the Islamic New Year. The central part of the masquerade is a parade through the village by a man with the skin and head of a mule, called *bǧila*. In the evening of the first day of the month, the younger children make a lantern out of palm leaves and set it on fire, singing 'butafo, butafo'. In the afternoon of the tenth day, children receive toys. They make a kind of palmleaf boat with which they go along the houses to collect dried meat (of the festive sheep) and eggs, singing

> *Mimun ystar 'alik* Mimun preserves you
> *aš bǧa Mimun?* What does Mimun want?
> *bǧa kardusa, buyūd wa ḵubiza* He wants dried meat, eggs and bread

Mimun is here the name for a kind of jinn. A girl gives the children dried meat of the festive sheep while a second girl throws water on their heads through the eye of the house. On *'ašūrā'* women visit the graveyard. The men are supposed to fast on this day, and some in the village actually do so. In the evening, unmarried men visit, together with the *bǧila*, the men who have been married in the past year. The married men have to give them a special kind of dried meat (*sliwna*). If not, they are thrown into the irrigation canal. From the participation of celibates, women and children as well as from the course of events, it can be concluded that the feast carries traits of a ritual of reversal, in which the less powerful in society are in temporary command and ridicule those on top (cf. Babcock 1978). Buitelaar (1991: 116) calls *'ašūrā'* 'a celebration of female power'. This at least has to be complemented by the power of the youngsters, and possibly by that of the Drawa. The main point here is that although one or two Drawa have acted as *bǧila* in the village, it is not altogether clear whether this is something of a rule. Contextual evidence is provided by way of a second masquerade that Laoust saw as closely associated with the 'carnival' of *'ašūrā'*. This second masquerade is held in some villages in the south on the second day of the Great Feast (Hammoudi 1993). In the village the Great Feast and 'ašūrā' are indeed linked: People at least save the dried meat from the festive sheep until it is distributed among the children at 'ašūrā'.

The Great Feast masquerade that is held in some villages west of the Dra Valley is centred around the figure of 'the man with the skin' (Būjlūd or Bilmaun). Two other personages figure in the masquerade, the Jew and the slave. Bilmaun has the skin of the festive sheep around his shoulders and horns on his head, his face is blackened, and he holds a large stick in his hands. He runs around the village, hitting everybody in reach, entering homes without asking for permission. Women let him cross the threshold and penetrate their house, even trying to be touched because of his fecundating quality. A beast on two legs, neither man nor woman, Bilmaun has left the human order and entered that of the jinns (idem, 216). Who dares play this ambiguous figure—being dangerous and attractive at the same time—in the village who may enter houses, harassing women and children?

> For several years Bilmaun has been played by members of an old but déclassé family. It belongs to a group that here is called assuqi and elsewhere aqabli or hartani. They are found just about everywhere throughout the Atlas and the southern oases; they are dark-skinned and either work the land or engage in labor involving water (e.g., well men or canal specialists). They exercise certain trades some of which, like smithing, are feared and disdained (Hammoudi 1993: 93).

Two men who have played Bilmaun in the village to which the quotation refers were traders in charcoal and wood, the others were a miner, a mason, a seasonal worker and someone who did every sort of trade. All were landless. In contrast to the other actors who were young men and adult bachelors, the Hartani actors were married men who played out their structural marginal status at the Great Feast masquerade.

'Ašūrā' is more than a feast of female or subordinate power. When we compare the rituals on this day with those performed for Prophet's birthday (maulid) we get the following arrangement:

'ašūrā': maulid
death: birth
women: men
children: elders
Drawa: Shurfa

Maulid literally is a birthday. It is also a day of men and of the collective consumption of food by men on the sacred ground of the village shrine. Instead, *'asūrā'* is a day of death, when women bring food to the cemetery and men fast. *Maulid* is the feast of the Shurfa, *'asūrā'* the feast of the Drawa in the village (similar to the 27th day of Ramadan). Yet the oppositions should not be read rigidly. In agreement with Pandolfo's analysis (1989), we may consider *'asūrā'* not as a feast of the death but as a celebration of the cycle of life and death. The masquerade and pouring of water testify to the fertilizing quality of this feast. *Maulid*, the Shurfa, represent a sacredness that would remain infertile without the fertility of *'asūrā'*, the Drawa. Therefore, the two celebrations are interdependent, similar to the two social categories that personify them.

The ritual practices of Drawa are connected to a view on human creation and the physiological and spiritual difference between Drawa and other humans. In this respect special mention has to be made of the relationship between Drawa and the plant *šiba* (*Artemisia absinthium*, or *absinth alsem*). The aromatic buds are used as a substitute for mint during the winter months. *Šiba* (litt. *šaybat al-'ajūz*, 'the white hair of the old woman'; cf. Bellakhdar 1978: 222) is in use as a medicine. Because of its power, one needs only a very small branch of the buds. This is also the reason why villagers state you should not put *šiba* in tea as often as you would do with mint. Its aroma is supposed to go to your head, just like alcohol does; for this reason others do not use *šiba* at all. The buds of *šiba* make you feel dizzy and lose self-control. In the village, *šiba* is cultivated by only one person, Hammed Hazzabin. Other families buy it at the market. In the nearby villages, the plant is cultivated by numerous families, but it is said that only Haratin can plant it. Any other person would get sick and eventually die. This seems to be in agreement with a note by Westermarck (1926 i: 261) that '[a]n unclean individual like a Jew may make the plants in a vegetable garden grow by touching them with a slick or flicking their leaves with his fingers'. This does, however, not explain what it is about *šiba* that endangers humans. *Artemisia* is in its different varieties attributed with special qualities in many cultures. In Morocco *šiba* is used as a medicine against the evil eye during giving birth (Bakker 1993: 199). Also in the Native American cultures *Artemisia* is used a medicine, and again in particular for 'female' diseases such as problems with giving birth.

Lévi-Strauss argues in *La pensée sauvage* that in the North American pharmacopoeia *Artemisia* is symbolically opposed to the 'male' plant *Chrysothamnus*, used as a remedy against male urogenital diseases. Both plants are an anomaly in natural classification and approached as ambiguities. These cautious observations may serve as a lead in further research into the natural classification and special status of *Artemisia absinthium* in southern Morocco. Here, they at least give a clue to the special symbolic relation between Drawa and *šiba*. Both represent an anomaly in their respective classifications, have a taboo status and are attributed with superhuman qualities. Where *šiba* as a 'female plant' is said to awaken a man's energy and instincts, Drawa are attributed with an extraordinary amount of this energy.

In the previous chapter *nafs* was defined as the entirety of organic instincts, opposed to the rationale (*ʿaql*) and patience (*sabr*) of men. As such, control over one's passions was seen to be a core element in the complex of civilized conduct. Otherwise, when men let passions rule their life, they follow the spirit of the devil (*nafs aš-šaiṭān*). It also became clear that *nafs* is a necessary faculty of every human being. Without it, human life would not be possible. This has to be taken quite literally. *Nafs* is the fecundating quality that makes lifeless objects come to life. In God's creation, one *nafs* represents one human being. When born, everybody has *nafs*. It is the energy needed to act, and ideally in the course of growing up it is balanced and tamed by reason. Besides standing for the human instinct, another image of *nafs* is *breath*. Both coincide in the dogma that through God's breath life was blown into Miriam's (the Virgin Mary) fruit—as my neighbour in the village brought forward in a discussion about the immaculate conception of the Christ child. *Nafs* then is the life-giving energy, the spirit that makes humans come alive; indeed, the term is used when sexuality and human reproduction come to mind. Sometimes *nafs* is used interchangeably with *rūḥ*, although one may find in written texts interpretations that distinguish the two.

A few words are needed on the difference between the two concepts, *nafs* and *rūḥ*. When asked, most villagers found it difficult to explain the difference, if any.[15] *Nafs* is the vital energy of humans.

---

[15] The tanners in the study of Jemma (1971: 55) state that the hide has two souls: *Rūḥ* is the soul of ingenuity and *nafs* is the vegetable soul, the life force.

One man explained: 'When a person is not yet married though already old enough to do so, people joke that perhaps he doesn't have any *nafs*'. Here virility would be the fitting translation. *Nafs* problems can then be solved with almonds or dates. Some people have a lot of extra *nafs* (*nafs ḍāʿif*). *Rūḥ* is the spirit, the entity that remains after a person has breathed his last (*nafs*). Where *nafs* is also human breath, *rūḥ* is closely related to the wind (*riḥ*) and odour (*rīḥa*) with which it shares the same root. Wind, then, is a soul without a body (Legey 1935: 47). *Riḥ* is also the name for the rhythm in trance seances to exorcise a specific type of jinn, but it can also be a synonym for jinns, in particular those of the wind. *Rīḥa* was used to denominate the bad effect of the odour of soap, the cause of an epidemic spread through the atmosphere, and the cause of the epidemic disease of palms called *bayud*. *Rīḥa* has a positive effect in the case of incense. In short, *nafs* is a natural instinct, connected to the body; *rūḥ* is the spirit that survives after the body has died.

Drawa, perhaps dark-skinned people in general, are said to be especially endowed with *nafs*. Drawa are seen as strong, energetic persons, more capable of bearing hard labour and more resistant against sickness. They grow fast and are already fully grown men when they are fifteen years of age. Two Moroccan sayings refer to this belief. The first says that 'a black man, with all his faults, is stronger than a white man'; the second states that 'a black man has a rib and a cup of blood more than a white man' (Westermarck 1930: 132). Haratin are specialists of the earth and fecundation and associated with a protective and life-giving force. This has partly to do with the dark colour of their skin, which they have in common with ʿAbīd. Through their *nafs* or *nafs*-loaden activities Drawa are able to raise (*tlʿa*) the spirit of others. In their occupations this theme returns. Tanning is an occupation associated with cleansing dead corpses with the aid of water. Water not only purifies but is said to bring dead corpses back 'alive' in the form of hides. It is thus taken here as a life-bringing substance, comparable to blood (Jemma 1971: 73). Tanners and potters bring *nafs*, the life-bringing energy, into the skins and soil to make them into hides and pottery.[16] Not only the

---

[16] Here, the correspondence with human creation is striking: God made all human beings out of clay and by means of his breath, God gave life to these clay humans. It is said that by rubbing your wrists against each other you can still smell the soil.

Hartani executors of these trades but also their clients consider the
work as a life-bringing task. The water in which the blacksmith
quenches the metal object is used by women in fertility rites. The
tanner is thus considered as '[the] master [*maître*] over all fertility'
(idem, 15–16). Hides are used in different marriage, rain and fertility rites in the Maghreb. For example, in the Dra Valley, tanners' hides are used as a underlay in the night of defloration (idem,
60). In the village the midwife receives the skin of the sacrificed
animal.

The ritual experience

> Certain things can only be expressed in rituals (Rappaport
> 1979: 174).

These analytic notes on the positive contribution of Drawa to the
cycle of life should not make us lose sight of the practical, ritual
means by which the distinctive qualities of Shurfa and Drawa are
experienced. Every individual ritual makes participants share in a
unique fusion of sensory experiences. Structural similarities between
the rituals help to convey the message of social and cultural import
transmitted by Drawa and Shurfa as reciters and bearers of *baraka*.
Rites of passage simultaneously express in a dramatic way the transition and change of status of an individual and exemplify the boundaries and interdependence of the central social categories through
time (men: women; youngsters: elders; Shurfa: Drawa). At the same
time, by way of the central positioning of the social and cultural
boundaries in the rituals, their permeability is revealed.

A ritual practice in which the fertility theme returns is the musical performance of Drawa at the festivities of rites of passage. At
weddings, villagers invite musicians from nearby villages to play in
the evening. In particular the group of musicians called *'Aissawa* are
essential to a successful feast. *'Aissawa* consist of a number of drum
instrumentalists, playing a tambourine (*bandir*) and a conical, one-
handed drum (*darabukka*), and a *gita* player. The *gita* is a kind of
oboe, played by members of the *'Aissawa* and *Hamadša* brotherhoods
in their ritual seances. These two brotherhoods are known for their
large membership of dark-skinned, lower class people. As the metal
castanets belong to the music of the descendants of slaves, the *gita*
is said to be the Hartani instrument *par excellence*. At all the mar-

riages I have attended, ʿAissawa musicians were invited. The close association of Haratin with reed instruments returns in the itinerant groups of poet-musicians of the High Atlas (*Imdyazen*). Such a typical *Imdyazen* group consists of four members: The leader-poet, two assistants and a flute-player. While the first three members are generally light-skinned Berbers, the flute-player is always a Hartani (Roux 1928: 232). The flute-player also acts as the buffoon who sports with the audience, sometimes taking on a transvestite role. The monopolization of this disreputable role corresponds with a substantial larger share of the payment than the two assistants.

In the village many voice objections against the participation of the ʿAissawa musicians. Music and singing in general are ambiguously appreciated in Islamic doctrine. This is why one speaks of the *recitation* of religious texts. To call it singing would be a negation of the sacred ambience of *silka-s* and reduce recitation to a corporeal instead of spiritual activity: 'It has thus become convention to name the psalmodic recitation of the Koran a "lecture", notwithstanding the melody and vocal variations . . .' (Lièvre 1987: 19). Likewise, the female ululations should only be performed at certain specific ritual moments, when they cannot be left out.[17] The objection to the ʿAissawa is largely because of the *ġita*. It is said by villagers that the *ġita* makes humans lose control over their senses (*ʿaql*), letting their passions (*nafs*) take over. The devil seduces humans by playing the *ġita*. Thus, to curse your enemy, you tell him to play the *ġita*, the *nafir* and the *ṭbal* (large drum) (Chottin 1927: 380); all three instruments are or were played by Drawa in the village.

At the same time, a person needs extra breath—and again the word *nafs* is used here—to play the *ġita*. Being a reed instrument, one definitely needs considerable effort to get any sound out. Its use is heavily debated by *Islamists* and purists. In comparison, at the seances of the *Ḥamadša* religious brotherhood consisting, according to Crapanzano (1973: 86–87; cf. note 3, chapter two), to a large extent of migrated Haratin, the *ġita* belongs to the 'hot' part of the ritual, enticing people to start dancing when they hear their own individual *riḥ* or rhythm. ' "The ghita talks to me" and "the ghita

---

[17] Once I witnessed how a woman explained marriage, the topic of our conversation, to a deaf and dumb woman by way of making the gesture of an ululation with her mouth and hands.

speaks to my jinn" are common descriptions of the ghita's effect' on participants of these seances (idem, 203). One may wonder why, then, do people invite the musicians to the village. Apparently, the music is considered to be dangerous, but nevertheless an essential part of the rituals. Just like the female ululations, the *gita* 'fertilizes' the ritual, so to speak, with a successful outcome and brings about the transition from nature to culture.

The attribution of a fertile quality to the Drawa via their corporeal activities is a positive result of their ambivalent status: They control some of the means to mediate between the human and natural world. Their intermediate position between this world and the subterranean world as well as between nature and culture returns in their practical knowledge and capacity to protect and heal people from illnesses.

The power to heal

In the local conception of illness and healing, we find a special concern with the boundaries and openings of the human body. Thus, according to villagers, the constitution of a human being is determined by a continuous internal flow of bodily substances. Everything that enters the body through the five senses may influence this internal flow in a positive or negative way. The use of an odour such as perfume, soap, toothpaste or shampoo, even when used by another person, interferes with and usually lengthens the healing process of wounds. These cleaning substances are therefore considered polluting and having a negative effect on the healing process (that is, purification) of a person. Blisters on your feet are useful because through it a substance (denoted as *nafs*) that causes rheumatism leaves the body. In the rites of passage the internal unity of the five senses returns. The ritual performances consist of an intricate and sometimes playful stimulation of the five senses. More generally we may note, in the words of Tambiah (1985: 1), how,

> [rituals are] amalgams or totalities constituted of both word and deed, of speech interlaced with the manipulation of objects, of a simultaneous and sequential use of multiple media of communication (auditory, tactile, visual, and olfactory) and of presentational modes (song, dance, music, recitations, and so on).

Sight, sound and smell are represented in the use of certain colours, different kinds of burning incense, recitation and music. Touch, or the lack of it, is represented in the carriage of liminars and the wearing of certain amulets on the body. Although food is an essential part of rituals, ritual elements in which taste as such plays a role are much more scarce. There are the almonds in the marriage ritual and the presentation of the *baraka*-laden food in the feasts that celebrate the Prophet's birthday and on the 27th day of Ramadan. Salt is an important ingredient of the food and considered to have a purifying effect. At rituals, the contributions of Drawa by way of music, incense, and transportation consist of the penetration of the five senses of the liminars with the objective to purify, protect or fertilize them.

The close interconnection between illness and an impure state of the body returns in the common explanation people give of their diseases: These are often explained by attributing them to a previous contact with jinns, the spirits of the subterranean world. A person can be slapped, possessed or pointed at by a jinn (cf. Crapanzano 1973: 152–57), which will be evident from the type of disease.[18] Healing can then be defined as the process by which a patient is freed from an attachment to a certain jinn, a process in which Haratin play a central role. Healers, such as the herbalist and the cauterization specialist know how to reclaim the body from the jinns and the harmful, impure substances; ashes, henna, salt and tar (*qatrān*) are some of the substances used to remove impurities. These substances are widely known for their capacity to heal and the protection they offer to humans against diseases connected to the jinns.

A medical practice in which healing is synonymous with purification is cauterization (*kawā*), a practice that has existed a long time in Arab medicine. In the Dra Valley, it is said that to be able to cauterize successfully, a person has to be in the possession of a quality that not equals but can be compared to the *baraka* of Shurfa. The cauterization specialist (*kawwāy*) looks for the exact location on the body to place a piece of sulphur, which he then lights. The burn is not treated but left open to heal, resulting in clearly visible scars. Through the heat the substance that causes the illness is thought to

---

[18] Diseases also can be inflicted by means of sorcery and the evil eye.

leave the body. Cauterization is used in particular with respiration problems. The heat of the fire is said to drive away 'the cold' (a generic term for a number of different illnesses) and helps 'to raise the breath' of humans. *Bu jnib* is one of the respiration-related illnesses that can be cured through cauterization. The disease has been described as 'the pain in the side that obstructs breathing' and is felt like 'a mass of flesh that moves around in the belly' (Bakker 1993: 181, 210). The *kawwāy* sets bones (*jabr*) as well. The *kawwāy* uses palm branches to set bones but also uses hot iron poles as a kind of soldering-iron. Once I assisted the Drawi healer of the nearby village, who performed a combination of cauterization and bonesetting on a sick donkey. His healing method, sticking hot iron poles at strategic spots in and through the skin of the donkey, was aimed at the removal of impure substances from the body that caused the illness. First, he rubbed crumbled charcoal on the spot. Next he took a piece of skin and stuck a hot pole through it, muttering *bismillah*. After sticking through a second pole, he took a knife and made a cross and two long cuts on and around the spot to be treated. The healer completed the session by wrapping a bandage around the leg.

I have never seen cauterization being performed on humans, but I did see the remaining scars. All *kawwāy-s* consulted by villagers are Drawa from villages surrounding Aduafil. Villagers visit a Drawia in a nearby village who uses cauterization as a prophylactic treatment for small children. She employs an iron pole to burn the child's skin at certain spots (chest, back and head). The treatment wards off some future dangers. A touch on top of the head with a heated iron pole aids in closing the fontanel. A touch on the chest between the nipples makes the child capable of lifting heavy loads. Horizontal lines along the body protect the child from certain diseases and respiration problems in general.

Other female healers and helpers in the village include the *'arīfa* ('she who knows'), an elderly Drawia who checks the virginity of girls, and the midwife.[19] The *'arīfa* ascertains on request whether a girl is still a virgin. In northern towns, mothers let their daughters be inspected by a doctor who then provides a certificate that can

---

[19] See on the female magicians as doctors, Bakker (1993: 107): 'In the *Maghreb*, there is a preference to look upon extratribal black women as magicians (. . .). The magicians who work as doctors, or rather countermagicians (in Doutté's words), are often women who use burnings (*kouweia*-s)'.

be shown to eligible marriage candidates. Also *'arīfates*, women who have been appointed by the Ministry of Interior, check whether there has been any trace of sexual intercourse. Their judgement has legal ramifications (Naamane 1994:194–195). This does not apply to the village *'arīfa*, although her work is of the same import. The midwife prepares a woman for giving birth, by medicinal and magical means; she also looks after mother and child in the first days after birth.

Hammed and his son are the barbers of the village. They have to be distinguished from the village phlebotomist (*ḥajjām*). The phlebotomist shaves as well, but he does so only to be able to cup a patient. He now and then cups blood for money at the bi-weekly market in the administrative centre. The blood he cups is considered to be bad, causing physical but mostly mental illnesses. Many a man lets himself be cupped during the summer because it is said to relieve the pressure of the summer heat. When it concerns a sick patient, the cupped blood will be examined: Inspection of the blood can tell the source of the disease, symbolized in a specific kind of evil jinn. Blood-letting heals through the purification of body and mind. But when the blood falls into the wrong hands, it can be used in magical practices aimed at causing harm to the patient. Therefore, and because contact with the cupped blood is dangerous to humans, the blood is afterwards poured into the ground at a spot where humans are not likely to pass. Clearly, then, blood-letting is a precarious task and not without danger to the phlebotomist. However, when once in a quarrel the danger of cupped blood was spelled out by a patient, the phlebotomist objected by stating fiercely that the blood is not dangerous at all, considering the fact that the phlebotomist of the Prophet Muhammad even drunk his blood.[20] Nevertheless, it is said that the former phlebotomist, the brother of the present one, died because of the polluted and jinn-infected blood of one of his patients.

In agreement with the pattern of Drawa fulfilling tasks that bring them into contact with organic fluids, one would expect the village phlebotomist to be a Drawi; however, this is not the case. The phlebotomist is a Sharif from the village, who took on this job after the death of his brother, who in turn had followed in his father's

---

[20] Also the *ḥajjām* of Mulay Idriss, Sidi 'Abdallah al-Hajjām, is said to have had the habit of drinking the blood of his patients (Herber 1937).

footsteps. Being a Sharif, the man who acts as phlebotomist has taken on some of the ambiguous qualities that are typical for Drawa but fit equally with his task. First, his appearance differs: He wears a long grey beard, which is not worn by any other man in the village or, for that matter, in the oasis. He dresses in blue trousers instead of the usual white ones. Secondly, he is the only adult and married Sharif who takes on some of the responsibilities otherwise performed only by Drawa. He serves and aids Hammed with sacrifices. At feasts he is the only Sharif to work with the bellows to make a fire. He has furthermore worked as field-guard, while his son is the only non-Drawi who has acted as usher of the groom.

In the village I have not noticed any particular knowledge of medicinal herbs among Drawa, but the neighbouring oasis of Tissint, located along the bed of the Dra River, is widely known for its Hartani herbalists. Bellakhdar *et al.* (1992: 209) mention 145 herbalists, of which 105 originated in one village. The herbalists collect more than 80 different herbal medicines or buy them in the north of the country. Some are ambulant traders and healers, others remain in the south. All return home for the annual saint's day of the village saint. From the Ktawa Oasis, a delegation of clients and migrated descendants visits their saint's feast.

Maher (1974: 25) notes that '[a]ll the spice and potion dealers, the *tabub* or healers, the men and women sorcerers whom I came across were *haratn*'. This is in agreement with Doutté's statement that every doctor in North Africa is 'nearly always someone with a marginal social position'. Bakker notes that the dark-skinned cauterizers in the Middle Atlas where she did fieldwork, 'were quite poor and lived in deplorable circumstances'. They were strangers to the region and came from the Ait 'Atta, where they were treated as slaves. One of these cauterizers also washed and buried the dead (Bakker 1993: 105, 265–266). The Drawi herbalists and healers are, however, not the only medicinal specialists in the oasis. Literate healers, and among them is the Sharifian *fqīh* of the village, write amulets. These amulets can be worn on a certain spot on the body, or placed at a strategic location in the house. The amulets can also be drunk, by putting the written paper into water, or inhaled, by writing something on a piece of cotton, burning it and inhaling the smoke. In these practices, the belief in the unity of the five senses and the human body returns. There is also the modern *médecin* or *tbib* in the oasis centre. Lastly, there are the healing seances of the religious brotherhoods, in which Haratin make up for a large part of the membership (Crapanzano 1973; Naamouni 1993). With respect to the relationship between the different types of healers, the following observations of two separate healing practices in early modern Europe are remarkably fitting. First, medicinal practices were performed by priests or literati. Second, there were,

> illiterate diviners, herbalists, midwives, bonesetters, and 'surgeons', many of the last doubling as barbers, who engage in blood-letting, cupping, pulling teeth, and the like. These lower-class and outcaste practioners lack a standardized body of knowledge and a scholarly orientation (Sjoberg cited in Blok 1981: 111).

Many of the healing practices of Haratin take place in public. People use specialists such as the *kawwāy* and phlebotomist in combination with other healers. The work of other healers is more of a private affair, taking place 'behind the scenes of men's communal social life' (Elias 1997 ii: 324). This division between the public and private domain is reminiscent of other professions performed by Drawa in the village. A second difference is the manual treatment versus the treatment with amulets. Third, the public practice is mainly based on knowledge originating in experience, while the other derives from scriptural knowledge. According to Bellakhdar (1978: 109–110), in southern Morocco along the classic Arab medical tradition an informal, medical practice developed which was informed by practices from south of the Sahara, with dark-skinned slaves acting as brokers. In time both traditions got to some extent mixed. Yet, the official 'art of the ancients' remains the truthful science and more prestigious than the 'crypto-medicine which is fed by subterranean sources in the popular culture'.

Milk and magic

> The milk from a *hartaniya's* breast is supposed to have curative properties ... (Maher 1974: 25).

Let me summarize the content of this chapter thus far. Drawa are specialists in the handling of impure substances and purification. They mediate between humans and the spirits of the subterranean world and play important roles in rites of passage as companions and assistants of liminars. Their healing practices are related to the purification of a body, reclaiming it from a specific jinn. They are attributed with an extraordinary energetic substance (*nafs*) which is translated into a fertile quality. All these features of Drawa as cultural brokers, between symbolic oppositions such as impure: pure; ill: healthy and nature: culture, acting alongside their Sharifian counterparts, return in the practice of colactation of Drawi and Sharifian babies.

In chapter four the phenomenon of milk kinship bonds between Shurfa and Drawa was described as a rite of incorporation, connected to an elaborate ensemble of exchanges between Sharifian patrons and Drawi clients. The reason for addressing the topic here once again is that an explanation that focuses solely on the patron-client bond disregards the importance of the act of colactation. The creation of milk kinship bonds is obviously the result of colactation, but milk kinship is not always the main reason for colactation. One indication for not disregarding colactation is that it is emphasized in the statements of villagers. They explain how their children were nursed by women from other households because the biological mothers had insufficient or bad milk. Furthermore, because they lacked the financial means to buy fresh or powdered milk, these mothers turned to a female friend with the request to nurse their child. Thus, in the stories of villagers colacation is presented as an instrumental act, one that will disappear—and already has, as some incorrectly added—when all villagers are able to feed their children in a preferable way. Lacking in their statements is the symbolic meaning of the exchange of breastmilk, that is, colactation. Colactation often only happens a few times, not enough to keep the baby alive, supposedly the primary reason for the act in the first place. For example one Sharifa thought that the early death of three of her children was caused by the poor quality of her own milk. When she gave birth to a fourth child, she let him be nursed by her Drawia girlfriend, Hammed's wife Aisha. She had nursed the boy four or five times, after which the biological mother took over. Apparently, five times were sufficient for the child to grow up and become a ten-year-old boy, a milk brother of the youngest son of Aisha and Hammed. The next time the Sharifa gave birth, her milk was considered healthy enough to nurse the child herself. From this we can conclude that while bad mother's milk can be the reason for the death of a nursing infant (cf. Creyghton 1981), mother's milk can at the same time be attributed with a curative or prophylactic quality that might help in solving the high rate of infant mortality for children under two years of age. This high

level is unfortunately typical for Moroccan society, with the south of
the country having the highest rate. The main causes are the almost
complete lack of proper sanitation, the dearth of vaccinations and
the subsequent infections that are caused by contact with dirty water
and soil. Dehydration is another problem caused by excessive diar-
rhoea, bad food and incorrect remedies.

The curative quality of mother's milk also takes effect when either
a small quantity is consumed or when it is not taken orally. In the
region, mother's milk is used as a remedy, especially for eye diseases.
For example, Abdelhadi was once hit by a stone, and went home
with one swollen eye. There his older sister told him to put some
of her breastmilk on his eye. Another boy developed an eye disease
after a heavy sandstorm. When he went on a family visit in another
village at the time of the infection, his aunt gave him some milk to
put on his eye. After a few days the infection had disappeared.[21] In
chapter four we saw how mother's milk has the power to forge long-
term affective social bonds between villagers. Additionally, it is attributed with the power to cure or protect. Where does this power
come from?

Sometimes, contact with organic, bodily substances, that in general
leads to an impure state, is considered to have a protective or healing
effect. Similarly, as an earlier quotation of Westermarck indicated,
sacredness or *baraka* can be spoiled very easily. Exactly because organic substances move within the 'margins or ill-defined states' of
the symbolic classification system, they may become the object of
taboo or attributed with specific negative or positive powers. The
blood of the Great Feast sheep is used in medicine or smeared on
the door as a protection against a jinn attack. Human breath is polluting but is also used for the transfer of *baraka*. Saliva is used in
the treatment of 'spit and touch healers' (Bakker 1993: 179–182). Sweat
produced during the carriage of a dead man to the graveyard can
heal the effects of prayers said in an impure state (to remove the
stale sprinkles that become ever-burning spots in the afterlife). Likewise,
mother's milk has ambiguous value. Milk is healthy and pure, but
can sometimes become the source of illness or even death. Even so,

---

[21] The same practice was described by Champault (1969: 278) in the Tabelbala
Oasis: 'An eye inflamed by conjuctivitis and obstructing normal treatment or an
eye injured by a thorn, knows no better remedy than mother's milk directly instilled
into the eye'.

another woman's breastmilk can have the power to heal. Colactation is here a powerful ritual of reversal in which Drawa participate.

In the creation myth of the dark-skinned *Gnawa*, it is said that with the conception of a child, the mother supplies the flesh and the father the bone structure (Pâques 1991: 41). The father gives the spirit (*rūḥ*) which turns the child of a Sharif into a Sharif and the child of a slave into a slave. Both father and mother contribute to the *nafs* of the child, the father through his semen, the mother through her milk. This might well be the fundamental idea underlying the existence of milk kinship: 'The wet-nurse can transmit her innate properties to the child she feeds . . .'. It furthermore explains why the powerful Shurfa of Ouezzane in the north of the country are said to be 'blackened' through the close contact with their servants (who are 'people originating in the oases of the River Dra'). Either they have slept with their black concubine or they have drunk the milk of their wet-nurse (idem, 72). Where the father determines descent through his semen, the mother influences character and health through her milk. In the Dra Valley conception is seen as a process whereby a woman becomes impure, blackens, at the moment that male semen has 'polluted' the pure flow of water in her womb. These months are meaningfully called 'the months of desire' (Pandolfo 1989: 18). Mother's milk transmits the energy (*nafs*) of the mother onto the child which has a life-long effect.[22]

Given that Drawa are said to be strong and energetic, translated in the statement that they have more *nafs* than other persons, and given that through mother's milk *nafs* may reach the child, I conclude that the milk of Drawa is said to be a healing or prophylactic substance for Sharifian children. In the village, my Sharifian neighbour was nursed as a child by the aunt of Hammed Hazzabin. At the time he was given the Drawi name Najem, which was changed to Muhammad after the nursing period. A comparable case is presented by Dwyer (1978). To prevent a premature death, a mother from the southern town of Taroudannt (near Agadir) gave her new-

---

[22] The association of Drawa with mother's milk returns in a special sanctuary in Marrakesh, located in an old tannery that is now known as 'the bride's garden'. When the tanners still worked there, they were attributed with a fertile power and therefore played an important role in the marriage rituals. At present, the garden is still inhabited by Drawa and women who paint the hands and hair of brides with henna. The sanctuary located in the garden is only visited by women who have nursing problems (Jemma 1971: 17–19).

born daughter the name of Mbarka, a name exclusively associated with dark-skinned Moroccans. Only on the day the daughter was going to marry did the mother change the name into one more fitting to a light-skinned woman. Again, Dwyer comments that dark-skinned humans, and apparently their names as well, have the ability to protect others from evil and sickness. The same was stated by Abdelhadi when I asked him about the reasons for the milk kinship practices. Drawa have 'something important' that gives humans strength and that Shurfa lack, comparable with the *baraka* of the Shurfa.

Both Shurfa and Drawa have a special place in the cosmology and are considered to be 'not quite like other people'. Shurfa, however, are widely respected while Drawa face contempt. The *baraka* of Shurfa is based on descent and proven qualities, that is, on the ancient conceptual pair of *ḥasab wa nasab* (esteem based on achievements and esteem based on descent). In a study on 'traditional healing', Bakker notes that this form of *baraka* is only the best known type of numinous power in Moroccan society (1993: 204–219). In chapter five, it was indicated that the gift of *baraka* takes place in a submissive relationship between saint and disciple. Bakker mentions 'ambiguous baraka' as *baraka* that is donated by jinns. To obtain this, healers first have to go through a chaotic period in which they enter into a turbulent fight with the jinns. It is only then that they are able to control the spirits and are considered as 'carriers of *baraka*'. 'Nevertheless it is an ambiguous *baraka* which still smells of *bas*', evil power (Bakker 1993: 214).[23] The exact difference in attributed supernatural power of Shurfa and Drawa could well be found in the different acquisition and application of *baraka*. The power that is attributed to Drawa is then based on their contact with the netherworld of jinns, crossing the boundaries between nature and culture—uniting these cultural categories in the fulfillment of their occupations—and is subsequently impure. The continuous dependence on the jinns of people who are associated with this ambiguous *baraka* corresponds with the more general dependence and subordination which determine the status of Drawa.

---

[23] In light of the close relationship of smell ('the result of non-belonging') and ambiguity, as noted by Van Beek (1992), Bakker's phrasing is quite to the point.

Conclusions

Cultural ideals define that which distinguishes man from nature, containing practical knowledge and guidelines on purity and defilement. The Drawa in the village mediate between the natural and cultural domains of human existence. As specialists of impurity, they offer purification and protection from impurities and assist individuals who are going through a crucial phase in the cycle of life. They protect their Sharifian fellow villagers from having to perform certain impure activities or aid in the re-establishment of their purity. The complex of purity and impurity was seen to be connected with the cosmological order. The intermediate world between nature and culture was thus not only populated by Drawa but also by 'the spirits of the subterranean world', named jinns. Here, once again the close interdependence between Shurfa, mediators between men and the supernatural world, and Drawa, mediators between men and the subterranean world, has been exemplified. Both are attributed with a superhuman quality and are necessary to the well-being of society. The supernatural blessing of Shurfa, *baraka*, is well known and regularly mentioned. Compared to the Shurfa's *baraka*, the supernatural quality that can sometimes be evoked by Drawa (as occupational and ritual specialists) is hardly mentioned. It opposes the qualities of the Shurfa and hinges on liminality, the reversal of normal situations and conceptions and is rooted in the netherworld of the jinns. This reversal of normal practices explains why Drawa can be attributed with prophylactic properties. They know ways to purify children or protect them against possible illnesses through defilement. The transfer of *nafs* (energy and force), for example through breastmilk, provides the essential fuel for his or her future lifepath.

There are several indications that this account has wider resonance. For northern Morocco, Jamous (1981, 1982) has examined the social and cultural mediation of Shurfa in Riffian society. There Shurfa share their mediating qualities with a second, less respected, category of people, the sorcerers. They are situated at the lower end of the social ladder: 'One fears [the sorcerer] but also despises him for his deficiencies, his subhumanity (*sous-humanité*) and his involvement with the subterranean world with which he stands in direct contact'. Calling the sorcerer a social marginal is emphasizing only one dimension of his identity. Marginality indeed constitutes his weakness—he does not have the right to own property and people avoid regular social contact—but also his forceful magical power (Jamous 1981: 208). Rasmussen (1992) provides a similar analysis of the ambivalent relationships between two types of cultural brokers in Tuareg society. In the introduction of this book, Casajus (1987: 291, 305) was cited in his qualification of the *Inadan* as 'free men of a special category', being needed but also despised: These *Inadan* work as blacksmiths, craftsmen, midwives and specialists of rites of passage. Rasmussen considers the *Inadan* tasks in connection with the mediating functions of marabouts. The 'smith is the counterpart of the marabout', with both having contradictory ritual powers: 'Both smiths and marabouts mediate between people (. . .) as they mediate between people and nature' (1992: 106). Where marabouts oppose and compartmentalize sacred and secular powers, 'the blacksmith bridges them' (idem, 107). The spiritual power of the marabout, called *baraka*, complements the spiritual power of the smith, called *ettama*. We are dealing here, in Rasmussen's words, with 'a conjunction of opposites', echoing Bourdieu's 'reunion of contraries' (1977: 132 *et passim*). The conceptions which position both Shurfa and Drawa as cultural brokers suggest the existence of a cosmological order in which the Shurfa and Drawa fulfil opposed, yet equally necessary, tasks. The mediative, numinous powers of Shurfa and Drawa are complementary: Life in the oasis consists of the transitional process of ricocheting between the two poles they represent. Life thus consists of acting out the bond that lies between reason and passion, birth and death, men and women, and Shurfa and Drawa.

CHAPTER EIGHT

CONCLUDING REMARKS

A number of authors has registered the radical effects of colonial and post-colonial state formation in the Saharan regions of Morocco. Pacification of the transhumant herdsmen, a rapid population growth and a migration stream towards the towns on the western plains— in some cases dating from pre-colonial times—have changed the outward appearance and economies of the oases. What were the implications of these processes for the oasis hierarchies composed of religious specialists, freemen, and unfree and semi-free cultivators? This book concentrated on a group of people at the lower end of the hierarchy, its members considered to be 'not quite like other people'. Was the French captain Meric right when he reported in 1935 that, although the Haratin as freemen of a special category were still considered to be 'an inferior race' in the eyes of other inhabitants of the oases, the socio-economic changes brought about by pacification and modern administration would soon lead to erasure of all traces of inequality (cited in Herzenni 1990: 13)?

An analytic description of the opinions, casual remarks and daily pursuits of inhabitants in one oasis bears out that hierarchical ideas continue to be transmitted and instilled in everyday life. Social relations between Drawa (Haratin) and fellow inhabitants of the oases remain coloured by a complex of condescending notions. To understand the persistence of these notions, Dumont was followed in the contention that whatever happens at the extremes of a hierarchy is essential for its understanding (1980: 76). The focus in this book on the relations between the descendants of the Prophet (Shurfa) and the cultivators and occupational specialists of humble descent (Drawa) has been an attempt to give the dialogical nature of these relations between the poles of the oasis hierarchy its proper place. Zooming in on the daily interaction of inhabitants in one locality offered in particular the possibility to identify a configuration of 'saints and servants' in structuring relations between individuals in the oasis.

The configuration of saints and servants is based on regular exchanges between a saint or his descendants and the laity. Material contributions in the form of land, services and agricultural goods are exchanged for scriptural assistance, legal advice and supernatural mediation. The saint's numinous force *baraka* is a superior currency in this exchange relationship and is transmitted in a submissive relationship. The division of labour and the exchange of goods and services are thus keys to the ideological underpinning of the social hierarchy. In agreement with their special status, the descendants of the saint command a workforce to take care of agricultural work and other tasks to liberate themselves from the material aspects of life. The exchange relationship between the descendants and those who work in their service involves labour, agricultural knowledge, services and material goods. Similar to the relationship between the saint and the oasis inhabitants, the servants of the sanctuary accept spiritual subordination and a possible feminized stature in exchange for an honourable existence in proximity to the sacred descendants of the saint.

The hierarchical interdependence between saints and servants hinges on practices which go back and forth between rapprochement and dissociation, or incorporation and exclusion. The *double-bind* between saint and servant not only applies to the fulfillment of tasks in and around the sanctuary, but also to the production and reproduction of respective identities. Since, for example, the village is basically conceptualized as sacred territory, the profane servants when stressing their origins emphasize at the same time their 'outsidership'. In stressing closeness to the saints, one also emphasizes social distance. This is because the tasks of servants imply rapprochement with the saintly families, bringing them behind the family façade, but even so emphasize the servants are different from the 'common people' who would never be allowed to enter the private sphere of home and family. The descendants of the saint from their side emphasize their independent stature and remain on the whole silent about their dependence on the servants for the fulfillment of innumerable tasks in the sphere of social and cultural mediation. The intricate network of milk kinship bonds that originate in the servant's gift of mother's milk is another example of the strong interdependent relations that the descendants of the saint maintain with their subordinate fellow villagers.

There are at least two important reasons to consider these findings on the configuration of saint and servant here in a broader perspective. The first is the view, propounded by Hammoudi in *Master and Disciple* (1997), that the *cultural model* of master-and-disciple, with submission, exchange, service and the inversion of gender as essential ingredients, pervades Moroccan society as a whole.

> If the royal institution and its legitimacy function in and through the hegemony of sainthood, as has been noted [by Geertz, RE], it seems logical to consider the master-disciple relationship in Sufi initiation as the decisive schema for the construction of power relations (Hammoudi 1997: 85).

In Morocco, the authoritarian régime, headed by the king as exemplary centre, precedes over an elaborate network of patron-client relations, blocking in this way the emergence of a truly autonomous civil society. Hammoudi sketches a bleak picture of authoritarian power relations in Morocco and elsewhere in the Arab world, yet the tone of the conclusion is hopeful: In certain sectors of society one can identify the germs of 'a radical individualization that could provide the future with the foundations of a civil society' (idem, 158). The possible existence of a civil society is also the second reason to consider my findings in a broader perspective.

The local field of opinion in the oasis and Casablanca is related to an extensive public domain in which discussions on the current state of affairs in the country take place. This civil society—here broadly defined as an autonomous sphere for public opinion (Taylor 1997: 259 *et passim*)—is 'the locus for debate, discussion, and dialogue in the contemporary Middle East' (Norton 1995: 25). Gellner observed that civil society, when strictly defined as an ensemble of autonomous associations (such as trade unions and social movements), has not been developed to the full in the Arab world (Gellner in idem, 8). Yet, the expansion of education and the mass production of books, magazines and cassettes has led to the emergence of a non-localized domain in which opinions are presented and transmitted.

The rise of mass-education has been instrumental in the emergence of the field of opinion. In the oasis, the spread of 'generalized, diffused, and popularized literacy' (Wagner 1993: 269; cf. Eickelman 1992) has produced a first generation of literate youngsters. In the village the ancient school was focused on memorization of the Koran. I thus noticed some adult Shurfa were functionally illiterate, which meant they were able to recite the Koran but faced difficulties in reading everyday texts. At present, young people follow primary and secondary schooling in the oasis and in some cases elsewhere in the valley. Young Drawa and Shurfa alike contest the art of memorizing Koran texts if this implies misunderstanding of their content. Mass-education has eroded the Shurfa's religious authority as well as their function as 'literacy mediators' (idem, 26). It remains the case, however, that in the village Drawa drop out of school at an early age, whereas many Sharifian families send their sons to one of the universities in the north of the country. Shurfa continue to act as teachers at the public primary school.

TV programmes, newspapers and cassettes transmit in evocative ways notions that can be appropriated to formulate objections against persistent social cleavages. Television triggers off 'critical conversation and reflection' and provides 'opportunities for viewers to discuss sensitive subjects by ostensibly talking about "something else" that is on television' (Ossman 1994: 115). The illiterate Drawi Abdelhadi drew Nelson Mandela in his talks on the social divisions in the village and attested thus of the intercontinental traffic in meaning in which the local field of opinion is set. In Casablanca, his brother Ibrahim found in *Islamist* cassettes and videotapes from Algeria the ideological ammunition in his fight against descent-based social distinctions.

It has been argued here that the establishment of the oasis population in unequal categories is embedded in a cultural idiom that maintains a relative autonomy from changing economic and political conditions. Likewise, central in the field of opinion is the voicing of social problems in a cultural idiom. People do not mechanically reproduce *idées reçues* but reformulate and transform cultural notions with clear objectives but within given conditions. In discussing social classes, they make use of concepts such as etiquette, civilization, tradition and learning. Usage of the cultural concepts is general but interpretations may diverge. Dwyer notes in an examination of Moroccan proverbs on power and freedom that 'apparently fixed forms of cultural expression could unite people on one level while also, on another, providing them with symbols and a vocabulary that might be used as weapons in their struggles against one another' (1991: 123). In the oasis, the specialized tasks of Drawa touch upon a wide-ranging ensemble of cultural ideals that explain and prescribe the behaviour of man towards his physical and mental functions, as well as towards fellow humans. Drawa, although facing difficulties in complying with these ideals, find ways to counteract and reinterpret them. Some propound alternative ways of behaviour, disputing

long-standing cultural ideals. For example, some Drawa, inspired by
fundamentalist ideas, grow a beard, international symbol of fundamentalism *par excellence*, when still young and refuse to address Shurfa
in the manner they learned as a child.

'Dreams of elsewhere' (Ossman 1994: 25) link the field of opinion to the formation of identities. Occidentalism and modernity offer
the stuff of which these dreams are made of. Already in colonial
times, the emancipation of Haratin was couched in modernist terms.
On the eve of independence, the French captain Moureau (1955:
10) witnessed a slow and silent emancipation in the southern oases.
Young urbanized Haratin pressed their parents with subversive ideas
of social equality. In the towns the emancipation of Haratin was
supposed to assume enormous proportions:

> Once arrived in the town, the whole framework in which [the Hartani]
> has lived seems vanished as if by magic. Our Hartani finds himself
> the equal of the Berber or Arab who have always considered them-
> selves superior to him. (. . .) Having been set free, he develops a mas-
> sive sense of pride and the need to show to others his newly-acquired
> emancipation: He exchanges his traditional clothes for European clothes
> in glaring colours so as not to pass unnoticed (Moureau 1955: 9).

It needs however to be said that notwithstanding 'modern dress',
urban migrants faced new forms of social inequality induced by colonial urban segregationist policies. Likewise, in the rural south the
French authorities supported ancient élites or brought new ones to
power. We should therefore be careful about the colonial representation of the emancipation of Haratin in modernist terms. To the
French military ethnologists, the disintegration of various forms of
bonded labour was symbol and proof of the inevitable passing of
traditional society. These authors of a number of unpublished reports seemed convinced their presence in the country contributed to
the rapid spread of the Enlightenment ideal of social equality and
individuality.

Present-day periodic migrants and students may look like Moureau's
stereotypic Hartani who literally put on a new identity as modern
urban Moroccan. They indeed change clothes when arriving or leaving the village. In discussions on the lack of electricity or a proper
sewer system, they compare life in Casablanca, Marrakesh or Agadir
with life in the village. In their talks, a traditional, or natural, life
is contrasted to the civilized, urban lifestyle of *Casa*. A modernist
ethos is responsible for their portrayal of the 'great tradition' of

Shurfa as 'little tradition' and part of the national folklore. In the towns, the flipside of this ethos is the traditionalization of daily life as seen in the reintroduction of 'antiquated family titles' such as *mulay* for the descendants of the Prophet (Hammoudi 1997: 35). The prevailing tendency, however, is that, whereas contemporary anthropologists avoid usuage of the conceptual pair of great and little tradition, urban and rural literates object against the cult of saints and the stature of the Shurfa by relegating it to the domain of little traditions. Migrants who have worked in France often dismissed interest in the sanctuary and the coexistence of saints and servants as an interest into the past. Hayeur (1991) in a study on the urban élite of Rabat encountered similiar reactions: Her interlocutors advised her not to look at Rabat, the town where social distinctions are kept alive. This town represented 'the Morocco of the past', which had already been surpassed by Casablanca, 'the Morocco of tomorrow'. With strategies to look either into the past or into the future— reminding here that *Islamists*, while not exactly opposed to modernist discourse or technology, nevertheless opt for a restoration of the past—one may well ask what to do with 'the Morocco of today' where the social and cultural differences still hold true.

GLOSSARY

'Abd pl. *'Abīd*: slave; descendant of slave
'abra: measure of capacity
'ain d-dār: open space in the centre of qṣar house
'Aissawa: musical group with ġita player; religious brotherhood named after Mahammad bin Isa al-Mukhtari
'Alawī: descendant of the Prophet; ruling dynasty in Morocco
'ālim: litt. 'expert'; irrigation guard
'āmma: commonality; the people
'āmmī pl. *al-'awāmm*: commoner
'aql: reason, social understanding
'ar: shame; compulsion
'arīfa: female expert in matters of virginity, pregnancy and giving birth
'arūbī: country dweller
'ašūrā': tenth day of the month Muharram; celebration of Islamic New Year
'āzab: bachelor; young man
'īd al-fiṭr: celebration of the breaking of Ramadan fast
'irḍ pl. *a'rāḍ*: honour, good repute
'ušr: tithe
adab: civilized conduct, refinement, culture
aḥidūs: Berber wedding dance
ajr: recompense, religious merit
amur: alliance pact of Middle Atlas tribes
aṣḥāb: companions, friends
aṣl pl. *uṣūl*: root, origin, descent
Asūqī: litt. 'marketeer'; synonym for Hartani (*off.*)
aswad pl. *sūdān*: black; black man (*off.*)
bakūr: incense
bandir: tambourine
baraka: sacred blessing
bard: cold; coldness; illness
barkūkš: couscous of large grains
bġila: attribute (usually donkey head) of 'ašūrā' feast (from *baġla*, female mule)
bismillah: In the name of God
blad: country, region of origin
Būjlūd and *Bilmaun*: litt. 'man in skins'; main figure of High Atlas masquerade
bulfaf: liver pikes
dahir (*ẓahīr*): decree
darabukka: a conical, one-handed drum, open at the small end
darb: dead-end street
Darqāwa: religious brotherhood, founded by 18th-century religious teacher of Idrissī descent Mulay Larbi Darqawi
dimuqrāṭiya: litt. 'democracy'; straight policy (opp. of zigzag)
ḏabīḥa: blood sacrifice
fḍīla: most excellent day of Ramadan fast (27th night)
fiṭra: alms, given on day of 'īd al-fiṭr
fqīh: leader of prayers; Koranic teacher
ġita: oboe, played at festive occasions

ġaraḍ: aim, goal
ġusl: major ritual ablution
Gnawa: religious brotherhood popular among ʿAbīd
gunʿa: black cloth with colourful stitchings, worn by women in the south
ḥaḍāra: civilization, settledness
ḥadaṯ: ritual impurity
ḥajjām: phlebotomist, barber
ḥalāl: that which is allowed; legal
Hamadša: religious brotherhood founded by 18th-century teacher Sidi Ali bin Hamdush
ḥarām: forbidden; taboo
ḥarmal: African rue (Peganum harmala)
ḥarrāṯ: ploughman
ḥurma: sacredness; sanctity
Ḥurr pl. *Aḥrār*: freeborn; freeman
ḥuzma: litt. 'bundle'; measure of capacity
Idrissī: descendant of the Prophet via Mulay Idriss
iḥtirām: deference, respect
Imalwan: tribal name, among Berber-speakers denoting specific category of Haratin
Imdyazen: High Atlas musical group
jabr: setting of broken bones (by *jābir*)
jallāba: long hooded robe
jamāʿa: collectivity; village council
janāba: major ritual impurity
kabb: litt. 'to pour'; ritual distribution of almonds at marriage ceremony
kaḥīl: black man (*off.*)
kalām: word, speech; influence, authority
kawā: to cauterize (by *kawwāy/-a*)
kisāʾ: type of garment worn by Sharifat
ḵaddām/ -a: worker; maid
ḵali: empty, uninhabited; maternal uncle
ḵammās: litt. 'one fifther'; sharecropper
ḵāṣṣa: élite; people of distinction
ḵatan: son-in-law; bridegroom
ḵāṭiba: marriage broker, matchmaker
ḵatn: circumcision
ḵuad: incense *mélange*
ḵud min ḥlīb: milk siblings via colactation
lalla: honorific title for female Shurfa
maiz al-ʿunṣurīya: racism
maġrīb: prayer at sunset; Northwest Africa
maulid: celebration of the birth of the Prophet
mausim: annual saint's day
milk: type of private ownership of land
muʿallim: master of a trade
mulay: litt. 'my lord'; honorific title for Shurfa
mustawan: (educational or civilizational) level
mwalin al-arḍ: litt. 'inhabitants of the earth'; euphemism for jinns
nafir: trumpet, in particular for Ramadan
nafs: soul; spirit; life; individual; desire
nār: fire
nisba: linguistic form and type of denomination
nīya: truthful intention; faith
nūr: light
qablī pl. *qabāla*: litt. 'southerner'; synonym for Haratin

qabīla: tribe; village council; community
qānūn pl. *qawānīn*: a law that has been formulated apart from the Shariah
qarāba muqarrab-s: closeness; close companions of the Prophet
qaṭrān: tar
qṣar: walled village in the pre-Sahara zone
rā'i: date-palm guard
rajul: adult man
ribāṭ: military castle and monastery
ridā': foster relationship
rīḥ: wind; musical rhythm
rīḥa: smell, odour
rūḥ: breath of life; soul; spirit
sakira: to subject; to reduce to servitude
sidi: sir
silka: Koran recitation
silsila: spiritual or ancestral chain of authoritative Koranic teachers
snisla: recitation and stamp-foot dance
Sūdān: litt. 'blacks'; region south of the Sahara
sūq: market
ṣabr: self-control; patience
ṣadaqa: alms, charitable gift
ṣāliḥ: saint
ṣaum: the Ramadan fast
šahāda: profession of faith
šaraf: honour; nobility
šarīk: (irrigation) associate
šiba: alsem (Artemisia absinthium)
šibanī: old man
šik: holy man
širk: polytheism; idolatry
Šwašīn: ethnonym for agriculturalists in Tunisian and Lybian oases
tabādul: exchange
taḍa: alliance pact in Middle Atlas
tafargant: alliance pact, among southern tribes involving the exchange of breastmilk
tamašgala: wage for cutting and picking dates
tarik: history
tilmīḏ: pupil
tiqa: trust
tiwīza: corvée service
ṭahūr: purity; circumcision
ṭarīqa: religious brotherhood; religious tradition
ṭbal: large drum
ṭulṭ: one-third tenancy
umma: community of Islamic believers
walima: communal dinner among youngsters
walīy: saint; a man close to God
wazīr/-a: assistant of bride and groom
wudū': minor ritual ablution before prayer
wuld: boy
zakāh: alms prescribed in Islamic law
zarda: communal dinner
zāwiya: tomb for saint; sanctuary; lodge
ziyāra: visit to sanctuary; gift to descendants of saint

REFERENCES

Abitbol, Michel
  1988 Maraboutism and state formation in Southern Morocco. In: S.N. Eisenstadt, Michel Abitbol & Naomi Chazou (eds.), *The Early State in African Perspective. Culture, Power and Division of Labor.* Leiden: E.J. Brill, 134–47.

Abitbol, Michel (ed.)
  1992 *Communautés juives des marges sahariennes du Maghreb.* Jerusalem: Institut Ben-Zvi.

Abu Zahra, Nadia
  1982 *Sidi Ameur. A Tunisian Village.* London: Ithaca Press.
  1997 The Rain Rituals as Rites of Spiritual Passage. In: Idem, *The Pure and the Powerful: Studies in Contemporary Muslim Society.* Reading: Ithaca Press, 3–33.

Abu-Lughod, Lila
  1986 *Veiled Sentiments. Honor and Poetry in a Bedouin Society.* Berkeley: The University of California Press.

Abun-Nasr, Jamil M.
  1987 *A history of the Maghrib in the Islamic period.* Cambridge: Cambridge University Press.

Africanus, Leo (Jean-Leon L'Africain)
  1981 *Description de l'Afrique.* 2 vols.; translated from Italian by A. Epaulard. Paris: Maisonneuve.

Agnouche, Abdellatif
  1987 *Histoire politique du Maroc. Pouvoir-Légitimités-Institutions.* Casablanca: Afrique Orient.
  1992 Les Chorfa face à l'état de droit' dans le Maroc contemporain. In: Jean-Claude Santucci (ed.), *Le Maroc Actuel. Une Modernisation au Miroir de la Tradition?* Paris: CNRS, 273–83.

Allport, Gordon W.
  1958 *The Nature of Prejudice.* New York: Doubleday Anchor Books [first edition 1954].

Altorki, Soraya
  1980 Milk Kinship in Arab Society: An Unexplored Problem in the Ethnography of Marriage, *Ethnology* 19, 2: 233–44.

Amard, Pierre
  1997 *Textes Berbères des Ait Ouaouzguite (Ouarzazate, Maroc).* Edités et annotés par Harry Stroomer. Aix-en-Provence: Edisud 'Bilingues'.

Anderson, Benedict
  1991 *Imagined Communities. Reflections on the Origin and Spread of Nationalism.* London, New York: Verso [second revised edition].

Appadurai, Arjun
  1986 Is Homo Hierarchicus?, *American Ethnologist* 13, 4: 745–61.
  1988 Putting Hierarchy in its Place, *Cultural Anthropology* 3, 1: 36–49.

Armstrong, R.
  1967 The Nightwatchmen of Kano, *Middle Eastern Studies* 3, 3: 269–82.

Asad, Talal
  1983 Anthropological Conceptions of Religion: Reflections on Geertz, *Man* 18: 237–59.

Ayad, Mustapha & Jean Le Coz
  n.d.   Vers une nouvelle ere hydraulique au Maroc? In: Moulay Ismaïl & Pierre
         Carrière (eds.), *Aspects de l'agriculture irriguée au Maroc* [*Espace Rural* no. 25],
         15–41.
Azam, Capt. R.
  1946   *Sedentaires et nomades dans le Sud-Marocain: le coude du Dra*. Paris, CHEAM
         no. 1009 [unpublished paper].
  1947   *La structure politique et sociale de l'oued Dra*. Paris, CHEAM no. 2039 [unpub-
         lished paper].
Babcock, Barbara (ed.)
  1978   *The Reversible world. Symbolic inversion in art and society*. Ithaca, London: Cornell
         University Press.
Bailey, F.G.
  1969   *Stratagems and Spoils. A Social Anthropology of Politics*. Oxford: Basil Blackwell.
Bakker, Jogien
  1993   *The Lasting Virtue of Traditional Healing. An Ethnography of Healing and Prestige
         in the Middle Atlas of Morocco*. Ph.D. thesis, Vrije Universiteit, Amsterdam.
Bakker, Johan de
  1991   *Slaves, Arms, and Holy War. Moroccan policy vis-à-vis the Dutch Republic during
         the establishment of the 'Alawi dynasty (1660–1727)*. Ph.D. thesis, Universiteit
         van Amsterdam.
Banks, Marcus
  1996   *Ethnicity: Anthropological Constructions*. London, New York: Routledge.
Barth, Fredrik
  1960   The system of social stratification in Swat, Northern Pakistan. In: E.R.
         Leach (ed.) *Aspects of Caste in South India, Ceylon and North-West Pakistan*.
         Cambridge: Cambridge University Press, 113–45.
  1969   Introduction. In: Fredrik Barth (ed.), *Ethnic groups and Boundaries. The Social
         Organisation of Culture Difference*. London: George Allen & Unwin, 9–37.
Bateson, Gregory & Mary Catherine Bateson
  1987   *Angels Fear. Towards an Epistomology of the Sacred*. New York: MacMillan.
Becker, Howard S.
  1973   *Outsiders. Studies in the Sociology of Deviance*. New York: The Free Press/
         Macmillan.
Bédoucha, Geneviève
  1984   Un noir destin: travail, statuts, rapports de dépendance dans une oasis du
         Sud-Tunisien. In: M. Cartier (ed.), *Le travail et ses répresentations*. Paris:
         Editions des Archives Contemporaines, 77–121.
  1987   'L'eau, l'amie du Puissant'. Une communauté oasienne du Sud-Tunisien. Paris:
         Gordon and Breach Science Publishers/Editions des archives contempo-
         raines.
Beek, Walter E.A. van
  1992   The dirty smith: Smell as a social frontier among the Kapsiki/Higi of
         North Cameroon and North-Eastern Nigeria, *Africa* 62, 1: 38–58.
Beg, M.A.J.
  1969   Khassa. In H. Gibb *et al.* (eds.), *The Encyclopaedia of Islam*. New Edition.
         Leiden: E.J. Brill, 1097–1100.
Belghazi, Hammou
  1997   Le rituel comme action sanctifiante des liens intergroupes: Le cas de 'Tada'
         au Maroc, *Hespéris-Tamuda* xxxv, 2: 121–30.
Bellakhdar, Jamal
  1978   *Médecine traditionnelle et toxicologie ouest-sahariennes. Contribution à l'étude de la
         pharmacopée marocaine*. Rabat: Editions techniques Nord-Africaines.

Bellakhdar, Jamal *et al.*
1992 *Tissint. Une oasis du Maroc présahararien. Monographie d'une palmeraie du Moyen Dra.* Rabat: Al Biruniya.
Berland, Joseph C.
1982 *No five fingers are alike. Cognitive Amplifiers in Social Context.* Cambridge, MA: Harvard University Press.
Berque, Jacques
1938 *Etudes d'histoire Maghrébine.* Tanger, Fes: Les Editions Internationales.
1982 *Ulémas, fondateurs, insurgés du Maghreb. XVIIe siècle.* Paris: Sindbad.
Bisson, Jean & Mohamed Jarir
1988 Ksour du Gourara et du Tafilelt. De l'ouverture de la société oasienne à la fermeture de la maison. In: Pierre Robert Baduel (ed.), *Habitat, Etat et Société au Maghreb.* Paris: CNRS, 329–45.
Blok, Anton
1969 Variations in patronage, *Sociologische Gids* 16: 365–78.
1981 Infame Beroepen, *Symposion* 3, 1/2: 104–28.
1989 Chimney-sweepers as symbolic mediators. In: Jeremy Boissevain & Jojada Verrips (eds.), *Dutch Dilemmas. Anthropologists look at the Netherlands.* Assen: Van Gorcum, 164–84.
1996 Mestieri infami, *Ricerche Storiche* xxvi, 1: 59–96.
Blok, Anton & Andrew Buckser
1996 Nicknames as symbolic inversions, *Focaal* 28: 77–94.
Blok, A. & H. Driessen
1984 Mediterranean Agro-Towns as a Form of Cultural Dominance, With special Reference to Sicily and Andalusia, *Etnologia Europaea* xiv, 2: 111–24.
Bollig, Michael
1987 Ethnic relations and spatial mobility in Africa: A review of the peripatetic niche. In: Rao (ed.), 179–228.
Boughali, Mohamed
1987 *Espaces d'ecriture au Maroc.* Casablanca: Afrique Orient.
Bourdieu, Pierre
1965 The sentiment of honour in Kabyle society. In: J.G. Peristiany (ed.), *Honour and Shame: The Values of Mediterranean Society.* Chicago, London: The University of Chicago Press, 192–241.
1977 *Outline of a Theory of Practice.* Cambridge: Cambridge University Press [first French edition 1972].
Bourgeot, André
1975 Rapports esclavistes et conditions d'affranchisement chez les Imuhag (Twareg kel Ahaggar). In: Claude Meillasoux (ed.), *L'esclavage en Afrique Précoloniale.* Paris: François Maspero, 77–97.
Bourqia, Rahma
1991a L'etat et la gestion du symbolique au Maroc precolonial. In: R. Bourqia & N. Hopkins (eds.), *Le Maghreb: Approches des mécanismes d'articulation.* Casablanca: Al Kalam, 137–51.
1991b Review of Lawrence Rosen (1984), *Hesperis-Tamuda* vol. xxix–1: 159–61.
Bousquet, G. H.
1971 Hada<u>th</u>. In: B. Lewis *et al.* (eds.), *The Encyclopaedia of Islam.* New edition. Leiden: E.J. Brill, vol. iii: 19.
Bovill, E.W.
1978 *The Golden Trade of the Moors.* Oxford: Oxford University Press [second edition, revised and with additional material by Robin Hallett].
Böwering, Gerhard
1984 The *Adab* Literature of Classical Sufism: Ansârî's Code of Conduct.

In: Barbara Daly Metcalf (ed.), *Moral Conduct and Authority. The Place of Adab in South Asian Islam.* Berkeley: The University of California Press, 62–87.

Brandes, Stanley
1987 Reflections on honor and shame in the Mediterranean. In: D.D. Gilmore (ed.), *Honor and shame and the unity of the Mediterranean.* Washington: American Anthropological Association, 121–34.

Brémond, Général
1950 *Berbères et Arabes. La Berbérie est un pays Européen.* Paris: Payot.

Briggs, Lloyd Cabot
1960 *Tribes of the Sahara.* Cambridge, MA: Harvard University Press.

Brown, K.L.
1976 *The People of Salé. Tradition and Change in a Moroccan City, 1830–1930.* Cambridge, MA: Harvard University Press.
1982 The 'Curse' of Westermarck. In: Timothy Stroup (ed.), *Edward Westermarck: Essays on his Life and Works.* Acta Philosopica Fennica 34. Helsinki: Societas Philosophica Fennica, 221–59.

Bruck, Gabriele vom
1996 Being worthy of protection. The dialectics of gender attributes in Yemen, *Social Anthropology* 4, 2: 145–62.
1998 Disputing descent-based authority in the idiom of religion: The case of the Republic of Yemen, *Die Welt des Islams* 38, 2: 149–91.

Brunel, René
1926 *Essai sur la confrerie religieuse des Aissaouas au Maroc.* Casablanca: Afrique Orient [fascimile edition 1988].

Brunot, Louis
1926 La Politesse et les Convenances chez les Marocains, *Bulletin de l'enseignement public* 73: 3–31.

Brunschvig, R.
1962 Métiers vils en islam, *Studia islamica* xvi: 4–61.

Buitelaar, Marjo
1991 *Fasting and Feasting in Morocco. An Ethnographic Study of the Month of Ramadan.* Ph.D. thesis, Katholieke Universiteit Nijmegen.
1993 De Koran in het dagelijks leven in Marokko. In: M. Buitelaar & H. Motzki (eds.), *De Koran. Ontstaan, interpretatie en praktijk.* Muiderberg: Coutinho, 111–23.

Bujra, Abdalla
1967 *The Politics of Stratification. A Study of Political Change in a South Arabian Town.* Oxford: Clarendon Press.

Burgat, François
1995 *L'islamisme au Maghreb. La Voix du Sud.* Paris: Payot.

Burke III, Edmund
1972 The Image of the Moroccan State in French Ethnological Literature: a New Look at the Origin of Lyautey's Berber Policy. In: Gellner & Micaud (eds.), 175–99.

Camps, Gabriel
1970 Recherches sur les origines des cultivateurs noirs du sahara, *Revue de l'Occident Musulman et de la Méditerranée* 7: 35–45.

Carnegie, Charles V.
1996 The Dundus and the Nation, *Cultural Anthropology* 11, 4: 470–509.

Casajus, Dominique
1987 Crafts and Ceremonies: The Inadan in Tuareg Society. In: Rao (ed.), 291–310.

Chafi, Mohamed
1989 Le nom de famille au Maroc, *Revue Juridique et Politique indépendance et coopération* 43, 1: 3–17.

Chaker, Salem
  1987 L'Affirmation identitaire Berbère à partir de 1900. Constantes et mutations (Kabylie), *Revue de l'Occident Musulman et de la Méditerranée* 44: 13–33.
Champault, D.
  1969 *Une oasis du Sahara Nord-Occidental. Tabelbala.* Paris: CNRS.
Chapelle, F. de la
  1929 Une cité de l'oued Dra' sous le Protectorat des nomades, *Hespéris* ix, 1: 29–42.
Charsley, Simon
  1996 'Untouchable': What is in a name?, *Journal of the Royal Anthropological Institute* 2: 1–23.
Chassey, Francis de
  1977 *L'etrier, la houe et le livre. 'Sociétés traditionnelles' au Sahara et au Sahara occidental.* Paris: Editions Anthropos.
Chebel, Malek
  1984 *Le corps dans la tradition du Maghreb.* Paris: P.U.F.
  1993 *L'imaginaire Arabo-Musulmane.* Paris: P.U.F.
Chottin, A.
  1927 Note sur le 'Nfir', *Hespéris* vii: 376–80.
Clancy-Smith, Julia A.
  1994 *Rebel and Saint. Muslim Notables, Populist Protest, Colonial Encounters (Algeria and Tunisia, 1800–1904).* Berkeley: The University of California Press.
Claudot-Hawad, Hélène
  1990 Honneur et politique. Les choix stratégiques des Touaregs pendant la colonisation française, *Revue du Monde Musulman et de la Méditerranée* 57, 3: 13–47.
Cole, John W. & Eric R. Wolf
  1974 *The Hidden Frontier. Ecology and Ethnicity in an Alpine Valley.* New York: Academic Press.
Colin, G.S.
  1971 Ḥarṭānī. In: B. Lewis *et al.* (eds.) *The Encyclopaedia of Islam.* New edition. Leiden: E.J. Brill, vol. iii, 230–31.
Combs-Schilling, M.E.
  1989 *Sacred performances. Islam, Sexuality, and Sacrifice.* New York: Colombia University Press.
Coon, Carleton S.
  1951 *Caravan. The Story of the Middle East.* New York: Holt and Company.
Crapanzano, Vincent
  1973 *The Hamadsha. A Study in Moroccan Ethnopsychiatry.* Berkeley: University of California Press.
Creyghton, M.L.
  1981 *Bad Milk. Perceptions and Healing of a Children's Illness in a North African Society.* Ph.D. thesis, Universiteit van Amsterdam.
  1992 Breast-feeding and *Baraka* in Northern Tunisia. In Maher (1992), 37–58.
Dahiru, Yahya
  1981 *Morocco in the sixteenth century. Problems and patterns in African foreign policy.* Harlow, Essex: Longman.
Daniel, E. Valentine
  1984 *Fluid Signs. Being a Person the Tamil Way.* Berkeley: The University of California Press.
Daniel, Gimaret
  1988 *Les Noms divins en Islam.* Paris: C.E.R.F.
Darif, Mohamed
  1993 La 'question' Berbère, *Al Bayane* (Special Tamazight) 4–5–1993.
Delaney, Carol
  1991 *The Seed and the Soil: Gender and Cosmology in Turkish Village Society.* Berkeley: University of California Press.

Dermenghem, Émile
  1954 *Le culte des saints dans l'islam maghrébin.* Paris: Gallimard.
Despois, Jean
  1961 Le Sahara et l'écologie humaine, *Annales de géographie* 382, 70: 577–84.
DeVos, George & Marcelo Suárez-Orozco
  1990 *Status Inequality. The Self in Culture.* Newbury Park: Sage Publications.
Dirks, Nicholas R.
  1994 Ritual and Resistance. Subversion as Social Fact. In: Nicholas R. Dirks,
        Geoff Eley, and Sherry B. Ortner (eds.), *Culture/Power/History. A Reader in
        Contemporary Social Theory.* Princeton, NJ: Princeton University Press, 483–
        503.
Dollard, John
  1949 *Caste and Class in a Southern Town.* New York: Doubleday Anchor Books
        (first edition 1937).
Domínguez, Virginia R.
  1986 *White by Definition. Social Classification in Creole Louisiana.* Nee Brunswick, NJ:
        Rutgers University Press.
Donoghue, John D.
  1957 An Eta Community in Japan: The Social Persistence of Outcaste Groups,
        American Anthropologist 55: 1000–17.
Dostal, Walter
  1985 *Egalität und Klassengesellschaft in Südarabien. Anthropologische Untersuchungen zur
        sozialen Evolution.* Horn: Verlag Ferdinand Berber & Söhne.
Douglas, Mary
  1966 *Impurity and Danger. An Analysis of Concepts of Pollution and Taboo.* London:
        Penguin.
  1975 *Implicit Meanings. Essays in Anthropology.* London: Routledge and Kegan Paul.
  1996 *Natural Symbols. Explorations in Cosmology.* London, New York: Routledge
        [first edition 1970].
Doutté, Edmond
  1908 *Magie et religion dans l'Afrique du Nord.* Paris: T. Maisonneuve & P. Geuthner.
Dumont, Louis
  1980 *Homo Hierarchicus. The Caste System and its Implications.* Chicago, London:
        The University of Chicago Press [complete revised English edition; first
        French edition 1966].
Dunn, Ross E.
  1977 *Resistance in the Desert. Moroccan Responses to French Imperialism, 1881–1912.*
        London, Madison, WI: The University of Wisconsin Press.
Durkheim, Emile & Marcel Mauss
  1963 *Primitive Classification.* Chicago, London: The University of Chicago Press
        [first French edition 1903].
Dwyer, Daisy Hilse
  1978 *Images and Self-Images. Male and female in Morocco.* New York: Columbia
        University Press.
Dwyer, Kevin
  1982 *Moroccan Dialogues. Anthropology in Question.* Baltimore, London: The John
        Hopkins University Press.
  1991 *Arab Voices. The Human Rights Debate in the Middle East.* London, New York:
        Routledge.
Eickelman, Dale F.
  1976 *Moroccan Islam. Tradition and Society in a Pilgrimage Center.* Austin: University
        of Texas Press.
  1979 The Political Economy of Meaning, a review article, *American Ethnologist*
        6, 2: 386–93.

1981   *The Middle East. An Anthropological Approach.* Englewood Cliffs, NJ: Prentice-Hall.

1984   New interpretations in North African society. In: Jean-Claude Vatin (ed.), *Connaissances du Maghreb. Sciences sociales et colonisation.* Paris: CNRS, 279–289.

1985a   Introduction: Self and community in Middle Eastern societies, *Anthropological Quarterly* 58, 4: 135–40.

1985b   *Knowledge and Power in Morocco. The Education of a Twentieth-Century Notable.* Princeton, NJ: Princeton University Press.

1992   Mass higher education and the religious imagination in contemporary Arab societies, *American Ethnologist* 19, 4: 643–55.

El Mansour, Muhamed

1990   *Morocco in the Reign of Mawlay Sulayman.* Outwell, Wisbeck: Menas Press.

1991   Sharifian Sufism: The religious and social practice of the Wazzani Zawiya. In: E.G.H. Joffe and C.R. Pennell, *Tribe and State. Essays in honour of David Montgomery Hart.* Cambridge: Menas Press, 69–83.

Elias, Norbert

1971   *Wat is sociologie?* Utrecht, Antwerpen: Het Spectrum [first English edition 1970].

1994   Introduction. A Theoretical Essay on Established and Outsider Relations. In: Elias and Scotson 1994, xv–lii [first Dutch edition 1977].

1997   *Über den Prozeß der Zivilisation. Soziogenetische und psychogenetische Untersuchungen.* 2 vols. Frankfurt am Main: Suhrkamp [first edition 1939].

Elias, Norbert & John L. Scotson

1994   *The Established and the Outsiders. A Sociological Enquiry into Community Problems.* London: Sage Publications [first edition 1965].

Ennaji, Mohammed

1994   *Soldats, Domestiques et Concubines. L'Esclavage au Maroc au XIXe siècle.* Casablanca: Eddif.

Epton, Nina

1958   *Saints and Sorcerers. A Moroccan Journey.* London: Cassell.

Evans-Pritchard, E.E.

1949   *The Sanusi of Cyrenaica.* Oxford: Clarendon Press.

Faath, Sigrid

1992   Rechte und Freiheiten der Staatsbürger im 'Hassanismus'. In: Sigrid Faath and HansPeter Mattes (eds.), *Demokratie und Menschenrechte in Nordafrika.* Hamburg: HansPeter Mattes Verlag; Edition Wuquf, 365–432.

Fakhry, Akhmed

1982   *The Oases of Egypt: vol. I: Siwa Oasis.* Cairo: The American University in Cairo Press [first edition 1973].

Fernea, Elizabeth Warnock

1975   *A Street in Marrakech.* Garden City, NY: Doubleday Books.

Filali, Latifa

1984   *Le Tafilalt precolonial. Essai d'etude socio-économique à la recherche des origines historiques du déséquilibre régional.* 2 vols. Thèse 3ème cycle. Paris.

Flamand, Pierre

1959   *Les communautés israélites du sud-marocain. Essai de description et d'analyse de la vie juive en milieu berbère.* Casablanca: s.d.

Free, Anthony

1996   The Anthropology of Pierre Bourdieu. A Reconsideration, *Critique of Anthropology* 16, 4: 395–416.

Gaborieau, Marc

1983   The Cult of Saints among the Muslims of Nepal and Northern India. In: Stephen Wilson (ed.), *Saints and their Cults. Studies in the Religious Sociology, Folklore and History.* Cambridge University Press, 291–308.

Gal, Susan
1995 Language and the 'Arts of Resistance', *Cultural Anthropology* 10, 3: 407–24.
Geertz, Clifford,
1960 The Javanese Kijaji: The changing role of a cultural broker, *Comparative Studies on Society and History* 2: 228–49.
1971 *Islam Observed. Religious Development in Morocco and Indonesia*. Chicago, London: The University of Chicago Press [first edition 1968].
1973 *The Interpretation of Cultures. Selected Essays*. New York: Basic Books.
1976 *The Religion of Java*. Chicago, London: The University of Chicago Press [first edition 1960].
1979 Suq: the bazaar economy in Sefrou. In Geertz, Geertz and Rosen 1979, 123–313.
1983 *Local Knowledge. Further Essays in Interpretive Anthropology*. New York: Basic Books.
Geertz, Hildred
1979 The Meanings of Family Ties. In: Geertz, Geertz and Rosen 1979, 315–79.
Geertz, Clifford, Hildred Geertz & Lawrence Rosen
1979 *Meaning and order in Moroccan society. Three essays in cultural analysis*. Cambridge: Cambridge University Press.
Gellner, Ernest
1969 *Saints of the Atlas*. London: Weidenfeld and Nicolson.
1981 *Muslim Society*. Cambridge: Cambridge University Press.
Gellner, Ernest & Charles Micaud (eds.)
1972 *Arabs and Berbers. From Tribe to Nation in North Africa*. London: Duckworth.
Gellner, Ernest & John Waterbury (eds.)
1977 *Patrons and Clients in Mediterranean Societies*. London: Duckworth.
Genovese, Eugene D.
1972 *Roll, Jordan, Roll. The World the Slaves Made*. New York: Pantheon Books, Random House.
Gerholm, T.
1977 *Market, mosque and mafraj. Social inequality in a Yemeni town*. University of Stockholm: Department of social anthropology.
Gilroy, Paul
1997 Diaspora and the Detours of Identity. In: Kathryn Woodward (ed.), *Identity and Difference. Culture, Media and Identities*. London: Sage, 299–346.
Gilsenan, Michael
1977 Against patron-client relations. In: Gellner and Waterbury (eds.), 167–83.
1982 *Recognizing Islam. Religion and Society in the Modern Arab World*. New York: Pantheon Books.
Goffman, Erving
1959 *The Presentation of Self in Everyday Life*. New York: Doubleday Anchor Books.
1963 *Stigma. Notes on the management of spoiled identity*. Englewood Cliffs, NJ: Prentice-Hall.
Goldberg, H.E.
1983 The Mellahs of Southern Morocco. Report of a survey, *The Maghreb Review* 8, 3–4: 61–9.
Golvin, Louis
1960 *La Mosquée: ses origines, sa morphologie, ses divers fonctions, son rôle dans la vie musulmane, plus spécialement en Afrique du Nord*. Alger: Institut d'Etudes Superieures Islamiques d'Alger.
Goudsblom, Johan
1987 Het onderzoek van civilisatieprocessen. In: J. Goudsblom, *De Sociologie van Norbert Elias*. Amsterdam: Meulenhoff, 147–66.
1989 The Formation of Military-Agrarian Regimes. In: Johan Goudsblom,

E.L. Jones & Stephen Mennell (eds.), *Human History & Social Process*. Exeter: University of Exeter Press, 79–92.

Guha, Ranajit
  1982   On Some Aspects of the Historiography of Colonial India, *Subaltern Studies I. Writings on South Asian History and Society*. Ed. by Ranajit Guha. Delhi: Oxford University Press, 1–8.

Gupta, Akhil & James Ferguson
  1992   Beyond 'Culture': Space, Identity, and the Politics of Difference, *Cultural Anthropology* 7, 1: 6–24.

Haas, Hein de
  1995   *Oasen, zand erover? Een milieugeografische studie naar maatschappij en landgebruik in een Marokkaanse oase. Agadir-Tissint, provincie Tata*. M.A. thesis, Universiteit van Amsterdam.

Hajji, Mohamed
  1977   *L'activité intellectuelle au Maroc à l'époque Sa'dide*. Rabat: Dar el Maghrib [Thèse, Université de Paris-Sorbonne].

Hammoudi, Abdellah
  1970   L'évolution de l'habitat rural dans la vallée du Draa, *Revue de Géographie du Maroc* 18: 33–45.
  1977   Segmentarité, stratification sociale, pouvoir politique et sainteté. Reflexions sur les theses de Gellner, *Hespéris-Tamuda* 15: 147–79.
  1980   Sainteté, Pouvoir et Société: Tamgrout aux XVIIᵉ et XVIIIᵉ siècles, *Annales E.S.C.* 3–4: 615–41.
  1985   Substance and Relation: Water Rights and Water Distribution in the Ḍrā Valley. In: Ann Elizabeth Mayer (ed.), *Property, Social Structure and Law in the Modern Middle East*. Albany, NY: State University of New York Press, 27–57.
  1993   *The Victim and its Masks. An Essay on Sacrifice and Masquerade in the Maghreb*. Chicago, London: The University of Chicago Press [first French edition 1988].
  1997   *Master and Disciple. The Cultural Foundations of Moroccan Authoritarianism*. Chicago, London: The University of Chicago Press.

Hamnett, Ian
  1967   Ambiguity, Classification, and Change: The Function of Riddles, *Man* 2, 3: 379–92.

Hart, David
  1972   The Tribe in Modern Morocco: Two Case Studies. In: Gellner & Micaud (eds.), 25–58.
  1981   *Dadda 'Atta and his Forty Grandsons. The Socio-Political Organisation of the Ait 'Atta of Southern Morocco*. Cambridge: Menas Press.
  1982   Masmuda, Sinhaja and Zanata. A three ring circus, *Revue d'Histoire Maghrébine* 27–28: 361–65.
  1984   *The Ait 'Atta of Southern Morocco. Daily Life and Recent History*. Cambridge: Menas Press.
  1993   Four Centuries of History on the Hoof: The Northwest Passage of Berber Sheep Transhumants across the Moroccan Atlas, 1550–1912, *Morocco* 3: 21–55.
  1994   Faulty models of North African and Middle Eastern tribal structures, *Revue du Monde Musulman et de la Méditerranée* 68–69: 225–38.
  1996   Segmentary models in Morocco, *Journal of the Royal Anthropological Institute* 2, 4: 721–22.

Hayeur, Mariette
  1991   *Les Rbatis-Bourgeoisie de Rabat. Identité et luttes de classements*. Thèse, Université de Montreal.

Heine, Peter
    1990   Qui est donc cette dame? Oder: Die heiligen des Atlas. In: Werner Diem
           und Abdoldjavad Falaturi (eds.), *Zeitschrift der Deutschen morgenländischen
           Gesellschaft*. XXIV. Deutschen Orientalistentag. Stuttgart: Franz Steiner
           Verlag, 254–63.
Herber, J.
    1922   Techniques des poteries rifaines du Zerhoun, *Hespéris* ii, 3: 241–52.
    1937   La légende de Sidi Abdallah el Hajjem, *Hespéris* xxiv, 3: 183–91.
Hergemöller, Bernd-Ulrich
    1990   Randgruppen der spätmitteralterlichen Gesellschaft-Einheit und Vielfalt.
           In: Bernd-Ulrich Hergemöller (ed.), *Randgruppen der Spätmittelalterlichen Ge-
           sellschaft. Ein Hand- und Studienbuch*. Warendorf: Fahlbusch Verlag, 1–51.
Herzenni, Abdellah
    1990   Eléments de stratification sociale dans une oasis du Sud: Aneghrif, région
           de Tata. In: Adellatif Bencherifa & Herbert Popp (eds.), *Le Maroc: Espace
           et société. Actes du colloque Maroco-Allemand de Passau 1989*. Passau: Passavia
           Universitätsverlag, 11–22.
Herzfeld, Michael
    1985   *The Poetics of Manhood. Contest and Identity in a Cretan Mountain Village*. Princeton,
           NJ: Princeton University Press.
Hodgson, Marshall G.S.
    1974   *The Venture of Islam. Conscience and History in a World Civilization. Vol. I. The
           Classical Age of Islam*. Chicago: The University of Chicago Press.
Howe, Leo
    1991   Rice, ideology, and the legitimation of hierarchy in Bali, *Man* 26, 3: 445–67.
Hunwick, John
    1992   Black Africans in the Mediterranean World: Introduction to a neglected
           Aspect of the African Diaspora. In: Savage (ed.), 5–38.
Jackson, Don D.
    1968   *Communication, Family and Marriage*. Palo Alto, CA: Science and Behavior
           Books.
Jackson, James Grey
    1968   *An Acount of the Empire of Morocco*. London: Frank Cass [first edition 1814].
Jacques-Meunié, D.
    1947   Les oasis des Lektaoua et des Mehamid, *Hespéris* xxxiv: 397–429.
    1951   Sur le culte des saints et les fêtes rituelles dans le Moyen Dra et la région
           de Tazarine, *Hespéris* xxxviii: 365–81.
    1958   Hierarchie sociale au Maroc Présaharien, *Hespéris* xlv: 239–69.
    1973   La vallée du Dra au milieu du xxᵉ siècle. In: *Maghreb et Sahara; Mélanges
           offertes à Jean Despois*. Paris: Société de Géographie, 103–92.
    1982   *Le Maroc Saharien des origines à 1670*. 2 vols. Paris: Librairie Klincksieck.
Jager Gerlings, J.H. & D.G. Jongmans
    n.d.   *Van Bron tot Bron. Onder de Berbers van de Marokkaanse Sahara*. Amsterdam:
           Scheltens & Giltay.
Jamous, Raymond
    1981   *Honneur et baraka. Les structures sociales traditionnelles dans le Rif*. Cambridge,
           Paris: Cambridge University Press, Editions de la Maison des Sciences de
           l'Homme.
    1992   From the death of men to the peace of God: violence and peace-making
           in the Rif. In: J.G. Peristiany and Julian Pitt-Rivers (eds.), *Honor and Grace
           in anthropology*. Cambridge: Cambridge University Press, 167–91.
Jansen, Willy
    1987   *Women Without Men. Gender and Marginality in an Algerian Town*. Leiden: E.J.
           Brill.

1995 'Eet! en ik zal zeggen wie je bent': eetgedrag en persoonlijkheid in de Arabische wereld. In: Marjo Buitelaar & Geert Jan van Gelder (eds.), *Eet van de goede dingen! Culinaire culturen in het Midden-Oosten en de Islam.* Bussum: Coutinho, 89–103.

1996 Sociale aspecten van de rechtsregels omtrent melkverwantschap. In: Susan Rutten (ed.), *Recht van de islam* (13). Maastricht: RIMO, 61–87.

Jansen, Willy (ed.)
1985 *Lokale Islam. Geloof en ritueel in Noord-Afrika en Iran.* Muiderberg: Coutinho.

Jemma, D.
1971 *Les tanneurs de Marrakech.* Paris: CNRS.

Joffé, George
1991 The zawiya of Wazzan: relations between shurafa and tribe up to 1860. In: E.G.H. Joffé and C.R. Pennell, *Tribe and State. Essays in honour of David Montgomery Hart.* Wisbech: Menas Press, 84–118.

Joly, A.
1905 L'ouerd des Ouled Sidi Bounou, *Archives Marocaines* vii: 288–329.
1906 L'industrie à Tetouan, *Archives Marocaines* viii: 196–329.

Julien, Ch.-André
1956 *Histoire de l'Afrique du Nord. Tunisie—Algérie—Maroc. Des origines à la conquête Arabe (647 ap. J.-C.).* Paris: Payot [first edition 1936].

Juynboll, Th.W.
1965 Djanāba. In: B. Lewis *et al.* (eds.), *The Encyclopaedia of Islam.* New edition. Leiden: E.J. Brill, vol. ii: 440–41.

Kapchan, Deborah A.
1996 *Gender on the Market. Moroccan Women and The Revoicing of Tradition.* Philadelphia: University of Pennsylvania Press.

Keenan, J.
1977 *The Tuareg. People of Ahaggar.* London: Allan Lane.

Khare, R.S.
1984 *The Untouchable as Himself. Ideology, Identity, and Pragmatism among the Lucknow Chamars.* Cambridge: Cambridge University Press.

Khatib-Chahidi, Jane
1992 Milk Kinship in Shi'ite Islamic Iran. In: Vanessa Maher (ed.), *The Anthropology of Breast-feeding. Natural Law or Social Construct.* Providence, Oxford: Berg, 109–32.

Klein, Martin A.
1992 The Slave Trade in the Western Sudan during the Nineteenth Century. In: Savage (ed.), 39–60.

Koran
n.d. *The Koran.* Translated into English from the original Arabic by George Sale. London: Warne and Co.

Kraus, Wolfgang
1991 *Die Ayt Hdiddu. Wirtschaft und Gesellschaft im Zentralen Hohen Atlas. Ein Beitrag zur Diskussion segmentärer Systeme in Marokko.* Wien: Verlag der Östereichischen Akademie der Wissenschaften.

Lahlou, Abdellatif
1986 *Croyances et manifestations magico-religieuses au Maroc.* Thèse 3ème cycle, Université de Provence (Aix-Marseille).

Laoust, Emile
1934 L'habitation chez les transhumants du Maroc central iii, *Hespéris* vxiii, 1: 109–56.
1993 *Noces Berbères. Les cérémonies du mariage au Maroc.* Paris: Edisud.

Le Goff, Jacques
1977 Métiers licites et métiers illicites dans l'Occident médiéval. In: Idem,

Pour un autre Moyen-Age. Temps, travail et culture en occident: 18 essais. Paris: Gallimard, 91–107.

Le Roy Ladurie, Emmanuel
1979 *The Territory of the Historian.* Hassocks: The Harvard Press [first French edition 1973 and 1978].

Leach, Edmund
1964 Anthropological Aspects of Language: Animal Categories and Verbal Abuse. In: Eric H. Lenneberg (ed.), *New Directions in the Study of Language.* Cambridge, MA: The M.I.T. Press, 23–63.
1967 Caste, class and slavery: the taxonomic problem. In: Anthony de Reuck and Julie Knight (eds.), *Caste and Race: Comparative Approaches.* London: J. & A. Churchill, 5–16.
1978 *Cultuur en communicatie. Een inleiding tot de analyse van culturele gebruiken.* Baarn: Ambo [first English edition 1976].

Legey, Françoise
1935 *The Folklore of Morocco.* London: George Allen & Unwin [first French edition 1926].

Leriche, A.
1951 Les Haratin (Mauritanie), *Bulletin de Liaison Saharienne* 6: 24–29.

Lesne, Marcel
1966 Les Zemmour. Essai d'histoire tribale, *Revue de l'Occident Musulman et de la Méditerranée* 2, 2: 111–54.

Lévi-Provençal, E.
1922 *Les historiens des chorfas.* Casablanca: Afrique Orient [fascimile edition 1991].

Lévi-Strauss, Claude
1962 *La pensée sauvage.* Paris: Librarie Plon.

Lewis, Bernard
1990 *Race and Slavery in the Middle East. An Historical Enquiry.* New York, Oxford: Oxford University Press.

Lièvre, Viviane
1987 *Danses du Maghreb d'une rive à l'autre.* Paris: Karthala.

Long, Debbi
1996 *Milky Ways. Milk kinship in anthropological literature and in a Turkish village community.* M.A. thesis, Katholieke Universiteit Nijmegen.

Lorcin, Patricia M.E.
1995 *Imperial Identities. Stereotyping, Prejudice and Race in Colonial Algeria.* London, New York: I.B. Tauris.

Maher, Vanessa
1974 *Women and Property in Morocco. Their changing relation to the process of social stratification in the Middle Atlas.* London: Cambridge University Press.

Maher, Vanessa (ed.)
1992 *The Anthropology of Breast-feeding. Natural Law or Social Construct.* Providence, Oxford: Berg.

Mann, Michael
1986 *The Sources of Social Power. Volume I: A History of Power from the Beginning to A.D. 1760.* Cambridge: Cambridge University Press.

Marçais, P.
1951 Note sur le mot 'hartani', *Bulletin de Liaison Saharienne* 4: 10–15.

Marchesin, Philippe
1992 *Tribus, Ethnies et Pouvoir en Mauritanie.* Paris: Karthala.

Marcus, M.A.
1983 *Townsmen and Tribesmen. Identity, History and Social Change in Eastern Morocco.* Ph.D. thesis, University of New York.
1987 'Horsemen are the fence of the land': Honor and history among the

Ghiyata of Eastern Morocco. In: D.D. Gilmore (ed.), *Honor and shame and the unity of the Mediterranean*. Washington: American Anthropological Association, 49–60.

Marcy, G.
1936   Tādaa. L'alliance par colactation chez les Berbères du Maroc Central, *Revue Africaine* 368–369: 957–74.
1949   *Le Droit Coutumier Zemmour*. Paris: Larose.

Marlow, Louise
1997   *Hierarchy and egalitarianism in Islamic thought*. Cambridge: Cambridge University Press.

Marmon, Shawn
1995   *Eunuchs and Sacred Boundaries in Islamic Society*. New York, Oxford: Oxford University Press.

Maryanski, Alexander & Jonathan H. Turner
1992   *The Social Cage. Human Nature and the Evolution of Society*. Stanford, CA: Stanford University Press.

Mas, Paolo de
1978   *Marges Marocaines. Limites de la cooperation au développement dans une région périphérique: le cas du Rif*. La Haye: Nuffic; IMWOO; Projet Remplod.

Mauss, Marcel
1969   *The Gift. Forms and Functions of Exchange in Archaic Societies*. London, Henley: Routledge & Kegan Paul [first French edition 1925].

McMurray, David
1993   Haddou: A Moroccan Migrant Worker. In: Edmund Burke III (ed.), *Struggle and Survival in the Middle East*. London, New York: I.B. Tauris, 376–93.

McNaughton, Patrick R.
1988   *The Mande Blacksmiths. Knowledge, Power, and Art in West Africa*. Bloomington, IN: Indiana University Press.

Meillasoux, Claude
1991   *The Anthropology of Slavery. The Womb of Iron and Gold*. Chicago, London: The University of Chicago Press [first French edition 1986].

Memmi, Albert
1962   *Portrait d'un juif*. Paris: Gallimard.

Mercer, J.
1982   *Die Haratin. Mauretaniens Sklaver*. Göttingen: Gesellschaft für bedrohte Völker.

Metcalf, Barbara Daly
1984   Introduction. In: Barbara Daly Metcalf (ed.), *Moral Conduct and Authority. The Place of Adab in South Asian Islam*. Berkeley: The University of California Press, 1–20.

Meyers, Allan Richard
1974   *The 'Abid l-Buchari: Slave soldiers and statecraft in Morocco. 1672–1790*. Ph.D. thesis, Cornell University.

Mezzine, Larbi
1987   *Le Tafilalt. Contribution à l'Histoire du Maroc aux XVIIᵉ et XVIIIᵉ siècles*. Rabat: Publications de la faculté des lettres et des sciences humaines.

Migdal, Joel S.
1988   *Strong Societies and Weak States. Society Relations and State Capabilities in the Third World*. Princeton, NJ: Princeton University Press.

Miller, James A.
1984   *Imlil. A Moroccan Mountain Community in Change*. Boulder, CO: Westview Press.

Ministère
1981   *Rapport de synthese; Etablissement d'un plan directeur de mise en valeur agricole de la vallée du Drâa moyen*. Rabat: Ministère de l'agriculture et de la réforme agraire.

Mintz, Sidney W. & Eric R. Wolf
  1967   An Analysis of Ritual Co-Parenthood (Compadrazgo). In: Jack M. Potter, May N. Diaz, George Forster (eds.), *Peasant Society. A Reader*. Boston: Brown and Company, 174–99.
Mitchell, Timothy
  1990   Everyday metaphors of power, *Theory and Society* 19, 5: 545–77.
Montagne, Robert
  1930   *Villages et kasbas Berbères. Tableau de la vie sociale des Berbères sédentaires dans le Sud du Maroc*. Paris: Librairie Felix Alcan.
  1953   *Révolution au Maroc*. Paris: Éditions France Empire.
Monteil, Capt.
  1948   *Le Peuplement des Qsar du Bani*. Paris, CHEAM no. 1307 [unpublished paper].
Mouline, Said
  1991   *Habitats des qsour et qasbas des vallées présahariennes*. Rabat: Le Ministère de l'habitat.
Moureau, Cap.
  1955   *Les sociétés des oasis. Une race du Bani: Les Haratins. Parallele entre son evolution et celle des outres races des Bani*. Paris, CHEAM no. 2431 [unpublished paper].
Munson, Jr., Henry
  1993   *Religion and Power in Morocco*. New Haven, London: Yale University Press.
Murdock, George Peter
  1959   *Africa. Its People and their Culture History*. New York: Mc Graw Hill.
Naamane, Soumaya
  1994   *De schaamte ontsluierd. Vrouwen uit Casablanca over huwelijk, seksualiteit en erotiek*. Amsterdam: In de Knipscheer [first French edition 1987].
Naamouni, Khadija
  1993   *Le Culte de Bouya Omar*. Casablanca: Editions Eddif.
Niclausse, Capt. M.
  1954   *Rapports entre nomades et sedentaires dans le coude du Draa: La Raïa*. Paris, CHEAM no. 2306 [unpublished paper].
Nicolas, F.J.
  1977   L'origine et la signification du mot *hartani* et de ses equivalents, *Notes Africaines* 156 (oct.): 101–06.
Nieuwkerk, Karin van
  1991   'A Trade like any Other'. Female singers and dancers in Egypt. An anthropological study of the relation between gender and respectability in the entertainment trade. Ph.D. thesis, Universiteit van Amsterdam.
Nijst, A.L.M.T. et al.
  1973   *Living on the edge of the Sahara. A study of traditional forms of habitation and types of settlement in Morocco*. The Hague: Government Publishing Office.
Noin, Daniel
  1965   Types de habitat dans les campagnes du Maroc, *Revue de Géographie du Maroc* 8: 101–108.
  1970   *La Population Rurale du Maroc*. Paris: P.U.F.
Norén, Lars
  1985   *Toneel 1*. vertaling Karst Woudstra. Amsterdam: International Theatre Bookshop [introduced by Magnus Florin].
Norton, Augustus Richard
  1995   Introduction. In: Augustus Richard Norton (ed.), *Civil Society in the Middle East*. Leiden: E.J. Brill, 1–25.
Ohnuki-Tierney, Emiko
  1981   *Illness and Healing among the Sakhalin Ainu: A Symbolic Interpretation*. Cambridge: Cambridge University Press.
  1984   Monkey Performances. A Multiple Structure of Meaning and Reflexivity

in Japanese Culture. In: M. Bruner (ed.), *Text, Play and Story. The Construction and Reconstruction of Self and Society.* 1983 Proceedings of the American Ethnological Society. Washington, D.C.: American Ethnological Society, 278–314.

1990   Monkey as metaphor? Transformations of a polytropic symbol in Japanese culture, *Man* 25: 89–107.

Ortner, Sherry B.
1973   On Key Symbols, *American Anthropologist* 75: 1338–46.
1995   Resistance and the Problem of Ethnographic Refusal, *Comparative Studies in Society and History* 37: 173–93.

Ossman, Susan
1994   *Picturing Casablanca. Portraits of Power in a Modern City.* Berkeley: University of California Press.

Ouali, Abdelillah (direction) & Brahim Derami (interviews)
1994   *De Belofte.* TV documentary. Nederlandse Moslim Omroep.

Ouhajou, Lekbir
1986   *Espace hydraulique et société. Les systèmes d'irrigation dans la vallée du Dra Moyen (Maroc).* Thèse, Université de Montpellier III.
n.d.   Les rapports sociaux aux droits d'eau. Le cas de la vallée du Dra. In: Moulay Ismaïl and Pierre Carrière (eds.), *Aspects de l'agriculture irriguée au Maroc* [*Espace Rural* no. 25], 87–100.

Palmen, Connie
1995   *De Vriendschap.* Amsterdam: Prometheus.

Pandolfo, Stefania
1989   Detours of life: Space and bodies in a Moroccan village, *American Ethnologist* 16, 1: 3–23.
1997   *Impasse of the Angels. Scenes from a Moroccan Space of Memory.* Chicago, London: The University of Chicago Press.

Pâques, Viviana
1964   *L'arbre cosmique dans la pensée religieuse et dans la vie quotidienne du Nord-Ouest africain.* Paris: Institut d'Ethnologie, Musée de l'homme.
1991   *La Religion des Esclaves. Recherches sur la confrérie marocaine des gnawa.* Bergamo: Moretti & Vitali.

Parish, Steven M.
1996   *Hierarchy and its Discontents. Culture and the Politics of Consciousness in Caste Society.* Philadelphia: University of Pennsylvania Press.

Pascon, Paul
1979   Segmentation et stratification dans la société rurale Marocaine, *Bulletin economique et social du Maroc* 138–139: 105–19.
1984   *La Maison d'Iligh et l'histoire sociale du Tazerwalt.* Rabat: SMER.

Pascon, Paul & Mohammed Ennaji
1986   *Les paysans sans terre au Maroc.* Casablanca: Les Editions Toubkal.

Pedersen, J.
1989   Masdjid. In: C.E. Bosworth *et al.* (eds.), *The Encyclopaedia of Islam.* New Edition. Leiden: E.J. Brill, vol. vi: 644–706.

Peters, Emrys
1990a   The tied and the free. In: Idem, *The Bedouin of Cyrenaica. Studies in Personal and Corporal Power.* ed. by Jack Goody and Emanuel Marx. Cambridge: Cambridge University Press, 279–84.
1990b   Debt Relationships. In: Peters 1990a, 287–92.

Pitt-Rivers, Julian
1976   Ritual kinship in the Mediterranean: Spain and the Balkans. In: J.G. Peristiany (ed.), *Mediterranean family structures.* Cambridge: Cambridge University Press, 317–34.

Pletsch, A.
  1971   *Strukturwandlungen in der oase Dra. Unterschungen zur Wirtschafts- und Bevölkerungs-entwicklungs im Oasengebiet SüdMarokkos.* Marburg: Im Selbstverlag des geographischen Institutes der Universität Marburg.
Pouillon, François
  1993   Simplification ethnique en Afrique du Nord: Maures, Arabes et Berbères (xviiiᵉ–xxᵉ siècles), *Cahiers d'Études Africaines* 33, 129: 37–49.
Rabinow, Paul
  1975   *Symbolic Domination. Cultural Form and Historical Change in Morocco.* Chicago, London: The University of Chicago Press.
Rachik, Hassan
  1990   *Sacre et sacrifice dans le Haut Atlas Marocain.* Casablanca: Afrique Orient.
Raheja, Gloria Goodwin
  1989   Centrality, Mutuality and Hierarchy: Shifting aspects of inter-caste relationships in North India, *Contributions to Indian Sociology* 23, 1: 79–101.
Rao, Aparna
  1987a   The concept of peripatetics: An introduction. In: Rao (ed.), 1–32.
Rao, Aparna (ed.)
  1987b   *The Other Nomads. Peripatetic Minorities in Crosscultural Perspective.* Köln, Wien: Böhlau VerlagRapport.
Rappaport, R.A.
  1979   *Ecology, Meaning and Religion.* Richmond: North Atlantic Books.
Rasmussen, Susan J.
  1992   Ritual Specialists and Power in Tuareg Society, *Man* 27, 1: 105–28.
Rassam, Amal
  1977   Al taba'iyya: Power, patronage and marginal groups in northern Iraq. In: Gellner & Waterbury (eds.), 157–66.
Redfield, Robert
  1967   *Peasant Society and Culture.* Chicago, London: The University of Chicago Press [first edition 1956; 1967 edition published together with *The Little Community*].
Reysoo, Fenneke
  1985   Een collectieve besnijdenis in Noord-West Marokko. In: Willy Jansen (ed.), *Lokale Islam: geloof en ritueel in Noord-Afrika en Iran.* Muiderberg: Coutinho, 42–50.
  1991   *Pèlerinages au Maroc. Fête, politique et échange dans l'islam populaire.* Neuchâtel, Paris: Éditions de l'Institut d'ethnologie/Éditions de la Maison des sciences de l'homme.
Robb, Peter
  1995   Introduction. South Asia and the concept of race. In: Peter Robb (ed.), *The Concept of Race in South Asia.* Delhi: Oxford University Press, 1–76.
Rodriguez-Manas, Francisco
  1996   Agriculture, sūfism and the state in tenth/sixteenth-century Morocco, *Bulletin of the School of Oriental and African Studies* lix, 3: 450–71.
Roff, William R. (ed.)
  1987   *Islam and the Political Economy of Meaning. Comparative studies of muslim discourse.* Berkeley: The University of California Press.
Rohlfs, Gerhard
  1874   *Adventures in Morocco and journeys through the oases of Draa and Tafilalet.* London: Sampson Low, Maston, Low and Searle.
Rosen, Lawrence
  1972   The Social and Conceptual Framework of Arab-Berber Relations in Central Morocco. In: Gellner & Micaud (eds.), 155–73.

1979   Social identity and points of attachment: approaches to social organization. In Geertz, Geertz and Rosen (1979), 19–52.

1984   *Bargaining for Reality. The Construction of Social Relations in a Muslim Community.* Chicago, London: The University of Chicago Press.

Roth, Anne Macy
1995   *Building bridges to Afrocentrism. A letter to my Egyptological colleagues.* WWW text.

Rouach, David
1990   *'Imma. Ou rites, coutumes et croyances chez la femme juive en Afrique du Nord.* Paris: Maissoneuve & Larose.

Roux, A.
1928   'Les Imdyazen' ou Aêdes Berbères du groupe linguistique Beraber, *Hespéris* viii, 2: 231–51.

Ruf, Urs Peter
1998a   *'Notre origine est reconnue!' Transformations d'identité et de hiérarchie sociale en Mauritanie vues par le bas.* Working paper no. 308. Universität Bielefeld. Fakultät für Soziologie.

1998b   *Dams and Ramparts, Cattle and Goats. Symbolic capital and the Central Mauretanian Slaves and Häratin Struggle for Emancipation and Autonomy.* Working Paper no. 287. Universität Bielefeld. Fakultät für Soziologie.

Sagnes, Lt. Col.
1949   *Introduction à la connaissance du Maroc.* Casablanca: Imprimerie Reunies.

Salmon, G.
1906   Sur quelques noms de plantes en Arabe et en Berbère, *Archives Marocaines* vol. viii: 1–98.

Sanders, E.R.
1969   The Hamitic Hypothesis; Its Origins and Functions in Time Perspective, *Journal of African History* 10, 4: 521–32.

Savage, Elizabeth (ed.)
1992   *The Human Commodity. Perspectives on the Trans-Saharan Slave Trade.* London: Frank Cass [special issue of *Slavery & Abolition* 13, 1].

Schama, Simon
1989   *Citizens. A Chronicle of the French Revolution.* New York: Vintage Books.

Schroeter, Daniel J.
1992   Slave markets and Slavery in Moroccan Urban Society. In: Savage (ed.), 185–213.

Scott, James C.
1977   Patronage or exploitation? In: Gellner and Waterbury (eds.), 21–39.

1985   *Weapons of the Weak. Everyday Forms of Peasant Resistance.* New Haven: Yale University Press.

1990   *Domination and the Arts of Resistance. Hidden Transcripts.* New Haven: Yale University Press.

Seligman, C.G.
1930   *The Races of Africa.* London: Thornton Butterworth.

Shabeeny, El Hage Abd Salam
1967   *An Account of Timbuctoo and Housa. Territories in the interior of Africa.* With notes, critical and explanatory by James Grey Jackson. London: Frank Cass & Co.

Shilling, Chris
1997   The Body and Difference. In: Kathryn Woodward (ed.), *Identity and Difference. Culture, Media and Identities.* London: Sage, 63–120.

Silverman, Sydel F.
1966   An ethnographic Approach to Social Stratification: Prestige in a Central Italian Community, *American Anthropologist* 68: 899–921.

1977   Patronage as myth. In: Gellner and Waterbury (eds.), 7–19.
Simmel, Georg
1950   The Stranger. In: Idem, *The Sociology of Georg Simmel*. Edited by Kurt H. Wolff. New York, London: Free Press, 402–08.
Spencer, William
1978   Berber. In: Richard V. Weekes (ed.), *Muslim Peoples. A World Ethnographic Survey*. Westport, CO: Greenwood Press, 99–110.
Spillmann, G.
1931   *Districts et tribus de la haute vallée du Draᶜ*. Paris: Honoré Champion [Villes et tribus de Maroc vol. ix: Tribus Berbères, vol. iii].
1936   *Les Aït Atta du Sahara et la Pacification du Haut Dra*. Rabat: Editions Felix Mancho/l'I.H.E.M.
St Bon, Cpt. de
1938a   *Monographie sur les districts Ait Atta de Nekob, du Tazzarine et du Taghbalt*. Paris, CHEAM 224 [unpublished paper].
1938b   *Les populations des confins du Maroc Saharien*. Paris, CHEAM no. 27 bis [unpublished paper].
Swanson, John Theodore
1978   *The Not-Yet-Golden Trade: Contact and Commerce between North Africa and the Sudan, to the Eleventh Century A.D.* Ph.D. thesis, Indiana University.
Tambiah, Stanley Jeyaraja
1985   *Culture, Thought, and Social Action. An Anthropological Perspective*. Cambridge, MA, London: Harvard University Press.
Tax-Freeman, Susan
1979   *The Pasiegos. Spaniards in no man's land*. Chicago, London: The University of Chicago Press.
Taylor, Charles
1997   *Philosophical Arguments*. Cambridge, MA: Harvard University Press [first edition 1995].
Teine-Cheikh, Catherine
1989   La Mauritanie en noir et blanc. Petit promenade linguistique en Hassaniya, *Revue du Monde Musulman et de la Méditerranée* 54: 90–105.
Terrasse, Henri
1950   *Histoire du Maroc. Des origines à l'établissement du Protectorat Français*. Casablanca: Editions Atlantides.
Testart, Alain
1998   L'esclavage comme institution, *L'Homme* 145 (janvier/mars): 31–69.
Thomson, A.
1987   *Barbary and Enlightenment*. Leiden: E.J. Brill.
Toutain, Georges
1971   *Sur une evolution economique de la vallée du Draa*. ORMVA Ouarzazate, Maroc [unpublished report].
Tozy, Mohammed
1987   *Champ et contre champ politico-religieux au Maroc*. Doctorat d'Etat, Aix-Marseille, 1984. Microfilm Université de Lille III, 1987.
1990   Le Prince, le clerc et l'etat: La restructuration du champ religieux au Maroc. In: Giles Kepel and Yann Richard (eds.), *Intellectuels et militants de l'Islam contemporain*. Paris: Seuil, 71–101.
Turner, Victor
1969   *The Ritual Process*. Chicago: Aldine.
1974   *Dramas, Fields, and Metaphors*. Ithaca: Cornell University Press.
Vajda, G.
1971   Ḥām. In: B. Lewis *et al.* (eds.), *The Encyclopaedia of Islam*. New Edition. Leiden: E.J. Brill, vol. iii, 104–105.

Vallet, Michel
1990 Les Touaregs du Hoggar: Entre décolonisation et indépendances (1954–1974), *Revue du Monde Musulman et de la Méditerranée* 57, 3: 77–90.

Van Gennep, Arnold
1960 *The Rites of Passage.* Chicago, London: The University of Chicago Press [first French edition 1908].

Veen, K.W. van der
1971 Counterpoint, Ambivalence and Social Structure. In: *Buiten de grenzen. Sociologische opstellen aangeboden aan prof. dr. W.F. Wertheim, 25 jaar Amsterdams hoogleraar, 1946–1971.* Meppel: Boom, 300–16.

Venzlaff, Helga
1977 *Der Marokkanische Drogenhändler und seine Ware.* Wiesbaden: Franz Steiner Verlag.

Vincent, Bernard (ed.)
1979 *Les marginaux et les exclus dans l'histoire.* Paris: Cahiers Jussieu.

Vinogradov, Amal Rassam
1974 *The Aït Ndhir of Morocco. A study of the social transformation of a Berber tribe.* Ann Arbor: The University of Michigan.

Wagner, Daniel A.
1993 *Literacy, Culture, and Development. Becoming Literate in Morocco.* Cambridge: Cambridge University Press.

Waterbury, J.
1972 *North for the Trade. The Life and Times of a Berber Merchant.* Berkeley: The University of California Press.

Watt, W. Montgomery
1988 *Bells inleiding tot de Koran.* Utrecht: De Ploeg [first English edition 1970].

Webber, Sabra J.
1997 Middle East Studies & Subaltern Studies, *MESA Bulletin* 31: 11–16.

Wehr, Hans
1976 *The Hans Wehr Dictionary of Modern Written Arabic.* ed. by J.M. Cowan. New York: Spoken Language Services.

Welte, Frank Maurice
1990 *Der Gnâwa-Kult. Trancespiele, Geisterbeschwörung und Besessenheit in Marokko.* Frankfurt am Main: Peter Lang.

Wensinck, A.J.
1993 Nadjis. C.E. Bosworth *et al. (eds.), The Encyclopaedia of Islam.* New edition. Leiden: E.J. Brill, vol. vii: 870.

Wertheim, W.F.
1964 *East-West Parallels; Sociological Approaches to Modern Asia.* The Hague: W. van Hoeve.

Westermarck, E.
1914 *Marriage Ceremonies in Morocco.* London: Macmillan.
1926 *Ritual and belief in Morocco.* 2 vols. London: Macmillan.
1930 *Wit and Wisdom in Morocco. A Study of Native Proverbs.* London: George Routledge & Sons.

Weulersse, Jacques
1946 *Paysans de Syrie et du Proche-Orient.* Paris: Gallimard.

Wolf, Eric R.
1956 Aspects of Group Relations in a Complex Society: Mexico, *American Anthropologist* 58: 1065–78.
1966a Kinship, Friendship, and Patron-Client Relations in Complex Societies. In: Michael Banton (ed.), *The Social Anthropology of Complex Societies.* London: Tavistock, 1–22.
1966b *Peasants.* Englewood Cliffs, NJ: Prentice-Hall.

INDEX

PLATES

Figure 1: A view on the Outside Quarter from the top of the minaret

Figure 2: A collective prayer on the day of the Great Feast. Note the imam with
the staff of the founder of the community

Figure 3: A portrait of a Sharif at the wedding of his son. Note the staff and slate of the ancestral saint

Figure 4: A portrait of a Hartani—crier and gravedigger—serving tea for his guests

Figure 5: A leather-worker from a neighbouring settlement poses in front of a tan-pit

Figure 6: A slaughterer and his son show their ability to sacrifice a goat on the morning of the Great Feast

Figure 7: A servant distributes almonds to the guests at a marriage party

Figure 8: Musicians from a nearby village parade through the village on the
occasion of a circumcision